The Things That Really Matter

The Things That Really Matter

Philosophical conversations on the cornerstones of life

Michael Hauskeller with

Alexander Badman-King, Drew Chastain,
Lewis Coyne, Jane Heal, Troy Jollimore,
Holly Lawford-Smith, Christine Overall,
Elaine Scarry, Helen Steward, Alison Stone,
Brian Treanor and Panayiota Vassilopoulou

First published in 2022 by
UCL Press
University College London
Gower Street
London WC1E 6BT

Available to download free: www.uclpress.co.uk

ISBN: 978-1-80008-219-9 (Hbk.)
ISBN: 978-1-80008-218-2 (Pbk.)
ISBN: 978-1-80008-217-5 (PDF)
ISBN: 978-1-80008-220-5 (epub)
ISBN: 978-1-80008-221-2 (mobi)
DOI: https://doi.org/10.14324/111.9781800082175

'Philosophy, like life, must keep the doors and windows open.'

William James

Contents

Contributors

Michael Hauskeller is Professor of Philosophy at the University of Liverpool and author of *Biotechnology and the Integrity of Life* (Routledge, 2007), *Better Humans? Understanding the enhancement project* (Routledge, 2013), *Sex and the Posthuman Condition* (Palgrave Macmillan, 2014), *Mythologies of Transhumanism* (Palgrave Macmillan, 2016) and *The Meaning of Life and Death* (Bloomsbury, 2019).

Alexander Badman-King is a Postdoctoral Research Fellow at the University of Exeter and author of *Living-With Wisdom: Permaculture and symbiotic ethics* (Routledge, 2021).

Drew Chastain is Visiting Assistant Professor of Philosophy at Loyola University New Orleans and author of a number of papers on meaning in life and spirituality, including 'Deep personal meaning: a subjective approach to meaning in life' (*The Journal of Philosophy of Life* 11/1 (2021): 1–23), 'Can life be meaningful without free will?' (*Philosophia* 47/4 (2019): 1069–86) and 'Gifts without givers: secular spirituality and metaphorical cognition' (*Sophia* 56/4 (2017): 631–47).

Lewis Coyne is Associate Lecturer at the University of Exeter. He is the author of *Hans Jonas: Life, technology, and the horizons of responsibility* (Bloomsbury, 2020) and co-editor of *Moral Enhancement: Critical perspectives* (Cambridge University Press, 2018).

Jane Heal is Emeritus Professor of Philosophy at the University of Cambridge. She is the author of *Fact and Meaning* (Blackwell, 1989) and *Mind, Reason and Imagination* (Cambridge University Press, 2003). Recent work on the importance of the first-person plural is in 'On underestimating *us*' (*Think* 54/19 (2019): 1–12).

Troy Jollimore is a poet and philosopher and currently Professor of Philosophy at California State University. He has published four volumes of poetry and is the author of *Friendship and Agent-Relative Morality* (Routledge, 2001), *Love's Vision* (Princeton University Press, 2011) and *On Loyalty* (Routledge, 2012), and is currently editing a collection of essays on loyalty for Oxford University Press.

Holly Lawford-Smith is an Associate Professor in Political Philosophy at the University of Melbourne. She teaches classes on everyday morality, the ethics of immigration, feminism, the intersection of metaphysics and ethics, and hate speech. Her past research interests have included political feasibility, collective responsibility and climate ethics, and her current research interest is feminism. Her second book, *Gender-Critical Feminism*, is due to be published by Oxford University Press in 2022.

Christine Overall is Professor Emerita of Philosophy at Queen's University, Kingston, Ontario, and is an elected Fellow of the Royal Society of Canada. She is the editor or co-editor of five books and the author of six. Most of her publications are in the areas of feminist philosophy, applied ethics and philosophy of religion. She is particularly interested in the social aspects of human identity, such as sex/ gender, sexuality, race, age, (dis)ability, class and religion.

Elaine Scarry teaches at Harvard where she is Cabot Professor of Aesthetics and the General Theory of Value. Her work has two central subjects: the nature of physical injury and the nature of human creation. Her writings include *The Body in Pain* (Oxford University Press, 1985), *On Beauty and Being Just* (Princeton University Press, 1999), *Dreaming by the Book* (Princeton University Press, 1999) and *Thermonuclear Monarchy* (W. W. Norton, 2014).

Helen Steward is Professor of Philosophy of Mind and Action at the University of Leeds and is a Fellow of the British Academy. She is the author of *A Metaphysics for Freedom* (Oxford University Press, 2012) and *The Ontology of Mind* (Oxford University Press, 1997). Her interests lie mainly in the philosophy of action and free will, the philosophy of mind, and the metaphysical and ontological issues which bear on these areas. She is currently writing a book on causation.

Alison Stone is Professor of European Philosophy at Lancaster University and author of seven books, among them *Being Born: Birth and philosophy* (Oxford University Press, 2019), *Feminism, Psychoanalysis, and Maternal Subjectivity* (Routledge, 2011) and *An Introduction to Feminist Philosophy* (Polity Press, 2007).

Brian Treanor is Charles S. Casassa Chair and Professor of Philosophy at Loyola Marymount University. He is the author of *Melancholic Joy: On life worth living* (Bloomsbury, 2021), *Emplotting Virtue* (SUNY, 2014) and *Aspects of Alterity* (Fordham University Press, 2006).

Panayiota Vassilopoulou is Reader in Philosophy at the University of Liverpool and co-editor of *Thought: A philosophical history* (Routledge, 2021) and *Late Antique Epistemology* (Palgrave Macmillan, 2008). She publishes widely on Neoplatonism and Aesthetics and has developed numerous research projects funded by the Arts and Humanities Research Council, the British Academy, the British Society of Aesthetics, the EU and the Wellcome Trust aimed at engaging non-academic readers with philosophical research and practice.

Introduction

This book is dedicated to the memory of Mary Midgley.

In September 2018 I received (through my Liverpool colleague Rachael Wiseman) a personal invitation to attend the launch of the Mary and Geoff Midgley Archives at Durham University in early November. I was delighted because Mary Midgley had long been one of my philosophical heroes, and yet I had never met her. So this was a wonderful – and, given her age, most likely my last – opportunity to finally do so. As it turned out, it was already too late. Mary died in October 2018, a few weeks after her 99th birthday, and like many others I am still mourning her passing.

There are many reasons why I liked Mary so much, as a person, a writer and a philosopher. I liked her for her wit, her warmth, her level-headedness and her moral clarity; her ability to steer clear of all unnecessary technicalities and cut straight to the chase, focusing on the big picture rather than getting mired in the details of any particular argument – which is an occupational hazard for us academic philosophers because it can all too easily become an end in itself. Mary knew what's what, neatly separating the wheat of our common ways of thinking – in philosophy, science and life – from the chaff. She had little patience for what she liked to call 'humbug'. Using vivid, striking images and comparisons to illustrate the points she wanted to make, she encouraged her readers to think hard about what really mattered and *why* it mattered.

One of the things that really matters is, according to her, philosophy itself, which is 'not just grand and elegant and difficult, it is also needed'.[1] Philosophers have an important and indeed essential job to do. Their 'business is not – as some people mistakenly think – merely to look inward. It is to organize what concerns everybody. Philosophy aims to bring together those aspects of life that have not yet been properly connected so as to make a more coherent, more workable world-picture. And that coherent world-picture is not a private luxury. It's something we all need for our lives.'[2]

In fact, we all have *some* kind of world-picture already, which informs how we think and feel about things, what we value, what facts we consider relevant and what we make of them, and then also, as a result of all this, how we live our lives. The trouble is that our picture of the world, the pattern of thought that guides us through life, tends to be rather confused and full of blind spots and contradictions. It lacks coherence and clarity and often gets things wrong, which is not surprising since the world is complex and indeed confusing in its complexity. So while we may all have our own personal philosophy of life – which of course we may share with many others – we don't always have a good one. But even good philosophies are usually one-sided: 'Even the most useful, the most vital of such patterns of thought, has its limits. They all need to be balanced and corrected against each other.'[3]

This is where philosophy as a discipline comes in – or I should say, philosophy as a shared *practice*, because philosophy is not, contrary to what many people (including many academic philosophers) take it to be: 'one specialized subject among many, something which you need only to study if you mean to do research on it. Instead, it is something we are all doing all the time, a continuous, necessary background activity which is likely to go badly if we don't attend to it. In this way, it is perhaps more like driving a car or using money than it is like nuclear physics.'[4]

To practise philosophy is to pay attention to how we think and what we do, and then to try to sort out the problems and conflicts that we discover there to help us think better and as a result also live better. Because the way we live reflects the way we think, philosophers sort out problems by suggesting 'new ways of thinking which call for different ways of living'.[5] Philosophy, then, aims not at truth, at least not primarily, but at helping us 'to make sense of the world . . . and so to find ways of life that are acceptable to others and also worthwhile for themselves'.[6]

Some of the problems that need sorting out will have been with us for a long time; others will be new because, for better or worse, the world doesn't stand still. Tackling the old problems is just as important as tackling the new ones, but tackling the new ones is especially challenging because it requires us to enter uncharted territory. It is philosophy's job to draw a map for the new territories that keep popping up in our conceptual landscape and to help us navigate them safely. This is why philosophers need to always stay on their toes, ready to revise their previous assumptions and conclusions and areas of interest if and when the situation requires it. Doing philosophy 'is not a matter of solving one fixed set of puzzles. Instead, it involves finding the many particular ways of thinking that will be most helpful as we try to explore this constantly changing world. Because the world – including human life – does constantly change, philosophical thoughts are never final. Their aim is always to help us through the present difficulty.'[7] This, however, is not a job for a specialist. Philosophers need to look at 'life as a whole'[8] because the problems they are meant to solve are entangled with many other problems, so that the widest possible context is needed to sort them.

This book should be read as an attempt to provide such a wide context and draw the map that Mary Midgley is talking about. It has a rather unusual format, containing a series of philosophical conversations I have had, in writing, over the past three years with friends and colleagues about some of the questions that we all, in one way or another, wrestle with if we are at all concerned about what kind of world we inhabit and what our own role – as living, thinking, feeling beings – in all this is. The issues those questions pertain to are the cornerstones of our life. They are fundamental in the sense that they define our existence and make us who and what we are. They apply, as time goes by.

There are 14 conversations in total, on 'meaning', 'agency', 'body', 'gender', 'age', 'self', 'goodness', 'evil', 'death', 'birth', 'love', 'faith', 'beauty' and 'sacredness'. The list of topics covered is clearly not exhaustive. Others could be added that are equally fundamental ('happiness' comes to mind, for instance, or 'time' and 'truth'), and I hope that someday I will be able to discuss those as well.

What prompted me to have those conversations in the first place was a certain dissatisfaction with the way we academic philosophers tend to conduct our business. To be successful we need the recognition of our peers, and the easiest way to gain this recognition is by carving out a niche for ourselves. Generalism is not a good strategy if you want to make a career in Philosophy. So we start out by studying the existing literature on a particular topic (or aspect of a topic) and trying to add something original to it: a new perspective or argument, a new way of looking at or dealing with a problem. Next, we develop our original insight into a clearly defined position and once we have done that, we spend the rest of our working life defending it against objections from our colleagues, trying to show why we are right and they are wrong. Professional philosophers typically make a name for themselves by standing for something and becoming the go-to people for certain ideas. It helps if our ideas are controversial, even outrageous, because that makes them more recognisable.

This need for not only specialisation but *entrenchment* has always bothered me because it seems to me that philosophers should not seek to stand for anything except intellectual honesty and the sincerity of their endeavour to understand. Ideally, we should keep moving with the flow of our thinking, wherever it leads us and, importantly, wherever the thinking of *others* leads us. Our own thinking is, after all, always limited and one-sided. We all have our biases and blind spots. Philosophers are too often entrenched in camps just as politicians are, which is not as it should be. What we need is a kind of philosophical bipartisanship and a sustained commitment to practising what Erik Parens calls 'binocularity'.[9] We need to do more than read and think in our armchairs. We need to actually talk to other people and, more importantly, *listen* to them and try to see things the way they look from their point of view. Even where we disagree with them, they usually have good reasons for their views that are worth considering and exploring.[10]

Putting this idea into practice, this book uses a method of doing philosophy – *conversationalism* – that is quite uncommon in contemporary Western academic practice but that has lately been proposed by Jonathan Chimakonam as 'an emerging method of thinking in and beyond African philosophy'.[11] As a method, conversationalism is more than just an informal exchange of opinions between two people, nor does it resemble a Socratic, 'maieutic' dialogue, which aims at establishing, once and for all, the truth or falsity of certain clearly defined positions. In contrast, conscious of the provisionality of all philosophical truths, the conversational method 'prioritises the sustenance of the engagement over the outcome of such engagements'[12] and understands itself as a creative struggle that through a constant reshuffling of ideas keeps leading to fresh insights. It opens up rather than closes down the process of thinking.

This method is in line with an understanding of philosophy that was articulated and practised most forcefully by Mary Midgley. According to her, philosophy is like 'exploring an unknown piece of country, something which is much better done co-operatively than in competition'[13] and that requires its practitioners to 'follow the argument . . . wherever it runs', even if that means we 'finally catch it in a territory quite far from the one where it started'. This is because, as Mary quips, 'arguments are altogether much more like rabbits than they are like lumps of gold. They can never be depended on to stay still.'[14]

Each of the following 14 chapters is a shared exploration of an aspect of our lives that is of fundamental importance to us. The aim was not to make an argument for or against a particular position, but to take the topic in different directions and see where they lead – to follow the rabbit wherever it runs – and thus open a space for discussion and further reflection instead of bringing it to an end (by refuting all views except the one that one wishes to endorse). In this way, this book practises and showcases thinking as an open-ended process and a collaborative endeavour where its participants benefit from talking to each other rather than against each other, featuring real conversations, where ideas are explored, tested, changed and occasionally dropped.

None of those explorations should be taken as conclusive. No attempt has been made to cover everything that one might think would be important to discuss in relation to a particular issue. Almost always, when we came to the end of our conversations, I and my co-authors felt that there was a lot more to discuss. Our discussions could also have started differently, could have continued differently, and could have ended differently. Yet this is precisely what made it such an exciting and rewarding project. We never knew at the beginning of our conversations where we would end up.

That said, the conversations in this book, while avoiding overly technical language, come with all the flesh and bones of a proper philosophical discussion and are firmly situated in the academic discourse on the topic they focus on, which is acknowledged and referenced in the notes to each chapter. The notes are for those readers who want to investigate the issues discussed further and in a more systematic and analytical way than we have done. That was, of course, deliberate. Our strategy was to keep it simple and to avoid theorising as much as possible. Theoretical constructs can certainly be helpful and illuminating, but they can also be a distraction because one can easily end up explaining and discussing those constructs instead of the phenomena they are meant to shed light on. However, while not attempting to summarise the existing debate, the chapters still use it as a foundation to add fresh perspectives and considerations that are designed to stimulate further debate and, in some cases, a deliberate redirection of research interests in the respective areas.

The Things That Really Matter is, in short, thinking in motion, both personal and universal. While the topics discussed are relevant to all of us, they are being discussed by particular people, each with their own personal history and circumstances. Thinking doesn't happen in a vacuum, in an insulated space of reason. Where there is thinking, there is also a thinker, and that thinker is always more than just a thinker. To acknowledge the embeddedness of our thinking in our lives is not a weakness. It anchors thought in lived reality. Accordingly, whatever I and those I have had the good fortune, pleasure and honour to exchange my thoughts with have to say in the following chapters, we say it – as Mary Midgley recommended we do – both 'as a fully instructed professional and as a whole human being'.[15] I am very grateful to all of them.

Liverpool, September 2021

Notes

1. Midgley, *Utopias, Dolphins and Computers*, 1.
2. Midgley, *What Is Philosophy For?*, 73.
3. Midgley, *Utopias, Dolphins and Computers*, 10.
4. Midgley, *What Is Philosophy For?*, 81.
5. Midgley, *What Is Philosophy For?*, 59.
6. Midgley, *Utopias, Dolphins and Computers*, 63.
7. Midgley, *What Is Philosophy For?*, 6.
8. Midgley, *What Is Philosophy For?*, 58.
9. Parens, *Shaping Our Selves*, 10, 33.
10. See Earp and Hauskeller, 'Binocularity in bioethics'.
11. Chimakonam, 'Conversationalism as an emerging method of thinking in and beyond African philosophy'.
12. Chimakonam, 'Conversationalism as an emerging method of thinking in and beyond African philosophy', 17.
13. Midgley, *Utopia, Dolphins and Computers*, 47.
14. Midgley, *What Is Philosophy For?*, 16–17.
15. Midgley, *Utopias, Dolphins and Computers*, 28.

Bibliography

Chimakonam, Jonathan O. 'Conversationalism as an emerging method of thinking in and beyond African philosophy', *Acta Academica* 49/2 (2017): 11–33.
Earp, Brian D., and Michael Hauskeller. 'Binocularity in bioethics – and beyond', *American Journal of Bioethics* 16/2 (2016): W3–W6.
Midgley, Mary. *Utopias, Dolphins and Computers*. London: Routledge, 1996.
Midgley, Mary. *What Is Philosophy For?* London: Bloomsbury, 2018.
Parens, Erik. *Shaping Our Selves: On technology, flourishing, and a habit of thinking*. Oxford: Oxford University Press, 2015.

1
Meaning

with Drew Chastain

Michael Hauskeller: Living a meaningful life matters to us, at least to the extent that most people, if given the choice, would prefer a life that has some kind of meaning to one that does not. Yet it is surprisingly difficult to say what exactly makes or would make our life meaningful.[1] In Douglas Adams's *The Hitchhiker's Guide to the Galaxy*,[2] it takes the supercomputer Deep Brain millions of years to come up with an answer to the 'ultimate question of life, the universe, and everything'. Famously, that answer, eagerly awaited by everyone, is 42. Naturally, this is rather disappointing because it doesn't seem to explain much, if anything, and at any rate doesn't seem to be the *kind* of answer that people are looking for when they ask that question. But what exactly *are* we looking for? What kind of answer would we consider satisfactory? What kind of answer would we even be willing to accept as an answer to our question? A mere number is clearly not going to do the trick, but what would? The trouble is that we don't really know what answer would satisfy us, which is hardly surprising since it is not quite clear what exactly the 'ultimate question' actually is.

Let us assume that the 'ultimate question of life, the universe, and everything' is a question about *meaning*. We want to know what all this is *about*, or in other words what the 'meaning of life' is, and by 'life' we usually mean everything that exists (the universe and all that is in it), but in particular our own existence. When we wonder about the meaning of life we wonder *why*, to what *purpose*, we are here, or what the *point* of our being here is. For some reason it seems important to us that there is such a point, that our life 'means' something. What is puzzling about this, however, is that it is far from clear how life should be able to mean anything at all. There certainly are things in this world that can mean something. Words and sentences mean something. A map and a road sign mean something. Even a person's look, posture or action can be meaningful.[3] What all these have in common is that they carry a message for those who can read it. They tell us something about something else, something that is not immediately present but to which what is present points.

A word or a sentence has meaning because it is intended to be understood as more than just squiggles or sounds. It has meaning because it has the power to bring to mind what is absent, if only in those who understand the language. Those who don't are left with the squiggles and the sounds. A look or a smile can also convey a message, and it 'means' something if and only if it is meant to do that. Meaning is never accidental. A footprint in the sand can tell me something (for instance that someone recently came this way), but it does not 'mean' anything unless it has been left there deliberately for me or someone else to find and draw conclusions from. For something to have meaning, there must be someone who means something by it. If nothing is *meant* by a thing then that thing has no meaning, at least not in the sense that a word or a sentence has a meaning.[4] Accordingly, unless human life and the world as we find it also carry a secret message that we are meant to understand, which does not seem likely, they don't mean anything either.

For the natural world out there to have a meaning, it would have to be like a text, as the ancient metaphor of the 'book of nature' suggests, and that text would have to be written by some supreme godlike being. But if it does contain a secret message, then we have so far failed to decipher it. And if there is no God who has used the world as his writing pad, so that there is no hidden message to be discovered by us, then it seems that the world, or life, must be considered utterly meaningless. In that case the question 'what does it all mean?' or 'what is the meaning of life?' would not only be unanswerable, it would in fact be a question that it makes no sense to ask in the first place, simply because life, like everything else in the world that is not the product of human intelligence, is not the kind of thing that can have meaning. We could just as well ask what the colour of life is. Is it green or red or blue? Of course it is none of these, nor any other colour. Questions about the colour of life cannot be answered, not because we don't know the answer, but because the question does not make any sense, and the same seems to be the case when we ask questions about the meaning of life.[5]

*

Drew Chastain: More broadly, I think the question of the meaning of life is the question of life's intelligibility. Can we make sense of it? Language and signs and symbols are paradigm examples of things that can have meaning, but life needn't fit that linguistic model in order to have some kind of intelligibility. Music can also have intelligibility without being a symbol – that is, music apart from any lyrics.[6] We can make sense of music, but it's not clear that music refers to anything, and a series of notes can make sense even if there is not someone who intended that series of notes. The intelligibility of life consists largely (I wouldn't say entirely) in having a purpose or point, a kind of *practical* intelligibility, this being a question of what we are supposed to be doing in life.[7] But I'm afraid that even if we are able to grasp the *question* of life's meaning in this way, we are still not set up for fully satisfying *answers*, even if there is a God.

To see this, let's say there is an author of all reality, including me, and imagine that, because I've been worrying over the question of the meaning of life, God decides to visit me one day to inform me of the purpose of my existence. God tells me that everyone is important and everyone has a unique purpose and that mine is X (he also asks me not to reveal it to anyone, so I will keep it a secret). Before God leaves, I beg for an answer to an additional question because my worry was not only about the meaning of my own life but about all life and reality, and, being very gracious, God informs me that the purpose of it all is Y (and again, he asks me to keep it secret).

Though of course this would be a very exciting day for me and I would feel very special to have been entrusted with the knowledge of the point of all reality by the source of reality itself, I'm afraid that it's very possible that my concern about the meaning of life could still find its way back into my soul. I can still ask, why X; that is, why is X the purpose of my existence? And, while it may be that the answer to the question of the purpose *of the purpose* of my own existence points us to Y, or the purpose of all existence, I can still ask, why Y? And why is there a God who sets purposes for existence? If there is a God, and especially if God visited me personally to help settle my doubts, it may seem very ungrateful of me to demand more answers, but then it really isn't my fault – that's how humans were created: to ask questions. Human reflection inevitably leads us outside of the frame of practical assumptions that guide us in everyday life, and outside of this frame, for better or for worse, we encounter problems that we are then unable to resolve.[8]

I remember experiencing my first serious intellectual grapplings with the question of meaning when I was in high school learning about Darwin's theory of natural selection, which tells us not only that we evolved from 'lower' life forms, but also that we don't need to appeal to a divine plan to explain that.[9] And it wasn't just grappling. I was coping. I realised that I had to *accept* that there is no God and that life unfolds randomly or arbitrarily, so that there's just a blind push forward without any pull toward some cosy destiny that could make sense of it all. Reconsidering this problem of meaning that I was experiencing then, I now want to ask the causal 'why' instead of the 'why' of purpose. In particular, why is natural selection a meaning problem – or, more precisely, why is lack of meaning in this sense experienced as a *problem* at all? Why was my teenage self coping, and why am I still coping, with the possible arbitrariness of life? To be coping is to feel vulnerable or threatened or traumatised by one's situation, like when one loses a job or a loved one dies. It makes sense that one would have to cope with material changes to one's life that directly affect one's physical and emotional security, but how does a mere reconceptualisation of our cosmic circumstance stir up a whirlwind of disorientation and distress, when no loved one has died and no job has been lost?

Some experience more distress over arbitrariness than others, but I think the problem that we feel in relation to arbitrariness is that there is no basis for saying what we are *supposed* to be doing. Some can certainly find this freeing.[10] In the absence of pre-established rules and purpose, we can create the rules and create our own purposes. But, though I'm able to accept that there is no creator God guiding us to desirable destinations, I also cannot find complete comfort in self-creation. However empowering a picture of self-creation may be, there is still something empty in viewing myself as the one who must create something out of nothing. If the question of meaning is not just a question but a *problem* with which I must cope, I think it is the emptiness (or other uncomfortable moodiness) I feel when I've lost the backdrop to my life that helps me to understand what I'm supposed to be doing.

That's why so many 'answers' to the question of the meaning of life don't satisfy. Certainly not the answer '42'. That gives me no guidance at all. The meaning I'm looking for is a practical one that grounds me and points me in some direction or other. But the deeper problem is that, for the reflective mind, the problem of meaning never really goes away once it has been identified. Human reflection is always capable of unearthing the roots of any orientation that we can feel anchored in, leaving us once again exposed to the absurd abyss of arbitrariness. So, what begins as an innocent intellectual question of the meaning of life becomes the practical question of how to live life with the intellectual question forever unresolved.

*

Michael Hauskeller: I think you are right that our concern about the meaning of life is at its core a concern about the world's intelligibility.[11] We want to understand what all this – our life, our very existence, the existence of everything – is all about, and find it difficult to accept that it may ultimately be about nothing at all; that things simply are what they are for no good reason at all. We are unwilling, or perhaps constitutionally unable, to accept the arbitrariness of things and thus we keep trying to make sense of what is going on in the world. But there are various ways in which we can make sense of things, and most of them do not really seem to get us anywhere, or at least not where we want to be.

We can certainly answer the question 'Why are we here?', or equally 'Why am *I* here?', by citing scientific evidence about the evolution of life and the origin and development of individual organisms. Yet while an understanding of the natural causes that have ultimately led to our existence may help us to make sense of it in the same way that a previously unexplained phenomenon (for instance an aurora) can be made intelligible by identifying the natural causes that have given rise to it (such as disturbances in the magnetosphere caused by solar wind), any kind of purely causal explanation must still remain unsatisfactory because it does not solve the problem. Even if the explanation were such that we can now see clearly how one thing has led to the next, so that there wasn't any room for chance anywhere along the way and everything had to turn out exactly as it did, the explanation would still be unsatisfactory because even though every single step in the history of the universe may have been necessary, none of it explains why there is something rather than nothing and why the laws of the universe are the way they happen to be.[12] No matter how comprehensively everything that happens is determined by what happened before, the entire necessary sequence of events is still unexplained and appears arbitrary.

Causes are, of course, not the same as reasons, and sometimes we need a reason to properly make sense of what is happening. If you badmouthed me behind my back and I demanded an explanation from you, asking 'Why did you do that?' (or 'What is the meaning of this?'), you would not really answer my question if you told me that what led you to do this was a combination of your genes, your upbringing, past experiences, and the affordances and constraints of the moment. 'Yes, I understand that,' I might say in response, 'and I am sure that is all very interesting, but what I wanted to know and what you haven't told me yet is *what reason* you could possibly have for doing something like that to me.' However, the reason I would be looking for in this particular situation is *not* a purpose. If you said that you did it in order to hurt me, then I would have learned something about the purpose of your action, but I would still not understand *why* you did it. For that, I would have to know what you think I have done to deserve being treated like this. Perhaps I seriously offended you in some way. If I did, then that would explain both why you badmouthed me and why you wanted to hurt me – that is, both your action and its purpose. '*Now* I understand,' I might then say. Things are making sense now.

Yet the reason given here is not an intention (or a future event that the action is meant to bring about) but something that happened in the past and is something that has (at least partly) *caused* the action that I demanded an explanation for. But it is a special kind of cause: one that stands in an intelligible, transparent relation to its effect. The connection is no longer just a given, a bare fact of nature that could conceivably have been very different than it is. That you are trying to hurt me because I hurt you makes sense, in a very human kind of way that is different from the way it makes sense that my shin hurts when you kick it. This is why the revelation of a divine purpose for the universe as a whole or for me personally would not solve the problem of meaning any more than a scientific explanation of our existence can.[13]

For my life to have meaning it is not sufficient for there to be a purpose to it, which can seem just as arbitrary as a sequence of natural causes. If God revealed his plans to me, this might explain certain features of the world that I previously failed to understand (for instance why there is so much evil in the world), but it would only satisfy the desire I express when I wonder about the meaning of life if it were no longer possible for me to ask 'why this plan rather than a different one?'. In other words, it would have to be immediately clear to me that this plan is indeed the only plan that makes sense.

That is why I am intrigued by the example you have used to cast doubt over my claim that only things that are *intended* to mean something can mean something. Your example was music. You point out, rightly, that a musical composition does not (unlike a sentence) necessarily refer to anything (just like life or the universe), and also that a series of notes can make sense without there being any intention behind them (just like life and the universe). I think you are on to something here. So how exactly does music make sense despite not being about something? I am not sure that intention, or at least an orientation towards a prefigured goal, is completely irrelevant here. It seems to me that a combination of musical notes makes sense only as long as we regard them as the product of a composition and that it would no longer make sense if this particular combination of notes were perceived as a product of pure chance. In this respect it would be similar to a poem that seems to make perfect sense, but would cease to do so if it were discovered that it was in fact produced by a toddler who randomly pressed the keys of a desktop without having any clue about what they were doing. The poem would then have no meaning at all, just as a cloud that happens to look like a dog has no meaning, precisely because the fact that it has for a while assumed the shape of a dog is entirely coincidental.[14] And yet, we may want to say that the meaning of the music resides in the architecture of the sound alone – that it neither needs to tell us anything about something that is not itself (like a sentence or a traffic sign), nor does there need to be a particular intention or purpose behind it. All that is necessary for it to make sense is that its elements are *evidently* in tune with each other: that it exhibits a certain rightness and fittingness, perhaps even goodness, that the ear can detect and that presents itself to us unquestionably. We can experience this without being pointed in any particular direction or being told how to live our lives. Purposelessly purposeful, as Kant thought all beautiful things are.[15] Perhaps when life is meaningful, it is meaningful in the same way.

*

Drew Chastain: There is the question of how things make sense, and then there is the question of how things can make sense in such a way that the deepest problem of meaning is solved. You've made it clear that, even when we know purposes and brute causes, we can still have a need for meaning that seeks the reasons people have for doing things. We humans exist in an interpersonal world and the interpretation of reasons is indispensable for social navigation. But does this mean that the deepest problem of meaning consists in the frustration of the belief that events have that kind of reason? It is certainly a problem for meaning if the world isn't governed by reasons – a problem which can even infect our view of human action. There is the possibility that the conscious reasons we impute to our own actions are not the real causes of them.[16] The reasons we give may only be interpretations for our actions that we provide after the true causes found in the neurophysiological processes of the body play themselves out; a possibility which has a way of eroding our faith that life has meaning.

Having reasons as a kind of psychological state is an important part of our experience of agency and of the interpersonal social world in which we make sense of action and identity. Another way in which reasons might matter for meaning is that we can agree and disagree with other people's reasons. We make sense of things not only with our explanations of things (causes, purposes, reasons), but also by any way in which we can be grounded and oriented. If I agree with someone else, then I am *with* that person, and if I disagree with someone else, then I am in that way *against* that person. Agreeing and disagreeing with others can ground me, helping me to locate where I am socially, and identify who I am. It's cosier to be with other people because then I have a sense of connection to others – I can feel safe and accepted with a sense of belonging – but even opposition can provide me with a sharp sense of identity and orientation in life, helping me to make sense of what to do in life: that is, giving my life meaning.

If explanations matter for meaning, I think it is because of the way that explanations help to keep us oriented, but we don't always need the extra orientation of explanation to have meaning. Imagine an everyday example of seeing someone walking down the street. You can make sense of this even if you do not know the cause, purpose or reason for the person walking down the street. It can simply be someone walking down the street. You can make sense of it, yes, but then, is such a grasp of events enough for us to have meaning in life? Perhaps it could be if we didn't demand more, in which case the question becomes why do we demand more? And is there good reason to demand more? When my reflections on meaning turn in this direction (and there are so many directions such reflections can turn!), I find myself appreciating the Buddhist perspective. At the core of Buddhism is the idea that we are the cause of our own suffering and dissatisfaction because we view ourselves as separate from the surrounding reality (ego) and need control (agency), clinging to certain ways we want things to be and disrupting the flow of life and our own contentment in the process.[17] If we could be content with things as they are, whatever that may be, then the question of the meaning of things wouldn't arise, at least not seriously. Like the Zen Buddhist, we could simply laugh at the need for meaning. What if, metaphorically speaking, there is nothing more to life than seeing shapes in the clouds?

I have to confess, though, that personally I am often in a state of dissatisfaction. I often don't feel quite in tune with what I'm doing. To account for my dissatisfaction, I can point to cosmic arbitrariness, or I can point to all the things that go wrong in life or aren't quite to taste, lowering the estimation of the value of life bit by bit. Many things that were once deeply engaging to me lose their lustre through repetition and disappointment. In many ways a state of dissatisfaction with life seems appropriate, as it did to the pessimist Schopenhauer.[18] Today we face climate change which may severely limit human opportunity in the near future, along with the explosion of the human population, making each human life seem a bit less significant than before, and of course human activity is the reason for climate change, so it's easy to get disgusted with our own kind.

I have trouble determining whether the erosion of orientation and motivation in my own life has more to do with the lack of ultimate explanation or the specific circumstances of my life in these present times, and it could also be that my own personality just happens to lean in a more pessimistic direction (which would help to explain why I think about meaning so much!). But I tend to think that lack of ultimate explanation is a deep meaning problem – that is, the kind of meaning problem that disrupts orientation and motivation, or the practical intelligibility of life – only if there are more circumstantial problems already exercising one's mind. Given problematic circumstances, the reflective mind naturally seeks ultimate explanations, and in seeking hard yet finding none, the underlying circumstantial problems for meaning get exacerbated. I think that for many, faith in ultimate explanations (or not thinking too hard about them) is a way to keep the pessimism in check, but, as I see it, the real meaning challenge we face is optimism without explanation.

*

Michael Hauskeller: But what if we finally realised that an ultimate explanation is simply impossible or at least inconceivable? Should we then not be able to give up the search and be content, just as we might be if it turned out that a key we had desperately been looking for could never be found because it had never been lost in the first place? Reasons are indeed important to us. We want them to play a causal role in our life. The realisation that all our deliberations may be nothing but a sham – because before we make the conscious decision to act in a certain way, or at least before we become *aware* of it, our brain has already initiated that action – can spark a crisis of meaning because if this is true then it may appear pointless to think about what to do in and with one's life. If my actions are caused by physical events in my body and those events are caused by other such events, so that everything I do can be fully explained solely by the chain of those events, then reasons are no longer needed.

Yet if reasons are no longer needed to explain what I do, then *I* am no longer needed because what I am, or at least seem to be more than anything else, is this conscious self that thinks and plans, hopes and despairs, wills and decides, which now, in a physicalist and deterministic universe, appears to be condemned to irrelevance. We tend to associate meaning with agency. Agency is the power to make a difference.[19] If we cannot make a difference, life appears pointless, and if it is pointless, it is meaningless. In order to be able to make a difference we need at the very least to be able to make our own choices.[20] We resent being merely passive spectators, following what is happening in the world (including our own actions) as though we are watching a play, or a film, or reading a novel, where whatever happens in it, good or bad, we are completely powerless to influence it in any way.

However, even if reasons did play a causal role in how events unfold, be it only with regard to our own actions or also beyond, this would not necessarily address the problem of our perceived lack of agency. Even if we have good reasons for acting as we do, we may not be free to act in any other way because it is only because of what and who we are that we have those reasons in the first place. Even if we believe that at least the human world is still governed by reasons (or reason), we may still feel powerless and without real agency when we consider the completeness of the causal chain that links our actions back to the conditions that precede them. This would also explain why, in our desire to live a meaningful life, we feel threatened by the vastness of the universe, in terms of both space and time. Given how unimaginably large and long-lasting the universe is, there is little if any chance that anything we do will make any sort of difference in the long run.[21] In a few million years, or perhaps even much earlier, the world will probably be exactly the same as it would have been if we had never existed.

If agency is the power to make a difference and ultimately nothing we do is likely to make one, then we lack agency even if we are entirely free to make our own choices based on the reasons we choose to embrace and adopt. And if we lack agency and without agency we cannot live a meaningful life, then our life is meaningless, with or without reasons. This is also connected to our desire for an intelligible world. It is difficult to understand why we should have the impression that we are (to some extent) in charge of our lives if we are not. Why would we be able think about how to live our lives? Why can we contemplate things like the nature of the world we live in and the meaning of life if it makes no difference whatsoever? This, we feel, makes no sense.

But of course it is not entirely true that what we do in this life makes no difference. It may make no difference *in the long run*, but it may still make plenty of difference in the short and medium term. And why should a shorter-lived difference not matter? Why should we value only differences that are ever-lasting? And even if it were true that we have no real choice in what we do or don't do, it would still be we who would be doing it. A lot of things may happen that would never have happened without us. So in that sense we *do* make a difference.[22]

I am wondering, though, whether in order for our lives to be meaningful we *have* to make (or at least be able to make) a difference at all. What if we really had no power to influence the course of events – if our role really were merely that of a spectator who cannot do anything but watch as time (as well as life and world) goes by? We don't usually think or feel that a film or a novel is meaningless just because we cannot influence the events in it, nor do we think or feel that our watching the film or reading the book is meaningless. On the contrary, what often happens is that we forget, for a time, our own existence, immersing ourselves instead fully in those fictional worlds, losing ourselves almost entirely in the events we see unfolding before our outer or inner eye.

Something similar happens when we immerse ourselves in a piece of music. That is not meaningless, even though there is no exchange of reasons here. Yet there is still some kind of grounding, as you call it: the creation of a connection, a belonging, a being-with. Can we not experience the universe and our role in it in a similar way? Perhaps not necessarily by agreeing with everything that happens in it (which seems to be the Buddhist way and is also what Nietzsche[23] advised we do to find meaning in life), but occasionally also by disagreeing (as Camus[24] encouraged us to do). In any case, what is needed is a constructive dialogue of sorts (not dissimilar to the one you and I are having right now, with each other as well as with the reader), but not so much a dialogue that aims at finding ways of making a lasting impact on the world (forming it in our image), rather one that co-develops a mutual responsiveness for the way in which the other inhabits and constitutes the world. Optimism without good reason is not the real problem at all. Rather, such optimism is in fact the solution to our concerns about meaning. As I see it, the Buddhist perspective is not so much that nothing means anything and therefore we shouldn't care, but rather that life is meaningful, or perhaps we should better say *significant*, precisely because it is not meaningful – that is, it contains no message to be deciphered and no purpose or underlying rationale to be understood. Perhaps it all really is just shapes in the clouds. I find this rather appealing.

*

Drew Chastain: What is 'connection'? I would like to focus in on that term.[25] I think a sense of connection is deeply important to meaning in life – it is the very depth of life's meaning. It is more basically important than goals and reasons and projects and desires, or any kind of active agency. When we sense a lack of meaning, the absence of goal orientation is most conspicuous – our first thought is, what is the point? what is the purpose? – but lying less detectably beneath this surface problem is a deeper problem of a lack of connection: our ungroundedness, alienation, emptiness, fakeness or boredom. What meaning is there in a goal if there is not a sense of connection with self, or with the world or with others in one's pursuit of that goal? And, even while active agency is a common and generally reliable way of getting connected, we can certainly experience connection without goals and purposes. As I sit and listen to the frogs on the pond, taking the dampness of the recent rain into my lungs, I get some distance from the day's frantic errands and, even as today's goal orientation slips away, somewhat more palpably a sense of meaning returns. But what is it? What more can we say about this sense of connectedness?

We are definitely working with metaphor here, because physical connectedness does not guarantee the sense of connection we want to illuminate. While telephonic and digital forms of communication can keep us closer to others than we otherwise would be, one can also be alone in a crowded room. Likewise, connection is not guaranteed by spiritual contact, understood in a supernatural way. If there is such a thing as demonic possession, this involves spiritual contact but the very opposite of a sense of connection. So I think we must look for a psychological phenomenon that undoubtedly depends upon physical or spiritual contact in various ways, but is not entirely conceptually reducible to contact. Also, despite the external relation emphasised by the metaphor of connection, I think that an internal relation is just as important. The externally oriented metaphor is appropriate because a sense of connection involves the experience of a return to the world or a return to others, but at the same time there must also be a return to self.

But what does *this* – a return to, or connection with, self – mean? There's a lot to explore here, but I don't think that connection to self is achieved merely by enacting an *idea* of who or what you are. It is more like enabling the flow of what your embodied subjectivity actually needs to express or experience in a given situation, whether this fits your idea of yourself or not. Sometimes this will be experienced as active agency, sometimes as passivity, sometimes experienced through emotion, sometimes through contemplation, sometimes experienced by being with others, sometimes by being alone, sometimes just by being here now.

Whatever connection is exactly, and even if I am right that it is the deeper thing we miss when we experience meaninglessness, my darker, pessimistic side still worries that the value of a sense of connection can wane over time – not just my own personal taste for it but connection's real desirability. I think that the underlying problem is that I have to continue the story of me.[26] Connection matters because *I* feel disconnected. But how many times can I value reconnection? This vessel for meaning gets chipped and scuffed. It wants to be filled a thousand times, perhaps more, but then it wants to be dashed into a hundred pieces in the fireplace. I cannot really aspire to be like a cloud, continually changing shape – at least not so radically as those vapours in the sky. As it is, when I look in the mirror, I find that same persisting human being: the one who I must be my whole life, with his ever-lengthening history, who can make less and less sense of the arrows of goals and the anchors of connection.

Put another way, agency loses its oomph. You say that agency is the power to make a difference. I think that's one aspect. But I think there is a value in agency – that intentional action mode – not just for what it can do, but also for the way it changes our experience of life when it overtakes us. I find myself desiring agency not just to make a difference but also to experience more emphatically that I am someone. As we grow up, which psychologically can take decades, there is an experience of agency in transformation and growth and finding one's potential, which isn't just the agency of performing a task, but the agency of becoming oneself and feeling one's power. This could be called an uphill experience of agency, or we could say it is like a tree reaching its full height as it gains more and more perspective on the world into which it could not help but break forth. But over time the reflective mind gets the overall story – this is me, breaking forth into the world – and that basic storyline gradually loses its tension.

Even if one commits one's life to helping others, or raising children, so that one lives a life that is not all about 'me', I think this problem of the slow disenchantment with the story of me gets delayed, but it's still there. With the slackening of suspense, my capacity for the uphill experience of agency also loses its energising potential. The downhill then looks more appealing: the wrap-up, the fade-out, a desire for nothingness, when meaninglessness feels better than meaning, or more true. A general point I keep coming back to in our dialogue is this: I don't think that the possibility of justified pessimism goes away with any analysis of meaning or any metaphysical or circumstantial description of the world. I think each of us has a voice inside, enabled by our reflective capacity, which asks, 'why more?'. One becomes a pessimist to the extent that one allows oneself to hear this voice and then comes to appreciate how difficult a truly satisfying response is.

*

Michael Hauskeller: Perhaps there is no truly satisfying response to the question of meaning. The moment it occurs to us to ask the question 'why more', thus demanding that we be given a *reason* to go on living, we are lost. When the oomph has gone, something other than reason is needed to restore it. Life is only ever truly meaningful when it is *unquestioningly* meaningful – when things matter not because we have convinced ourselves with compelling arguments that they do, but because we never feel the need for an argument in the first place. Meaninglessness only becomes a problem for the sceptic. In that respect it is like the problem we have when we doubt the existence of an external world, the reliability and trustworthiness of our senses or our reasoning, or the objectivity of moral values. Once we have articulated the doubt, there is no way back; at least not through theorising.[27] It is impossible to prove, beyond any doubt, that there really is an external world, that whenever we are certain about something we cannot possibly be wrong, or that the actions we consider morally wrong really *are* wrong.

Fortunately, it is rather rare for us to seriously entertain any of those doubts. Even philosophers, who make a living from raising and debating such doubts, are normally quite happy to live their lives as if our ordinary assumptions about how the world works are all perfectly justified and undeniably true. And when they do, they find themselves, like David Hume when he took a break from his sceptical writings to dine, chat and play backgammon with his friends, quickly cured of their 'philosophical melancholy and delirium'.[28] (This is the saving grace of our profession: we rarely mean what we say.) Those, however, who *do* mean it are the lost ones: they face a gulf that has opened between them and the world and that they have no way of bridging. They are stranded on the other side of everything, deprived of the connection that keeps most of us grounded in the world. This connection is indeed neither physical nor spiritual. I would call it, for lack of a better word, existential. Instead of entertaining a merely theoretical doubt, they let their doubts transform their experience of the world. Instead of merely saying 'This appears real to me, but is it really?', 'This appears true to me, but is it really?', and 'This appears (morally) wrong to me, but is it really?', they internalise their doubts to such an extent and in such a way that things do no longer even *appear* real, true, or right and wrong to them.

The same happens when we start doubting that our lives have meaning. It can be a merely theoretical exercise, which is designed to (still rather playfully) test the strength of the connection, but it can also be more serious. If it is the former, we say 'This matters to me, but does it really?', but if the latter, then this changes to 'This does not matter to me, and nor does anything else'. And right at the top of the things that no longer matter to me is what is real and what is not, what is true and what is not, and what is good and what is not. This is why when the world loses its meaning for us, it appears chimerical, indifferent, a fake. It is the very *realness* of things that is at stake here, and that includes our own realness for ourselves. We are no longer connected and that is precisely why we no longer even find it desirable to be connected.

When everything appears meaningless, then meaningfulness, too, appears meaningless. When nothing matters, the mattering of things does not matter either. In that situation, reason is helpless. What is needed is a leap of faith, although that sounds too deliberate. It might be more accurate to say that what is needed is something that pulls us back to the other side – a lucky break, the good fortune of coming across something that breaks through and rebuilds our connection to the world. Things must reimpose their significance on us, reclaim their intelligibility, speak to us again in a language that we can understand, like they speak to non-human animals when they live a life that suits their needs and interests, perfectly in tune with their environment, never doubting that what they do matters and that their life is worth living.[29]

*

Drew Chastain: Lately in the philosophy of life's meaning, the trend is to ignore the general question of pessimism altogether, although this was a problem placed front and centre by earlier writers such as Leo Tolstoy and Albert Camus. The question of why we should live despite meaninglessness or absurdity is present even in the more recent reflections of Richard Taylor and Thomas Nagel.[30] But, for twenty-first-century philosophers of life's meaning like Susan Wolf, this core problem of meaning vanishes.[31] The task is no longer to grapple with reasons why we feel defeated by life. Instead, we are invited to line up lives side by side to determine whether these lives are more or less meaningful as judged by someone taking an external standpoint on them.[32]

For instance, what do we conclude if we reflect on the lives of Mahatma Gandhi or Oprah Winfrey, versus, say, a destitute person whose unlucky background and personal decisions led her to engage almost exclusively in trivial acts her whole life, only to die an early death from drug addiction? On the contemporary approach to meaning in life, the lives of the former have more meaning mainly because they are oriented toward activities having more value, while the latter's unfortunate life is less meaningful, if not meaningless, because she failed to pursue sufficiently worthwhile engagements. This approach to meaning in life certainly captures one way in which we make judgements about whether life (or a life) is meaningful, but my sense is that it doesn't capture the deeper question, and for that reason it comes off as a rather superficial analysis of meaning.

I think that the deeper question is experienced from the first-person perspective, or the internal standpoint.[33] It is the existential question of why I should live, rather than the more thin, comparatively evaluative question of whether so-and-so's life can be said to possess enough value for it to be deemed meaningful by an external observer. These questions are certainly related – when I wonder why I should live, I wonder about my life's value, thus taking an external standpoint on my own life. But if the internal question is absent, it is not clear what's at stake when we are making the external judgement. This is one problem with the contemporary approach. Another problem is that, from the internal standpoint which gives depth to the question of life's meaning, the answer to the question of whether I should live may well be highly subjective and there really may be no good answer at all. Ultimately, I am not personally greatly invested in relativism or nihilism, but a good, honest response to the question of why I should live has never been able to free itself of these haunting possibilities. As long as this is the case, no external standpoint has earned the right to project its presumptive judgements onto others.

On the other hand, as you say, the pessimistically posed question of why I should live seems to have its source in the sceptical stance, and the problem of meaning seems to easily dissolve as soon as one's practical engagements with life distract us from unanswerable scepticism. Perhaps we should drop the 'deep' question and just pursue our best guesses at what's worthwhile even if we can't answer the sceptic by providing a philosophical foundation for objective value. I feel the force of that point, but at the same time this opportunity for open dialogue has helped me to see that I don't think the sceptical or pessimistic stance is without substantive motivation. Existential concerns are real. In my view, problems such as death and the possibility of ultimate purposelessness or the absence of personal free will are more real than the problem of knowledge, though the contemporary approach to meaning in life treats such existential concerns as unimportant. But we shouldn't sideline these concerns. Instead, we should try to better understand what makes these problems for meaning, or else we lose touch with why meaning matters in the first place.

That said, I should make clear that I am not really a pessimist per se, even if I take pessimism seriously and experience the drag of scepticism about meaning in my own life. I've come to think of myself as a

Janus-faced 'ambivalentist', who is both pessimistic and optimistic about life itself, not just my own life, struggling with the basic question of whether the difficulties of life are worth it. On the optimistic side of things, I have found that I personally feel most life-affirming when I'm feeling creative, constructive and connected. I like how you say that our shifts from scepticism to affirmation are not really a leap of faith but a matter of luck, because I think it is largely the case that authentic optimism finds us, while forced optimism can suffer from fakeness. But at the same time, as we gain more insight into our sources of optimism, we can include a bit of strategy and wisdom in our search for meaning, rather than leaving it all to fate.

Notes

1. For a concise overview of the contemporary analytical debate on both the meaning *of* life and meaning *in* life and the difficulties of agreeing on what exactly the term 'meaning' means when applied to people's lives, see Metz, 'The meaning of life'.
2. Adams, *The Hitchhiker's Guide to the Galaxy*.
3. See Nielsen, 'Linguistic philosophy and "the meaning of life"'.
4. This is known as the 'endowment thesis'. See Morris, *Making Sense of It All*, 56: 'Something has meaning if and only if it is endowed with meaning or significance by a purposive agent or group of such agents.' We do, however, sometimes use the word 'meaning' in a broader sense that does not depend on there being an agent who intends that that meaning be there and be understood. For instance, we can say that the footprint in the sand 'means' that somebody must have left it there, even if leaving it was not intentional. This is what H. P. Grice called the *natural* sense of meaning, contrasting it with its more common and more fundamental *non-natural* sense in which words and sentences can have meaning which can always be traced back to an agent's intentions. See Grice, 'Meaning'.
5. Of course, when a question appears unanswerable because it doesn't seem to make any sense in the context in which it is asked, we may simply have to improve our understanding of the question. See Thomson, 'Untangling the questions', 42.
6. Koopman and Davies ('Musical meaning in a broader perspective', 261) challenge the linguistic model of musical meaning, arguing that music has meaning through its dynamic structure rather than by referring, representing or expressing as words do.
7. For more on my own view about meaning as practical intelligibility see Chastain, 'Can life be meaningful without free will?'.
8. These reflections owe something to Thomas Nagel ('The absurd', 141), who says that if 'we can step back from the purposes of individual life and doubt their point, we can step back also from the progress of human history, or of science, or the success of a society, or the kingdom, power, and glory of God, and put all these things into question in the same way'.
9. Of course, these were some of my initial reactions in my youth – I don't mean to indict evolutionary theory as emptying the world of meaning. For some counterbalancing perspective see Levine, *Darwin Loves You*.
10. See Camus, *The Myth of Sisyphus*, 53: 'It was previously a question of finding out whether or not life had to have a meaning to be lived. It now becomes clear, on the contrary, that it will be lived all the better if it has no meaning.'
11. That the meaning of life consists in nothing but 'the information a person needs to make sense of it' and hence its intelligibility for a particular person has recently been argued by Thomas, 'Meaningfulness as sensefulness'. According to Thomas, the more relevant information I have about the world, the more I can make sense of it, and the more I can make sense of it, the more meaningful my life is. The problem with this interpretation of meaning is that it frames an experienced absence of meaning as an epistemological rather than an existential crisis.

12. Kurt Baier ('The meaning of life', 82) has argued that even though 'no type of human explanation can help us unravel the ultimate, unanswerable mystery' of why there is something rather than nothing, this should not bother us because once we understand how things hang together – that is, how they fit into the system of rules that govern the universe – no further explanation is required. Once we know how things work, we know everything there is to know about the world, and since this still leaves room for human purposes, and meaning in life consists in having such purposes, a commitment to a scientific, naturalistic worldview does not prevent anyone from living a meaningful life.

13. For the opposite view that only a divine purpose for the world and our existence in it can make human life meaningful, see for instance Craig, 'The absurdity of life without God' or Hill, 'The meaning of life'.

14. Or, as Hilary Putnam (*Reason, Truth, and History*, 1–21) put it, it doesn't 'represent' anything: if a line drawn in the sand which appears to be a picture of Winston Churchill turns out to have been made accidentally by an ant's random crawling around in it, is not really a picture, or representation, of Churchill at all because the ant was never aware of Churchill's existence in the first place and, accordingly, had no intention of depicting him.

15. Kant, *Critique of the Power of Judgement*, Third moment of the analytic of the beautiful, §17: '*Beauty* is an object's form of *purposiveness* insofar as it is perceived in the object *without the presentation of a purpose*.'

16. As has been argued, in a string of publications, by Benjamin Libet. See for instance his 'Do we have free will?'. For a critique of Libet's conclusions see for instance Seifert, 'In defense of free will'.

17. See Gowans, 'The Buddha's message'.

18. See Schopenhauer, 'Additional remarks on the doctrine of the suffering of the world'.

19. For a detailed discussion of 'agency' see the next chapter in this book.

20. See Midgley, *Evolution as a Religion*, 14: '[P]eople often find plenty of meaning in their lives if they are working for their own purposes in harmony with those around them.'

21. This thought plunged Leo Tolstoy into a deep existential despair. 'Today or tomorrow,' he wrote in his *Confession*, 'sickness and death will come . . . to those dear to me, and to myself, and nothing will remain other than the stench and the worms. Sooner or later my deeds, whatever they may have been, will be forgotten and will no longer exist. What is all the fuss about then? How can a person carry on living and fail to perceive this? That is what is so astonishing! It is only possible to go on while you are intoxicated with life; once sober it is impossible not to see that it is all a mere trick, and a stupid trick.' (21) Tolstoy's sentiment is echoed by many contemporary writers, including those who support a supernatural account of meaning in life which makes it dependent on the existence of God. See for instance Craig, 'The absurdity of life without God'. Joshua Seachris ('Death, futility, and the proleptic power of narrative endings') calls the underlying intuition that in order for things to be worthwhile and meaningful they have to *last* (forever) the 'staying-power intuition'.

22. I have developed this argument further in Hauskeller, 'Out of the blue into the black'.

23. Nietzsche, *Ecce Homo*, passim. For a more detailed account of Nietzsche's philosophy of life see 'The joy of living dangerously' in Hauskeller, *The Meaning of Life and Death*, 113–32.

24. 'Rebellion is the common ground on which every man bases his first values. I rebel – therefore we exist' (Camus, *The Rebel*, 28).

25. I develop an analysis of the concept of connection, suggesting how an experience of connection supports meaning in life, in Chastain, 'Deep personal meaning'.

26. To aid in thinking through this phenomenon of telling oneself stories about oneself, see Velleman's exploration of the notion of a narrating self (in response to Daniel Dennett) ('The self as narrator'). While Velleman is pondering the ontology and function of self-narration, I am expressing the concern that this sense-making ability that self-aware beings have can still fall short of supporting motivation to keep going in life, no matter how much value is attributed to oneself in one's self-narrative, and even if one's self-narrative is hitched to a fairly robust narrative of the meaning of life itself. Compare Seachris, 'The meaning of life as narrative'.

27. Descartes tried this in his *Meditations* and failed spectacularly.

28. Hume, *A Treatise of Human Nature*, book I, section 7.2.

29. On the meaningfulness of the life of non-human animals see Hauskeller, 'Living like a dog'.

30. The relevant works by Tolstoy (*A Confession*), Camus (*The Myth of Sisyphus*) and Nagel ('The absurd') have been cited in previous footnotes. Richard Taylor makes the pessimistic point that life is objectively meaningless because it is a cyclical, repetitive activity that ultimately comes

to nothing, but he adds that life can be made subjectively meaningful if it is in you to do what you are doing ('The meaning of life', 128–31).

31. Wolf ('The meanings of lives', 71) advises that pessimists upset by their cosmic insignificance simply 'Get Over It'.

32. See Wolf, *Meaning in Life and Why It Matters*.

33. My inspiration here comes from Thomas Nagel (*Mortal Questions*, chapter XI), who includes the internal standpoint in the overall analysis of the problem of meaning in life.

BIBLIOGRAPHY

Adams, Douglas. *The Hitchhiker's Guide to the Galaxy*. London: Pan Books, 1979.

Baier, Kurt. 'The meaning of life'. In *The Meaning of Life*, edited by E. D. Klemke and Steven Cahn, 76–102. New York/Oxford: Oxford University Press, 2018.

Camus, Albert. *The Rebel*, translated by Anthony Bower. Harmondsworth: Penguin, 1962.

Camus, Albert. *The Myth of Sisyphus and Other Essays*, translated by Justin O'Brien. New York: Vintage International Books, 1991.

Chastain, Drew. 'Can life be meaningful without free will?', *Philosophia* 47 (2019): 1069–86.

Chastain, Drew. 'Deep personal meaning: a subjective approach to meaning in life', *Journal of Philosophy of Life* 11/1 (2021): 1–23.

Craig, William Lane. 'The absurdity of life without God'. In William Lane Craig, *Reasonable Faith: Christian truth and apologies*, 57–75. Wheaton, IL: Good News Publishers/Crossway Books, 1994.

Descartes, René. *Meditations on First Philosophy*. Oxford: Oxford University Press, 2008.

Gowans, Christopher W. 'The Buddha's message'. In *The Meaning of Life*, edited by E. D. Klemke and Steven M. Cahn, 27–34. New York/Oxford: Oxford University Press, 2018.

Grice, H. P. 'Meaning', *The Philosophical Review* 663 (1957): 377–88.

Hauskeller, Michael. 'Living like a dog: can the lives of non-human animals be meaningful?', *Between the Species* 23/1 (2019), Article 1. https://digitalcommons.calpoly.edu/bts/vol23/iss1/1 (accessed 1 December 2021).

Hauskeller, Michael. *The Meaning of Life and Death: Ten classic thinkers on the ultimate question*. London: Bloomsbury, 2019.

Hauskeller, Michael. 'Out of the blue into the black: reflections on death and meaning'. In *Exploring the Philosophy of Death and Dying: Classic and contemporary perspectives*, edited by Michael Cholbi and Travis Timmerman, 262–8. New York and London: Routledge, 2021.

Hill, Daniel. 'The meaning of life', *Philosophy Now* 35 (2002): 12–14.

Hume, David. *A Treatise of Human Nature*. Harmondsworth: Penguin Classics, 1985.

Kant, Immanuel. *Critique of the Power of Judgement*. Revised edition. Cambridge: Cambridge University Press, 2002.

Koopman, Constantijn, and Stephen Davies. 'Musical meaning in a broader perspective', *The Journal of Aesthetics and Art Criticism* 59/3 (2001): 261–73.

Levine, George. *Darwin Loves You: Natural selection and the re-enchantment of the world*. Princeton, NJ: Princeton University Press, 2006.

Libet, Benjamin W. 'Do we have free will?', *Journal of Consciousness Studies* 6/8–9 (1999): 47–57.

Metz, Thaddeus. 'The meaning of life', revised 2021. In *Stanford Encyclopedia of Philosophy*. https://plato.stanford.edu/entries/life-meaning/ (accessed 1 December 2021).

Midgley, Mary. *Evolution as a Religion*. London and New York: Methuen, 1985.

Morris, Thomas. *Making Sense of It All: Pascal and the meaning of life*, 56. Grand Rapids, MI: William B. Eerdmans Publishing, 1992.

Nagel, Thomas. *Mortal Questions*. Cambridge: Cambridge University Press, 1979.

Nagel, Thomas. 'The absurd'. In *The Meaning of Life*, edited by E. D. Klemke and Steven M. Cahn, 137–46. New York/Oxford: Oxford University Press, 2018.

Nielsen, Kai. 'Linguistic philosophy and "the meaning of life"', *CrossCurrents* 14/3 (1964): 313–34.

Nietzsche, Friedrich. *Ecce Homo*. Revised edition. London: Penguin, 1992.

Putnam, Hilary. *Reason, Truth, and History*. Cambridge: Cambridge University Press, 1981.

Schopenhauer, Arthur. 'Additional remarks on the doctrine of the suffering of the world'. *Parerga and Paralipomena*, volume 2, translated by E. F. J. Payne, 291–305. Oxford: Clarendon Press, 1974.

Seachris, Joshua. 'The meaning of life as narrative', *The Journal of the Society of Humanist Philosophers* 20 (2009): 5–23.

Seachris, Joshua. 'Death, futility, and the proleptic power of narrative endings', *Religious Studies* 47/2 (2011): 141–63.

Seifert, Josef. 'In defense of free will', *Review of Metaphysics* 65/2 (2011): 377–407.

Taylor, Richard. 'The meaning of life'. In *The Meaning of Life*, edited by E. D. Klemke and Steven M. Cahn, 128–36. New York/Oxford: Oxford University Press, 2018.

Thomas, Joshua Lewis. 'Meaningfulness as sensefulness', *Philosophia* 45 (2019): 1555–77.

Thomson, Garrett. 'Untangling the questions'. In *Exploring the Meaning of Life*, edited by Joshua W. Seachris, 40–47. Chichester: Wiley-Blackwell, 2013.

Tolstoy, Leo. *A Confession*, translated by Jane Kentish. London: Penguin, 2008.

Velleman, J. David. 'The self as narrator'. In *Autonomy and the Challenges to Liberalism: New essays*, edited by John Christman and Joel Anderson, 56–76. Cambridge: Cambridge University Press, 2005.

Wolf, Susan. *Meaning in Life and Why It Matters*. Princeton, NJ: Princeton University Press, 2010.

Wolf, Susan. 'The meanings of lives'. In *Introduction to Philosophy: Classical and contemporary readings*, 4th edition, edited by John Perry, Michael Bratman and John Martin Fischer, 62–74. Oxford: Oxford University Press, 2007.

2
Agency

with Helen Steward

Helen Steward: I first became interested in the power I call 'agency' through thinking about the problem that determinism is supposed to present for free will.[1] Not everyone agrees on how exactly free will should be characterised. For some it involves the power to do otherwise than one in fact does; for others it attaches to loftier notions like self-determination and autonomy.[2] But there seemed, at the time, to be general agreement that free will should be thought of as a power specific (at any rate so far as its manifestations on earth are concerned) to human beings – and that the 'problem' which determinism presents is one which arises only in connection with certain human-specific powers. In particular, virtually none of the literature on free will ever mentioned the capacities of non-human animals.

But to me, the idea that a universe containing the activities of creatures such as chimpanzees, dolphins, elephants and dogs might safely be regarded as entirely deterministic seemed as strange as the idea that one containing human beings might be so. Surely, I thought, at least some animals do things in contexts in which it is right to say that they could have done otherwise (than do those things). Think of a cow meandering around a field, going this way and that; or two squirrels rolling and tumbling around in play; or birds selecting nesting material. In all these cases, and many others like them, it seemed to me, we perceive the exercise of various powers which seem, on the face of it, just as difficult to square with determinism as do the morally loaded human choices on which the philosophical free will literature tends to focus. I felt convinced that a certain degree of freedom attached to all these animal activities – and I was interested in exploring further whether that thought could be justified.

It is not surprising, of course, that the free will debate has tended, historically, to focus on capacities unique to human beings. That debate, like most other longstanding philosophical debates, has its roots in a religious context which took the special status of human beings entirely for granted – they were creatures made in God's image and so creatures which of course should be expected to have unique metaphysical powers, and to be 'outside' nature in certain respects. But stripped of that religious context, the supposition that it is human agency *alone* that presents problems for determinism looks much more problematic. What on earth could it be about us humans, specifically, that presents an obstacle to determinism? What is it about our mode of functioning *in particular* that makes it look as though a certain kind of flexibility must be present in nature? Libertarianism can come to look foolishly anthropocentric and anti-naturalistic when it alleges that it is *just us*, alone in the natural world, who have managed to escape the shackles of an otherwise thoroughgoing determinism. I was interested in the prospect of developing a more naturalistic style of incompatibilism that might attempt to root a determinism-disrupting freedom somehow in animal biology. We already have reason to suspect that life introduces surprising new properties to the world – I wanted to argue that agency might be one of them.

A concept I have made use of in the development of my ideas about agency is the concept of 'settling'.[3] The vision of the universe that determinism offers us is one in which everything that happens is settled in advance by things that have already happened or which are otherwise already fixed (such as the laws of nature or God's prescription). If determinism is true, nothing that happens is ever newly settled at the time at which it occurs – since everything that happens is *already* settled – and nothing can be (newly) settled *at t* that was already settled prior to *t*. But I think our natural conception of action supposes actions themselves to be settlings of the hitherto unsettled – things such that it is up to the agent *at the time of action* whether or not they will occur. Actions simply cannot be settlings in this sense, if determinism is true. And so if I am right that it is in fact essential to the concept of an action that it be a settling by its agent of what is hitherto unsettled, then there is a conflict not only between human-specific powers of 'free will' or 'freely willed action' and determinism, but between agency itself and determinism. Actions themselves then cannot be accommodated by the deterministic universe. This view I call 'agency incompatibilism' and I think it offers a much more palatable version of libertarianism than do many traditional versions of incompatibilism.

Is it right to think that it is essential to the concept of an action that it be a settling by its agent of what is hitherto unsettled? There are of course conceptions of actions on which this wouldn't be true. Some think, for example, that inanimate entities can act – that water acts, for instance when it dissolves salt.[4] I don't mind, of course, if people want to use the language in that way. But I do want to insist that there is another concept for which no better term suggests itself than 'action', which is such that water is not the sort of thing that could be engaged in it. Nothing is ever up to water. When water 'acts' on salt, what is occurring is an inevitable inter-action, and there is nothing at all strange about the supposition that all of the fine details of this interaction are settled in advance of its actual occur-rence (though as a matter of fact, the supposition could be false),[5] by facts about the distribution of the salt, the temperature of the water, the shape of the container in which the water is held, etc. My interest is in a concep-tion of action and agency which draws a fundamental distinction between the 'doings' of things like water and another class of doings, the ones which manifest what I should like to call the *two-way power* of agency.[6]

*

Michael Hauskeller: It is indeed important to distinguish between the way an inanimate object can be said to 'act' or do things and the way we humans and also many (if not all) animals do. Ordinary language tends to blur or even ignore that difference.[7] I can be hit by a rock, but I can also be hit by another person, but what the rock does is in fact quite different from what the person does when they perform an act of hit-ting. It is an altogether different category, a different *sense* of doing, and what makes it different clearly has something to do with the difference between the power we think rocks have (and the power we think they lack) and the power both people and many non-human animals appear to have. 'Two-way power' is a good term for this: it is the power to do *or* not do a certain thing. In contrast, inanimate objects like rocks have only one-way power: the power to do a certain thing without the power not to do it. When prompted in a certain way (e.g. you pick it up and throw it), the rock will act in a certain way (i.e. follow the trajectory of your throw and hit me). It has the power to do so, but not the power not to do so. We, on the other hand, and generally all proper agents, also have the power when prompted in a certain way (e.g. I annoy you) to act in a particular way (e.g. you throw a rock to hit me) or not to act in that particular way (i.e. not throw it and do something else instead). In other words, we have the power to act in *more than one* way. Or so it appears to us.[8]

Yet even though we strongly feel that we have the power to do otherwise than we in fact do, we are also very much aware that this power is far from unlimited. What freedom we have, we have within the limits of our nature. We can be fairly sure that there are certain actions that somebody we know (be it a human or a non-human animal) is not going to perform. It is extremely unlikely that the colleague I'm having a relaxed chat with during my lunch break will suddenly start screaming and destroying the furniture, or that my beloved dog will suddenly, in the middle of her morning walk, turn on me and tear me apart. Clearly, this is not physically impossible for them and it wouldn't break any known laws of nature if they did it, but, *being who and what they are*,[9] it is just not something they would do, and if they did do it we would immediately assume that they must have lost control over their actions and that something else must have stripped them of their agency and made them behave in that otherwise inexplicable manner.[10]

In that sense their actions are more or less predictable.[11] They are free to do certain things or not to do them, but they are not really free to do just about anything or not to do it. There are options, but those options are quite limited and determined by the situation and the nature and history of the agent. This is why there is a certain degree of reliability in our interactions with other agents. Accordingly, agency is in practice not the power to do something that goes against our nature. It is the power to do a certain range of things that lie *within* our nature to do (and to not do the things that do not lie in our nature to do).

But how do we know that we have such a power? It certainly *feels* like we could have done otherwise, and when we observe the behaviour of other people and animals it certainly gives the impression that they, too, could have done otherwise, since we are unaware of anything that would have *compelled* them to act the way they did. At the same time, however, it seems impossible to verify any of this. I can never know whether I or anyone else really could have done otherwise because there is no way to test the hypothesis.[12] In order to do so I would have to be able to go back in time and recreate exactly the same situation, which we know is impossible. Doing something different now than we did last time does not prove anything, because we are no longer in the same situation. The circumstances have changed. So perhaps, despite appearances, we are not free to do otherwise than we in fact do after all.

If you are right that true agency (the kind that both human and non-human animals have but rocks don't) is not compatible with determinism, then it follows either that determinism is false or that there is no such thing as true agency. Yet determinism is not so easily abandoned.

The trouble is that no matter how strongly we feel that we and others have the power to settle certain things, it is difficult to see how this should be possible. It seems that this would require a suspension not only of determinism, but also of our belief in the universal validity of the principle of causality, which is fundamental to our thinking and which makes a commitment to determinism appear inevitable.[13] Whatever happens must have been caused by something, and whatever caused it to happen must have been caused by something else. Nothing comes from nothing. Things are connected by chains of cause and effect. If that were not the case and things could happen that have not been caused by anything, then anything could happen at any time. Yet this, as far as we know, is not the way things work. And even if it were possible for things to happen for no good reason at all, unconnected to and undetermined by anything that happened before, it would not help us to understand the possibility of agency any better. We don't, after all, want to say that what we do hasn't been caused by anything at all. What we want to be able to say is that it has been caused by *us*, which of course begs the question: what has caused us to be the way we are? And if there is something that has caused us to be the way we are (as we must assume), then it seems that we could not in fact have acted otherwise than we in fact did.

*

Helen Steward: I agree, of course, that agency does not consist in the power to do just anything. There are things I physically cannot do; there are also many things I could not (as we might say) bring myself to do – and this latter sort of restriction might be just as significant in ruling certain things out for me as are the laws of physics. That is in fact one reason why I think it is very important to characterise the two-way power that is essentially involved in agency not as a power to do A or B, for some specified independent pair of distinct options, but rather as the power, implicit in any active exercise of agency, not to have undertaken that very exercise of agential power.

The 'A or B' way of thinking about things has led some philosophers to argue that when we face decisions which are easy for us, because, for example, the reasons all speak in favour of one option and against the other, nothing goes on which is incompatible with determinism – we are determined by our reasons to do A, say (and would be unable to 'bring ourselves', perhaps, to do the unpalatable B).[14] But this would be a mistaken inference. There may indeed be a sense in which it may be impossible for me to do B, if there is a great deal to be said against doing it and nothing at all in favour. But this does not mean that my action (when I 'do A') is determined. That I am determined by my reasons on a given occasion doesn't imply that my action (when I undertake it) is deterministically caused. What's determined by the agent's reasons is, for a start, not a token event, but a fact – 'that the agent will (try to) do A' (at some point, in some way, on some occasion – much normally remaining to be settled).[15] And the nature of the determination is not of the brute event-causal sort by means of which the fall of one domino can determine that the next will fall too. It is the agent (and not events inside her) who is said to be determined by her reasons – and what we mean in saying that is merely that the agent formed her intentions on the basis only of the assessment of the relative power of the various reasons at work. Reasons are not causal players which are independent of the agent and her power of action at all – they are merely considerations she responds to in deciding what to do. Their 'power' is metaphorical and utterly dependent upon hers.

Talk of 'determination by reasons' presupposes that an agent with agential powers will be effecting any necessary action. It is not at all the same kind of determining as is implicit in the doctrine of determinism. What determinism would imply is that the actual (token) action I undertake was necessitated to happen, exactly as it did, exactly when it did, etc. And the fact that my reasons for doing something can be overwhelmingly strong does not imply that anything like this is true.

You ask the important question of how we know we are not determined. I agree that in a sense it may be impossible to verify the fact, with respect to any given occasion, that we could have done a different thing. But it is arguable that we are also unable to verify such important and foundational things as the existence of the external world and the existence of other minds.[16] There may be things we have to take for granted in philosophy, despite their unverifiability – and it has always puzzled me a bit that external-world scepticism and what one might call free-will scepticism have been treated so very differently in philosophy (at any rate in recent years). We are permitted to assume the existence of the external world, it seems, despite the fact that no one has really (at least in my estimation) come up with an argument that shows that its existence is more likely than not! But we are *not* permitted likewise to assume the existence of free will (in the sense of alternative agential possibilities). We must worry that determinism might be true, because it is perfectly consistent with all our 'evidence'. But so is the non-existence of the external world, given a certain conception of what that evidence amounts to.[17] In my view, the denial of real, in-the-moment alternate possibilities deals a blow to our ordinary worldview of much the same sort of magnitude as the denial that the external world exists. Nothing we believe can remain in place if this has to go. If it has to go, there are no agents, there is no (real) thinking, there are no (real) choices or decisions, there is no moral responsibility. There is just 'the dull rattling-off of a chain forged innumerable ages ago'.[18] This is very far from being the world we think we inhabit.

In abandoning determinism it would of course be very problematic if, as you say, we were forced to abandon any principles we ought to take to be obviously true. But I deny that we are forced to do so. You say that we would be forced to abandon the idea that 'whatever happens must have been caused by something'. But there are a number of important points to make about this claim. One is that it appears to be false! There do seem to be spontaneous events in nature (such as radioactive emission events) – we cannot just assume that every event has a cause.[19] A second is that 'caused by' and 'determined by' don't mean the same thing. An agent's doing something may have a variety of causal explanations – and that may enable us to identify a number of things that were the causes of that agent's doing that thing. But that doesn't mean that those causes either individually or jointly determined that the agent's action would occur. A third and final point is that our mental models of how causation works may well not be up to the job of encoding the hugely rich and complex variety of causal (including inter-level) relationships that exist in nature. I've tried to argue, for instance, that it might be possible for a whole to affect its own parts[20] – and that actions might precisely be instances in which whole animals bring about activity in their own sub-systems.

*

Michael Hauskeller: It would indeed be a blow to our ordinary worldview if we accepted determinism as true and became convinced that whatever we do is always something we have no choice not to do. Going about our daily business, we naturally assume that many of the things we do we could just as well not do.[21] And when we reflect on our experience, we still feel very strongly that very often we *do* have a choice. We may not, as you say, always have a choice about *what* to do, but even then we still seem to be able to choose *when* to do it and *how* to do it.

We feel equally strongly about the existence of an external world and the existence of other minds, even though the evidence we have in this regard is ultimately inconclusive, so that we can no more prove their existence than we can prove the existence of free will and (true) agency.

So why, you wonder, is scepticism about the existence of the external world or other minds far less common than scepticism about (or even denial of) the existence of free will? It seems to me that this can be easily explained by the fact that while there is very little that militates in favour of the non-existence of an external world and other minds other than our inability to prove their existence beyond any philosophical doubt (which may or may not be *reasonable* doubt), the denial of free will (and hence true agency) follows directly from our commitment to the law of causality and the difficulty of understanding what we actually *mean* by 'free will' or the 'power to do otherwise than one in fact does'.[22]

There is something rationally compelling about determinism that is absent from the denial of an external world or other minds. We may find it difficult – perhaps even impossible – to give up our instinctive belief in the reality of choices, but most people will find it at least equally difficult to abandon their epistemic commitment to the principle of causality. This commitment is in fact so fundamental to how we think about and experience the world that Kant can be excused for concluding that it can only be accounted for if we assume that causality is, just like space and time, not something we happen to come across in our experience of the world, but rather an essential and indeed necessary aspect of the *way* we experience it. Causality, in other words, is not one of the many contents of conscious experience, but part of its very *form*.[23]

It is of course possible that Kant was wrong to assume that the principle of causality is universally valid so that nothing could ever happen without a cause. Perhaps some things do happen without a cause, for instance quantum events or other events occurring at a subatomic level such as the so-called 'spontaneous emission' of electromagnetic radiation. Then again, perhaps they don't and we simply haven't been able (so far) to find the cause.[24] Yet, as noted before, even if we accept the possibility of uncaused events, this does not bring us any closer to understanding the supposed two-way power of agency. Whatever actions are, they cannot be (or be like) spontaneous, entirely uncaused eruptions of a physical nature, because if they were, they wouldn't be actions. For an event to be an action, it must not be uncaused; it must be caused by the agent. And that is the difficulty we face when we try to understand agency. It seems to require something that is in fact conceptually far more difficult to grasp than the suspension of the principle of causality. What we need to get our heads around is not causation or its absence, but the possibility of self-causation. A true agent, it seems, is, like the God of some philosophers: *causa sui* – her or his own cause.[25] Is this something we can really make sense of?

In order to understand agency, we need to carve out a space for the agent to genuinely settle things: things that are neither uncaused nor causally determined by anything but the agent herself. You attempt to create that space by making a distinction between reasons and causes, and also between causation and determination. I want to believe this works, but I'm not sure it does. Reasons are not 'causal players', you say, but merely considerations the agent (freely) responds to. I take this to mean that they don't compel us to act in any particular way. But then, are we free to ignore the relative strength of the reasons that appear to us, so that even though we have most reason to do A, we are still free to exercise our agency by doing B or at any rate *not* doing A? And what about non-human animals, which we believe are also agents? Do they, too, 'consider' reasons for acting in a certain way and reasons for not acting that way? Does talk about reasons and how reasons are different from causes help us understand how animals exercise their agency?

Sometimes, when I am walking my dog and I decide it's time to go home and I call her, she does not come right away but stands still, as if considering whether she should heed my call or ignore it. Then, after a few seconds, she makes up her mind and settles the matter, by either running towards me or staying where she is and continuing to do what she was doing before I called her. I very much doubt that she was engaged in an assessment of the relative weight of reasons to stay or go. So what exactly was going on when, for a few seconds, she was undecided and then, suddenly, she was undecided no longer?

*

Helen Steward: I am sure you are right that the reason why scepticism about free will is so much more commonplace than (genuine) scepticism about the external world has something to do with the difficulty we have in understanding how free will can be consistent with something else we think we have reason to believe in – something you call 'the law of causality'. But what does the law of causality say, exactly? Since it rules out free will, it seems important to be very clear what the principle says. As I have said, if it is the claim that every event has a cause, it seems not to be true. Is it perhaps, then, the claim that all *non-random* events have causes? But no one is denying that actions have causes. Among the causes of my getting up may be my realising that it's time to go for my train, for instance. But this doesn't imply that having realised this, I couldn't possibly have done anything else, does it?[26]

Perhaps, then, the thought is rather that all non-random events must have causes which *necessitate* them – causes which are such that no other event could have resulted from them. Perhaps it's tempting to suppose that unless causes are necessitating in this way, there must always be an *element* of randomness about the question whether the result occurs or does not occur. But now we need to know more about what it is for an event to be 'random'. I think it is probably true of events in the inanimate world that if they are not necessitated, then there is something about their occurrence which will have to amount to happenstance – if the event might not have occurred, then however *probable* its occurrence, there still seems to be a chance element involved. But are we allowed to suppose without argument that this principle governs the whole of reality – including the animate world and the actions that it contains? That, it seems to me, is to beg the very question at issue. The question at issue is *precisely* whether it is true that all non-random events must have causes which necessitate them. And it might be argued that actions constitute a major exception to this principle.

We already know, don't we, that any event which is an action is (to that extent) in a sense *not* a random or chance occurrence – for when something is an action, we know already that it was the agent's doing – and that is (in everyday contexts) sufficient to allay the ground-floor question, 'why did *that* happen?'. That is not, indeed, the question we will generally want to ask when we seek to understand a happening in the domain of action: what we will want to ask is normally something of the form 'why did he do *that*?'.[27] The metaphysics is not what puzzles us – what may puzzle us in an everyday context is the agent's motivation. It is not at all like a case in which, for example, a book suddenly falls off a shelf and we wonder what has triggered it. We don't generally have the triggering worry *at all* in connection with things we have identified as actions. Perhaps that is because we already encode actions cognitively in a way that does not presuppose the need for any trigger.

Nevertheless, you may say: as metaphysicians, we *ought* to be puzzled! Can actions just start? How? You say that for an event to be an action, it must be caused by the agent. But I would argue that this is a mistake.[28] If actions are caused by agents, we must ask the question: is there room, or is there not, for the question *how* the agent has caused them? If we say 'yes', we seem to be off on an infinite regress, since the only ordinary way we have of understanding how agents cause things (when they do so intentionally, anyway) is by way of action. A second action would therefore be required to understand the means by which the agent brought about the first one. On the other hand, if we say 'no', we seem committed to agents causing things without actually *doing* anything – and that seems incoherent. So I think we must resist the idea that agents cause actions. Rather, actions just *are* agents' causings of *other* events – events like arm-raisings and leg-extensions, for example – and also the further effects of these things, like windows being opened and goals being scored.[29]

Still, you may say, actions *begin*. Surely no event in nature can *just begin*! Of course, actions require underlying neurological activity, and to that extent I would agree that we need some sort of account of how the causal principles which govern the underlying neurological hardware are to be rendered consistent with the idea that whether or not an action occurs is up to its agent at the time of action. Ultimately, it seems to me, what we need to understand is not self-causation, exactly, but rather whole–part causation. We need to understand how a whole animal can make something happen in one of its parts – and that requires a better understanding than we currently have of *top-down* causation.[30] I don't think this is easy to come by. But nor do I think there's any a priori reason for thinking it must be impossible. Indeed, I rather think there are a priori reasons for thinking it must be possible! For unless it is, it seems very difficult to understand how the integration of sub-systemic activity which is so obviously a feature of animal life can be maintained. I am now sitting typing at my computer, for example. The muscles which keep me from slumping must be engaged, as must my sense of balance. The knowledge I have of how to move my fingers to hit the right keys at the right time, to type the words I want to write, must be active. I must screen out distracting noises in order to concentrate. And all these things must happen *at the right time* and *in the right order*. Coordination is required. How is it possible to understand such coordination unless wholes are somehow able to influence their parts – to make it the case that the parts are working harmoniously together?

*

Michael Hauskeller: Yes, I can see that, but does that really help us understand the possibility and nature of agency? After all, most of those coordinated and integrated sub-systemic activities do not seem to be controlled and directed by me at all. 'I' do not make any decisions about, say, my blood circulation or my digestive processes, and yet they are certainly an essential part of the system that I am, tirelessly working to ensure that system's continued existence. Nor do I normally engage my sense of balance or the muscles that keep me from slumping when I sit and write.

These things are clearly coordinated and integrated, but I am not the one who is doing the coordinating and integrating, at least not the I that we are wont to take ourselves to be. I am not even sure it is entirely correct to say that *I* am coordinating the movement of my fingers when I am typing these lines. From my perspective as a conscious, decision-making being, those things just happen, which means they are not actions – or if they are, then I am not really the agent of those actions. There may well be top-down causation, but it is far from obvious who or what is at the top here. The whole may well influence its parts, but which whole or what kind of whole is ultimately in charge? Is my conscious self the 'whole animal' that is keeping it all together? Is my conscious self that which performs that whole animal's actions, that which settles things, or is it just another sub-system that is engaged by that animal to cause certain events? And would it really matter if it were? Do I, or my conscious self, *have* to be in control for those actions to be mine?

Let us look again at what is going on when we make a decision to do something rather than not to do it. I am asleep in bed, the alarm clock rings, I wake up, remember that I have to catch a train, and get up. We can then say that I am getting up *because* I remember that I have to catch a train, or that my remembering this *causes* me to get up. But surely, you say, I could have stayed in bed, *despite* having a good reason to get up. So even if my remembering the train I have to catch *causes* me to get up, it does not *necessitate* my getting up, because I was still free not to. It is hard to disagree with that. However, I don't think anyone, not even the most committed determinist, would claim that a single contributing cause, *on its own*, necessitates a certain outcome. Rather, what is being claimed is that the *whole situation* was such that no other outcome was possible.[31] If I am getting up, and getting up at this particular moment, I am doing this not *solely* because I remember the train I want to catch, but because, in addition, I am sufficiently awake, my bladder feels unpleasantly full, the central heating is already on so that there's no cold room to deter me, I happen to be the kind of person who hates being late, I am hungry and if I don't get up right now I won't able to eat anything before leaving, catching the train is very important to me because I know that if I miss it I won't be able to attend the interview that might get me the job that I desperately want to have, and so on and so forth. There may be a large number of aspects of the given situation that jointly determine what I do, some of which I am consciously aware of and many others that I am completely ignorant of, and none of which would on its own necessitate anything. So strictly speaking a single event is never the determining cause of an effect: it is always the entire state of affairs at a particular moment in time that *determines* what happens next. Single events can only ever be contributing factors. So if we ask 'why did I get up?' the full answer would have to list all those different factors, which is impossible. This is why we tend to focus on the most obvious, conspicuous or interesting one: because I remembered that I had a train to catch.

Do we now really want to say that despite all these factors coming together to jointly cause me to get up at this moment (and thus to cause my causing), I could *still* have done otherwise? That it was still 'up to me' to get up or not to get up? But was it not up to me anyway (namely to the whole animal that I am)? Did I not *decide* to get up, even though, given the situation I was in, I could not really have done otherwise and it would have made no sense whatsoever if I had? I did not, after all, get up against my will or against my inclinations. Nobody made me get up or manipulated me to do something that I didn't really want to do. On the contrary, getting up is *exactly* what I wanted to do. So why must we insist that I could just as well not have done what I in fact did? What exactly do we *gain* by that?

*

Helen Steward: I think there has been some misunderstanding here. I didn't mean to claim that the example I gave of typing, as a case which necessarily involves the integration and coordination of various sub-systems, would count as a case of integration and coordination all of which is *done by the agent*. I agree with you that of course much of the coordination which goes on in this case is certainly sub-agential. I only meant to claim that if there were such integration and coordination, it might be an example of something we could reasonably think of as *top-down causation*. And just because *some* such integration and coordination is clearly sub-agential (as you say), it wouldn't follow that *all* of it is.

Once one has had the thought that biological organisms are in general characterised by a hierarchical form of organisation in which top-down (as well, of course, as bottom-up) causation has a role to play, it doesn't seem such an enormous step (at any rate to me) to think that agential control might be, as it were, the topmost form of control in the hierarchy – a way in which a minded organism can respond with *discretion* to rapidly changing environmental information, balancing such things as short-term and long-term priorities, individual gain and social approval, selfish wants and the needs of others, against one another. Do we know that evolution has not found such a discretionary capacity to be an improvement on any deterministic system that might be envisaged for producing effective and appropriate actions under the complex conditions presented by the ecological niche human beings occupy and the huge part played in that niche by social bonds and social forms of organisation? If so, how do we know? What I dispute is that there is any obvious 'principle of causation' known to be true by us in advance that would rule it out.

I don't in fact disagree with you that there can be circumstances in which the fact that an agent will do some particular kind of thing (φ) in a given situation (e.g. get up soon after their alarm clock has gone off, once they remember that they have a train to catch) is pretty much settled by facts pertaining to that agent's overall constellation of reasons, traits, etc. (together with the absence of certain potential interfering factors, such as physiological impediments). But what I would want to deny is that we can move easily from a recognition of this kind of general settledness and predictability concerning the sorts of things agents will be apt to do under certain conditions to the idea that therefore human agency is consistent with the thesis of universal determinism, from which it follows not only that the *general lineaments* of an agent's doings are determined from time to time by prior circumstances of various kinds, but also that every last detail of timing, trajectory, expression, speed, etc. is thus determined, as the agent moves through the world. That is a much stronger thesis and it requires much more than just the general recognition that (i) what is rational to do is sometimes obvious and (ii) in such cases there is no realistic possibility of the agent's doing otherwise than taking the rational course of action, provided some catastrophic failure of her agency (such as a sudden paralysis) doesn't occur.

The thesis of universal determinism requires that *absolutely everything* is already settled. And it is this totalising deterministic picture that I find very difficult to believe is really consistent with the power to make interventions into the world of which we are truly the source. That there may often be general facts about me, my reasons and my situation which make it more or less impossible to imagine why I would do anything other than φ in a given situation (and hence 'determine' what I do) is something I am absolutely prepared to accept. But the individual actions and activities by means of which I respond to those reasons cannot in my view be themselves the upshot of deterministic processes. It seems important that I have to *execute* those processes, at a time of my choosing and in a way which I control – and these things are essential to the phenomenon of agency. If my so-called 'action' is just produced by neural firings, which in turn were produced by prior neural firings, and those by still earlier events, the whole chain being necessitated, then agency seems to me not to be what we generally take it to be – a power to *settle* things at the time of action as we move through the world. Like other source incompatibilists, I think this picture turns agency into an illusion.

I agree, then, that we don't *gain* anything from having the power to do things we haven't the least inclination to do. But from my point of view, the question of what we would gain from having this power is the wrong question. That question already assumes that there could be a 'we' even in the absence of any power, on the part of those individuals, to settle things. It assumes that there could be subjects with interests (things to 'gain') who nevertheless lacked the capacity to make events go one way when they really could have gone another. But my question is whether the whole conceptual scheme which surrounds the idea of agency can be made sense of without beings who can settle things, be the source of things. Once such beings are in existence, of course, it is of no *further* help to them to be able to do things they don't want to do, haven't decided to do, can see no reason to do, and so on. But they have to be *in existence* in order to be the sorts of beings to whom things can be of help in the first place – and that is the thing which in my view requires alternative possibilities – although not alternative possibilities of the kind which are usually thought to be required for freedom and/or moral responsibility.

*

Michael Hauskeller: I must admit that I find it most difficult to wrap my head around this whole issue. Like you, I cannot bring myself to accept that everything we do, and everything that happens in the world, has been settled all along. Ironically, I feel that I have no choice but to believe in free will – or, more precisely, the power to settle things myself – just as I have no choice but to believe in the existence of an external world and other minds. This is not because the alternative is not conceivable, but because it is part of the fabric of reality as it presents itself to me and generally to beings such as us. The future, I feel very strongly, has not been settled yet. If it had, it wouldn't be the future; it would be merely a kind of past in disguise – a past that we haven't had the chance to become aware of yet. And if the present didn't give us the chance to settle things that hadn't been settled before, then the present would also be merely a version of the past – one that we could observe but not affect in any way. The present, however, appears to be real, which is to say, full of real possibilities, as the past is full of roads not taken that could have been taken when the past was still the present. There are things we can decide, things we can settle ourselves, things that are up to us.

And yet, when I start thinking about it, I am struggling to understand how this is supposed to work and what exactly it means to be the kind of (moderately) free agent that I take myself (and other people, but also non-human animals like my dog) to be. This is because determinism seems rationally compelling to me. Then again, I'm not sure we should worry too much about it. Our discussion of agency has been haunted by the seemingly awful and repulsive spectre of determinism, looming darkly over our ability to act. In a desperate attempt to escape its clutches, we have insisted that it is not real – that it is one of those monsters that reason has a tendency to conjure up. But perhaps we should simply pay less attention to it and understand agency on its own terms. If we did that, we might no longer feel the need to conceive of agency as the power to do otherwise than one in fact does, which is a power we can never be sure we have, nor is it one that it would be particularly desirable for us to have. That is why I asked earlier what we would gain from such a power.

In very simple terms, I exercise my agency when I do what I want to do. This is a power I clearly have. I share this power with other people and other animals. This does not of course mean that it is *always* possible for me to do what I want to do, but very often it is. What I do *not* seem to have is the ability to do what I do *not* want to do, but I do not usually consider this a problem because I have no good reason to want a power that allows me to do what I do not want to do. As long as I am free to do what I want to do, I have all the freedom I need and care about. I do not feel any less free just because I am not free to want what I don't want, or not to want what I want. And if I had that kind of freedom, if I were free to *decide* what I want (which is not the same as figuring out what I want when I am unsure about it), then there would be no *me* that could make a decision. For I am someone, and I am someone because there are things I want to do and things I do not want to do. There are things that interest me, that I care about, that move and engage me in particular ways. If that were not the case, I would be no one. But in order to *do* something, we first need to *be* something. And while we can choose what we do, we cannot choose what we are. Nobody is their own creator.

What and who we are (as a particular kind of biological organism and as individuals) is, to a large extent, not up to us. We find ourselves in the world, shaped physically and mentally by our genes, our history and our environment, none of which is in our control, and we become *someone* through the combined effect of all these forces – a superject rather than a subject. And *then* we act, on that basis: free agents not because we can do otherwise than we in fact do, but because we do what, being what we are, we feel we have to do. Sometimes the clearest expression of agency is not the arbitrary ('I did this, but could just as well have done that'), but the necessary. Martin Luther, when asked to renounce his teachings by the German emperor Charles V, is supposed to have refused with the words: 'Here I stand. I can do no other.' This is not a declaration of failed agency. It may in fact, on the contrary, be an articulation of agency's very essence.[32]

Notes

1. For the results of those reflections see my book *A Metaphysics for Freedom*.
2. These different conceptions of free will have generated two different versions of the position generally known as 'incompatibilism' (the view that determinism is incompatible with free will). One is called 'leeway incompatibilism' and argues that *having the capacity to do otherwise* is incompatible with determinism. The other is called 'source incompatibilism' and argues that *being the source of one's own actions* is incompatible with determinism. The most influential recent argument for leeway incompatibilism is that offered by van Inwagen in *An Essay on Free Will*. Roderick Chisholm in 'Human freedom and the self' and Robert Kane in *The Significance of Free Will* both offer arguments for source incompatibilism. For an argument that the two kinds of incompatibilism are in any case connected see Timpe, 'Source incompatibilism and its alternatives' and my 'Frankfurt cases, alternate possibilities and agency as a two-way power'.
3. See in particular my *A Metaphysics for Freedom*, chapters 2 and 3. The notion of settling has some affinities with the STIT ('sees to it that') operator, introduced by Belnap et al. in *Facing the Future*.
4. For a view of this kind see Alvarez and Hyman, 'Agents and their actions'.
5. Why would it be false? It would be false because in a world which contains settlers of matters, those settlers can intervene to prevent and interrupt things that would otherwise occur. See Anscombe, 'Causality and determination' for persuasive arguments.
6. For reflections on the concept of a two-way power see Alvarez, 'Agency and two-way powers'; Frost, 'What could a two-way power be?'; and my 'Agency as a two-way power: a defence'.
7. And not only ordinary language. Notoriously, Actor-Network Theory postulates a fundamental symmetry between human and non-human actors, which includes things as diverse as 'microbes, scallops, rocks, and ships' (Latour, *Reassembling the Social*, 11), and assigns agency to all of them in equal measure. For an introduction see Latour, *Reassembling the Social*; for a critical defence see Sayes, 'Actor-Network Theory and methodology'.
8. There is a school of thought that claims that our sense of agency is in fact deceptive. We *think* we act (freely), when in fact we don't. See for instance the collection of papers in Caruso, *Exploring the Illusion of Free Will and Moral Responsibility*.
9. Compare Midgley, *Beast and Man*, 327: freedom, 'in the sense in which we really value it, does not mean total indeterminacy, still less omnipotence. It means the chance to do *what each of us has it in him to do* – to be oneself, not another person.'
10. For the connection between what we are and how we act, the extent to which our behaviour is predictable, and how this limited predictability affects the dispute between determinism and anti-determinism, see Danto and Morgenbesser, 'Character and free will'.
11. Mary Midgley wrote: 'It is quite easy to be unpredictable, if you don't mind acting crazily. But freedom does not require craziness. Nor does it require omnipotence . . . To be unpredictable, not only to other people but to oneself, is to have lost all control over one's destiny. That is a condition as far from freedom as rolling helplessly downhill' (*Wickedness*, 102–3).
12. See Northcott, 'Free will is not a testable hypothesis'.
13. See for instance Mackie, *The Cement of the Universe*. For an opposing view see for instance Anscombe, 'Causality and determination' and Friedman, 'Analysis of causality in terms of determinism'.
14. For views of this sort see in particular van Inwagen, 'When is the will free?' and Ekstrom, *Free Will*.

15. For a much more detailed discussion of the ontological categories of 'event' and 'fact' see my *The Ontology of Mind*.
16. For further reflections on the parallels between the free will problem and scepticism about the external world see my 'Free will and external reality'.
17. For the classic version of this argument see Descartes, *Meditations* I and II.
18. See James, 'The dilemma of determinism'.
19. See https://en.wikipedia.org/wiki/Radioactive_decay (accessed 1 December 2021) for a brief introduction to the notion of spontaneous radioactive decay.
20. See my *A Metaphysics for Freedom*, chapter 8.
21. And it would be hard, perhaps impossible, not to make that assumption, given how much of our interaction with other people and often also non-human animals relies on it. See Strawson, 'Freedom and resentment'.
22. For a discussion of the various problems the concept of free will faces see for instance Slote, 'Understanding free will'.
23. Kant, *Critique of Pure Reason*, A195–6.
24. For an overview of the current debate on events that appear to have no cause see Svozil's *Physical (A)Causality*, which is dedicated to Kant.
25. See for instance Morden, 'Free will, self-causation, and strange loops' and Strawson, 'Free agents'.
26. See Anscombe's 'Causality and determination' for vigorous arguments against the equation of causality with determination.
27. See Hornsby, 'Action and causal explanation'.
28. Many philosophers have made this argument. For a classic version see e.g. Davidson, 'Agency'.
29. For views along the same lines see Bishop, *Natural Agency* and O'Connor, 'Agent causation'.
30. For discussions of 'top-down' or 'downward' causation see Campbell, 'Downward causation in hierarchically organised biological systems' and the papers collected in Andersen et al., *Downward Causation*.
31. And this whole state of affairs naturally includes not only physical states, but also agential states such as an agent's beliefs and desires. See List, 'Free will, determinism, and the possibility of doing otherwise'.
32. This example is also discussed by Dennett, *Elbow Room*, 133.

Bibliography

Alvarez, Maria. 'Agency and two-way powers', *Proceedings of the Aristotelian Society* 113 (2013): 101–21.
Alvarez, Maria, and John Hyman. 'Agents and their actions', *Philosophy* 73 (1998): 219–45.
Andersen, Peter Bøgh, Claus Emmeche, Niels Ole Finnemann and Peder Voetmann Christiansen (eds.). *Downward Causation*. Aarhus: Aarhus University Press, 2000.
Anscombe, Elizabeth. 'Causality and determination'. In *Collected Philosophical Papers*, volume 2, 133–47. Oxford: Blackwell, 1981.
Belnap, Nuel, Michael Perloff and Ming Xu. *Facing the Future*. Oxford: Oxford University Press, 2001.
Bishop, John. *Natural Agency*. Cambridge: Cambridge University Press, 1989.
Campbell, Donald T. 'Downward causation in hierarchically organised biological systems'. In *Studies in the Philosophy of Biology: Reduction and related problems*, edited by Francisco Jose Ayala and Theodosius Dobzhansky, 179–86. London/Basingstoke: Macmillan, 1974.
Caruso, Gregg D. (ed.). *Exploring the Illusion of Free Will and Moral Responsibility*. Lanham, MD: Lexington Books, 2013.
Chisholm, Roderick. 'Human freedom and the self'. *The Lindley Lectures*, Department of Philosophy, University of Kansas; reprinted in *Free Will*, edited by Gary Watson, 2nd edition, chapter 1. Oxford: Oxford University Press, 2003.
Danto, Arthur, and Sidney Morgenbesser. 'Character and free will', *The Journal of Philosophy* 54/16 (1957): 493–505.
Davidson, Donald. 'Agency'. In *Essays on Actions and Events*, 43–61. Oxford: Oxford University Press, 1980.
Dennett, Daniel. *Elbow Room*. Cambridge, MA: MIT Press, 1984.

Descartes, René. *Meditations* I and II. In *The Philosophical Writings of Descartes*, volume II, edited by John Cottingham, Robert Stoothoff and Dugald Murdoch. Cambridge: Cambridge University Press, 1984.

Ekstrom, Laura. *Free Will: A philosophical study*. Boulder, CO: Westview Press, 2000.

Friedman, Kenneth S. 'Analysis of causality in terms of determinism', *Mind* 89/356 (1980): 544–64.

Frost, Kim. 'What could a two-way power be?', *Topoi* 39 (2019): 1141–53.

Hornsby, Jennifer. 'Action and causal explanation'. In *Simple-Mindedness*, 129–53. Cambridge, MA: Harvard University Press, 1997.

James, William. 'The dilemma of determinism'. In *Essays in Pragmatism*, 37–64. New York: Hafner, 1970.

Kane, Robert. *The Significance of Free Will*. Oxford: Oxford University Press, 1996.

Kant, Immanuel. *Critique of Pure Reason*. Translated and edited by Paul Guyer and Allen W. Wood. Cambridge: Cambridge University Press, 1997.

Latour, Bruno. *Reassembling the Social: An introduction to Actor-Network Theory*. Oxford: Oxford University Press, 2007.

List, Christian. 'Free will, determinism, and the possibility of doing otherwise', *Noûs* 48/1 (2014): 156–78.

Mackie, John Leslie. *The Cement of the Universe: A study of causation*. Oxford: Clarendon Press, 1974.

Midgley, Mary. *Beast and Man: The roots of human nature*. Hassocks: Harvester Press, 1978.

Midgley, Mary. *Wickedness: A philosophical essay*. London: Routledge & Kegan Paul, 1984.

Morden, Michael. 'Free will, self-causation, and strange loops', *Australasian Journal of Philosophy* 68/1 (1988): 59–73.

Northcott, Robert. 'Free will is not a testable hypothesis', *Erkenntnis* 84/3 (2019): 617–31.

O'Connor, Timothy. 'Agent causation'. In *Agents, Causes and Events: Essays on indeterminism and free will*, edited by Timothy O'Connor, 173–200. New York: Oxford University Press, 1995.

Sayes, Edwin. 'Actor-Network Theory and methodology: just what does it mean to say that nonhumans have agency?', *Social Studies of Science* 44/1 (2004): 134–49.

Slote, Michael. 'Understanding free will', *The Journal of Philosophy* 77/3 (1980): 136–51.

Steward, Helen. *The Ontology of Mind: Events, processes and states*. Oxford: Oxford University Press, 1997.

Steward, Helen. *A Metaphysics for Freedom*. Oxford: Oxford University Press, 2012.

Steward, Helen. 'Free will and external reality: two scepticisms compared', *Proceedings of the Aristotelian Society* 118/2 (2019–20): 1–20.

Steward, Helen. 'Agency as a two-way power: a defence', *The Monist* 103/3 (2020): 342–55.

Steward, Helen. 'Frankfurt cases, alternate possibilities and agency as a two-way power'. In *Fifty Years of Responsibility without Alternate Possibilities*, edited by Geert Keil and Romy Jaster. Special Issue of *Inquiry* 2021: https://doi.org/10.1080/0020174X.2021.1904639.

Strawson, Galen. 'Free agents', *Philosophical Topics* 32 (2004): 371–402.

Strawson, Peter F. 'Freedom and resentment', *Proceedings of the British Academy* 48 (1962): 1–25.

Svozil, Karl. *Physical (A)Causality: Determinism, randomness and uncaused events*. Cham: Springer, 2018.

Timpe, Kevin. 'Source incompatibilism and its alternatives', *American Philosophical Quarterly* 44/2 (2007): 143–55.

van Inwagen, Peter. *An Essay on Free Will*. Oxford: Clarendon Press, 1983.

van Inwagen, Peter. 'When is the will free?', *Philosophical Perspectives* 3 (1989): 399–422.

3
Body

with Lewis Coyne

Michael Hauskeller: For all we know, there are no free-floating spirits: we are all embodied beings. And yet we routinely talk as if our bodies are not really essential to what we are – as if the connection between us and our bodies is merely accidental. We do know, of course, that we are pretty much stuck with the body we have, but we still fantasise about swapping bodies with others,[1] acquiring new bodies, and even getting rid of our bodies altogether, be it by continuing our existence in a bodiless form after our death[2] or by uploading our minds to computers before our death in order to gain some kind of 'digital' existence.[3] While the fact that we can *imagine* this kind of thing may not in any way prove that we can *actually* live without a body (which is what the French philosopher René Descartes claimed),[4] it is certainly suggestive of the possibility. We cannot deny that we all, as a matter of fact, have bodies; but we also feel that bodies are not really what we are – that what we really are is not our body, but something that inhabits that body, something inside, something that is in principle detachable from the body. This seemingly immaterial something is traditionally called 'the soul' or, perhaps more commonly today, 'the mind'.

Now if this is what we really are, then the body may indeed be best understood as a mere 'vessel': nothing more than a 'mortal shell' or, even more drastically, the soul's tomb, as the Pythagoreans, echoed by Plato, declared the body to be (*soma sema*)[5] – which strongly suggests that we are somehow impaired and curtailed in our freedom by our body and that we would be better off, or at any rate freer, without one.

This idea of the body as something that, for some unknown reason, we are intimately connected with but that is still distinct from what we really are of course has roots in our own personal experience. For one thing, we often feel insufficiently represented and indeed let down by our bodies. There is so much we want to do and so much we cannot do because our bodies are so weak and frail. Often it seems as if the only thing standing in the way of our fully becoming what we feel we truly are is our own body. Then there is also the fact that we can actually see and touch our body, just as we can see and touch other objects in the world out there. Being visible and touchable (as well as audible and smellable), the body is clearly also an object – one among others, a thing really – and we know ourselves to be not *merely* an object, not a thing, but (at least primarily) a *subject*: unlike mere objects, we are thinking beings; we are world- and self-aware.

In addition, we very much *use* our body as a tool, or rather a well-stocked tool box. 'Tool' is actually what the Greek word 'organ' (*organon*) means, and rightly so because our organs function as tools: we use our eyes to see, our ears to hear, our hands to handle things, our feet and legs to walk, just as we use other things – a knife to cut things, a vehicle to move around and so on. All these tools, both those that form part of our body and those that do not, help us do and get what we want, but they are not us. Rather, we are the ones who use those tools. This is why we can even replace parts of our body without compromising our identity. If for instance one of my hands is cut off, I have one tool fewer at my disposal, but I am not suddenly split in two parts – the hand part and the rest-of-my-body part. By having my hand separated from my body I am not being separated from myself. While I am certainly losing part of my body, I am not losing a part of me in the sense that I am now less me than I used to be.

And yet, despite all the evidence that speaks in favour of there being a difference between us and our bodies, doubts remain; and those doubts, too, are rooted in our experience. If you break my knife or crash my car, I don't feel it directly as something that is being done to me. I can shrug it off as being of little concern to me. In contrast, if you break my nose or shatter my kneecap, it is difficult if not impossible for me to remain indifferent to what is happening, because by inflicting damage on my body you are also, directly, inflicting damage on me. What goes on in my body goes on in me. If you hurt my body you are hurting me, because if my body hurts *I* hurt. And it is not just our body's pain that we feel directly as our pain. Unsurprisingly, our body's pleasure is very much our pleasure, but also, although perhaps less obviously, my emotions are very much my body's emotions.[6] When I am tired my body is tired; when I am angry my body is angry; when I am in love my body is in love. We think, feel and indeed live in and through our bodies. In that sense, we do not *have* a body: we *are* that body.

So what is it? Do we have a body or are we that body? Or is it perhaps both: are we the body that we have? But isn't that a contradiction? How can we both have something and be what we have? Isn't that like saying that we are both identical with our body and not identical with it – that we both are our body and are not our body?

*

Lewis Coyne: The German philosopher Martin Heidegger once said that the 'body phenomenon is the most difficult problem'.[7] I'm not sure that it is the *most* difficult problem, but Heidegger was rightly perplexed by exactly the dilemma that you identify: the body both appears to be something that we *have*, somewhat like a tool, and also appears to be what we *are*.[8] How can we make sense of this apparent contradiction? We might be tempted to follow Descartes, who famously argued that while he could doubt the existence of his body, he could not doubt that he existed as a mind, for the mere act of doubting was enough to prove it.[9] As he put it: *cogito, ergo sum* (I think, therefore I am).[10] Although he did ultimately accept the reality of his body, Descartes' method led him to believe that we are thinking things that merely *have* bodies: a theory that has exerted great influence over Western intellectual history ever since.[11]

What Descartes overlooked, however – or at the very least undervalued – is the fact that much of our lives, even for philosophers, is spent not in thought, but rather in engagement with people and things in the world.[12] Reflection on how we encounter such beings and the world opens a window onto the peculiarity of the body and undermines Descartes' position.

Say, for example, that I am walking across a pebble beach in search of a stone to skim on the water. As everyone knows, I will consciously be looking for a circular, flat stone, as these are best able to hit the water without sinking. But my goal here will also be defined, in ways that may not even be explicit, by the possibilities made available by my body, and in particular by my hands. Without really thinking about it I will be looking for a stone of the right size and heft, which essentially means the right size and heft *for me* to hold and throw. This act of sorting takes place prior to conscious deliberation: I do not perceive each pebble and then examine it for its size, comparing it to that of my hand; I see certain pebbles *as* graspable for me, overlooking those that are not. Going on alongside this I walk across the beach, my feet finding the right places to fall.

Again, the 'right places' are not identified through a deliberative examination of various possibilities; they are simply perceived as right for my feet and stride. As such, in my encounter with the pebble beach my body not only determines what is possible for me, but in fact structures the world as I perceive it in accordance with those possibilities. Here we can best speak of the subject not as – or at least not primarily as – a thinking thing, but rather as an acting thing; not an 'I think', but an 'I can', and the body not as an impediment to freedom, but rather as the condition of freedom, opening up the world to us as a horizon of possibilities.[13] It is because we live *as* the body in this way that we feel we *are* a body.

As you rightly point out, however, the possibilities of the body sometimes fail to live up to our hopes and expectations, and here it reveals a wholly different aspect. Most notably there are times when we fantasise about precisely what is impossible for us. Who has not dreamt of being able to fly, or climb great heights and run great distances with ease, and then felt their own body as limited in comparison? Undoubtedly these fantasies are influenced by our cultural milieu, such as science fiction films and comic-book tales of superheroes. Yet the latter may themselves spring from a universal human preoccupation with the limitations of the body and the possibilities offered by other corporeal forms. Folklore and myths from across the world feature animals revered for their remarkable abilities, as well as humanoids with heightened powers, and even gods that take animal form to carry out tasks impossible for humans.[14] The oldest known representative artworks also show a fascination with non-human bodies, depicting, almost without exception, the forms of various animals and occasionally even human–animal chimeras.[15] All of the above reflects the other way in which our bodies appear to us: as a restricted set of possibilities, a hindrance on the mind which can float away from it through thought and imagination. It is because of this power of freely roaming thought that we can also be said to live *in* the body, underpinning the sense that we *have* it.

Such are the two ways in which we are embodied: living as the body, and living in the body. Indeed, human existence itself can almost be described as a kind of oscillation between these two modes of being.[16] If this is correct then the answer to your question – whether we have a body or are a body – does then seem to be 'both'. But are we simply resigned to this contradiction? By no means: we can attempt to explain how it is possible, and one means of doing so, I suggest, is through a comparison with other kinds of living beings.[17]

Ever since Darwin's theory of evolution by natural selection was accepted as the best scientific account of humanity's origins, we have grown accustomed to thinking of ourselves as a kind of animal – or at least, as an offshoot from the animal kingdom. This knowledge brings to the fore the aspects of our lives that are shared by animal, and in particular mammalian, life. We find safety in warmth, howl when in pain, nurse and rear our young, live alongside others with varying degrees of ease and animosity.[18] And yet there are clearly ways in which human beings are quite distinct: no other animal has the mastery of fire, reflects the world in objects of aesthetic appreciation or has language (as opposed to signals) as an integral part of its existence. Could these differences be explained by the peculiar way in which we humans are embodied? I ask this question not only with regard to our anatomical form – including opposable thumbs, an upright stance, and so on – which no doubt does play a pivotal role in accounting for our capacities and achievements.[19] I instead wonder whether it is the fact that we both live as the body and live in the body that sets us apart from animals, and ultimately accounts for the cultural and psychological achievements mentioned.

*

Michael Hauskeller: I suppose you are right that even those non-human animals closest to us are unlikely to ever experience that curious detachedness from their bodies that plays such a prominent role in our own existence. Non-human animals, as a rule, live *as* their bodies and not *in* them.[20] So this does indeed distinguish us as a species. There are, however, many different characteristics that distinguish humans from other animals – you already mentioned some of them – and I am not sure this is the one that somehow constitutes, as it were, the essence of being human. (In fact, I rather doubt that there is such a thing as the human essence.[21]) In any case, it is worth spelling out what it means to experience oneself as having a body rather than being a body, and what exactly it is that prompts or allows us to conceive of ourselves and our bodies in that peculiar way.

When we think of ourselves as having a body, what happens is that we distance ourselves from what we are, that is, as bodies. We take a step back from the reality of our existence, from everything that binds us to the world as it actually is in its concrete materiality, from all our dependencies and vulnerabilities, our existential embeddedness. And we are able to do this only because we have a highly developed 'sense of possibility', as Robert Musil called it,[22] which allows us to abstract from what is actually there and consider (and then, if we wish, also aim for) what is not there but conceivably could be there. In other words, we are able to imagine all sorts of things that do not exist, at least not yet. In a way, absences are as real for us as presences. This gives us an enormous power: the power to change the world.

It is pretty obvious, though, that some of the things that our sense of possibility conjures up are not really possible at all. Unlike non-human animals, we sometimes imagine (as possible) what is *actually* impossible, such as travelling back in time or communicating with the dead. The idea that we can somehow separate ourselves from our bodies and go on living without them, or replace them with a different one, may well fall into the same category: we can imagine it, but it is factually impossible. This would also solve the problem we identified earlier: how we can appear to both be and have a body. For a solution is indeed required because it strikes me as *logically impossible* to both be and have a body. This is because having a body entails not being that body, and we cannot both be and not be a body. If being a body and having a body are both modes of being, they seem to be mutually exclusive. Yet what is entirely possible is that we sometimes *feel* distinct from our body and sometimes not. This is quite compatible with our never really 'having' our body at all. We would simply be frequently deceived by our imagination (our strong 'sense of possibility') into thinking that we do. The notion that we can become separate from our body would then just be an illusion or a fantasy. We would, just like all the other animals, live as bodies rather than in bodies.

Naturally, we may find this hard to accept because being a body comes with a price that many of us are rather reluctant to pay, which is death. Bodies, or at any rate the kind of bodies that we happen to have or be, are mortal. If we only *had* our bodies, there would still be hope. Having a body holds the promise of a possible escape route from our existential dependencies. If we are not, or at least not entirely, identical with our bodies – if the real me is somehow beyond the reach of the physical universe and its destructive forces – we may still survive the demise of our body. But if we really are our body, then there is no way out. The death of our body will be *our* death, just as the life of our body is our life. So clearly the question whether we are our body or have our body is not just of academic interest. The stakes are high for all of us. This may explain why the illusion, if indeed it is one, of there being an essentially bodiless (and for this reason potentially immortal) self that merely uses a particular body to interact with the material world is so persistent.

There is of course another possibility that we should at least consider: that we are not at all mistaken about having a body; we are mistaken about *being* one. Even if we are certain that two states of affairs (in this case: being a particular body and not being that body) are mutually exclusive, this does not tell us anything about *which* of the two states actually obtains and which does not. Perhaps it is not our sense of possibility that misleads us, but our sense of reality. Perhaps it is our constant active engagement with the material world in which we find ourselves that deceives us into thinking that we are no more than the bodies we use for that purpose. Perhaps Descartes was right all along and we are (nothing but) thinking things. Is there anything we can say to prove Descartes wrong, or at least to show that we have little reason to believe he was right?

*

Lewis Coyne: It is true, to be sure, that one cannot both have a body and be a body at the same time. As you say, to have something presupposes that it is separate from oneself, and so to claim that one also *is* this thing would be self-contradictory. Note, however, that I suggested that our having a body and being a body are just feelings, or impressions, that we have about ourselves, and it is of course psychologically possible to feel contradictory things. These feelings are based on our two modes of being: living as the body and living in the body. It is the latter that underpins the former. The question then is whether it is logically possible to both live as and live in the body equally. Again, however, the answer would appear to be no, and for exactly the same reason as before: to live in implies a separation between the self and the body that to live as denies. Hence what we are searching for is a reason to believe that one mode of being is in fact foundational, and ultimately underpins the other, merely subsidiary mode.

One answer, as you note, is essentially Cartesian: we are thinking things that live in the body, and only mistakenly believe that we are that body on the basis of the derivative mode of being that is living as the body. This brings us to the question you raise of whether there is any-thing we can say to prove Descartes wrong. I think we can argue with some confidence – which is usually as much confidence as philosophy permits – that he was probably wrong, and the justification for believing this is partly philosophical and partly scientific.

The philosophical reasons to reject Descartes' mind–body dualism centre on the purported relation between those two entities. Despite his claim that the body and the mind are fundamentally different things – one material, the other immaterial – they are evidently interrelated, and uniquely so: if my body is struck, my mind feels the pain; if I will my limb to move, move it does. With no other object in the world do I have this twofold relation – a fact that Descartes himself recognised when conceding that we are not in our bodies in the way that 'a pilot [is] in his ship'.[23] To explain exactly how the mind and body could interact with one another, despite being different kinds of thing, Descartes supposed that the pineal gland in the brain acted as a point of contact.[24] The problem with this explanation, however, is that the pineal gland would then have to be both material *and* immaterial, which it obviously is not – indeed, it is impossible that anything could be.

The second major reason to reject the Cartesian answer is simply that our worldview has drastically changed since the early modern era. Descartes' understanding of the mind drew heavily on the Christian idea of an eternal soul, distinct from the world of nature. After Darwin, however, we must assume that humanity and its mental faculties are *part of* nature, or at least an outgrowth of it, and therefore seek self-understanding on that basis.[25] From our post-Darwinian perspective the idea of a mind that merely has a body, interacting in ways that were already hard to account for, appears yet more implausible.

The more attractive solution is the other one you described: that our living as the body is fundamental, and our living in the body merely derivative. Now, if, as we have supposed, animals exclusively live as their bodies, then we must ask what distinguishing feature or features we have that allow us to temporarily suspend our immediate engagement with the world. What allows, in other words, for what you called our sense of possibility? Although there are probably several factors simultaneously responsible, the best single candidate, to my mind, is *language*.[26] As users of language we are capable of more than signalling (although we also, of course, do a great deal of this). Signalling is an outward expression of an inner feeling: the snarled warning of a dog, the contented purr of a cat, the genuine smile that reveals good intent. This is real communication, no doubt – but in language proper words signify *ideas*. Thus the word 'book' (and its equivalents in other languages) names the idea of the book as such. Although this idea is formed from encounters with actual books, which are brought together under the label 'book', the idea itself is available to us as an object of contemplation totally independently of the books from which it was derived. We can then take this idea and freely manipulate it in our imaginations, including in ways that would be physically impossible to enact. And the same is true, of course, of any other entity that we have an idea of, ourselves included. The fact that I can call myself 'I' means that I have an idea of myself, and can scrutinise myself and imagine myself in all sorts of ways as a result. I have, in other words, the power of self-consciousness.

With self-consciousness comes, of course, an awareness of our eventual death. This knowledge once again reveals the ambiguity of the body, albeit in a new and more urgent light. You note that if we only *had* our bodies there would still be hope, as then our 'real' selves might be able to survive the deaths of the bodies that housed them. I quite agree. Equally, however, if we only *were* our bodies, there would be no scope for existential anguish, as we would lack the self-reflection necessary for knowledge of our own mortality. To put it another way: if our only mode of being were living as the body, existing in a permanently unfolding present, then we would not be preoccupied with ourselves and the fact that at some point in the future we must die. Animals, to be sure, are well-served by instinct to fear threats to themselves and their group. But can we really call this an *awareness* of their *own mortality*? If we cannot, then perhaps we would have been better off as a species to remain animals: death would still await us, of course, but we would not live with it as an ever-present possibility.

*

Michael Hauskeller: An interesting question for sure, but I feel we are drifting a bit off topic here. Also, I am not entirely satisfied yet by the proposed solution to the contradiction that we have identified, which is that we *are* our bodies, just like non-human animals are their bodies, but what distinguishes us is a particular cognitive capacity, namely self-consciousness (rooted in language and the ability to operate with abstract ideas), that allows us to assume a certain degree of detachedness from what we are, which in turn deceives us into thinking, falsely, that it might actually be possible for us to exist without our bodies, or within a different body.

It is true that the dualist position (that has us existing *in* a body rather than *as* a body) is hard to reconcile with what we know about the world. As far as we are aware, when our body dies, we die. If there is a spirit or soul – some immaterial substance that forms the core of our being – that is set free when our body dies, it must continue to exist in some other dimension of reality to which we have no access. Those who are dead seem to be gone for good, at least from this world, which strongly suggests that the death of our body is indeed the death of us. And if the death of our body is our death, then the life of our body is our life. However, I don't think that the two reasons you provide for why we should reject the dualist position are conclusive. Of course, it is difficult to understand how it should be possible for an immaterial, non-physical substance (if that is what we really are) to interact with the body, which is part of the physical world. But just because we haven't yet figured out how to explain this interaction does not mean that such an interaction is impossible. There are many things in this world that we know are real and that we do not understand and cannot explain. Modern science is full of unsolved riddles.[27] Neither is the fact that we have evolved naturally a compelling reason for rejecting dualism. Perhaps it is not just us, but *everything* that exists that has this dual nature. Perhaps all things merely *have* a body, while the essence of their being is immaterial.

Let us have another look at something I pointed out at the beginning of our conversation. Not only do we use our body in many situations, like an extremely adaptable multi-purpose tool, we can also lose and indeed replace parts of our body without, apparently, losing parts of ourselves. How is that possible if I and my body are one and the same? It seems that I can lose a leg and still be me, and not be less me than before. I can lose another leg and still be me. I can lose both of my arms too. I can lose my eyes and my ears. I can have an artificial lung implanted and even an artificial heart and still be, not only partially but wholly, me. None of the parts that I can lose or replace seem to be essential to what I am, with one possible exception, which is our brain, and even that can be at least partially replaced (an artificial hippocampus is already being tested).[28] Should we then say that what we are is actually not our (entire) body, but our brain? But that seems odd, too, and in some ways more implausible than to say that we are our entire body. We live in the world as bodies, we engage and interact as bodies, we love and hate each other as bodies. But we do not do all these things as brains. In many ways I live my life as a body, but I do not seem to live my life as a brain. So if most of our body is expendable or replaceable and therefore not an essential part of what we are, and if what remains (the brain) is not something we can easily identify with, then it would appear that we are not our body after all. Instead, we seem to have it.

This would also explain why so many people feel alienated from their bodies. It is increasingly common for people to assert that the bodies they happen to have do not really reflect what they are. When we are getting old and our bodies begin to show it, we often find it difficult to reconcile the image we see when we look in a mirror with the more youthful image that we have of ourselves in our heads. We then feel betrayed by our bodies because instead of lending expression to what we are they seem to conceal it: we look old even though we still feel young(ish), and this experience is then reinterpreted first as 'We are old on the outside, but young on the inside', and finally as 'Our *bodies* are old, while *we* are still young'. Yet while this still makes some kind of sense – we can perhaps meaningfully distinguish being physically young or old from being mentally so – there are other assertions indicative of an alienation from one's body that prove more challenging to our understanding. If I am, in my bodily constitution, a man, but feel that what I *really* am is a woman, or if I am white, but feel that what I *really* am is black, then what appears to be claimed here is not simply a mismatch between my body and my (immaterial) self, but a mismatch between my *actual* body and my *true* body. Both sex and skin colour are, after all, physical attributes. So what is being claimed here is that what I only *have* is this particular body, while what I *am* is not something non-physical, but, instead, a different (not yet realised) body. And I am not sure this makes any sense at all.[29]

*

Lewis Coyne: I admit that the above arguments against Descartes do not constitute absolute, knock-down criticisms. Were his theories not plausible, at least up to a point, they would have long since gone the way of old Scholastic puzzles such as whether angels are sexed beings or not (once a hotly debated question). And more than that, Cartesian substance dualism resonates with a deep – perhaps universal – desire to comprehend ourselves as merely having, rather than being, bodies. Why we have this psychological need one can only guess (your suggestion that it has something to do with awareness of our own mortality is surely on the right lines), yet the proliferation of dualistic religions throughout history and across the world attests to its force, and despite everything I have said against Descartes I of course feel it too.

Nevertheless, I find the evolutionary argument against Cartesian substance dualism rationally persuasive, primarily for its parsimony. Perhaps I can put it more convincingly this way. We have already supposed that animals simply live as their bodies, and have already argued that human beings, who evolved from non-human animals, both live as and live in their bodies. Now, since logic dictates that one of those modes of being has to be fundamental, then one of two possibilities has to be true. Either we human beings really live in our bodies, and therefore represent a rupture with the remainder of the animal kingdom, or else we really live as our bodies, just like other animals. The problem with the first option is one of continuity: we evolved from non-human animals and yet exist in a way that is fundamentally at odds with our closest relatives. How are we to explain this radical departure? To be sure, nature presents us, as you say, with many unexplained phenomena. Yet the gap in our understanding of how humans alone could exist in their bodies is significant enough to prima facie count against the suggestion. Far more parsimonious is the second option: that humans, just like animals, in truth live as their bodies. The problem with this explanation is comparably minor: we have to explain how human beings can also experience themselves as living in their bodies, which is precisely what we have sought to do by pointing to the human capacity for self-consciousness grounded in the possession of language and its concomitant grasp of ideas.

The latter position may also be able to shed some light on the phenomena that you describe, in particular the facts that we can lose certain parts of our bodies and yet feel no less of a self, and that ageing can lead people to feel subjectively alienated from their objective body. Recall the distinction drawn above between the acting self, the 'I can', and the ego, the 'I think'. The former is the self living as the body, finding its way through the world in accordance with bodily possibilities, whereas the latter is the self living in the body, roaming freely in thought and imagination. Now, if I lose a limb, for example, then the latter mode of being is indeed unaffected; I will carry on thinking just as before. But the former mode – living as the body – *is* affected. Whereas I could formerly move in and interact with the world in a great many ways, some of these possibilities are now objectively closed off to me, which can affect my living as the body in two possible ways.

On the one hand, the 'I can' may simply readjust to accommodate the new, restricted set of possibilities presented by the body: the staircase that previously appeared climbable now confronts me as an obstacle, for instance. On the other hand, the 'I can' may (at least for a time) remain just as it was courtesy of a phantom limb – a limb that is still felt to be there. But in that case the 'I can' is sure to be betrayed by the objective body, which can no longer engage with the world in the way that gave rise to the 'I can' as it originally was.[30] In either case, then, our living as the body is negatively affected, yet our living in the body remains intact. Resting on the cognitive capacity for self-reflection, the latter mode of being is only impaired by damage to the body parts chiefly responsible for cognition – namely, certain regions of the brain. It is on these grounds alone that the self can be thought of as co-extensive with the brain, in the fashion you mentioned.

It seems to me that something similar, albeit far less dramatic, may also be true of physical ageing. My first-hand experience of growing old is limited, but I have noticed that certain athletic feats which came easily 10 years ago are now more difficult for me: running for extended periods, or swimming widths of a pool underwater. In these cases the 'I can' finds itself let down by the objective body, which 'can' no longer, although once again the 'I think' of course remains perfectly intact. A different process is surely at work, however, in the way that our physical appearance lets us down with age, when we begin to notice wrinkles, a receding hairline and the like. For here the expectation that goes unmet seems to be based not on the 'I can', but rather on a mental image that we entertain of ourselves, one that once accurately reflected our objective body but now is at odds with it. As an idea, the latter is surely an *operation* of self-consciousness, of the 'I think', even though the thinking subject *itself* goes unaffected, as before.

The latter is close in structure, I suspect, to the Cartesian belief that one is not really this body, but rather a soul, spirit or mind simply encased within it. As a belief about ourselves this also depends on our self-consciousness. And as with our disappointment at noticing physical signs of ageing, the person who believes themselves to really be a soul or mind is perplexed, perhaps even outraged, by the persistent reminder that they are not free from the brute presence of the body. However, unlike the mental image of our objective body that ageing so rudely contradicts, the Cartesian understanding of the self does not reflect the way that I once was but am no longer. On the contrary, it may never have been true at all.

*

Michael Hauskeller: Right then. So let us assume that we are indeed bodies, just like any other animal, and that it is only because of our ability to think that it does not always seem that way to us. And paradoxically, as you point out, it is precisely when our bodies start diverging from the mental image we have of ourselves that we become painfully aware that we do not just inhabit those bodies but are in fact identical with them. As long as we are young, healthy, reasonably presentable, and at the height of our physical powers, we do not feel constrained by our body: it remains unobtrusive, a well-functioning tool, completely at our service. It is then, when we are most at one with our body, that the body appears least essential. It is only when it fails us that it dawns on us that we cannot escape it – that the fate of our body is in fact our fate. It is easy to distance oneself from a healthy body; it is much harder to do this when the body is in pain or dysfunctional, thus transforming the largely pre-conscious 'I *can*' into a very conscious 'I can't'.

Let us move on, though. We have established or at least (tentatively) agreed that we are bodies. I am my body, and you are your body. However, what we have not talked about so far is *what* exactly a body (or perhaps *our* body) is. The question that I posed at the start of our conversation, which we have been discussing ever since, was whether we *are* a body or (only) *have* a body. This somewhat echoes Descartes' question whether we are *res extensa* (an extended thing) or *res cogitans* (a thinking thing). But now we can see that Descartes may have got not only the answer wrong, but also the question. Even if we are indeed bodies, this does not mean that we cannot *also* be thinking things. These predicates are not mutually exclusive. And there is, in fact, no doubt that we *are* thinking things. Clearly, we are things that think – and not only in the narrow rationalistic, concept-using sense, but in the wider (Cartesian) sense of thinking, which is something like subjective awareness. We are thinking things in the sense that it is something that it is like to be the body that we are. We are thinking things in the sense that we are aware of the world and ourselves in it, that we feel pain and pleasure and all kinds of other things like fear, anger, love, desire or simply our being alive.

Yet if we are bodies *and* thinking things in this wide sense, then we can only conclude that the body, or at any rate the human body, is itself (not only an extended thing, but also) a thinking thing. But if the human body is a thinking thing, then should we not – based on the same considerations that led us earlier to conclude that if non-human animals are their bodies, then humans must also be – now conclude that perhaps *all* bodies are thinking things? Surely the argument from evolutionary continuity cuts both ways: if we must be bodies because non-human animals are bodies, then non-human animals must be thinking things because we are thinking things. And why not go further than that? Why stop with non-human animals? Plants have bodies or rather are bodies, so perhaps they are thinking things too,[31] although if they are, they are most likely thinking things in a more diffuse way, perhaps akin to the way we are still thinking things even when we are only-half awake or indeed fast asleep.

Whatever the body is, if we are it, then we know that it is not just an extended thing. And if that body is also a thinking thing, then it is a thinking thing by virtue of it being a body and not by virtue of it doing any actual thinking. What I am wondering, though, is whether all extended things are also bodies. Perhaps a body is a particular kind of extended thing. Our body, the body that we are, is an organised whole. If it were not, it could not be one particular entity, which we believe ourselves to be. For this body to be me it must have an organisational unity that sets it apart from other bodies and other extended things that are not part of that unity. The borders of our being may not be clearly defined, but it certainly seems that there are such borders, fluid and fuzzy as they may be. There are clearly extended things, including bodies, that are not me. But we know that sometimes what is part of me can stop being part of me, for instance when I lose an organ, a limb, or even something as small and seemingly insignificant as a hair or a fingernail. And if what is part of me can stop being part of me, then perhaps what is *not* part of me can *become* part of me, for instance a prosthetic arm or leg when it is integrated into the organisational whole that is my body.

*

Lewis Coyne: I agree that the argument from evolutionary continuity cuts both ways. Earlier I suggested that we have reason to think of living as the body as our primary mode of being because non-human animals, our closest relatives, appear to exist in precisely that way. As you rightly point out, though, this invites the question of whether that mode of being can also be traced *down* from animals, and, if so, where we then draw the line between those beings that exist in that way and those that do not.

One answer, which deserves some consideration, is that we should not draw a line at all. This would amount to the claim that *everything* that physically exists is a body, and that living as the body accordingly goes all the way down, to the atomic and even sub-atomic levels of nature. The advantage of this position – which owes something to Descartes' great antagonists, Baruch Spinoza[32] and Gottfried Leibniz[33] – is that we no longer have to explain how mind and matter interact with and relate to one another: they are simply construed as two facets of one and the same nature.[34] The disadvantage, however, is simply that it is hard to accept that sentience or subjectivity, however rudimentary, can be attributed to *every* physical entity. For if all bodies are thinking things, and if everything that physically exists is a body, then everything that physically exists is also a thinking thing. This conclusion stretches the limits of credulity: can we really say that electrons live as their bodies, or that there is something-that-it-is-like-to-be a quark? Perhaps – but at face value I find it hard to accept.

The problem with the above is evidently not the idea that 'all bodies are thinking things', but rather that 'everything that physically exists is a body'. To be sure, everything that physically exists is a spatially extended entity. But the body that our conversation is concerned with – the body that we have and are – is evidently a good deal more than this. In trying to establish more precisely what a body is, beyond its being a physical object, it might be instructive to recall the two modes of being that we called 'living as the body' and 'living in the body'. What these formulations share, apart from 'the body' being their subject, is the predicate 'living'. If we take this latter commonality seriously as a clue to defining the body, our attempt will be restricted to the domain of physical beings that are *alive*. Are there, then, any good reasons to think that living beings alone are bodies in the sense that you outline?

The strongest evidence for believing this to be the case has already been pointed toward, namely, your observation that '[o]ur body, the body that we are, is an organised whole'. This is entirely correct – but it still does not quite get to what is unique about living beings. The reason for this is that a being counts as organised if it possesses parts that play a functional role in fulfilling an end or ends of the whole. Evidently, this definition excludes a great many non-living physical beings: rocks, clouds, the sun, wind and rain, to name just a few. All are what we may call non-teleological, in that they lack *teloi*, or 'ends', which is another way of saying that they are not characterised by any kind of purpose.[35] Only organised beings, as indicated, can be so described. A chair, for instance, has parts (one or more legs, a seat and a back) that contribute to the fulfilment of its purpose, which is to be sat on. Saw it in half and the parts of the chair will cease to function, meaning that the chair itself no longer fulfils its purpose – a purpose which nevertheless remains the chair's defining characteristic.

Tools, furniture and machines are perhaps the clearest cases of organised beings, but the category also includes anything intentionally created by human hands, as, even if the purpose is not merely instrumental, *some* kind of purpose is by definition involved regardless. Even a painting, for example, consists of parts (paint and canvas) that serve to stimulate the eye and the mind, invite us to reflect on its themes and qualities, and thereby obliquely serve the purpose of enriching our inner lives.

While the chair and the painting are organised, however, neither is alive, and it is the latter that we have taken as our clue to defining the body. What, then, distinguishes an organised living being from an organised non-living being? The answer is that the former alone is *self-organised*. The chair and painting are created by humans, meaning that their parts are arranged by us in order to serve overarching purposes which are themselves bestowed upon the object. Matters are quite different with a living being, however. An organism generates its *own* parts (cells, organs and so forth), the functionality of which serves the purpose of its continued existence – a purpose that is not imparted from without, but is rather immanent *to* the organism.[36] Clearly, all organisms are brought into being through reproduction, but regardless of whether this occurs sexually or asexually, at no point in the development of a living being is a *telos* bestowed on it by a third party. It is, to reiterate, its *own* end, and the fact that complex organisms such as we only survive through symbiotic relationships with bacteria and the like does nothing to undermine this fact. Thus the living being is a categorically distinct kind of physical entity: one that is not only organised but also – and unlike an artefact – self-organised.[37]

Evidently we are such entities, and, since we have also agreed that we are our bodies, it would appear that our being organisms and being bodies amount to one and the same thing. If we extended this line of thinking to all organisms, then everything alive – but *only* things that are alive – would count as bodies. To my mind, this position has a fairly significant advantage over the one previously examined, namely that in placing a restriction on the domain of bodies it also places a restriction on the domain of thinking things. For if all bodies are thinking things, and if everything that is alive is a body, then everything that is alive is a thinking thing. Some people will still find this hard to accept, of course. Indeed, my earlier incredulity can be turned back against me by asking whether we can *really* say that bacteria live as their bodies, or that there is something-that-it-is-like-to-be a fungus. But if we understand 'being a thinking thing' in the very broad sense you suggest – as merely 'sentient', or 'having subjectivity' – then it strikes me as entirely plausible.

The tentative outcome of our conversation, then, is that bodies are identical with the physical form of living beings, and that such beings live *as* bodies – even though human beings, courtesy of our linguistically grounded capacity for self-consciousness, sometimes adopt the second, derivative mode of being that is living *in* our bodies. It is for the latter reason, we suggested, that human beings feel that we both have and are our bodies. If this is at least partly correct, then we can conclude that Heidegger was indeed wrong to say that 'the body phenomenon is the most difficult problem'. But it would seem, at least on the basis of our conversation, that an analysis of the body leads almost by necessity to the question of the mind, and ultimately to the phenomenon of *life*: perhaps the greatest problem of them all.

Notes

1. A common trope in many science fiction novels and movies, the idea was first brought up as a thought experiment by Locke, *An Essay Concerning Human Understanding*, 340. The thought experiment was meant to show that the identity of the person is independent of their body.
2. Among many popular accounts of life after death see for instance Tomlinson, *Exploring the Eternal Soul*.
3. See for instance Wiley, *A Taxonomy and Metaphysics of Mind-Uploading*, or Rothblatt, *Virtually Human*.
4. Descartes made this argument in his *Meditations on First Philosophy*, which I cite here in Sutcliffe's translation (Descartes, *Discourse on Method*, 156): '[I]t is certain that I, that is to say my mind, by which I am what I am, is entirely and truly distinct from my body, and may exist without it.'

5. Plato, *Gorgias*, 492e–3a.
6. For a comprehensive discussion of the extent to which and how emotions are enacted and embodied, see Colombetti, *The Feeling Body*.
7. Heidegger and Fink, *Heraclitus Seminar*, 146. Heidegger did, however, develop an account of the body in his *Zollikon Seminars*.
8. The body's alternating appearance as something that we have and something that we are – a distinction sometimes captured by the labels 'objective body' and 'lived body' – has been explored in great depth by philosophers belonging to the phenomenological tradition. See, for example, Merleau-Ponty, *Phenomenology of Perception*.
9. Descartes, *Discourse on Method*.
10. This canonical Latin formulation of the idea appeared in Descartes' *Principles of Philosophy*, originally published in 1644, seven years after his *Discourse on Method*.
11. Of course, Descartes' position is itself a variant of the body–soul dualism that can be traced back to Plato, Pythagoras and other Ancient Greeks, in addition to the Judeo-Christian tradition (and many non-Western intellectual traditions besides).
12. As Heidegger argued, a phenomenological analysis of our being-in-the-world reveals that beings are primarily revealed to us in and through practical engagement rather than disinterested reflection. See his *Being and Time*. It is only in the *Zollikon Seminars*, however, that Heidegger connects this idea to an account of the lived body.
13. My use here of the phrase 'I can' is indebted to Edmund Husserl, *Ideas Pertaining to a Pure Phenomenology*, 266.
14. Greek and Norse mythology are prime examples of sources of such stories.
15. I am thinking here of the Paleolithic cave paintings of Altamira, Lascaux and Chauvet-Pont-d'Arc in Spain and France, and Lubang Jeriji Saléh and Leang Tedongnge in Indonesia.
16. This is a point made with great sophistication and justified at length by Plessner in *Levels of Organic Life and the Human*.
17. This is, in part, the method employed by Plessner and other proponents of philosophical anthropology in their quest to solve the 'riddle' of human existence in a non-reductive naturalistic fashion.
18. On this point see 'Philosophical aspects of Darwinism', the second essay of Hans Jonas's *The Phenomenon of Life*.
19. For competing accounts of the existentially significant anatomical and morphological features of human beings see Alsberg, *In Quest of Man* and Gehlen, *Man*.
20. See Plessner, *Levels of Organic Life and the Human*, 237. Plessner distinguishes between the 'excentric positionality' of the human, which allows us to distance ourselves from our body, and the 'centric positionality' of the non-human animal, which does not.
21. See Hauskeller, 'Making sense of what we are'.
22. Musil, *The Man Without Qualities*, 10.
23. Descartes, *Discourse on Method*, 48.
24. Descartes, *Treatise on Man*, 95.
25. See Jonas, *The Phenomenon of Life*: 'Philosophical aspects of Darwinism'.
26. This has been argued at some length by Cassirer in *An Essay on Man*.
27. See Brooks, *13 Things That Don't Make Sense*.
28. https://futurism.com/a-new-device-could-make-memory-implants-a-reality (accessed 1 December 2021).
29. On this matter, see my conversation with Holly Lawford-Smith on gender in this volume, 65-83.
30. For full discussions of missing and phantom limbs and their meanings for a philosophy of the body, see Merleau-Ponty, *Phenomenology of Perception* and Goldstein, *The Organism*.
31. See Segundo-Ortin and Calvo, 'Are plants cognitive?'.
32. Spinoza, *Ethics*.
33. Leibniz, *The Monadology*.
34. For a sophisticated modern expression of this position see Whitehead, *Process and Reality*.
35. For classic philosophical accounts of organismic teleology see Aristotle, 'De Anima', in *Complete Works*, 641–92, and Kant, *Critique of Judgement*.
36. This is a distinction that I have elsewhere called 'immanent' versus 'transcendent' teleology. For a full discussion see Coyne, *Hans Jonas*, 20.
37. For a complete account of this idea see Jonas, *Organism and Freedom*.

Bibliography

Alsberg, Paul. *In Quest of Man: A biological approach to the problem of man's place in nature.* Oxford: Pergamon Press, 1970.

Aristotle. *Complete Works,* volume 1, edited by J. Barnes and translated by J. A. Smith. Princeton, NJ: Princeton University Press, 1984.

Brooks, Michael. *13 Things That Don't Make Sense: The most intriguing scientific mysteries of our time.* London: Profile Books, 2010.

Cassirer, Ernst. *An Essay on Man: An introduction to a philosophy of human culture.* New Haven, CT: Yale University Press, 1944.

Colombetti, Giovanna. *The Feeling Body: Affective science meets the enactive mind.* Boston, MA: MIT Press, 2017.

Coyne, Lewis. *Hans Jonas: Life, technology and the horizons of responsibility.* London: Bloomsbury Academic, 2021.

Descartes, René. *Discourse on Method and Other Writings,* translated with an introduction by F. E. Sutcliffe. Harmondsworth: Penguin, 1968.

Descartes, René. *Treatise on Man,* translated by Thomas Steele Hall. Cambridge, MA: Harvard University Press, 1972.

Gehlen, Arnold. *Man: His nature and place in the world,* translated by C. McMillan and K. Pillemer. New York: Columbia University Press, 1988.

Goldstein, Kurt. *The Organism: A holistic approach to biology derived from pathological data in man.* New York: Zone Books, 1995.

Hauskeller, Michael. 'Making sense of what we are: a mythological approach to human nature', *Philosophy* 84/1 (2009): 95–109.

Heidegger, Martin. *Being and Time,* translated by J. Stambaugh and D. J. Schmidt. Albany, NY: SUNY Press, 2010.

Heidegger, Martin. *Zollikon Seminars: Protocols – conversations – letters,* translated by F. Mayr and R. Askay, edited by M. Boss. Evanston, IL: Northwestern University Press, 2001.

Heidegger, Martin, and Eugen Fink. *Heraclitus Seminar,* translated by C. H. Seibert. Evanston, IL: Northwestern University Press, 1993.

Husserl, Edmund. *Ideas Pertaining to a Pure Phenomenology and to a Phenomenological Philosophy: Studies in the phenomenology of constitution,* translated by R. Rojcewicz and A. Schuwer. Dordrecht: Kluwer, 1989.

Jonas, Hans. *The Phenomenon of Life: Toward a philosophical biology.* Evanston, IL: Northwestern University Press, 1966.

Jonas, Hans. *Organism and Freedom: An essay in philosophical biology,* edited by J. O. Beckers and F. Preußger. Freiburg im Breisgau: Rombach, 2016.

Kant, Immanuel. *Critique of Judgement,* translated by J. C. Meredith and N. Walker. Oxford: Oxford University Press, 2008.

Leibniz, Gottfried Wilhelm. *The Monadology and other philosophical writings,* edited and translated by R. Latta. Oxford: Oxford University Press, 1898.

Locke, John. *An Essay Concerning Human Understanding,* edited by Peter Nidditch. Oxford: Oxford University Press, 1975.

Merleau-Ponty, Maurice. *Phenomenology of Perception,* translated by T. Carman. Abingdon: Routledge, 2012.

Musil, Robert. *The Man Without Qualities,* translated by Sophie Wilkins. London: Pan Macmillan, 2017.

Plato. *Gorgias,* translated by Walter Hamilton. London: Penguin, 2004.

Plessner, Helmuth. *Levels of Organic Life and the Human: An introduction to philosophical anthropology,* translated by M. Hyatt. New York: Fordham University Press, 2019.

Rothblatt, Martine. *Virtually Human: The promise – and the peril – of digital immortality.* London: St Martin's Press, 2014.

Segundo-Ortin, Miguel, and Paco Calvo. 'Are plants cognitive? A reply to Adams', *Studies in History and Philosophy of Science* Part A 73 (2019): 64–71.

Spinoza, Baruch. *Ethics,* translated by E. Curley. London: Penguin, 1996.

Tomlinson, Andy. *Exploring the Eternal Soul.* From the Heart Press, 2017.

Whitehead, Alfred North. *Process and Reality: An essay in cosmology,* 2nd edition edited by D. R. Griffin and D. W. Sherburne. New York: The Free Press, 1978.

Wiley, Keith. *A Taxonomy and Metaphysics of Mind-Uploading.* Seattle: Alautun Press, 2014.

4
Gender
with Holly Lawford-Smith

Michael Hauskeller: I am wondering what it means to be a woman or a man. Personally, I have never had any doubt that I am a man, nor have I ever had any problems with being one. I am neither proud nor ashamed of it. Nor do I think it is in any way a big deal. Being a man is simply one of many things that I have always assumed can be truthfully said about me, just as it can be truthfully said about me that I am Caucasian, or that I was born in Germany to German parents, or that I am human. Like these other descriptive attributes, I used to take my gender for a fact of life: some people are men, others are women, and I happen to be one of the former. However, it is not entirely obvious what 'being a man' actually means or entails and in what way and to what extent it defines my identity, making me who I am. Would I be a different person if I were a woman? And what would it take for me to be a woman? Could I conceivably be neither? Or both?

The main reason, I suppose, why I call myself a man and not a woman, and others see and treat me as one, is that I have certain physical attributes that identify me to myself and others as a biologically male, sperm-producing member of our species, for instance my sex organs, my beard, and a physique and facial features that are far more common in males than in females of our species. In other words, I look like a person needs to look if they wish to be immediately recognised as a man by others, especially since I also dress like a man is supposed to dress in our time and social environment and have the kind of haircut that is currently most typically found in men. Clearly, though, some of those attributes that allow others, or make it easier for them, to recognise me as a man are not essential to my being a man in the sense that without them I would no longer be one. At least in the kind of society in which we live, if I cut off my beard, I would still, unambiguously, count as a man. However, if I changed my haircut and the way I dress to a more 'womanly' appearance, people might initially be more hesitant to see me as a man, but in the end and if nothing else had changed they would probably settle on seeing me not as a woman, but as a man who dresses like a woman, the reason being that what people tend to see as the most if not the only essential condition of being a man is being in possession of the proper reproductive organs – that is, the kind of reproductive organs that the vast majority of biologically male humans possess. When pushed, people tend to identify gender (being a man or being a woman) with sex (being male or female).

Then again, we often talk and behave as if being a man requires more than just being male, and being a woman requires more than just being female. There are expectations that need to be met if someone wants to fully qualify as a man or a woman in their social environment; expectations regarding their behaviour as well as character. If for instance a man seems to lack the kind of courage and resolve that we think is merited and required in a certain situation, we tell him to 'man up', 'be a man' or 'grow some balls'. We even say this kind of thing, though probably less frequently, to women. What we do *not* usually say is 'woman up' or 'grow a vagina' (although, as you know, some feminists have strongly suggested we should say exactly that[1]).

Women can of course show courage and resolve as much as men do, but it seems that this is not part of their traditional role description. Men, on the other hand, are believed to have failed *as men* if they are not brave and determined;[2] if they are not, they do not meet the essential criteria for the job of being a man. Mechanical skills and today computer skills are also on the imagined list of essential criteria. The other day I watched an episode of the American TV show *Modern Family*, in which the dad, Phil Dunphy, was trying in vain to figure out how to get one of the smoke detectors in the house to stop beeping. What made his failure especially painful and humiliating for him was the fact that, in his own perception, this is the kind of thing that men are supposed to be able to fix, and he just couldn't do it. 'Changing the battery in a smoke detector is what they teach you in Man 101. So, of course, every time I hear that noise all I hear is, "Beep beep! You're not a man! Beep beep! You're not a . . ."'[3]

In his own estimation, Phil Dunphy is 'not a man' because he is not the way he has been trained to think men are supposed to be: skilful, tech-savvy. No doubt there is also a Woman 101, where women learn how to be good or true women, what to do and what not to do, and how to be and how not to be.

If gender were nothing but sex, statements like the one just cited would make little sense. Of course we can disagree with Phil Dunphy about what it means to be a man and how we need to behave in order to secure or maintain our manhood, but we are all likely to have *some* deeply ingrained understanding of what makes a man a man and a woman a woman that goes beyond mere biology. Does it, however, follow that gender can, if necessary or desired, be *completely* detached from sex? That I can be a woman despite having all the physical attributes of a male member of my species, or a man despite being biologically female? If this is so and we can safely ignore our physical constitution, how – given that there is no agreement on what makes a man a man and a woman a woman – do we decide who is what?

*

Holly Lawford-Smith: I think you're right to note that while people tend to identify gender (which you describe as being a woman or a man) with sex (which you describe as being female or male), there is also more to gender than sex. As you say, there are social ideas about being a woman and being a man that can lead to individual women and men feeling like failures as women and men.

Feminists since the very beginning have been interested in identifying those social ideas that contribute to the meaning of 'woman', in order to show that they do not actually have much to do with women as people.[4] Suppose our social idea of 'woman' at a particular time was that she is passive, submissive, weak; nurturing, caring, warm; she lives to serve others, particularly men and children. Feminists have argued that she might *look* that way, but this is only because she has been denied an equal education,[5] or denied the right to vote, or because she depended on marriage to a man for economic security,[6] or because nearly all intellectual culture (e.g. science, literature, the arts) characterised her as inferior, as lacking, and she believed it.[7] Or because she never had 'a room of [her] own' – a space to think and develop her own ideas.[8] Feminists aimed to show that the idea of 'woman' is something that has been created by men, and really does not have much to do with women themselves.[9] If they could articulate all those social ideas and *separate* them from women, then they could liberate women to truly be themselves, whatever that would mean.[10]

As far as I can see, this did not really happen with men, which is why your Phil Dunphy could still feel like a failure as a man for not being able to stop the smoke alarm from beeping. Men never really had a movement to identify all the social ideas about 'man' and work out how little they really had to do with men, the people. And I think that is part of the explanation for what is going on at the moment with changing ideas about sex and gender. I think because men have not done this work as a class, individual men are literally fleeing from the category 'man'. Some are trying to set up a new category, 'nonbinary' – a third gender, or no gender, depending on who you talk to – but some are fleeing *into* the 'woman' category. And this, predictably, is causing some problems for women.

You asked whether it follows from the fact that there is more to gender than sex that 'gender can . . . be *completely* detached from sex . . . [t]hat I can be a woman despite having all the physical attributes of a male member of my species'. I definitely do not think that is what the feminists were trying to do, but I think it is what modern trans activism is trying to do. Feminists were trying to decouple sex and gender in order to throw gender away.[11] They wanted to show that those ideas about 'women' did not have anything to do with actual women, and they wanted women to be free to express themselves exactly as they pleased – to be and do whatever they wanted. Furthermore, they thought it was no accident that the *content* of gender as applied to female people was subordinating. That was the whole point of gender – a thousands-of-years-old[12] set of ideas that had grown up as part of an ideology to justify male supremacy. No feminist in her right mind is going to look at a system like that and say, 'you know what, there's a lot of value in the content of gender here, so instead of throwing it away we should simply *detach* it from females, so that everyone has an equal opportunity to be subordinated'.

But that is what trans activism is trying to do (with quite a bit of success). There are men who *like* the content of gender applied to females and want it for themselves. If you read Julia Serano in *Whipping Girl*, or Andrea Long Chu in *Females*, or the testimonies of the hundreds of men gathered by Anne Lawrence and reported in *Men Trapped in Men's Bodies*, or some of the men interviewed by Janice Raymond for *The Transsexual Empire*, you will see this. So for them, we should not detach sex from gender in order to get rid of gender and liberate female people; rather we should detach sex from gender *a bit* in order to let some men have that gender too. And the worst part is that this *only* works if we detach it a bit rather than fully; men cannot be women if no women are women anymore. If we detach sex from gender and all the female people are liberated and thus no longer women, then *only* the men who liked the content of women's subordination would be 'women'. But for it to be intelligible that they actually *are* women, it probably cannot be only men in the category.

(Maybe it could if there was a long enough history to the category, with female people dropping out only gradually; but it seems to me that with a mass exodus of females the category would simply collapse.)[13]

Let me say as a final point for now that I have been using the terminology you introduced: 'woman' for gender and 'female' for sex. But I do not actually agree with it. I agree with the sex/gender distinction because I think it is helpful to distinguish the physical subjects (for instance human females) that particular ideas about gender are applied to. But I do not think that a female person who is non-conforming relative to those ideas is not a woman. I think men's ideas about women do not have much to do with *women*. (Rather than, men's ideas about women do not have much to do with female people, therefore there are no/few women.[14]) I prefer to use 'female' and 'woman' synonymously to track the physical subject, and to refer to the ideas about gender that are applied to her as 'femininity'. If we had been using the terminology that way all along, we would be in a lot less trouble now. Saying that a man can be feminine, or can identify with femininity, is not difficult to understand, and no one would think this makes him a woman or makes him female. It is because we detached the idea of gender *and* called it 'woman' that we ended up in a situation where some people do think that you, Michael, could be a woman with your male body and male appearance, simply by identifying as a woman (which must mean, identifying with your man's understanding of what a woman is).

But I agree with the observation you made earlier – that even if you were to start presenting in a more feminine way, people would likely see you as a man who dresses as a woman, not think that you are suddenly in fact a woman. I think more men *should* present as women! Gender non-conformity is a good way to break down gender norms and make everyone freer. But this is work that *men* need to do to free *men* from the constraints of masculinity. They cannot do that work while claiming not to be men at all.

*

Michael Hauskeller: I am intrigued by your suggestion that people who are biologically male but self-identify as women may do so because they like the social role that is traditionally assigned to women and want that role for themselves. That does not make much sense to me, at least not if we see that role as subordinate and associated with passivity, submissiveness and weakness. If these were the attributes that defined a woman socially, then role-envy, if we may call it that, would be much more plausible as a motive in the case of women self-identifying as men, because it is easier to see something desirable in being, or appearing to be, active, dominant and strong rather than passive, submissive and weak. (Of course it is entirely possible that this is just my man's perspective speaking.) Even if the envy were focused on the in my view much more positive 'womanly' attributes of being nurturing, caring and warm, it would still be puzzling because there does not seem to be any good reason to think that one cannot be all that while still being a man (or, for that matter, be all that while being active, dominant and strong). There may be certain gender role expectations and stereotypes, but they are actually far less rigid today than they used to be. It is also not the case that trans women tend to be particularly passive, submissive and weak, nor are they, as a group, particularly nurturing, caring and warm.

If role-envy is indeed a causal factor here, then we should expect that there is some actual or perceived *advantage* to being a woman that certain men would like to share, and some advantage to being a man that certain women would like to share. And perhaps there are such advantages in each case. However, I do not think that this is what is going on here, at least not primarily. It is one thing to say that I want to enjoy the advantages of the gender role that society typically reserves for the other sex, and quite another to claim that I feel 'trapped in my body'[15] because I am *actually* a woman who happens to have been born with a biologically male body. It may be politically opportune to make such a claim because it gives a lot more weight to the demand that one be addressed and treated as a woman *despite* not being one in the biological sense (which in the common understanding is the *primary* sense of the word 'woman').[16] But the claim itself is ontological: it is about what I *am*, and not about what I want to be or have, or how people should or should not behave towards me. And that is what makes it so interesting philosophically: it is not at all obvious what exactly it is that is being claimed here. For that reason, it is also unclear what would make such a claim true or false.

Say I develop a strong conviction that the sex assigned to me at birth does not match my true gender identity. When I was born, people thought, based solely on the evidence of my sexual organs, that I was a boy, but now I have come to realise that I am in fact a woman. Why would I think that? One possible reason might be my sexual preferences. Perhaps I feel sexually attracted to men and not to women. But most men who feel sexually attracted to men do not think that this is because they are actually women. They are simply men who happen to be attracted to other men. So this cannot be it. What other options are there? Since my body is undoubtedly and unambiguously that of a male member of my species, the only other option seems to be that I *feel* like a woman. But what does *that* mean? Since biologically I am not a woman, I have no way of knowing what it feels like to be a biological woman (just as I have no way of knowing what it is like to be a bat[17]). Presumably, then, I am not really feeling like a woman; rather I am feeling how I imagine a woman feels. But why should I presume that there is a particular way that a woman feels that is different from the way a man feels? Do all women feel alike? Is there a special experiential quality to being a woman (which is unconnected to their female *bodies* and hence their *sex*), and a different experiential quality to being a man? And if so, what would that quality be?

*

Holly Lawford-Smith: You say role-envy cannot be the explanation for men identifying as women, because it is surely not that appealing to envy being *passive, submissive, weak* as opposed to *active, dominant, strong*. But you are overlooking the sexual domain. Women are sexual objects. Women are subject to the male gaze. According to sexist ideology, women are *for* fucking.[18] In an average casual heterosexual encounter, the man can expect to dominate in the bedroom, the woman can expect to be dominated. Thoroughgoing sexual objectification – by which I mean objectification which extends into all or most aspects of life, rather than being restricted to the bedroom – is something that men *cannot* experience as men. Men are the ones doing the gazing, the fucking and the dominating.

But what if you are a man who finds the thought of sexual subordination exciting? It would seem that the only way to truly secure this, not just in the bedroom but in your everyday life, is to *become* a woman. You can find this motivation in the writings of some men who identify as women. Andrea Long Chu is the most honest about it – she literally says that sissy porn made her trans.[19] I mentioned already the testimonies Anne Lawrence gathered from autogynephilic males (men who identify as women but who are not homosexual). Here are a couple, just to make the point: 'My sexual fantasies all include myself in female form, either being forced to become female or voluntarily. Frequently they involve a submissive element on my part: I am either forced to be a woman or forced to behave in a particularly submissive manner.'[20] And another: 'I have also questioned myself on whether I'm gay. But I just don't think so, as I have never really thought of having sex with a guy when I'm physically male. At the same time, I have also fantasized [about] myself being a woman and being gang raped.'[21]

What is fascinating about this is that it is actually consistent with a radical feminist analysis – Catharine MacKinnon thinks that women's subordination is primarily sexual. So the men who identify as women *because* they want to be sexually subordinated actually understand something of crucial importance about the politics of sex inequality. MacKinnon talks about the content and consequence of women's sexual subordination: male control of abortion, birth control, forced sterilisation, domestic violence, rape, incest, violence against lesbians, sexual harassment, prostitution, trafficking for prostitution and pornography.[22] Of course, there is something pretty grim about men finding sexual excitement in the thing that is the source of so much suffering for women.

I should clarify that I am not saying that all men who identify as women are doing so for sexual reasons. There is a lot of evidence from the sexology in the late 1980s through the 1990s that many men who identified as women had this motivation – basically all those who were not gay (this was before 'gender identity' took over as the sanitised explanation for all things trans).[23] But the fact that some, if not many, men who identify as women are doing so for sexual reasons helps to explain why the envy point stands even when we might otherwise consider it incomprehensible. It also helps to explain why so many women are angry about the vociferous trans rights movement, because it is literally pitting women's safety against men's sexual rights and elevating the latter.[24]

The other point you made was about hypothethical-you's claim to *be* a woman, and how that connects to knowing what it is like to be a woman. I think this claim, when men make it, is enormously hubristic, and reveals a complete dismissal of women. It is 'colonial' in the metaphorical sense – it treats 'woman' as a sort of conceptual *terra nullius*, that has no indigenous inhabitants. 'Here is an idea I have!', proclaims the man, 'I am *woman*.' The woman sitting next to him looks up and blinks hard a few times. Maybe he will see her there, and notice that *she* is woman, and wonder what they have in common? Maybe he will ask her? But he does not.

As I said earlier, men's idea of 'woman' really has little to do with women, and that is as true now, with men claiming that indeed they *are* women, as it was 600 years ago when Christine de Pizan wrote *The Book of the City of Ladies*, reflecting on all the denigrating things men had written into the scholarly texts about women at the time. In response to the former, feminism eventually emerged, and pushed back on men's ideas about woman. We should have the vote; we deserve an education; we need equal political rights; we need legal protection against discrimination, women said. But there is no 'feminist movement' against today's men identifying as women.[25] On the contrary, the feminist movement has *embraced* these men, and thrown out its definition of 'woman' and the attached sense of what feminism is and who it is for. It is also in the process of throwing out all the women who say, however cautiously, that something seems to have gone wrong here.[26]

*

Michael Hauskeller: You make it sound as if the whole transgender rights movement and especially trans activism is nothing but a clever ploy by men to extend and consolidate their dominion over women. I think that is too simple. While I appreciate the apparent absurdity of a man or biologically male person telling women what being a woman really means, and while finding the idea of sexual subordination arousing might indeed be a reason for some to seek a female gender identity, we should not forget that there are also a lot of trans *men* out there – that is, biological females who self-identify as men. And if a man should not presume to know what it is to be a woman, then I suppose the same must be true for women: they should not presume to know what it is to be a man. If men's ideas of 'woman' have, as you say, little to do with real women, then women's ideas of 'man' are unlikely to have much to do with real men.

But all this assumes that there is some radical, unbridgeable difference between men and women that makes it virtually impossible for either to understand the other.[27] I do not believe that, and, frankly, do not see any good reason to do so. While it is true that I, being a man, do not know what it is like to have a female body, with different sexual organs and different associated functions and experiences, surely this is only one aspect of what makes you, a woman, what you are. We may not share those particular bodily features, but there are plenty of other things that we have in common, perhaps many more than I have in common with most other men. I may not know what it is to be a woman, but I also do not know what it is to be, say, a New Zealander, or to be only 1.5 m tall, or to be born with a disability, or to have grown up in Italy, or to be super-rich. So in that sense it is rather trivial to say that I do not know what it is to be a woman, simply because I can say that about almost anything. Ultimately, I do not know what it is to be someone other than the person I in fact am. I can, however, imagine what it must be like to be in a very different situation, and while what I imagine might not be entirely accurate (since I have never actually been in that situation), it does not have to be completely wrong either. Why would my imagining what it is to be a woman be any different?

I think we need to resist the temptation to attach too much importance to the supposed differences between men and women, and instead insist that the *only* difference between men and women lies in certain features of their bodies (namely those that are connected to different sexual and reproductive functions), and that everything else is not in any way essential to being a woman or being a man. That includes what you say about men – that they 'are the ones doing the gazing, the fucking and the dominating'. Clearly, a woman can do that too, and in fact the vast majority of women objectify men sexually just as much as men objectify women. Non-objectification defines a woman no more than weakness or subordination does. We are all different from each other, and we all have a lot in common, too, both with those of our own sex and with those of the opposite sex.

For me, this makes it even more puzzling that so many people these days seem to believe that they have somehow been assigned the wrong gender, insisting that, even though their bodies are unambiguously male or female, what they *really* are is different from what their bodies say they are. What I would like to understand is what this claim, which is a claim about identity and not just preference, is based on. When I, a biological male, self-identify as a woman, what I am claiming is *not* that I wish I were a woman and that I would very much like people to treat me as one. Rather, what I am claiming is that I *am* a woman, and that precisely *because* I am, I have a *right* to be recognised and treated as one.[28] But my body is a male body, so what exactly is it that I think makes me a woman?

From our discussion so far it would seem that it is not enough to *feel* like a woman, for one thing because it would be difficult, if not impossible, for a biological male to know how women feel,[29] and for another because it seems rather unlikely that there really is such a thing as 'feeling like a woman', or in other words that there is something it is like to be a woman. So it seems to me that we can only make sense of that claim if we think that there is some sort of female *essence* that is present in women, including trans women, but not present in men – a bit like the traditional 'soul' that is believed to exist independent of the body, except that now that soul is seen as gendered. It is a revival of the old Cartesian dualism, which is problematic in its own right. But even if that does not trouble us, can we say anything more about that gendered soul, except that it is female or male? If so, are we doing more here than unduly essentialising certain social norms and expectations? And if not – if being a man and being a woman is a basic quality that cannot be analysed any further – how do we recognise it? Is it something directly intuited? I *know* I am a woman, I might say. But *how* do I know?

Let us assume I self-identify not as a woman, but as King Henry VIII. That would be absurd because I clearly am not King Henry VIII. But if my body's features and history are irrelevant for my identity, why can I not be him? What is different here from the case of a woman self-identifying as a man? Or, if that seems too farfetched, take race. I, a white person, self-identify as black. I do not think that happens very often, but it has happened,[30] and it is curious that such claims have been widely and vehemently rejected as preposterous.[31] Apparently a person who has all the physical attributes of a man can be a woman, but someone who has all the physical attributes of a white person cannot be a black person, no matter how they feel about it or how convinced they are of it. Yet what exactly is it that makes many people view those cases so differently?

*

Holly Lawford-Smith: I think the points you made towards the end, and the questions you ask, are bang on. Let me pick up on a couple of earlier things I disagreed with before I come back to that.

First, you said 'if men's ideas of "woman" have, as you say, little to do with real women, then women's ideas of "man" are unlikely to have much to do with real men'. I do not think that is right, because it presumes that there is symmetry in the knowledge base. But there is not. Men have literally written history. They have held most of the positions of power; they have written most of the laws, the science, the history books. They have produced most of the art, including the books, films, television and radio shows that represent women characters. They have given themselves a central place. Any woman alive today is likely to have been exposed, throughout her education and across her exposure to media and entertainment, to men's stories, men's accomplishments, men's thoughts and ideas. Women have an abundance of material on which to draw if they want to understand men. And we know from other minority groups that when there is a very serious social power differential – as there was between black and white people during slavery, and between men and women when women were economically dependent on men through marriage and the family – the class who are worse off tend to become experts in the class who are better off, because this helps them to survive.

So I think if a woman says she identifies as a man, there is a much stronger sense in which she could be getting something right – at least, she knows what it is, roughly, to be a man, and she is saying she wants a slice of that. Not so for the man who says he identifies as a woman.[32] There are so many examples of the ways we can be completely unaware of things just because they do not affect us – Caroline Criado Perez's book *Invisible Women* is absolutely crammed with examples of the ways women's issues have been invisible to men. Here is just one tiny example: when Apple developed HealthKit to track people's health, it managed to overlook menstruation. Probably because it was developed by men, and this just did not occur to them. I agree with you that this knowledge gap is not 'radical, unbridgeable'. I think if men wanted to, they could bridge it. But the extent of the problem we still have is striking, and I have not seen any evidence that trans women are better at bridging it than other men.

Second, you said 'in fact the vast majority of women objectify men sexually just as much as men objectify women'. Hah! I hope it does not seem too obnoxious to suggest that this might be an example of what I have just been trying to explain, namely some things being largely invisible to men, which allows them – here *you* – to assume the situation is roughly symmetrical for the sexes. Girls start being sexually objectified by boys and men around the age of puberty. They are routinely subject to sexualised comments about their bodies and appearance, from people they know, and from people they don't, for instance in street harassment and catcalling. Many teenage girls develop eating disorders or self-harming problems arguably as a result of this treatment. Pornography, which presents a particularly distorted view of women and girls as things for men to fuck, makes this situation considerably worse (I am sure you are aware that men tend to be the subjects, and women the objects, in most mainstream pornography). Advertising uses women's bodies and women's sexuality to sell products. In her representations in film and television woman is generally presented as something whose primary value lies in her appearance. *None of this* is true for men. I am sure you can find some examples of a handsome shirtless man being used to sell cologne or whatever, but this is nowhere near as pervasive as it is for girls – and with nowhere near the consequences. For even while men are objects, they are also subjects, and this is unfortunately often not true for women and girls. No wonder so many girls today are declaring themselves to *be* men!

Which, of course, takes us nicely to your point about trans men, and whether the existence of trans men shows that trans activism can't just be 'a clever ploy by men to extend and consolidate their dominion over women'. I think trans men's reasons are very different to transwomen's and have more to do with escaping the clutches of socialised femininity (and in some cases, escaping homophobia). It is the ideology that you can be whatever you identify as that has created the 'refugees' from sex categories, and perhaps what they have in common is that in both the female and the male case, trans individuals want *not that* – where 'that' is the stereotypes and expectations imposed on people of their sex. But their reasons for seeking asylum have very little in common apart from that. I think this started with men (nearly all transsexuals were male) and then the ideology created an opportunity for some women.

Finally! Your comments about dualism and gender essences seemed exactly right to me, and I find it amusing that this movement is billed as progressive when it is really just a return to the ancient Greeks.[33] I also have all the same questions you have, about how arbitrary it seems to be advocating self-identification for sex but not for race, and not for identifying as a specific person.[34] I cannot find the logic in it. It would be good if there was something I could say that would help us to advance on this point, but I really don't have anything to suggest. I think it is nonsense. Like you, I think the *unavoidable* differences between men and women are mainly, if not entirely, differences in our bodies (and differences in experiences that come from those, in context). But there are other *avoidable* differences that come from how sexist particular societies are or have been.

*

Michael Hauskeller: If I understand you correctly, what you are saying is basically that, because men have always been so dominant, women know very well what it is to be a man (mostly: to be in a position of power) – which is why women who self-identify as men are 'getting something right' – whereas men who self-identify as women have no idea what they are talking about because women have never been properly heard, so men cannot possibly know what it is like to be a woman. And yet you also said earlier that trans women are motivated by a (in your view twisted or at any rate misguided) desire to experience for themselves the submissive role that men think women should occupy. I do not quite see how these two claims can both be true; but the power dynamics between men and women are not really the issue here, at least not for me. You look at things from a gender-*political* perspective, whereas I try to do so from a gender-*metaphysical* angle. I want to understand what 'being a man' or 'being a woman' actually means in order to make sense of claims by some biological males that they are in fact women, by some biological females that they are in fact men, and by some biological males and some biological females that they are in fact neither. To understand and assess these claims (which pose exactly the same difficulty ontologically), their personal reasons for making such a claim are not really relevant. People do all sorts of things for all sorts of reasons. And there are also many different ways of being a woman and of being a man – or perhaps I should say, many different ways of being a person.

As far as I am concerned, people should be free to be whatever they want to be, provided they do not harm other people in the process. If a biological male wants me to address him as a woman, or a biological female wants me to address her as a man, or if they want me to call them 'they' because they identify with neither, I am happy to oblige and call him 'she', and her 'he', or both 'they', and treat them with the same respect I show to every other person. I do not need to know why they prefer that particular social identity ('man' or 'woman'), or prefer not to be burdened with any gender-related social identity at all ('nonbinary'); it is none of my business. I appreciate that this can cause problems in certain contexts (for instance when it comes to the use of public bathrooms or changing rooms,[35] or in sports where it raises issues of fairness in sex-segregated athletic competitions[36]), but apart from that we should respect people's choices to live and present themselves any way they want. But that does not mean I have to unquestioningly accept an identity claim that, on the face of it, is highly paradoxical.

It seems to me that while we can change our *social* identity – that is, the way we present ourselves, and through this possibly also the way we are perceived by others – we cannot change what we *are* simply by declaring ourselves to be something on the inside that we are not on the outside, especially if what we claim to be on the inside is something that can by its very nature only *exist* on the outside. We are embodied beings, and my sex is just as much a biological fact – that is, a fact about my *body* – as the colour of my skin, or my height, or my species affiliation. There is of course also the social role that is commonly associated with a particular sex – which is what we normally mean by gender – but that role is precisely *not* something that I am; it consists mainly in social expectations, which, even though we may have internalised them to a certain extent, we are ultimately free to reject. And that is indeed what many people do or try to do today. As you rightly say, 'gender non-conformity is a good way to break down gender norms and make everyone more free'. It may well be that the most effective way of doing this is by declaring oneself to be 'nonbinary'; declaring oneself to be a 'man' in a female body, or a 'woman' in a male body is probably less so because it might actually reinforce certain gender stereotypes. But all such attempts to reinvent oneself can easily be understood as acts of defiance – a refusal to be pigeonholed and an insistence that one is unique, uncategorisable, oneself rather than this or that – and as such they are quite understandable and legitimate.

However, the narrative that is often being used here to convince others of the legitimacy of such conversions (and of the rights claims and demands that are being tied to them) strongly suggests that gender is presented here not as a social construct or biological fact but as something much deeper and more foundational, and unconnected to both my body and my social role. It is made out to be an essential part of what I really, *truly* am, and something that I can *discover* myself to be. What puzzles me is this narrative of detached authenticity and self-discovery. It is one thing to reject the gender norms that society inflicts on us, and quite another to think that we or our true selves are somehow trapped in the wrong body, as though our body had no relevance to what we are. But it does. We can sometimes change what we are, but we are not free to be anything we want to be, and reality cannot be neatly separated from materiality (which, contra Plato, is *not* mere appearance).

*

Holly Lawford Smith: I agree with most of what you just said. I share your puzzlement about the idea that genders are essential parts of what we really, truly are; I too reject the bad metaphysics behind the idea that our bodies have little to do with our 'selves'. (By the way, if you haven't read it, Kasja Ekman's book *Being and Being Bought* notes that this kind of self/body dualism is used ideologically to support institutionalised surrogacy and prostitution – the use of the body becomes a good/service, rather than a selling/renting of the self.)

One thing I do not agree with is your optimism, I think, about the new gender category of 'nonbinary' being a good way to help to break down gender roles. Creating a third gender category does change *something*: there is a bit more freedom for the people who choose to opt into it. But it can also do what you noted straightforward swapping of categories could do (from man to woman or from woman to man), namely reinforce gender stereotypes. That is because nonbinary people, just like transgender people, make an exception of themselves: by saying *I am not my sex* they are in effect also saying, *this is not a way that someone of my sex can be*. The transgender person says he is more like the opposite sex; the nonbinary person says she is not like either sex.

But suppose the transgender person is a feminine male and the nonbinary person is an androgynous female. Why isn't 'feminine' a way to be a man, though, or 'androgynous' a way to be a woman? If you ask, they will say, it is! But *this* person just happens not to be merely a feminine man, he is in fact a woman (because he identifies as a woman).

So then you have two people side by side who are materially pretty much identical, but somehow one is trans and one is not, because they *identify* differently. If this catches on – which it seems to be doing, with huge increases in the numbers of girls reporting to gender clinics[37] – then it looks as though we are definitely going to be reinforcing feminine gender norms, because any woman with the slightest bit of a personality will suddenly be 'not a woman'. Maybe it looks like an improvement from the perspective of the female nonbinary person, who has applied an individual solution to a collective problem, but it is certainly not helpful for all the women left behind, who now have to fight to explain why they're *not trans* just because they like wearing trousers. (The Australian lesbian comedian Hannah Gadsby, who likes wearing trousers, talks in her show *Nanette* about being pressured to come out as trans.[38] The Danish comedian Sofie Hagen, who also enjoys trousers, came out last year as 'nonbinary', noting how annoying it was that people paid so much attention to her being a female in comedy.[39])

You said you were interested in the metaphysics of gender, and wanted 'to understand what "being a man" or "being a woman" actually means in order to make sense of claims by some biological males that they are in fact women, by some biological females that they are in fact men, and by some biological males and some biological females that they are in fact neither'. Orthodox/establishment feminist philosophers are moving away from a metaphysical understanding of 'being a woman' to a political one, probably because the metaphysical couldn't be made to work for their purposes (could not be made to do useful theoretical work *and* also not exclude anyone who wanted to be included). The problem with moving to the political is, *whose politics?* I find their politics repugnant. (The same problem exists for amelioration projects, where people talk about what 'we' want our words to do. What *we* is that?)

This means, for me, that we should keep it metaphysical, so in that sense I share your interest, as well as having a political interest. But if 'being a woman' is not just being female, then it seems that it involves turning *how women have been treated by men* into a social role for women to occupy. But I agree with Kathleen Stock's analysis that the move to thinking of 'woman' as a social role (rather than a person *in* a social role) was a mistake in the history of feminist thinking.[40] Being a woman turns out to be just being female, after all. Is this compatible with there being some contexts where we should go along with a man's claim to be a woman? Maybe. But it helps to make it more intelligible why some women do not want to do this. It is not only because it is not true, it is also that it *perpetuates* the idea that 'female' refers to sex while 'woman' refers to gender in the social role sense. (So that anyone in that role can be a woman, even a man.) Reclaiming the word 'woman' for female people, and reserving the use of sex-based pronouns for people who actually have the sex, are helpful tools in getting feminist theory and movement back on track as being fundamentally *about sex caste.*[41]

Notes

1. Frequently cited on the internet is this quote (which is commonly, but apparently wrongly, attributed to the actress Betty White): 'Why do people say "grow some balls"? Balls are weak and sensitive. If you wanna be tough, grow a vagina. Those things can take a pounding.'
2. See Kang, 'Does manly courage exist?'.
3. *Modern Family*, second season, episode 7: 'Chirp'.
4. There is extensive commentary on this point in Gilman's *Herland* (1912), as well as in Beauvoir's *The Second Sex* (1949).
5. Wollstonecraft, *A Vindication of the Rights of Woman*; Taylor Mill, 'Enfranchisement of women'; Mill, 'The subjection of women'.
6. Firestone, *The Dialectic of Sex*.
7. Pizan, *The Book of the City of Ladies*; Millett, *Sexual Politics*.
8. Woolf, *A Room of One's Own*.
9. Gilman's *Herland* is an early text that makes this point forcefully. Revealing the extent of the female sex's socialisation into subordination was a central concern of the second wave's radical feminists. For an overview see discussion in Lawford-Smith, *Gender-Critical Feminism*, chapter 2.
10. There is confusion today between this idea – the separation of sex (women) and gender (what women are socialised to be like) – and the *terms* we use to refer to sex and gender. Some use 'female' and 'woman' synonymously for sex, some use them synonymously for gender, and some use 'female' for sex and 'woman' for gender. The latter creates the possibility of a woman (gender) who is not female (sex). See further discussion below, and also Stock, *Material Girls*, chapter 1.
11. Many thought of themselves as 'gender abolitionists' or 'gender annihilationists'. See e.g. The Feminists, 'The Feminists'.
12. On the origin of patriarchy as a system see the fascinating discussion in Lerner, *The Creation of Patriarchy*.
13. There is consideration of a slow change to the categories of 'man' and 'woman', becoming mixed-sex over time, first in Bach, 'Gender is a natural kind with a historical essence', and later in George and Briggs, 'Science fiction double feature'.
14. For a comprehensive argument against this mistake in the history of feminism see Stock, 'Not the social kind'.
15. See Rubin, *Self-Made Men*, 150–1.
16. See Bettcher, 'Trapped in the wrong theory', 387: 'The point I'm pressing is that transsexual claims to belong to a sex do not appear to be metaphysically justified: they are claims that self-identities ought to be definitive in terms of the question of sex membership and gendered treatment. They are therefore political in nature.'
17. See Nagel, 'What is it like to be a bat?'.
18. See for instance Dworkin, *Intercourse*.
19. Chu, *Females*, 79.
20. Lawrence, *Men Trapped in Men's Bodies*, 47.
21. Lawrence, *Men Trapped in Men's Bodies*, 52.
22. This discussion appears in her paper 'Feminism, Marxism, method, and the state'.
23. See for instance the discussion in Blanchard, 'Typology of male-to-female transsexualism'; Blanchard, 'The concept of autogynephilia and the typology of male gender dysphoria'; and Bailey, *The Man Who Would Be Queen*.

24. See also Helen Joyce's discussion of this issue in *Trans*, chapter 2.
25. There are, however, occasional individual feminists speaking out. Early dissenters include Raymond (*The Transsexual Empire*) and Jeffreys (*Gender Hurts*). More recently, Schrier (*Irreversible Damage*) and Stock (*Material Girls*) are notable voices.
26. Perhaps the best example of this phenomenon is the enormous public backlash against J. K. Rowling's rather temperate essay on sex and gender published in 2020 ('J. K. Rowling writes about her reasons for speaking out on sex and gender issues').
27. Which is strongly suggested by the popularity of books such as Tanner's *You Just Don't Understand*.
28. See for instance Hines, 'The feminist frontier'.
29. See Burkett, 'What makes a woman?'.
30. See Brubaker, 'The Dolezal affair'.
31. See for instance Dembroff and Payton, 'Why we shouldn't compare transracial to transgender identity'.
32. I develop these ideas at greater length in the public essay 'Trans men are men (but transwomen are not women)'.
33. I say a bit more about this connection in 'What is a woman?'.
34. For a defence of treating the two together see Tuvel, 'In defense of transracialism'.
35. For a comprehensive overview of the debate see Barnett et al., 'The transgender bathroom debate at the intersection of politics, law, ethics, and science'.
36. See Bianchi, 'Transgender women in sport'.
37. For example, the case note for *Bell v Tavistock* states: 'The number of referrals to GIDS has increased very significantly in recent years. In 2009, 97 children and young people were referred. In 2018 that number was 2519' (para. 31, p. 8); 'in 2011 the gender split was roughly 50/50 between natal girls and boys. However, in 2019 the split had changed so that 76 percent of referrals were natal females' (para. 32, p. 8). https://www.judiciary.uk/wp-content/uplo ads/2020/12/Bell-v-Tavistock-Judgment.pdf (accessed 1 December 2021).
38. https://www.netflix.com/nz/title/80233611 (accessed 1 December 2021).
39. https://www.sofiehagen.com/newsletters/2020/2/26/also-im-not-a-woman-2019 (accessed 1 December 2021).
40. Stock, 'Not the social kind'.
41. A 'caste' is socially stratified group—the term is more usually applied within nations, stratifying racial groups. Some feminists use it to emphasize the social distinctions between the sexes. I make the case for reclaiming feminism as being about sex caste in *Gender-Critical Feminism*.

Bibliography

Bach, Theodore. 'Gender is a natural kind with a historical essence', *Ethics* 122/2 (2012): 231–72.
Bailey, Michael. *The Man Who Would Be Queen*. Washington, DC: Joseph Henry Press, 2003.
Barnett, Brian S., Ariana E. Nesbit and Renée M. Sorrentino. 'The transgender bathroom debate at the intersection of politics, law, ethics, and science', *Journal of the American Academy of Psychiatry and the Law* 46/2 (2018): 232–41.
Beauvoir, Simone de. *The Second Sex*. New York: Alfred A. Knopf, 1971.
Bettcher, Talia Mae. 'Trapped in the wrong theory: rethinking trans oppression and resistance', *Signs* 39/2 (2014): 383–406.
Bianchi, Andria. 'Trangender women in sport', *Journal of the Philosophy of Sport* 44/2 (2017): 229–42.
Blanchard, Ray. 'Typology of male-to-female transsexualism', *Archives of Sexual Behaviour* 14 (1985): 247–61.
Blanchard, Ray. 'The concept of autogynephilia and the typology of male gender dysphoria', *Journal of Nervous and Mental Disease* 177 (1989): 616–23.
Brubaker, Rogers. 'The Dolezal affair: race, gender, and the micropolitics of identity', *Ethnic and Racial Studies* 39/3 (2016): 414–48.
Burkett, Elinor. 'What makes a woman?', *The New York Times*, 6 June 2015. https://www.nytimes.com/2015/06/07/opinion/ (accessed 1 December 2021).
Chu, Andrea Long. *Females*. New York: Verso, 2019.

Criado-Perez, Caroline. *Invisible Women*. London: Chatto & Windus, 2019.

Dembroff, Robin, and Dee Payton. 'Why we shouldn't compare transracial to transgender identity', *Boston Review*, 18 November 2020. http://bostonreview.net/race-philosophy-religion-gender-sexuality/robin-dembroff-dee-payton-why-we-shouldnt-compare (accessed 1 December 2021).

Dworkin, Andrea. *Intercourse*. New York: Basic Books, 1987.

Ekman, Kajsa Ekis. *Being and Being Bought: Prostitution, surrogacy and the split self*. Melbourne: Spinifex Press, 2013.

Firestone, Shulamith. *The Dialectic of Sex*. New York: William Morrow, 1970.

George, B. R., and R. A. Briggs. 'Science fiction double feature: trans liberation on twin earth', 25 March 2019. https://philpapers.org/rec/GEOSFD (accessed 1 December 2021).

Gilman, Charlotte Perkins. *Herland*. New York: Pantheon, 1979.

Hines, Sally. 'The feminist frontier: on trans and feminism', *Journal of Gender Studies* 28 (2019): 145–57.

Jeffreys, Sheila. *Gender Hurts*. Abingdon: Routledge, 2014.

Joyce, Helen. *Trans*. London: Oneworld, 2021.

Kang, John M. 'Does manly courage exist?', *Nevada Law Journal* 13/2 (2013): 467–85.

Lawford-Smith, Holly. 'What is a woman?' *Medium*, 16th November 2019. https://hollylawford-smith.org/what-is-a-woman/ (accessed 1 December 2021).

Lawford-Smith, Holly. 'Trans men are men (but transwomen are not women)', *Medium*, 12 May 2020. https://hollylawford-smith.org/trans-men-are-men-but-transwomen-are-not-women/ (accessed 1 December 2021).

Lawford-Smith, Holly. *Gender-Critical Feminism*. Oxford: Oxford University Press, 2022.

Lawrence, Ann. *Men Trapped in Men's Bodies*. New York: Springer, 2013.

Lerner, Gerda. *The Creation of Patriarchy*. Oxford: Oxford University Press, 1986.

MacKinnon, Catharine A. 'Feminism, Marxism, method, and the state: an agenda for theory', *Signs* 7/3 (1982): 515–44.

Mill, John Stuart. 'The subjection of women'. In *Essays on Sex Equality*, edited by Alice Rossi, 123–242. Chicago, IL: University of Chicago Press, 1970.

Millett, Kate. *Sexual Politics*. Champaign, IL: University of Illinois Press, 2000.

Nagel, Thomas. 'What is it like to be a bat?', *The Philosophical Review* 83/4 (1974): 435–50.

Pizan, Christine de. *The Book of the City of Ladies*, translated by Rosalind Brown-Grant. London: Penguin, 1999.

Raymond, Janice. *The Transsexual Empire*. New York: Teachers College Press, 1994.

Rowling, J. K. 'J. K. Rowling writes about her reasons for speaking out on sex and gender issues', 10 June 2020. https://www.jkrowling.com/opinions/j-k-rowling-writes-about-her-reasons-for-speaking-out-on-sex-and-gender-issues/ (accessed 1 December 2021).

Rubin, Henry. *Self-Made Men: Identity and embodiment among transsexual men*. Nashville, TN: Vanderbilt University Press, 2003.

Schrier, Abigail. *Irreversible Damage*. Washington: Regnery, 2020.

Serano, Julia. *Whipping Girl*. Berkeley, CA: Seal Press, 2007.

Stock, Kathleen. *Material Girls: Why reality matters for feminism*. London: Fleet, 2021.

Stock, Kathleen. 'Not the social kind: anti-naturalist mistakes in the philosophical history of woman-hood', 24 February 2020. https://philpapers.org/rec/STONTS (accessed 1 December 2021).

Tanner, Deborah. *You Just Don't Understand: Women and men in conversation*. New York: Ballantine Books, 1990.

Taylor Mill, Harriet. 'Enfranchisement of women'. In *Essays on Sex Equality*, edited by Alice Rossi, 89–122. Chicago, IL: University of Chicago Press, 1970.

The Feminists. 'The Feminists: a political organization to annihilate sex roles'. In *Radical Feminism*, edited by Anne Koedt, Ellen Levine and Anita Rapone, 368–78. New York: Quadrangle, 1973.

Tuvel, Rebecca. 'In defense of transracialism', *Hypatia* 32/2 (2017): 263–78.

Wollstonecraft, Mary. *A Vindication of the Rights of Woman*. London: Arcturus, 2017.

Woolf, Virginia. *A Room of One's Own*. New York: Harcourt, Brace & World, 1929.

5
Age

with Christine Overall

Christine Overall: In talking about age, I'm also interested in age*s*, plural. I think age is an identity, just as gender, race, sexuality, class and (dis) ability are.

One's age is sometimes defined, roughly, in terms of demographic cohort membership: the Lost Generation (1883–90), the Greatest Generation (1901–27), the Silent Generation (1928–45), the Baby Boomers (1946–64), Gen X (1965–80), Millennials (originally called Gen Y; 1981–96), Gen Z (1997–2012), and now Generation Alpha (2013–). This classification is used primarily in the developed world, and maybe specifically North America.[1] Whether or not the members of each generation have much in common, they are often *seen* as being similar, and they may very well share the experience of certain landmark national and global events (such as the world wars).

It is, however, probably more common to identify oneself with a life stage defined in terms of age: children, adolescents, young adults, middle-aged, old. One's age is therefore much more than a number; it marks participation in a culturally familiar and well-defined stage of life, complete with roles, expectations, limitations and stereotypes. People often think of the trajectory of their lives in such terms as 'when I grow up', 'when I was young', 'when I get old'. We say things like 'she's only a teenager', 'he's all grown up', 'life begins at 40', 'he's pushing 60', 'they are in their 80s'.

Notably, the life stage 'old' usually encompasses the widest span of years. Thus, an old person could be anywhere from 60 or 65 to 105 – or more. In asking participants' age, many surveys, whether by academics or by corporations, include an age category of '65 and older'. The assumption seems to be that persons belonging to this group are entirely undifferentiated; there is no difference between a 70-year-old and a 90-year-old, for example. Whereas people who have lived for fewer years are thought to change in noteworthy ways from 10 to 20 and from 20 to 30, everyone who is 'old' is believed to remain both fixed and alike. The old are not thought to develop, grow or change in any psychological, social or culturally significant ways. This phenomenon is an expression of ageism.

Age is socially constructed, at least in this respect: the various life stages and their associated roles, expectations, limitations and stereotypes have changed over historical time and also vary from one social context to another.[2]

Philippe Ariès was the first to argue that the notion of childhood was invented – in Europe, during the 1600s; before that time, young human beings in that region were regarded as small adults.[3] Adolescence as a life stage is more recent, its origins often traced to the 1920s. My own maternal grandfather, born in 1896, seems never to have been an adolescent; in 1909, at the age of 13, he left school to take up full-time work, as was typical for young people in working-class London of the time, and five years later he was in the trenches in France, fighting on behalf of Canada and England.

With the growing need for more education and the declining availability of low-skill jobs, a new life stage is gradually developing: young, or 'emerging', adulthood. Partly because of increasing evidence about the slow maturation of the human brain, people in the decade or so past adolescence are granted more freedom and fewer responsibilities than in the past. They remain in school longer, they marry later, if at all, and their children are born later. During this time, young people in their 20s and even their early 30s are often considered to belong to a group called 'youth'. By contrast, when my mother and father were 18 or 19, they thought of themselves as adults, full stop, and were expected to have finished school, to get full-time jobs, to find a life partner, and to start reproducing. They were required to act like independent adults and to be responsible for themselves.

As for me, at 72 I am 'old' in social terms. I readily refer to myself as old for two reasons: first, because people generally, and younger people particularly,[4] inevitably *regard* someone in their 70s as old, and more importantly, because I want to reclaim and rehabilitate the word 'old' and not treat the term as a label to be shunned.

As I pointed out earlier, the life stage 'old' generally tends to be undifferentiated, although some sociologists and gerontologists distinguish between the young old, middle old, and old old, the boundaries of each of which are variously defined. My own view is that there are good reasons for defining 'old' by reference to life expectancy.[5] An individual who has lived longer than the age of life expectancy for her or his nation or region is old. But because of significant differences in poverty levels, nutrition, health care, workplace safety, and air and water pollution, life expectancy varies greatly from one country to another.[6] Hence, defining 'old' by reference to life expectancy would mean that what constitutes being old would differ from one nation to another. For example, since life expectancy at birth for women in Canada for 2020–5 is projected to be 84.74,[7] by my proposed definition I am not old.

Thus, while people's ages seem fixed because they can be measured in years, their social meanings vary from era to era and from society to society, and their associated life stages vary because of differences in the social and material conditions of living.

Although attempts to pass as belonging to a different gender, race, sexuality or socioeconomic class are frequently remarked upon and studied, *age passing* seems not to be considered significant, perhaps because it is so frequent. Passing or trying to pass as a different age is a common human practice, sometimes even mandated.

Thus, for very young people (up to the age of 16 or so, let's say) being older is often desirable, and they may try to pass as older – in order to drink alcohol, drive, get into 'adult only' venues, or just to be cool and fit in with an admired social cohort. But even more pervasive within dominant Western cultures is the assumption that old people will at least try to pass as young. Old people are expected to colour their hair or get hair implants, dress youthfully, take part in youthful activities, be physically active, continue to care about sex and try to have a lot of it, and so on. After about age 25, people are often complimented for looking younger than their chronological age.

The primary reason for age passing is that different values are attached to different ages: youth (but maybe not extreme youth) is generally regarded quite positively, while oldness of any sort is not, at least within dominant European and North American cultures. Just take a look at the sentiments expressed on most birthday cards.

And indeed, for older people there is plenty to be gained through passing as younger. Successful passing may mean acquiring or holding on to a job, or attracting or hanging on to a romantic partner. By contrast, there is (in most cases) nothing much, if anything, to be gained for a 30-year-old who tries to pass as 50, for example, or a 40-year-old as 60.

These asymmetries, too, are manifestations of ageism in action. But that's a topic for further discussion.

*

Michael Hauskeller: Age, you said at the beginning, is an identity. It defines who we are both in our own eyes and in those of others. There is good reason for this, too, because our biological age – how many years we have lived – tends to have a perfectly real and noticeable effect on what and how we are. As we get older and our bodies and minds mature, we learn to do certain things that we were not capable of when we were younger, and as we grow older still, we are bound to lose some of those abilities again, while (if we are lucky) gaining others.

We do not merely get older chronologically[8] – in the sense that the time we have spent in this world increases; we also *age* in the sense that our getting older leads us through different life stages, each of which comes with certain distinctive features linked to the natural development of our physical bodies.[9] This process of ageing has a certain direction, a certain (multi-layered) shape of rise and decline, of gaining and losing capacities, that, for beings such as us,[10] inevitably accompanies our getting older. In that sense, age is, just like our biological sex, not at all a social construction but an indisputable fact of our existence as human (and indeed living) beings. This is the reason why our rather desperate attempts to stay physically young (because we don't merely wish to *pass* as younger than we are when we have reached a certain age; we want to actually *remain* young for as long as possible) are all doomed to fail. It is also the reason why 'childhood' and 'old age' are to a large part *not* pure constructions, let alone 'inventions'. If anything, childhood was not invented, it was discovered. Children are not, in fact, small adults, and being old means more than simply having lived for a certain number of years.

Our age, then, is indeed part and parcel of our personal identity. It is one of the things that make us who we are, which is a strange thing to say really if we want to assume that what makes us who we are must necessarily be something that persists over time, making the middle-aged man I am today the same person I used to be when I was much younger and the same person I'm going to be when (or if) I am much older.[11] But that person is very much an abstraction. We exist in time. As physical, living, incarnate beings, we always have a particular age; we are always at a particular stage of our biological development. What we are, as a person and an individual, we are always *here and now*. In that sense, we cannot plausibly detach ourselves from our temporal incarnation and say 'my age doesn't matter: the real "me" is ageless'.

However, as you rightly pointed out, our *biological* age is only one aspect of this. How old we are in chronological and biological terms is one thing; what that *means* is quite another. I'm in my late 50s now and as such I share certain experiences with others of a similar age: a lot of life has already been lived and both body and mind have lost some of their youthful vigour. And as our body and mind are tiring, mortality is no longer an abstract concept: we feel it in our bones, our flesh, our skin. On the other hand, we are generally still quite capable, aided by the economic power and social status that many of us have managed to acquire over several decades of adult life. Clearly, though, this is not a given. Being in one's late 50s (or early 70s or any other age group) means different things for different people, depending on our personal circumstances and many other factors: whether we are healthy or not, a woman or a man, economically secure or financially struggling, successful in our professional career or stuck in a job that is not really going anywhere.

It is also important (for the way we experience our age and for what it means to us and others) *where* and *when* we are the age that we are. For me, being in my late 50s is probably in some ways different from what it was like for my parents or grandparents, let alone for someone who lived centuries ago, as it will also not be quite the same for people living in different cultures. What we share with others in our age group and what defines us as belonging to that group are, in addition to our being at a particular stage in our biological development, mostly certain cultural experiences, and here the past very much affects the present. I am not only a man in my late 50s living in the early 2020s; I am also someone who, among other things, was a teenager in the late 1970s and early 1980s, when there were no mobile phones around, no personal computers and no internet. The environment in which we happen to find ourselves at a certain age greatly affects what it means to be that age at that time, and what it means for a certain person to be a certain age at a certain time also affects what it means for the same person to be a different age at a later time.

*

Christine Overall: As you said, Michael, 'our biological age – how many years we have lived – tends to have a perfectly real and noticeable effect on what and how we are'. But *when* and *how* it has these effects certainly changes, and changes dramatically, from one era to another. Unlike my own grandmothers with me, I have never baked cookies for my grandchildren, or knitted them hats and sweaters. However, in the past year I have taken the boys canoeing, kayaking and pedal-boating. I have gone on hikes, run races, and played basketball and soccer with them. My grandparents did none of these things; they were not *capable* of doing them, even when they were younger than I am. So while my biological age may have a noticeable effect on what and how I am, that effect is very different from the effect of the same age on my grandparents, born in the 1890s.

Not only do the meanings of various ages change over time and place and milieu and society, but *those meanings themselves can change the way various ages are lived and physically manifested*. For example, when retirement was thought to be the end of an active and engaged life, and when old people were believed to be naturally frail and tired and incapable of strenuous physical activity, it is not surprising that that is what they became; they lacked the encouragement and opportunity to do more. And if children now are thought to be in need of constant protection and surveillance, kept safely at home, compared to the past when children were expected to be away from home all day playing, or to walk long distances to school on their own, then today's kids become literally incapable of navigating the outside world on their own – and any parent who enables them to do so is believed to be guilty of child neglect.[12] As Lenore Skenazy says, 'A child who thinks he can't do anything on his own eventually can't'.[13] Stages of development are not just givens; they are a function of nutrition, health care, parenting, education, ideologies, opportunities and restrictions.

As a type of identity, age is different from some other identities such as race or sex in the degree of mobility it provides (and necessitates).[14] We move, inexorably, from one age to another, from one life stage to another. In that respect, it is different from socioeconomic class, in which mobility is possible, though certainly not inevitable. This age and stage mobility renders ageism of any sort not just unjust but also irrational. To be ageist against young people or old people is to express an unwarranted bias against either one's past self or one's future self. Those who begrudge health care or social support to people over 65 may help to undermine the wellbeing of their own future selves.

But of course, age mobility is unidirectional only. As a result, there is an inherent asymmetry between the experiences of different ages. A young person can have little or no idea of what it's like to be old, at least not through immediate experience, whereas an old person has undergone the experiences of being young. Admittedly, it may be challenging for the old person to be *au courant* on the contemporary cultures of youth, and their challenges, problems and goals, but old age is an entirely unknown country when one is young. And not one that youth are in a hurry to explore. When one is young and feels immortal, old age as a life stage is hard to empathise with or even imagine.

As Madeleine L'Engle said, 'The great thing about getting older is that you don't lose all the other ages you've been.'[15] An old person can look back over the stretch of a lifetime and see what happened with some perspective. He can assess decades of choices, values and experiences. He knows that most things pass; nothing stays the same; and suffering is inevitable. He has seen that parents won't live forever, that a broken romantic attachment won't always hurt, that there are many kinds of love, that fertility has boundaries, that one's children won't always be little, that education and learning are possible at any age.

Perhaps here, if anywhere, in this decades-long life perspective, is where the supposed and much-vaunted wisdom of old age may be found. But I would be the first to admit that such wisdom is not inevitable, and perhaps not very common. We don't necessarily gain much insight as we get older.

*

Michael Hauskeller: Yes, you're right: stages of development and the way we live our age and how our age physically manifests itself are not fixed but can play out very differently in different circumstances. The plasticity of age expression, however, has limits. Many nine-year-olds may be perfectly capable of navigating the outside world on their own – or would be if we let them. But if you trust your three-year-old to do the same, it is very likely that they will prove you wrong, not because you haven't trusted them enough, but because they simply don't have the mental and physical capacities to do it successfully. And while you, at your current age and in your current mental and physical condition and despite being generally considered 'old', may still be perfectly capable of going kayaking with your grandkids, in a few years' time you may well find that you just can't do it anymore.

Acknowledging this has nothing to do with ageism. It is not ageist to think that our biological age affects what we can and cannot do. It clearly does, though admittedly it does not affect us all in the same way and at the same time. Not only can there be a huge difference (in terms of what one is still capable of) between a 65-year-old and a 95-year-old, there can also be a huge difference between two people of the same age. We are not all the same, we can choose to live our age in different ways, and we can refuse to let ourselves be defined by our age or by what people tend to think is appropriate for someone our age, and that may well, as you rightly point out, make a difference in terms of what we can and cannot do. And yet, it is still a fact that the average 20-year-old can do things that the average 70-year-old can only dream of.

Again: this is not ageism. Ageism, understood as unfair discrimination against someone purely because of their chronological age, occurs when it is assumed that they cannot do certain things or, worse, should not be *allowed* to do certain things because they are supposedly 'too old' or 'too young' *for the sole reason* that they have lived (or not yet lived) a certain number of years, and they are then as a result prevented from doing those things. This assumption is almost as discriminatory as the assumption that someone is not capable of performing a certain task because they are 'too black' or 'too female'. I say 'almost' because it seems to me that while people's race or the colour of their skin is completely unrelated to their abilities, and one's sex is never a reliable indicator of what an individual can or cannot do,[16] a person's age is more directly related to their abilities, so that it is not entirely unreasonable to expect that because of their age certain things will be, if not impossible, then at least more difficult for them to do. Particular individuals may of course always defy our expectations, and some of our expectations may be wildly off the mark anyway, but that doesn't mean that nobody can ever be too young or too old for anything or that age restrictions are always, as a practice, discriminatory.

For instance, the legal age of consent (to sex) in the UK and Canada is 16, which assumes that when you are younger than 16 you are not able to give meaningful consent to any sexual activities. In the US, the age of consent is 16 in some states, and 17 or 18 in others. The minimum age for buying and consuming alcohol in the UK is 18, in the US it is 21, and in Canada it is, depending on where you are, 18 or 19. These are obviously legal fictions because people's abilities don't change dramatically from one day to the next when they cross a certain age threshold or when they move to a different country. Are such fictions discriminatory, though? It would seem so since it is one's chronological age alone that is used here to determine whether a person is permitted to do particular things.[17] But it's not completely arbitrary either and it might simply be unfeasible to have no such restrictions and assess every case individually and based solely on actual competence.

Perhaps a greater problem than age-related legal restrictions that are based on certain presumed capacities (or the lack thereof) is what is deemed *appropriate* for certain ages: how people are supposed to dress, wear their hair, express themselves, occupy themselves, and generally behave both in private and in public. It is one thing to (rightly or wrongly) assume that someone in their 70s is not capable of going kayaking with their grandkids and quite another to believe that it is somehow not appropriate to do so and that it would be much more fitting if they baked cookies instead.

*

Christine Overall: I agree with your definition of 'ageism': 'Ageism, understood as unfair discrimination against someone purely because of their chronological age, occurs when it is assumed that they cannot do certain things or, worse, should not be allowed to do certain things because they are supposedly "too old" or "too young" for the sole reason that they have lived (or not yet lived) a certain number of years, and they are then as a result prevented from doing those things.'

My point is that because of the broad effects of ageism, at both ends of the life spectrum and sometimes also in between, the expectations of what people *can* do, and should be *allowed* to do, have limited them psychologically, intellectually, and sometimes also physically. For that reason, many of our explicit and implicit legal and social boundaries based on age are not only unjust but also, often, incapacitating.

One example is the legal voting age. When I was young, the voting age in Canada was 21. That was the era of young Baby Boomers, and fortunately we didn't accept that limitation. In 1970 the voting age was lowered to 18. To me, this is both fair and reasonable, given the capacities of 18-year-olds. (There may also be a case for lowering the voting age to 17 or even 16, but I won't try to make that here.)

Another example is compulsory retirement. When I was in administration at Queen's University, a few 65-year-old faculty members came to me, heartbroken, asking if there was some way they could stay in full-time employment. There wasn't: the institution was within its legal rights to force them to retire because at that time, in Canada, it was legally permitted to require workers to leave employment at 65. I was then in my 50s and unaffected by this cruel mandate, but I was saddened both by the grief experienced by those who were ejected from their jobs against their will, and by the very real loss to the institution itself of the tremendous teaching ability and administrative experience of these people. Once again, however, the Baby Boomers, now ageing, eventually rejected this ageist requirement. Retirement is no longer compulsory; instead, it is based, as it should be, on the individual's capacities for the job and their own wishes.

As a 72-year-old, I'm not all that unusual in engaging in activities like kayaking and canoeing with my grandsons. Plenty of geezers like me are doing such things.[18] However, because of ageism, we don't yet really know what's *possible* for both old people and young people – and many in between.[19] Just as societies did not know what women are capable of until we were disburdened of at least some of the legal, social, psychological and economic constraints holding us back, so also until people of all ages are disburdened of at least some of the legal, social, psychological and economic constraints holding them back, there will not be adequate evidence for what people of different ages can actually do. So, while there no doubt are biological limits on what people of different ages are capable of, there is much that we do not yet know about what those limits are. And because some of those constraints still exist, especially for middle-aged and old people,[20] I *don't* think everyone is entirely free to 'choose to live our age in different ways', and I *don't* believe people can always 'refuse to let [themselves] be defined by [their] age'.

You'll notice that I called myself and others in my age group 'geezers'.[21] That was deliberate. 'Geezer' is among a multitude of negative terms used for people who are old, such as 'crone', 'hag', 'biddy', 'codger', 'old bag', 'old bat', 'old-timer', 'little old lady', 'grumpy old man', 'fogey' and 'old coot'. I often refer to myself as a geezer just in order to reclaim the term.[22] As you know, I am forthright about my age; I acknowledge the years I've lived, and I describe myself as old. Yet people are usually shocked that I use terms like 'geezer' and 'old' for myself; they assume that I suffer from that quintessentially twentieth- and twenty-first-century syndrome, 'low self-esteem'. To comfort me, they respond, 'Don't call yourself a geezer! You're *not* old.' But I would need that reassurance (or attempted flattery?) only if being old were truly a bad thing. And I don't think it is; I don't see being old as something to fear, regret, deny or be ashamed of.[23] No age is inherently good or bad.

However, because being old is considered so regrettable or embarrassing that it must be hidden or denied, various euphemisms have sprung up in so-called polite English to talk about old people, including 'seniors', 'senior citizens' and 'golden agers'. Yet there are no 'junior citizens', and no one refers to younger life stages in terms of metals (silver? copper? bronze? lead?). I reject these terms for people my age.

*

Michael Hauskeller: I agree that we should not try to hide our age and that there is nothing inherently wrong or bad about any age. But it seems to me that this also requires acknowledgement of the physical and mental changes that we typically go through when we age, not all of them good.

Montaigne, in his essay on 'Age', after making some of the points you have been making as well ('To send men back into retirement before the age of fifty-five or sixty seems not very reasonable to me. I should be of the opinion that our employment and occupation should be extended as far as possible, for the public welfare'),[24] frankly admits: 'I hold it as certain that since that age my mind and my body have rather shrunk than grown, and gone backward rather than forward. It is possible that in those who employ their time well, knowledge and experience grow with living; but vivacity, quickness, firmness, and other qualities much more our own, more important and essential, wither and languish.'[25]

This judgement is based on honest self-observation, not prejudice. And yet Montaigne was only in his 40s when he wrote that. His essay starts with an anecdote about the younger Cato who, when he committed suicide at the age of 48, laughed off the pleas of those who thought that was too early an age to die, regarding it as 'quite ripe and quite advanced, considering how few men reach it'.[26] This may seem odd to us today, but it is very much in line with the definition of 'old' you suggested earlier on, which is based on life expectancy at a certain time and place. We are old when we have reached an age that few others have managed to reach or can expect to reach. Of course, for Montaigne this means that we should see living past that age as a rare privilege and all the time that may still lie ahead of us as borrowed.

In any case, you are right that in our culture there is a certain stigma to being 'old'. However, the use of euphemisms such as 'senior citizen' can perhaps be understood not as an expression of ageism but as an attempt to remove that very stigma. You may be comfortable referring to yourself as a 'geezer', but few would relish being called geezers (or any of the other pejorative terms you mentioned) *by others*, precisely because those terms clearly convey a certain dismissive, even contemptuous attitude towards us. And 'senior citizen' or 'golden ager' are only euphemisms if they are meant to conceal an ugly or unpleasant reality – if there is *in fact* nothing golden about old age. But if there is or if there might be if only, as you say, we removed the various constraints that hold us back when we have reached a certain age and are commonly regarded as 'old', then these terms are not euphemistic. They are rather linguistic tools designed to change our perception of old age, presenting it as a new phase in people's lives that offers new opportunities for living, for exploration and development, rather than a phase in which people are no longer good for anything much, not even for themselves.

But before we conclude our conversation, I would like to pick up on something you said earlier, namely that one of the advantages of old age is that we take, as it were, our youth, or at least the memory of it, with us. We have lived through it, whereas for the young being old (or even older) is an unknown, unexplored territory, which is why the young don't know what it's like to be old, while the old know very well what it's like to be young. And yet, you say, despite all the experience we gain over the decades, despite the widening of our perspective as we age, despite the fact that, in the words of Montaigne, 'knowledge and experience grow with living', we don't necessarily get much wiser or gain more insight. If that is true – and it certainly seems that way – what is all that experience good for? How come it doesn't make us wiser? And do we really know what's it like to be young when we are no longer young?

Of course we have memories of our younger self, but are those memories not tinted by our present perspective, which is that of a much older person? And when we still feel 'young inside', as we often do or think we do, do we then really feel the way we did when we actually *were* young? Or is saying or thinking things like that perhaps itself an expression of ageism in the sense that we mistakenly believe that, being as old as we are, we should be feeling differently, more mature perhaps, more secure, more in control and less crazy and foolish?

*

Christine Overall: Thank you, Michael, for this opportunity to discuss age, ages and ageing. It has been an illuminating conversation.

You have reiterated that we must not deny the changes that ageing brings, and I have never denied it. My claim is that the changes believed to be associated with certain ages are deeply affected by, and in part a product of, varying material conditions, social resources and cultural stereotypes.

I agree that most people would not want others labelling them a 'geezer' or any of the other terms I listed. Just like members of other beleaguered minorities, reclaiming culturally pejorative terms rightly belongs only to those who choose them for themselves. I deliberately call myself a geezer, partly for the shock value, but I am not in any way advocating that younger people start calling old people geezers.

You are probably right that terms like 'senior citizen' were an attempt to lend dignity to old age. I am, however, sceptical that they have been successful. Despite what I argue are the goods of ageing,[27] being old continues to be considered undesirable and even pitiable. Hence 'senior citizen' functions merely as a euphemism for something still regarded as too negative to name directly.

Different ages are accorded very different values. Young children seem to aspire to be older; they know that getting older means more freedom and more choices. The teens, 20s and 30s are generally esteemed: people are thought to be at the peak of their physical and cognitive powers, they are considered to be highly attractive and their lives are ahead of them. From there, according to many, it's a matter of decline. Despite assurances that 'life begins at 40', mid-life is often considered to be a time of crisis and regret for all the opportunities missed and time lost. From there one is old, and supposedly lives an undifferentiated, undistinguished life common to all those who are 65 to 105.

Given the negativity toward old age, and the high value accorded to youth, would I want to return to any of the first four decades of my life? Absolutely not – unless, perhaps, I'd also have, while there, the ability to do some things differently. But obviously, if I *were* able to act differently, I would not really have gone back to being the former me; I would be a different person, a person who did not make the kinds of choices and mistakes that the real Christine made.

This is not, I think, the expression of an ageist assumption that 'being as old as we are, we should be feeling differently, more mature perhaps, more secure, more in control and less crazy and foolish', as you put it, Michael. Though frankly, for the sake of safety in an ageist society, it's often in old people's *interest* to try to be mature and secure, and not to be 'crazy and foolish'. But old people can certainly continue to try to change and grow, be experimental, develop new relationships and new activities, and forge new meanings for their lives – provided they are offered the material conditions, resources and encouragement to do so, and are freed of the stereotypes that say all old people are the same and do not change.

We old people can even have fun and find joy in our lives! A study of over 300,000 adults in the United Kingdom, released in 2016 by the UK Office for National Statistics, showed that people between 65 and 79 had the 'highest level of personal wellbeing'. People who were 90 or older 'reported higher life satisfaction and happiness compared with people in their middle years'.[28] Similarly, according to Statistics Canada, Canadian 'seniors' are strikingly 'more satisfied with their lives than [are] adults in younger age groups. Men and women in their 60s, 70s and 80s had higher average life satisfaction scores than men and women aged 20 to 59'.[29]

This study of life satisfaction revealed in Canadians the same U-shaped curve of life satisfaction that is found in citizens of other nations, ranging from Denmark and Bulgaria to South Africa and Peru. According to Carol Graham and Julia Ruiz Pozuelo, 'Happiness declines with age for about two decades from early adulthood up until roughly the middle-age years, and then turns upward and increases with age. Although the exact shape differs across countries, the bottom of the curve (or the nadir of happiness) ranges from 40 to 60 plus years old.'[30]

One advantage (among several) of being old, in my experience, is that I can look backward and forward at the generations before and after me. I was fortunate to know all four of my grandparents very well. The oldest of them was born in 1893. From them, I received stories about my great-grandparents, only one of whom I knew. I am also close to my own grandchildren, who are likely to live, if human society survives and life expectancy remains stable, until at least 2100. If I'm very fortunate, and if I've inherited my mother's longevity (she's 95 and doing well), I may meet my great-grandchildren. Thus, I am connected, via my relatives, to two centuries of human life, and potentially to seven generations of family from the past and the future. An association with other generations is possible at any age, but it is potentially broader in old age. I can see myself as both a descendent and an ancestor, a beneficiary of the past and (I hope) a benefactor of the future.

*

Michael Hauskeller: We may indeed, as we age, become more aware of our role as a link, or mediator, between the past and the future, which I believe also makes it easier to accept the transient character of our existence – and that also means our finitude as an individual. While we may when we get older still have a lot to live for as well as a lot to contribute to the lives of others (and a lot more than is commonly acknowledged in an ageist society), one of the benefits of being 'old' – and perhaps one of the reasons why the curve of happiness or 'life satisfaction', after taking a downward turn in middle age, rises again in old age – is that we tend to feel less anxious about the fact that we have to die, even though we are now much closer to our biological expiry date than when we were younger.[31] And that may well be partially owed to our growing appreciation of our double role as both a descendant of those who arrived before us and an ancestor to those who have arrived and are going to arrive after us.

A beautiful illustration of that kind of appreciation can be found in Ray Bradbury's story 'The leave-taking', in which an old woman decides that she has lived long enough and that it's time to die. This is not because she feels that her life is no longer worth living – far from it. She has had a good life and her life is still good. She is not ill or ailing, and she is surrounded by a loving family who all try to convince her not to die. But she thinks it's best to leave while she is 'still happy and still entertained'. Besides, she says, the 'important thing is not the me that's lying here, but the me that's sitting on the edge of the bed looking back at me, and the me that's downstairs cooking supper, or out in the garage under the car, or in the library reading. All the new parts, they count. I'm not really dying today. No person ever died that had a family.'[32]

Social connectedness matters. It makes our lives more meaningful and increases life satisfaction.[33] And while it makes us more vulnerable to the death of others, it can take some of the sting out of our own mortality. And as we age, we naturally become more connected, not in the sense that we necessarily expand and deepen our connections to other people, because that does not always happen, but in the sense that the older we get the more we embed ourselves, ever more firmly, into the temporal structure of the world. You said that if you could go back in time to your 40s or 30s you wouldn't want to do it, or only if you could make different choices, in which case it would no longer be you. This is because the person you are now is the one who actually made those choices and not others. We gain an identity and become who we are over time, through the choices we make and through the connections we create because of them. The various connections we have thus far made in our life, social and otherwise, make us who we are.

The process of ageing is a process of becoming. Unlike the other identities you mentioned at the beginning of our conversation – gender, sexuality, race, class, (dis)ability – our age is *constantly* changing, and always in the same direction without any possibility of turning around. Whatever age we have today, tomorrow we will have a different age, and we will always be older than we are now. This would be so even if we somehow managed to halt and reverse the biological ageing process, as many hope and some strongly believe we will soon be able to do,[34] because it is not only our bodies that age, but also our minds.[35] Among other things, getting older also means gaining experience, changing and developing perspectives and attitudes, and most importantly being able to look back on an increasing number of things we have done and witnessed.

Ageing is essentially an accumulation of past. The older we get, the longer we have lived, and the longer we have lived, the more past we have gathered, while in a normal human – and that means mortal – life our future, the time we can hope to stay alive, dwindles. We tend to see this as a bad thing because we attach more value to the future than to the past. We associate past with loss but could just as well see it as something we have gained, that we have made our own, while the future is still a very uncertain possession. The past is money in the bank, as it were, something that cannot be undone and taken away from us. Accordingly, the older we get and the more past we have acquired, the richer we are. As Viktor E. Frankl put it, *'having been* is the surest kind of being'.[36]

Ageing, then – and by that I do not mean 'getting old', but the process of 'getting older', which starts with our conception – is not a bad thing. We can only be alive by being in time, and ageing means just that: being in time. To stay, as many appear to wish, 'forever young' would only be possible if we could somehow stop time, but the only way we can do that is by dying. 'If you really want to stay the same age you are now forever and ever,' your compatriot Margaret Atwood once remarked, 'try jumping off the roof: death is a sure-fire method for stopping time.'[37] The wish to retain one's youth forever amounts to the wish to stop living, and that means it is ultimately a concealed death-wish.

Notes

1. https://en.wikipedia.org/wiki/Generation#Western_world (accessed 1 December 2021).
2. See Overall, 'How old is old?'.
3. Ariès, *Centuries of Childhood*.
4. Arnquist, 'How old do you feel?'.
5. See Overall, 'How old is old?'.
6. World Bank, 'Life expectancy at birth, total'.
7. United Nations, 'Life expectancy at birth, females'.
8. For the distinction between chronological ageing, biological ageing and experiential ageing see Räsänen, 'Age and ageing'.
9. For the distinction between 'ageing' and 'getting older' see Kamm, *Almost Over*, 121–2.
10. In *Almost Over* (121–41), Kamm discusses F. Scott Fitzgerald's 'The curious case of Benjamin Button', in which the title character is born with all the physical features of an old man and then gradually gets younger (or rather less aged, while getting older in years) until he eventually disappears into the prenatal nothingness that the rest of us have come out of. See Fitzgerald, *Flappers and Philosophers*, 150–72.
11. This is in fact part of the standard definition of what it means to be a 'person' – namely, in the words of John Locke, 'a thinking intelligent Being, that has reason and reflection, and can consider itself as itself, the same thinking thing *in different times* and places' (*An Essay Concerning Human Understanding*, 2.27.9, my emphasis).
12. See Skenazy, 'I let my 9-year old ride the subway alone'.
13. Skenazy, 'Why I let my 9-year old ride the subway alone'.
14. Mobility within these other kinds of identities may not be impossible. There has been some debate as to whether mobility between races is possible (e.g. Tuvel, 'In defense of transracialism'). Novelist Ursula LeGuin (*The Left Hand of Darkness*; 'Coming of age in Karhide') chronicles a (to me) believable imaginary world in which the human inhabitants regularly change their sex (and their sexual identities), becoming able to impregnate sometimes, and at other times be impregnated. More recently, of course, there has been growing cultural and scholarly attention to and exploration of various kinds of gender changes (e.g. Bettcher, 'What is trans philosophy?').
15. Quoted in Heller Anderson and Dunlap, 'New York day by day'.
16. While it may be true that on average men are physically stronger than women, which is why female athletes do not usually compete against male athletes, there is no physical activity in which particular women do not outperform the vast majority of men.

17. This is why it has been suggested (Räsänen, 'Moral case for legal age change') that individuals who feel they have the competence that is being denied to them due to their chronological age should be allowed to contest and if successful change their legal age.
18. Of course, my ability to do these things is in part an expression of multiple forms of privilege: in adult life I have had resources, opportunities and support that many old people do not have.
19. People in mid-life are also rejecting the stereotypical expectations of and constraints on what they can do. See for instance Saner, 'A stunning second act!'.
20. Some bioethicists and social commentators, such as Leon Kass, Francis Fukuyama, Daniel Callahan, John Hardwig and Ezekiel Emmanuel, endorse the placing of limits on old people, by advocating that they gradually withdraw from society and cease using up attention and resources. See Overall, 'Aging and the loss of social presence'.
21. In common use, 'geezer' is often not gender-neutral. Nonetheless, I use it in regard to myself, a woman, because a) my use of the word is then more shocking, and b) I prefer not to endorse the gendering of nouns.
22. Think of some of the ways that queer people and people of colour have reclaimed formerly disparaging terms to name themselves.
23. Similarly, for second-wave feminists, reclaiming the term 'woman' was important (for example, Lakoff, *Language and Women's Place*, 20–7), because 'woman' had acquired so many negative associations as to be in need of euphemisms: 'lady' or 'girl'. Unfortunately, 'girl' seems to be used just as much now as it was 50 years ago, in cases where people would never use 'boy' for a man of the same age. The ubiquitous use of 'girl' is probably a persistent expression of ageism.
24. Montaigne, *The Complete Works*, 288.
25. Montaigne, *The Complete Works*, 289.
26. Montaigne, *The Complete Works*, 289.
27. Overall, 'Is aging good?'.
28. Office for National Statistics, 'Measuring national well-being'.
29. Statistics Canada, 'Life satisfaction among Canadian seniors'.
30. Graham and Pozuelo, 'Happiness, stress, and age', 226.
31. See Neimeyer and Van Brandt, 'Death anxiety'.
32. Bradbury, 'The leave-taking', 516 and 517.
33. For the (bidirectional) link between connectedness on the one hand and meaningfulness and life satisfaction on the other see Stavrova and Luhmann, 'Social connectedness as a source and consequence of meaning in life'.
34. See for instance Zealley and de Grey, 'Strategies for engineered negligible senescence'.
35. See Hauskeller, 'Forever young?'.
36. Frankl, *Man's Search for Meaning*, 124.
37. Atwood, *The Year of the Flood*, 316.

Bibliography

Ariès, Phillippe. *Centuries of Childhood: A social history of family life*. New York: Alfred A. Knopf, 1962.

Arnquist, Sarah. 'How old do you feel? It depends on your age', *New York Times*, 30 June 2009. http://www.nytimes.com/2009/06/30/health/30aging.html?ref=health&_r=0 (accessed 1 December 2021).

Atwood, Margaret. *The Year of the Flood*. London: Bloomsbury, 2009.

Bettcher, Talia Mae. 'What is trans philosophy?', *Hypatia: A journal of feminist philosophy* 34/4 (2019): 644–667.

Bradbury, Ray. 'The leave-taking'. In *The Stories of Ray Bradbury*, 515–19. New York: Alfred A. Knopf (Everyman's Library), 2010.

Fitzgerald, F. Scott. *Flappers and Philosophers*. London: Penguin Classics, 2010.

Frankl, Viktor E. *Man's Search for Meaning*. London: Rider, 2004.

Graham, Carol, and Julia Ruiz Pozuelo. 'Happiness, stress, and age: how the U curve varies across people and places', *Journal of Population Economics* 30/1 (2017): 225–64.

Hauskeller, Michael. 'Forever young? Life extension and the ageing mind', *Ethical Perspectives* 18/3 (2011): 384–404.

Heller Anderson, Susan, and David W. Dunlap, 'New York day by day; author to readers', *New York Times*, 25 April 1985, Section B, page 3. https://www.nytimes.com/1985/04/25/nyregion/new-york-day-by-day-author-to-readers.html (accessed 1 December 2021).

Kamm, F. M. *Almost Over: Aging, dying, dead*. Oxford: Oxford University Press, 2020.

Lakoff, Robin. *Language and Woman's Place*. New York: Harper Colophon, 1975.

LeGuin, Ursula. *The Left Hand of Darkness*. New York: Ace Books, 1969.

LeGuin, Ursula. 'Coming of age in Karhide'. In *The Birthday of the World and Other Stories*, 1–22. New York: HarperCollins, 2002.

Locke, John. *An Essay Concerning Human Understanding*, edited by Peter H. Nidditch. Oxford: Oxford University Press, 1975.

Montaigne, Michael de. *The Complete Works*, translated by Donald M. Frame. New York: Alfred A. Knopf (Everyman's Library), 2003.

Neimeyer, Robert A., and David Van Brandt. 'Death anxiety'. In *Dying: Facing the facts*, edited by Hannelore Wass and Robert A. Neimeyer, 49–88. New York: Taylor & Francis, 3rd edition 2018.

Office for National Statistics. 'Measuring national well-being: at what age is personal well-being the highest?', 2 February 2016. https://www.ons.gov.uk/peoplepopulationandcommunity/wellbeing/articles/measuringnationalwellbeing/atwhatageispersonalwellbeingthehighest (accessed 1 December 2021).

Overall, Christine. 'Aging and the loss of social presence'. In *Aging in an Aging Society: Critical reflections*, edited by Iva Apostolova and Monique Lanoix, 65–81. Sheffield: Equinox Publishing, 2019.

Overall, Christine. 'How old is old?'. In *The Palgrave Handbook of the Philosophy of Aging*, edited by Geoffrey Scarre, 13–30. London: Palgrave Macmillan, 2017.

Overall, Christine. 'Is aging good?' In *The Ethics of Aging*, edited by Christopher Wareham. Cambridge: Cambridge University Press, 2022 (forthcoming).

Räsänen, Joona. 'Moral case for legal age change', *Journal of Medical Ethics* 45/7 (2019): 461–4.

Räsänen, Joona. 'Age and ageing: what do they mean?', *Ratio* 34 (2021): 33–43.

Saner, Emine. 'A stunning second act!', *The Guardian*, 26 August 2021. https://www.theguardian.com/lifeandstyle/2021/aug/26/a-stunning-second-act-meet-the-people-who-changed-course-in-mid-life-and-loved-it (accessed 1 December 2021).

Skenazy, Lenore. 'Why I let my 9-year-old ride the subway alone', *The New York Sun*, 1 April 2008. https://www.nysun.com/opinion/why-i-let-my-9-year-old-ride-the-subway-alone/73976/ (accessed 1 December 2021).

Skenazy, Lenore. 'I let my 9-year-old ride the subway alone. I got labeled the "world's worst mom"', *The Washington Post*, 16 January 2015.

Statistics Canada. 'Life satisfaction among Canadian seniors'. 2 August 2018. https://www150.statcan.gc.ca/n1/pub/75-006-x/2018001/article/54977-eng.htm (accessed 1 December 2021).

Stavrova, Olga, and Maike Luhmann. 'Social connectedness as a source and consequence of meaning in life', *The Journal of Positive Psychology* 11/5 (2016): 470–9.

Tuvel, Rebecca. 'In defense of transracialism', *Hypatia: A journal of feminist philosophy* 32/2 (2017): 263–78.

United Nations. 'Life expectancy at birth, females (years)'. 2019. http://data.un.org/Data.aspx?q=life+expectancy+canada&d=PopDiv&f=variableID%3a67%3bcrID%3a124 (accessed 1 December 2021).

World Bank. 'Life expectancy at birth, total (years)'. 2019. https://data.worldbank.org/indicator/SP.DYN.LE00.IN (accessed 1 December 2021).

Zealley, Ben, and Aubrey D. N. J. de Grey. 'Strategies for engineered negligible senescence', *Gerontology* 59 (2013): 183–9.

6
Self

with Jane Heal

Michael Hauskeller: I am myself and nobody else. Or so it seems. And that is not only because each of us is in many ways different from everybody else. There is a more radical and fundamental difference between me and everyone else that has nothing to do with all the things that can truthfully be said about me and no other person. That fundamental difference is that I am *me*. When I think or talk about myself, I do this in the first person singular. For everything else, and that includes other people, I use the third person. Strangely, though, everyone else does the same. For me, 'I' am the one who is writing this; for other people it is 'he' who is. The difference seems to be one of perspective. I know (or at least do not doubt) that each one of those other people, to whom I refer as 'he', 'she' and 'they' (and occasionally, when I am communicating with them, as 'you') is also an 'I', namely for him or herself. I am 'I' for me, and you are 'I' for you. And if I didn't think you were, I wouldn't be talking to you, or at least wouldn't be trying to have a philosophical conversation with you. I would, instead, think of you and treat you like any other object in the world: as something that has certain properties, that is good for certain things and can be used in certain ways. But I don't do that, or at least not consistently so, because I see you not just as an object, but also as a subject.

With subjects we can do what we cannot do with objects: communicate. Yet the subject that you are is different from the subject that I am. The most conspicuous and perhaps most fundamental difference between me and you is the difference between self and other. We may be alike in many different ways. We could even be completely indistinguishable to an outside observer. Yet even though we also each think of ourselves as I, and we both acknowledge that the other does the same (so that we are, in other words, both *selves*), the fact remains that my self is not your self. We are *different* selves, and while I am self to myself, you are self to yourself, and while you are other to me, I am other to you. I am, therefore, both *a* self and *my*self, which is not the same, because not every self is, or seems to be, myself.

But do selves really exist?[1] Is a self a particular kind of thing, so that there are things (such as human beings) that are selves and others (such as tables and chairs) that are not?[2] There are reasons to doubt that, since the expression 'I', with which I signal my existence as a self, is clearly indexical, which is to say that who or what it refers to depends on the context, namely who says it. If Michael uses the term 'I', it refers to him; if Jane uses it, it refers to her. In this respect, the word 'I' functions in the same way as the words 'here' and 'now'. Wherever I am it is always *here*, and whenever I am it is always *now*. We are never not here or not now. Nobody lives in the past or the future. And while some people may live far away, if they do, they don't live far away from themselves, but only far away from us. But my 'here' is not your 'here', at least not exactly, and my 'now' *may* be your 'now', but it doesn't have to be.[3] For me, 'here' is always the place where *I* happen to be, and now is always the time when I happen to be. And for you, 'here' is always the place where *you* happen to be, and 'now' is always the time when you happen to be. Because of this semantic relativity it would be misleading to say that 'now' refers to a particular time or 'here' to a particular place. There is no time that is now and no place that is here. And perhaps, since the term 'I' is just as indexical as the terms 'here' and 'now', there is also no such thing as (a) self.

Then again, it may well be precisely because we are selves that there is a 'here' and a 'now' for us in the first place. There is, after all, no 'now' or 'here' for a table or a chair. The reason there is a 'here' and a 'now' for us is that we are the kind of beings that have not only the capacity but also a strong natural inclination to relate everything they experience back to their own existence in the world. We are constitutionally incapable of adopting a view from nowhere[4] (or everywhere, which is the same thing). For us, not all times and spaces are equal. It is what happens here and now that matters most, because what happens here and now is what happens to us. The here and the now are functions of the self, different ways in which the self articulates itself, different ways in which we mark our position in the world. And what makes it so strange that my self is not your self is the fact that the self, *qua* self, has no content. It does not seem to be this or that, one particular property or another, that makes me me, just as it is not what the eye sees that makes it an eye. It is the seeing that does. I am not myself because I am a particular person who does certain things, has a certain history, and a certain name and identity. I can accurately be described as that person, but that person is a 'he', not an 'I'. The self as such, then, transcends all possible descriptions of it.

*

Jane Heal: Yes. By reflecting on the questions 'What does "I" refer to? Who or what am I?' I can get myself into a state of mind where I find it strange that my self is not your self, and where I can debate whether I am (or have) a 'self'. But I would rather come at the puzzlements you mention in a different way. It is not a way which makes everything at once clear and easy. The route you sketch starts with distinctively human phenomena, like the use of the word 'I' and the vivid awareness of difference, which is part of some of our encounters with other people. The alternative route starts rather with acceptance of life of all kinds, as a real phenomenon, needing its own categories for description. But this starting point is a problematic one for us now, because we have such strong pressures to adopt atomism in our metaphysical thinking. And atomism cannot comfortably accommodate any kind of living being, let alone us. So we philosophers, in its grip, may be driven to very strange contortions in our efforts to give an account of central features of human life, such as the fact that we have thoughts and feelings and can talk to each other about them.

Living beings have characteristic ways of coming to be, growing, nourishing themselves, defending themselves from danger, reproducing and so on. In doing these things they manifest a drive to live effectively as the kind of thing they are, be it an amoeba, an oak tree, a cat or a human. And they succeed or fail in this, flourish or the opposite, according to whether the world around them offers or does not offer them what is required for their capacities for living to be developed and exercised.[5]

Living beings are thus intrinsically multifaceted. If a living being exists, there will be a great deal to say about it, specifying its way of life, its repertoire of responses to the environment, its current state and so forth. And the concepts we use to describe living beings and what they do (advance on nourishment, shrink from danger, reproduce, etc.) form an interdependent set, no one of which can be understood without the others. And where there is a living being there will always be a question about whether it is doing well or ill, whether its life is going on effectively or whether it is suffering damage or failing.

Terms like 'holism' and 'organic unity' exist in the tradition to gesture in the direction of these facts about living beings, as they present themselves in our everyday understanding. And it is an indication of how uneasy we are, philosophically, with that everyday understanding that these terms are in such bad odour.

Our metaphysical preconceptions in favour of atomism make problems for taking the everyday understanding of living beings, as unities, at face value. Atomism encourages us to divide living beings into two kinds: ones without and ones with 'consciousness'. The first are those (plants perhaps) which are merely complex assemblages of physical atoms – unified indeed, but only by physical and chemical forces, as a rock might be. We may speak of such things as 'flourishing' or 'doing poorly'. But this is to be taken metaphorically, as one might speak of a stalactite as 'flourishing', simply to record that it is growing. There is no unified item which could flourish or do poorly in any non-metaphorical sense.

The second kind of living beings are ones (us for example) where there is 'consciousness'. And here flourishing and doing poorly do get a real grip. But that (we think) is because of the conscious events now going on – pleasant or unpleasant feelings occurring, for example. In the context of our atomistic preconceptions, we may take these conscious events to be each a distinct item, the occurrence of which is logically independent of both bodily events and other conscious events. And now we are likely to get into trouble! We find ourselves wanting both to 'have' the conscious events and to stick them together across time. The idea of a 'self' (or 'ego' or 'subject') is one which, in our tradition since the seventeenth century, has been wheeled out to fill these roles. But there are many familiar problems here![6]

How might things go if we could bring ourselves to jettison atomistic presuppositions and take the everyday conception of living things at face value? It would allow us to think of the difference between conscious and non-conscious organisms as having to do with the nature and kind of their sensitive responses to the whole of their world, including themselves. Conscious beings are ones who are capable of the kind of sensitive response deserving the label 'awareness' or 'perception' of their world. So for them a window, perhaps a very small and clouded one, has opened onto the world, a world of already existing living creatures, some doing well, some not doing so well.

The content of consciousness, on this view, is in the simplest cases 'subjectless'. By this I mean that the best we can do to conjure up such content in English might be, for example, 'hunger, hunger – must eat', 'food', 'seize it!', 'lovely', 'safe now', etc. We do not need to include any 'I' in our attempt to capture the content of the consciousness. To do so would be to misrepresent what is going on as more complicated than it is. For the kind of living being imagined, the question of who or what is hungry, is aware of the food, is to do the seizing and so on just does not arise, and hence does not need specifying. There is no possible other hungry, aware, active being around except the living creature of whose consciousness these are the contents. But the representations are not 'subjectless' in the sense of not being about anything. They are about the situation of that living being.[7]

We need to include indexical elements, such as 'here' and 'now', in our reports of the contents of consciousness when we have living creatures aware of the layout of the space around them and with memory and imagination of the future. And 'I', 'you' and the like begin to seem appropriate when we are dealing with social animals, aware of each other, sharing food, mating, fighting, playing and the like.

And when language is on the scene, since 'I' is an indexical, I speak of myself when I use it and you speak of yourself. But if we think of how 'I' is used, in the light of the ideas sketched in the last few paragraphs, we will not be tempted to think that this could mean that I was or had some distinctive sort of thing called a 'self'. If we report some happening as 'a cat is washing herself', we are not tempted to postulate some extra and mysterious thing, some 'self' which the cat has and washes. Similarly when I refer to myself using 'I', it is just me which is referred to, not some extra, mysterious thing which I have and can refer to. I am indeed myself and no one else. But, on this line of thought, there isn't more to this truth than that this human being is different, in time, place, history, actions, from any other human being. And this human being is what I am.

*

Michael Hauskeller: I don't think that saying I am myself and nobody else is saying nothing more than that there is a difference between me (the person that I happen to be) and other people and things. The difference between Michael and Jane may be just that, but the difference between me and you is something else entirely. That difference is of a different kind than the difference between things in the world that can be accounted for by listing and comparing their individual characteristics, histories and circumstances. Those differences are easy to understand. Far less easy to understand is the difference between me and you, the difference between me and everything else. The mystery is not that I am *this* particular person. The mystery is that I *am* this person. It is the very *me*-ness of me.

But let us, as you suggest, take a step back – a step back from what you call atomism – and look at living beings that are other than human. Where is the self, or selfhood, in living beings that do not have the same 'vivid awareness of difference' that we have? It is true that for most if not all non-human animals the question of the self never arises. They are immersed in their world, sourcing food, avoiding predators, finding someone to mate with, playing, fighting and resting. They never have the occasion (or the conceptual resources) to reflect on their own position in the world. They never wonder how it is possible that now they are and once they were not, while others were, and that one day they will not be, while others will. Their existence is woven into the existence of every- thing else, as the existence of everything else is woven into theirs. So in *this* sense they may indeed be subjectless and selfless. Yet many of them are also conscious – not self-aware perhaps, but definitely aware of the world, or if not of the 'world', then of something, something unnamed and perhaps unnamable. And that awareness is not neutral, not just a mental mirror image of the world. It has direction and purpose and con- cern. There may be just 'hunger' and 'hurt' and the like, and not the more clearly self-referential '*I* am hungry' and '*I* am hurting', but that hunger and hurt is still experienced by someone, a particular living thing, and the hunger and the hurt it experiences, because it is experienced by it and nobody else, is not just a hunger and a hurt, but *its* hunger and *its* hurt. The hunger and the hurt, as total and world-consuming as it may be, is there for it, and it is there for it in a way that is very different from the way that same hunger and hurt is there for everybody else.

Non-human animals may not be able to contemplate their selfhood, but they most assuredly still *live* it. Naturally, that living is done by the whole animal, not by some distinct and potentially detachable entity we may refer to as that animal's 'self'. And its real, lived selfhood does indeed seem to have something to do with its ability to flourish, to do well and badly, and with the fact that there are things that can happen to it that can hurt and harm it, and others that can help it grow and pros- per. Animals share this with plants, even though we tend to assume that plants do not feel any pain or pleasure or are in any other way aware of the world. But they clearly do have a unity that unliving things appear to lack, and it is a unity that goes beyond the kind of unity that physical and chemical forces can create (unless these forces can also create the kind of unity that we exhibit). A tree can thrive or wither. It lives and dies as that particular tree that it is.

Non-living things don't do this. They may come into existence at some stage and then at some later stage cease to exist, but it makes no difference to them. And it makes no difference to them because there is no 'them' to whom it could make a difference, and there never has been. It is in that sense that non-living things are self-less, not because they are not conscious, but because they do not really exist *as* the thing they are. Their unity, which allows us to refer to them as one individual thing, is a borrowed one. It consists in our singling them out and giving them a name, which then serves to unify it for our mental operations, in recognition of the purposes that determine and structure our particular human form of life. Living things, however, are different. We may not be able to understand how exactly they do this, but it certainly looks as if they exist as and for themselves, even when they are amoebas or oak trees and very unlikely to be conscious, with no windows to the world, not even small and clouded ones.

*

Jane Heal: I cannot get a sense of what the mystery is which presents itself to you. Jane and Michael are different people. But that is straightforward for you – that is not the mystery. Rather it has to do with the fact that I am Jane and not Michael. (And for you, then, the mystery is that you are Michael and not Jane.) So it is the me-ness of Jane which is supposed to be the mysterious thing (for me at least). But I don't get it.

   I (Jane) exist. That is, for sure, a truth which is puzzling and challenging in various ways. Let me note some of them, so that we are clear that they are not the thing which puzzles you.

   First, it is puzzling that I exist, inasmuch as I am an example of a living being. And the fact that there are living beings – plants, other animals, ourselves – can present conceptual problems. I am still firmly enough in the grip of atomism and physicalism to find it natural to picture the universe as a vast assemblage of matter and energy laid out in space-time, governed by a set of laws which is, in some sense, 'complete'. And when that picture of things is prominent for me, I find myself bewildered and saying: How can it be that matter gives rise to life and consciousness? The universe is, it seems, in some sense thoroughly physical and it has no point of view on itself. Yet it contains beings which have a point of view on it, which find some things good and others bad, which are aware of the world, which flourish or suffer, which act for reasons.[8]

   I don't find it difficult to sympathise with the feeling that there is something mysterious or unintelligible here. I am, nevertheless, pretty much convinced that these conceptual cramps are the upshot of patterns of thought and talk which are not obligatory. So if we could lessen their grip, the bewilderment would lessen too. But lessening that grip, finding an alternative picture, takes a good deal of reflection. There is a direction of travel here, not a finished outlook.

And part of what needs to be done in travelling that route is articulating how the use of 'I' would be spelled out on such an alternative picture. The programmatic claim is something like this: '"I" is part of the repertoire by which a conscious, living being crystallises and expresses its stance to the world, thereby becoming self-conscious, in the context of its shared life with other conscious beings. It is not a label for some distinctive kind of entity.' But that is just a programmatic claim. What does it mean? How does it work in detail? Setting this out is challenging.

It seems to me that your puzzlement, insofar as I get any grip on it, is not in these areas. You are happy to see animals as I do, namely as having a point of view on the world, which presents things as urgent, for them. They live their selfhood, you say, even if they do not contemplate it. And that is a way of putting things which seems to me congenial, illuminating. That there exist beings of this kind, living, conscious and indeed self-conscious, is not your mystery. And it seems also that your worry does not have to do with the idea that 'I' refers to some distinctive sort of item, a 'self', which we seem to need to postulate but cannot understand.

Here now is a second line of thought which can be initiated by reflecting on the fact that I exist. One might say, 'How extraordinary it is that there exists something rather than nothing.' And one might add, 'And how extraordinary that part of the vast immensity which does exist, is our earth, and on it these tiny, evolved mammals, which are us. And how extraordinary that each of us has our own distinct, complex life, that there are these particular people, me and you and the many others we know.' And I can share a sense of amazement at that being how things are. But it seems to me that your puzzlement or mystery is also not focused in this area – is not to do with the remarkableness of there being a universe, and in particular there being the vast and strange universe we have become aware of, with all of us individual human beings as a tiny part of it.

So what is it which is the mystery; what is this me-ness of me? Can we generate an analogous worry about the hereness of here? (Perhaps you hinted at this in your first remarks with your mention of indexicals.) One might think, 'There are many places, which all exist and are equally real. But there is a further property which only one of them has, namely its hereness. How mysterious that this place, here (my study in Cambridge as it happens), should have hereness and Michael's study in Liverpool should not have any hereness!'

But doesn't seeing how the indexicality works do away with the idea that there is 'hereness' as an interesting property which one place might have?[9] And if it does, then seeing 'I' as an indexical, by which any self-conscious being can articulate its situation, similarly does away with the idea that there could be an interesting property of me-ness, which might have belonged to Michael, but as a matter of fact (and mysteriously) belongs to me, Jane. Doesn't fully grasping and acknowledging the reality of others, and their right to articulate their thoughts with 'I', do away with the temptation to think there is a mystery?

*

Michael Hauskeller: I don't dispute anybody's right to articulate their thoughts with 'I'. I don't dispute anyone's reality. On the contrary. What I find puzzling is that other people appear to be just as real as I am, and just as much they as I am me. Should this really be due merely to my atomistic prejudices or confusions? Am I bewitched by a language that has gone on holiday?[10] Maybe, but I am not convinced yet.

You are right that it is not very surprising, let alone mysterious, that I am I and not somebody else, just as it is not very surprising that I am here and not there, or now and not then. When else, where else and who else would I be? So in that sense it is utterly trivial to state that I am myself and nobody else. Nor is it very surprising that I am a conscious being, one that has, for whatever reasons, a subjective perspective on the world. Since this is the kind of being I happen to be, it is also the kind of being I am most familiar with, so if there is anything that should surprise us, it is the fact that there are also things in the world that are supposed to *lack* such a subjective perspective, such as tables or chairs, or atoms and elementary particles. (For the same reasons we should be surprised not that there is life on earth, but rather that there doesn't seem to be any life anywhere *but* on earth.) In terms of our ability to know and understand them, things that are there both for others and for themselves are less mysterious than things that are there only for others but not for themselves. Yet maybe we are wrong about that. Maybe there are no such things.[11]

However, before getting side-tracked and delving too much into the nature of physical reality let me try to start again to help both of us to understand better the nature of my puzzlement. I am myself and nobody else, I said. I have direct access only to my own thoughts and feelings and generally to the way the world appears to me, even though I know, or at least have no reason to doubt, that other people and living things have their own thoughts and feelings and perspectives on the world that are just as real as mine. Still, mine are more real to me (or more present, or perhaps simply real in a different way) than those of others. No doubt I have *some* access to other people's thoughts and feelings, to the extent that I interact with them and their thoughts and feelings manifest themselves through and in those interactions. While other people are not exactly an open book to me, they are not completely opaque either. Also, when I die, it is for all I know only I that dies, while everybody else will or at least may go on living. My death is *my* death and nobody else's, and the reason for this is that my life is my life and nobody else's. We may be connected in many different ways to other living things, but there also seems to be a very real disconnect between us. So in that sense I am myself and nobody else.

But this is where it gets interesting: in some ways I am also *not* just myself, but also everybody and everything else. We are all subjects (of experience), but there is no subject without an object, and that object is the world as we see and experience it. This is why Schopenhauer confidently declared the world to be 'my representation',[12] not (at least not primarily) in the sense that the world does not really exist and is some sort of illusion, but in the sense that to all intents and purposes *the* world is always *my* world and I am nothing without that world. It is not that the world's existence depends on me, namely causally, nor that my existence depends on the world. Rather, we are two sides of the same. I *am* the world that I experience and the world I experience *is* (the whole of) me. (So there is no need for positing an additional self here.) Now, if I were the only conscious being in my world, then the world would cease to exist when I cease to exist, because just as there cannot be a subject without an object, there cannot be an object without a subject either, so that a world perceived and experienced by nobody is nothing or at any rate indistinguishable from nothingness.

But I am not the only conscious being in my world. You, for instance, are part of my world (as I am part of yours), and you are conscious just as I am. But the existence of my world, which for me is the only world, would not be affected by your death, as the existence of your world would not be affected by my death. But if you continue to exist after my death and I continue to exist after your death, then we must assume that the world (or at least *a* world) will also continue to exist. But how is that possible? When I die, my world will disappear with me, and then it will be, namely for me, as if the world had never existed. If I am my world, and my world is *the* world, then there can be no other world, no world without me. If the world will indeed continue to exist no matter what happens to me, then it would seem that I must also continue to exist no matter what happens to me. So I guess what I fail to grasp is not so much how there can be such a thing as a self, or in other words how it is possible that I am, but rather how I can ever *not* be.

*

Jane Heal: So now, when I think about the interdependence of subject and object, I do begin to get some sense of where there might be a puzzlement. Some of the properties and relations which worldly items present themselves as having (being noisy, bright, hard, warm, far away, too heavy to lift and the like) are properties and relations which presuppose an experiencing subject. And an experiencing subject cannot exist without something to experience, even if it is only silence or the dark. So a world exhibiting these properties and relations is, necessarily, a world for a subject. And a subject is, necessarily, one who is aware of a world exhibiting properties and relations like these. Some of us may think that in the concepts of physics we have ways of characterising the world which do not presuppose an experiencing subject. But there are difficulties in spelling this out (connected with the worries about atomism mentioned earlier) which suggest that 'wholly independent physical reality' may be a more problematic notion than is often assumed.[13]

So what happens if we accept that subject and object are interdependent? The world being noisy, bright and the like seems to presuppose only one subject: me. But the world, as it in fact presents itself to me, contains not only the noisy and bright, but also houses, books, tables laid with places for six and so on. It presents itself as inhabited not just by me but by many other people as well. And indeed, there they are, reading the books and discussing them with me, sharing the meal and so on. And it seems that we are aware of the same world, that we read and discuss the same book, join in the same meal and so on. If we were right earlier to say that subject and object are interdependent, and if we are indeed aware of the same world, then the implication is that the subject with which the world is interdependent is not me but us.

The puzzlement you are probing is perhaps bound up with a sense that this idea cannot be right. We are very used to taking it that the first-person singular rather than the first-person plural provides the fundamental kind of subjectivity. And the picture that brings with it is of a deep reality in which we each have our own world. That world is, for each of us, correlative with our individual subjectivity, and is not bound up with the existence of others. You put this vividly when you write: '[T]he existence of my world, which for me is the only world, would not be affected by your death, as the existence of your world would not be affected by my death.' And if that is so, then the idea that you are part of the subject correlative with the existence of the (my) world is a mistake. And conversely for you, even if I disappear, the world is still there for you, unaffected, exactly as it was before.

Plainly, in some sense, this view is right. The death of one of us does not annihilate the world for the rest of us. But perhaps there is also some sense in which it is wrong. And the sense in which it is wrong may be the one which is needed to dissolve the puzzlement. If two people are in the middle of doing something important together – bringing up a child or writing a book for example – and one says to the other, 'the existence of my world would not be affected by your death', it seems to me that something has gone wrong! And perhaps not just morally but also metaphysically. Bereavement does affect the world, even if it does not wholly destroy it. A feature which the world used to have, being the site of our joint endeavour to bring up our child, write our book or whatever, it no longer has. There used to be a possible way for the world to be for me, which no longer exists. A rough analogy, to make this vivid: it is as if your not being there made a certain shade of red disappear or no longer be a possible object of sight. If what I can be as a subject is correlative with what the world can be as object, and if your death changes the world as object, then it changes me (or better, those of us who are left behind) as subject.

What another's death may do for me, my death may do for them – change their world, bring certain possibilities definitively to a close. And it seems to me that I can make sense of that. And what I make sense of is (some of) what makes contemplation of one's own death difficult, for example that my children will be left alone, and that I will not be there for them any longer.[14]

*

Michael Hauskeller: That is all true, but it still seems to be the case that when I die, the world disappears for me but does not disappear for you. In that sense the existence of your world remains unaffected by my death. Clearly, however, to the extent that I am part of your world, my death will change your world. We may then correctly say that your world is no longer the same world it used to be. It has now become a Michael-less world, or more precisely a world in which this particular subject-object that I am, although it may still play a role in your life, for instance by being remembered, is no longer around to converse with you or to do any of the other things people who are still alive can do to affect other people's lives. But isn't that rather trivial? Yes, my death would affect the existence of your world if by 'world' we mean the 'world as it is now', because *that* world – the world as it is now – would no longer exist without me being alive in it.

But the same may be said about any other change too, no matter what it is. In a way, every little change in my world transforms the world as it is now into a different world. Yet we would not normally say that because my world has changed it has been destroyed and then replaced by a new one. Only on an extremely atomistic reading of reality is change the same as replacement. To accept this reading, we would have to commit to the view that existence or being can only ever be instantaneous, that nothing can last for more than a moment, which is to say only for as long as it remains unchanged.[15] It would also require us to abandon the common idea that what changes are often things that, *as* those things, persist in time, which goes very much against the way we (have learned to?) experience the world. Indeed I'm not sure we could even make sense of the idea of a change that is not tied in any way to something that does not change and whose change it is (just as for there to be any movement there needs to be something that remains still and in relation to which the movement occurs).

My world changes all the time, but through all those changes it remains not only my world, but also the same old world that it used to be, just as I, in some for us clearly very important though admittedly not entirely clear sense, remain the same person that I was yesterday despite thinking, feeling and doing different things than yesterday. It seems to us that although we change all the time (because our individual world does, which defines what each one of us is by giving content to our otherwise empty subjectivity), it is still the same me who undergoes those changes and experiences them as such. Whatever I am, my experience of the world and myself is such that I cannot help believing that (or at any rate acting as if) I was already there yesterday and that there is a good chance I will still be there tomorrow. I regard myself (as well as you and any other subject) as temporally extended, a being in time, one that stubbornly persists through the myriad of tiny extinctions and rebirths of objective content that make up our lives as experiencing subjects.

The death or disappearance of another person is precisely such an extinction. The death of a particular person can no doubt have a considerable impact on our world, but this is the exception rather than the rule. The vast majority of other people live and die without affecting us, at least not noticeably. Their death makes no tangible difference to us. And even those whose death clearly does make a big difference to us are not so essential to our being that we or our world would actually end with their ending (even though it may sometimes feel like it). It only ends with our own death. That said, you are right that the world we find ourselves in is very much a shared world. My world is indeed our world. Not only is it, right from the start, a world brimming over with subjectivity, with selfhood, but we are also, every step of the way, creating this world together. It is not only the houses and books and tables set for six that speak loudly of a world shared with others but also relational qualities such as noisiness and brightness that presuppose more than just one subject.

Things that are noisy or bright only for me are not really noisy or bright at all. They would not even appear 'noisy' or 'bright' to me if there were nobody else around to whom they could appear and with whom I could communicate about them.[16] There is no saying how they would appear because to say it we would first have to name the things we are talking about, and the naming of things is one of the things we do together. We have co-created a world which is, despite all the differences between your and my world (which overlap, but also contain different things, things that the other is not aware of or pays little attention to) a shared world, one that we both live (and die) in. Should we then, as you seem to suggest, conclude that since subject and object, self and world, are co-extensive, we also share the same self (or if you prefer, the same experiencing and acting subject)?[17] Or is there a self in the plural just as there is a self in the singular, one that both you and I refer to when we speak of 'us'? And is that plural self that would reflect the world that we inhabit together – the world that you and I (and also my dog and I, but, importantly, not my sofa and I) share – perhaps more fundamental than the individual self? It would certainly be less atomistic to think so and perhaps more in line with what is going on when we engage in acts of co-creation such as this very conversation that we are having right now, leading to ideas and ways of expressing them that neither of us would have thought of on our own.

*

Jane Heal: Looking back over earlier parts of this exchange I find an idea which comes up several times and seems worth probing, namely that 'subjectivity is empty without a world'. What does that mean? Perhaps it just means that there cannot be a subject without a world of which it is aware. That's fine. And perhaps it just points to the fact that 'here is an instance of subjectivity' is a wholly schematic claim and does not tell us anything about the subject or what it is aware of. And that's fine too.

But perhaps it means that everything distinctive about an individual subject is to be supplied by some world, which is the object of its awareness and must be over against the subject which is aware of it. This idea presupposes that any object of a subject's awareness is necessarily other than that subject. And this results in a picture of things which I am very uneasy with. It seems to me that there are things which are in my world, and of which I am aware, but which are not other than me, but rather parts, states or aspects of me, constitutive of me. So my body, with its limbs and its sensory and intellectual capacities, memory and so forth, are not over against some pure, empty instance of subjectivity which is ('really') me, but *are* me. I am a real, solid thing, a human animal. And I am in and part of the world I am aware of, along with the other living creatures, that is, plants, non-human animals and other humans.[18]

To stabilise this view of things we need an account of self-awareness which is expressive or articulatory rather than observational. So we are back to thinking about how 'I' works, how first-person authority is possible and suchlike. To the extent that we can stabilise such a view of things – on which 'I' introduces something substantively in the world, and not an empty, merely observing, limit of some world – we can also resist the idea that there is something called 'my individual world', which may overlap with your world but is not identical with it and which disappears on my death. We can accept instead that the world which is the object of my awareness is the one and only world. And it, that very world, is also the object of your awareness.

The world conceived of this way is not necessarily the object of any actual awareness. It existed prior to the existence of any living creatures and will probably continue to exist even if there comes a time when all living creatures are extinct. Whatever we mean when we say 'subject and object are interdependent' cannot (on this way of looking at things) be in conflict with these claims. And there is no conflict if we take 'subject and object are interdependent' to mean, roughly, that the world does not come pre-conceptualised – that any concept in terms of which we could think of the world, including those of the maximally 'objective' and scientific kind, are still our concepts and not the world's concepts. When we describe the independent world, as it exists pre- and post-us, we do so in terms of our concepts. It follows that we necessarily do so in ways which implicate us. But those ways don't implicate us in the sense that we need to exist for our representation of the described (us-less) world to be true.

If all this is on the right lines, then what blinks out at my death is not a world, let alone the world, but me. With me gone, my take on the world is, of course, gone too. But my take on the world is not a world.

What we are aware of in the world is sometimes what we discover, using the concepts of natural science, which we have devised to be maximally independent of the contingencies of our nature as possible. ('Maximally independent' does not mean 'wholly independent'. They are still our concepts.) And what we are aware of is sometimes what we have invented and had an active part in creating – tables, meals, music, the book we are writing, our child's family life, for example. What we do, both as to discovery and as to invention, we do together, in smaller and larger groups. So the possibilities of what can be discovered or invented are limited by the resources which we, together, can bring to the enterprise. As an individual agent, what I can discover or invent is shaped by my resources. If I lose a limb or lose my sight, then what I can investigate or make is reduced; some options are just no longer there. And the same is true of us as co-operating agents. If someone close to me dies, then the discovering or creating we were doing together is deprived of his or her resources. The possibilities of the world are radically diminished, in a way which may make a vast difference to me, although very little difference to some stranger on the far side of the globe.

The view of things which emerges from this has, it seems to me, much in common with that of your last paragraph in your reply immediately above. And in the context of your presentation of that view, we could, as you note, now raise the (metaphysical) questions as to whether, or in what sense, I persist through time, given changes in my body, mind and world, and whether, in some sense, 'we share the same self'.

But I am inclined to think that life, as sketched in the picture we both seem to endorse, is quite a tough business. The picture presents us as capable of remarkable and admirable things, but also as muddled and finite, and liable to partial and selfish views. And it presents us as vulnerable to tragedy, in the collapse of our larger and more generous enterprises through the loss of the others with whom we were working. There seems to me considerable challenge in mustering resources to take on all this and to ponder what it requires of us. From my point of view, the metaphysical questions need attention and defusing only so far as getting entangled in them might divert us from engaging with life. I am inclined to think that there are no metaphysical mysteries here but rather paradoxes and tangles we get ourselves into because of our being drawn to pictures and ingenious verbal speculations. I don't see any hope of our ceasing to be drawn to these things, and we would lose much if we did cease to be drawn. But let's be aware of the pitfalls here and not give these speculations more importance than they deserve.

Notes

1. Various philosophers have claimed they do not. See for instance Unger, 'I do not exist' (then again, Unger also claims that tables and chairs do not exist either) or Metzinger, *Being No-One*. The existence of the self is, in any case, still hotly contested; see Siderits et al., *Self, No Self?*
2. That selves are simply persons – and that means, in effect, human beings – has been argued by Perry, 'Persons and selves'.
3. Such 'locating beliefs' are thus *essentially* indexical (Perry, 'The problem of the essential indexical').
4. Nagel, *The View from Nowhere*.
5. Michael Thompson explores these issues. A good place to start is 'The representation of life'. A book-length treatment of these ideas and some of their ramifications for ethics is his *Life and Action*.
6. Hume famously made vivid for us the idea of there being separate, simple 'ideas' or conscious events and the difficulty of sticking them together. For any reader unaware of these issues, the discussion of Hume in the *Routledge Encyclopedia of Philosophy* (online at https://www.rep.routledge.com (accessed 1 December 2021)) will provide an introduction to his outlook, his views on 'the self' and subsequent discussion of his ideas.
7. Elizabeth Anscombe articulates this outlook in 'The first person'. For one exposition of it see Heal, 'Pragmatism and Anscombe on the first person'.
8. There are hundreds of expositions of this supposed problem. One which is rigorous and systematic (and as a bonus includes an appendix with a good account of what 'the completeness of physics' means) is Papineau, *Thinking about Consciousness*.
9. For one influential formal treatment of the kind of meaning which indexicals have, and why they do not import properties like 'hereness', see Kaplan, 'Demonstratives'.
10. Wittgenstein famously declared that philosophy is 'a battle against the bewitchment of our intelligence by means of our language' (*Philosophical Investigations*, §109) and that 'philosophical problems arise when language goes on holiday' (§38).
11. I am sympathetic to Alfred North Whitehead's panpsychist or panexperientialist conception of material reality as being always to some degree both physical and mental so that subjectivity is not entirely absent even from things that are not alive. For Whitehead, *everything* that exists has windows to the world. It is just that our windows are exceptionally large and clean. This makes it easier to understand how it has been possible for high-level consciousness to arise from material substrates. Panpsychism, which has been much ridiculed in the past, is currently enjoying a renaissance in the philosophy of mind, having gained prominent supporters in Galen Strawson, David Chalmers and Philip Goff, among others. For a good collection of recent work see Brüntrup and Jaskolla, *Panpsychism*.
12. Schopenhauer, *The World as Will and Presentation*, volume 1, §1.
13. We engage here with the enormous topics of 'realism', 'idealism', 'pragmatism' and the like. For an approach I find illuminating and congenial see Lear, 'The disappearing "we"'.
14. I argue for the importance of the social world, particularly for action and ethics, in Heal, 'Other minds, facts and values'. A shorter version is 'On underestimating *us*'.
15. This idea is often associated with Buddhism. See for instance Allinson, 'The Buddhist theory of instantaneous being'.
16. To clarify: we obviously do not need to have other people around to have those experiences, but we need other people in order to conceptualise the world in a particular way to begin with. Brightness and noisiness are not objective features of the world, but ways of making sense of it. And this sense-making is a social process.
17. Arnold Zuboff ('One self') has argued that there is only one self that we all share. Accordingly, the boundaries between different people, insofar as we think of them as different selves, are illusory.
18. This is the view which Anscombe's paper points us to. It is also, of course, the view of Wittgenstein as explored in his *Investigations*.

Bibliography

Allinson, Robert E. 'The Buddhist theory of instantaneous being: the Ur-concept of Buddhism', *The Eastern Buddhist*, New Series 8/1 (1075): 133–48.

Anscombe, Elizabeth. 'The first person'. In *Collected Papers Volume II: Metaphysics and philosophy of mind*, 21–36. Oxford: Basil Blackwell, 1981.

Brüntrup, Godehard, and Ludwig Jaskolla (eds). *Panpsychism: Contemporary perspectives*. Oxford: Oxford University Press, 2016.

Heal, Jane. 'On underestimating *us*', *Think* 19/54 (Spring 2019): 9–20.

Heal, Jane. 'Other minds, facts and values'. In *Knowing and Understanding Other Minds*, edited by Anita Avramides and Matthew Parrott, 200–18. Oxford: Oxford University Press, 2019.

Heal, Jane. 'Pragmatism and Anscombe on the first person'. In *The Practical Turn*, edited by C. Misak and H. Price, *Proceedings of the British Academy* 210 (2017): 117–30.

Kaplan, David. 'Demonstratives'. In *Themes from Kaplan*, edited by Joseph Almog, John Perry and Howard K. Wettstein, 481–563. Oxford: Oxford University Press, 1989.

Lear, Jonathan. 'The disappearing "we"', *Proceedings of the Aristotelian Society*, supplementary volume LVIII (1984): 219–42.

Metzinger, Thomas. *Being No-One*. Cambridge, MA: MIT Press, 2003.

Nagel, Thomas. *The View from Nowhere*. Oxford: Oxford University Press, 1986.

Papineau, David. *Thinking about Consciousness*. Oxford: Oxford University Press, 2002.

Perry, John. 'Persons and selves', *Revue de metaphysique et de morale* 4/68 (2010): 455–73.

Perry, John. 'The problem of the essential indexical', *Noûs* 13 (1979): 3–21.

Roelofs, Luke. 'The unity of consciousness, within subjects and between subjects', *Philosophical Studies* 173/12 (2016): 3199–221.

Schopenhauer, Arthur. *The World as Will and Presentation*, volume 1, translated by Richard E. Aquila. New York: Pearson Longman, 2008.

Siderits, Mark, Evan Thompson and Dan Zahavi (eds). *Self, No Self? Perspectives from analytical, phenomenological, and Indian traditions*. Oxford: Oxford University Press, 2010.

Thompson, Michael. *Life and Action: Elementary structures of practice and practical thought*. Cambridge, MA: Harvard University Press, 2008.

Thompson, Michael. 'The representation of life'. In *Virtues and Reasons*, edited by Rosalind Hursthouse, Gavin Lawrence and Warren Quinn, 247–97. Oxford: Oxford University Press, 1995.

Unger, Peter K. 'I do not exist'. In *Perception and Identity*, edited by Graham F. Macdonald, 235–51. Ithaca, NY: Cornell University Press, 1979.

Wittgenstein, Ludwig. *Philosophical Investigations*. Oxford: Basil Blackwell, 1953.

Zuboff, Arnold. 'One self: the logic of experience', *Inquiry* 33/1 (1990): 39–68.

7
Goodness
with Alexander Badman-King

Alexander Badman-King: I once said to you that I find it bemusing that many people talk about how hard it is to ever know what is right and wrong, and I gave the example of one of my dogs as an instance where goodness *shines through*. I said how when I look at Bleddyn I don't have any doubt at all about goodness and badness, about what is right and what is wrong – it is just there in front of me. I wasn't talking about his, Bleddyn's, goodness, not his moral virtue as such, but the goodness in that situation. I talked about his background, about the abuse he suffered in early life, and about the safety and comfort we have been able to give him by adopting him. But the main thing I was talking about was the way in which that goodness is clear. It wasn't a calculation; my process of thought wasn't an overly cerebral one in which I was weighing up his past, his possible lives and the prices I had paid in order to bring him a better life. The goodness is an immediate thing, something apparent, something visible, something in his eyes. It is the darkness of the world he had known, and the light and warmth in the moment – it is all visible and all immediate.[1]

It is interesting how this kind of immediately visible quality of goodness (or badness), or right and wrong, interplays with the complexity of reflecting on the more abstract calculations of moral decision-making, and I am not always sure what the nature of that relationship is. We can imagine someone who is a very good sort of person, who simply has good instincts and who sees what is right and wrong in an immediate way, and who incorporates those immediate understandings in their life. They act unthinkingly in accordance with those impressions. And yet this person needn't be particularly intelligent, not in the usual sense. This good person might not need to be a human at all: we can imagine another animal being simply good; in fact, I'd suggest we don't need to imagine it, we can witness this simple goodness quite frequently.[2]

In the end, I want to be good. I think it is the thing I want most of all. I'm not sure, in fact, if I can make sense of a way of being which is not directed like this. Is it coherent for someone not to want to be good? Is it coherent for someone to want something more than being good?[3]

I suspect some people are tempted to think about this in terms of happiness, and the pursuit of happiness – that happiness is somehow the most valid thing to set as a primary goal and the driving motivation of life. Other people might want to be good *at* something, or good *for* something, rather than being good as such. Maybe these possible goals can give us a clue as to what being good is like and how being good *as such* is different from happiness and proficiency. I suspect that goodness as such might lie in a kind of combination of these things: that there might be something about both happiness and proficiency which is also common to goodness. *Flourishing* is a word which has been used in this context, and I suspect it goes some way towards the truth.[4]

When I look at Bleddyn, or any of the many animals and plants which live in my garden, the immediately apparent quality of the goodness amidst those lives does seem to have something to do with flourishing. What might it mean to flourish? Is there some other way of talking which might help us? Rather than use the language of 'flourishing', I am tempted to talk in terms of 'doing well', because there is a way in which flourishing might be too inward looking – it sounds like a very personal thing, it sounds like an individual organism being suited to its immediate environment, as opposed to something which might be talking about doing things for the sake of others, and I don't think we would want to leave altruistic, outward-looking behaviour out of our concept of goodness.

I think the garden is a good place to look, a good place to live if we want to understand goodness, if we want to be good – but there are other, very different places.[5] A war zone might be one: the front lines of death, destruction and injustice. When we hear stories of extraordinary courage, self-sacrifice and kindness in the face of extreme violence, we again get a clear impression of goodness, of something to which we should aspire. Someone like Mary Seacole caring for soldiers in the Crimean War, or perhaps Desmond Doss offering aid at the Battle of Okinawa, and countless others who face danger and death for the sake of others; there's something important here which must be included in our thoughts about goodness.

*

Michael Hauskeller: I may be one of those people who want to be good *at* something and also good *for* something. If I thought I was neither good at nor good for something, then not only might I find it difficult, perhaps impossible, to feel good about myself; I would also struggle to understand in what *way* I could still be good. We define ourselves to a large extent through our abilities and our achievements: what we can do (what we are good at doing) and what impact we have on the world we live in (what our doing is good for). This also tends to be the stand- ard by which we measure our as well as other people's goodness. We admire and value people who are good at doing certain things: we call them good musicians, good mathematicians, good teachers, good bakers, good plumbers, and we value them even more if what they are good at is also good *for* something other than itself: pleasing our senses, advancing science, helping us understand things, making sure we have good bread to eat and hot water in the house. This also seems to be the case with those that we tend to turn to when we look for examples of *moral* goodness. People like Mary Seacole and Desmond Doss are very good at doing things that are very good for many other people: they save lives, help others, make the world a better place, and that seems to be at least an important part of why we think of them as good. We would not do that if they were good at nothing and good for nothing.

And yet, I have no doubt that the goodness that you feel shines through in your dog Bleddyn is real, and that that goodness has noth- ing to do with the display of certain skills or any perceived utility. I often have the same feeling when I am watching my own dog, Lottie: the strong intuition that here there is true goodness. And this goodness is a quality both of her and of the situation in which I find myself with her. Naturally, this has nothing to do with her being exceptionally altruistic. She does not run around, Lassie-like, saving children and kittens. I doubt she has any intention to make the world a better place. Of course she has a few skills, like digging holes in the garden and chasing balls and squirrels, but that is not really good for anything much except her own pleasure. She is, however, a very gentle dog, showing no aggression (except very rarely and briefly to other dogs who sniff at her the wrong way), and she is good friends with our three cats, licking them affectionately and apparently not minding when they eat her food, instead waiting patiently until they are finished. She seems to care for them. I am also fairly sure that should she ever manage to catch one of the squirrels that she loves to chase she would do no harm to them. As a friend put it, she 'doesn't have a bad bone in her body'.

But here's the thing: even if she did occasionally harm other creatures, this would not necessarily change my view of her. I know, for instance, that our cats show no hesitation when it comes to preying on other, smaller animals. I am not deceiving myself: I know that if they can get hold of them, they are going to hurt and kill them. Do I see goodness in this? No, but I don't see evil either. There is a certain innocence to what they do, perhaps even a certain beauty. A fittingness. But the goodness I perceive in them too is more than that. It does not consist merely in their not being conscious of any difference between good and evil, right and wrong; not in the pure, guiltless affirmation of their own life and nature. More important is the way they interact with each other, with us and with the dog. How they clearly value the life they share with us, the company, the closeness. How they enjoy being touched and caressed, by our hands and Lottie's tongue; how they communicate with us and trust us; how, even when they stage a fight, they never hurt each other, or us, or Lottie, retracting their razor-sharp claws just in time, always tempering their bite, knowing exactly how far they can go without harming the other. There seems to be *some* understanding here of good and bad, right and wrong – some instinctive, species-transcending concern for the well-being of others, however selective it may be.[6]

*

Alexander Badman-King: Yes, I think you've found the right sort of place for this goodness, something about an awareness of others and being directed towards those others in a benevolent way.

Of course, as much as I want to exercise the kind of 'simple goodness' of which I spoke, it would be quite dishonest of me to suggest that I don't want to be good *at* things, or good *for* things. And, apart from all the more trivial things I would like to have greater proficiency in (mathematics and music are fairly high on that aspirational list), I suspect you're also correct that there is an important sense in which the battlefield altruists of whom we've been speaking do also have a very particular kind of proficiency and usefulness. They are good at saving people from death; they are good *at* and *for* those kinds of tasks. But do we think of their *motivation* as being a part of that skill? And should we judge that motivation in the same way that we judge the proficiency of the great mathematician or the prodigious musician? If someone finds it difficult to imagine self-worth without a sense of their own proficiency, do we think that one's attention should first be directed to the kind of motivations which the battlefield altruists are demonstrating, and then to the kinds of skills which the mathematician and musician are demonstrating? I suspect that the success of the cruel mathematician is far less important than the kindly (but mathematically useless) person.[7]

Maybe it would help to talk about bad dogs. We might not be inclined to judge the cats harshly for their killing. There seems to be something quite cattish about that violence, and we can probably imagine similar acts for which we would not judge dogs too harshly (I think my dogs are not so gentle as Lottie but I forgive them some of their barking and hole digging). But I think that in addition to the simple regard for others which these good creatures can and do demonstrate, we also find those that lack such a regard. I've met dogs like this – dogs that push other dogs around, that take food with no sense of the harm they cause, that, at times, seem genuinely malevolent. Despite their obvious limitations, when such animals seem to be so entirely blind to the interests of others and to be filled almost entirely with self-centred and violent impulses, I think we can rightly judge them to be morally bad.

I do think innocence is relevant to these judgements, though. A lack of proficiency seems to be important to the way we judge these creatures, and children or other people who lack certain (what we might call) 'intellectual' abilities. But aside from this mitigating factor, the awareness of others which you have perceived in Lottie and the cats (maybe we should say 'regard' for others) seems to me to be the same kind of thing (though perhaps to a different degree) as we witness in the battlefield altruist (and perhaps Lassie; but her heart never seemed to be in it much).

It is difficult to know what sort of language we should be using in this world of moral emotions, motivations and psychology. I'd suggest that, as philosophers, it is right that we should be enquiring as to whether these phenomena do have an important common characteristic which means they are of a *kind*, a kind which is importantly different from the kinds of proficiencies possessed by the mathematician or musician. 'Other-regard' seems a bit clunky and artificial, and since we already have a rich moral vocabulary, it might be better to talk in terms of 'goodness', 'simple-goodness', or maybe 'compassion', or even 'love'.

I think you are right to find that there's no need for overt self-sacrifice in order that we can clearly find this goodness; simple moments of mutual recognition and care (whether human or otherwise) are sufficient. This said, our expectations – the bar by which we judge this goodness – do seem to shift depending on proficiencies (we would think poorly of the child who murders songbirds for fun). So maybe the language of flourishing does have some use, because we can well imagine that being good *at* being a cat means something quite different from being good *at* being a human. But again I think this would drive us away from any possibility of finding continuity between the goodness of all of these creatures: of finding anything like goodness *as such*. Perhaps, though, there is another proficiency being demonstrated by good people (by all these persons, human or otherwise, through whom we witness goodness). Perhaps this common proficiency is just the proficiency of *being someone*. Perhaps there is something in the act of regarding (and the tendency to regard) other 'someones' that is crucial to a core proficiency in being someone. Maybe that's what they are good *at*, and they are good *for* other 'someones'. When we say someone is a 'good person', maybe we really do mean this in the same sort of way as when we say someone is a 'good musician'.[8]

What troubles me most here is that there might be an important sense in which this possibility of being a good person – this proficiency in *being someone* by being somehow caring of others – is heavily dependent upon intelligence. We don't need to think about the goodness of other animals here either: we can just think about our battlefield altruists. We can imagine, I think, scenarios in which there will be dilemmas on that battlefield where a clear and accurate analysis of the possibilities involved will be crucial to doing the right thing. When running into the line of fire to save a life (though kind and brave) is ultimately foolish. When a complex overview of the facts and a discerning power of judgement will make the difference between a hero and a dead idiot. So, is this another kind of proficiency upon which goodness depends? Perhaps all of these proficiencies are interdependent.[9]

*

Michael Hauskeller: Sometimes it is indeed difficult, or at least not immediately obvious, what the right thing to do is. In such cases, doing the right thing requires good judgement: the ability to correctly assess a situation and to understand what needs to be done in order to achieve a certain (good) outcome. But does it follow that a person's goodness also depends, as you say, on their proficiency, or in other words their ability to create good outcomes or, more generally, to make the world a better place? Take for example your 'dead idiot' who has run into the line of fire to save somebody else's life. Let's call him Fool Hardy and his more proficient counterpart Hero Hardy. The difference between Fool Hardy and Hero Hardy is that Hero Hardy succeeds where Fool Hardy fails and he does so because he has assessed the situation more accurately than his less fortunate alter ego. But of course Hero Hardy can only succeed in the same situation in which Fool Hardy fails if there is an alternative course of action that allows him to actually save the life that Fool Hardy tries in vain to save by running into the line of fire. If there is no alternative course of action, then Hero Hardy will simply stay put and not be a hero at all. He will not have proven himself to be superior in goodness either.

If, however, there *is* an alternative course of action available and Hero Hardy takes it, then he has certainly proven himself to be smarter than Fool Hardy and perhaps for that very reason also more proficient at being good, but I don't think he has proven himself to be *better* in that simple or moral sense of goodness that we are trying to track down. Fool Hardy may be a fool, but he is still a *good* (namely, as you point out yourself, kind and brave) fool, and there isn't any less goodness in him than there is in Hero Hardy. In fact, depending on the circumstances, we may even think of him as the better of the two, precisely because, in contrast to Hero Hardy, he is willing to risk and therefore potentially sacrifice his life to save that of another person. Of course, if it was obvious that his attempt to save that other person's life was doomed to fail, if there was *no way* he could have succeeded, then we may well ask what the point of his sacrifice was. But it is rarely the case in situations like the one described that we know in advance that it is *impossible* for a particular course of action to succeed.

Perhaps it is highly unlikely that Fool Hardy will manage to save that person and highly likely that he will lose his own life in the attempt, but as long as there is *some* chance of saving that person's life and unless there is indeed an alternative and better option to achieve his goal, making the attempt is just as much an expression of his goodness as of his apparent foolishness. Indeed, we are in conventional terms 'foolish' in this situation precisely because we let our actions be guided by our goodness – here, by our concern for the wellbeing and survival of another human being – rather than by our rational self-interest. And surely the hero in that situation is not the one who calmly assesses the situation and then comes to the conclusion that given the odds it is not really worth taking the risk. The hero is not the one who only does what he or she thinks is right if and when it is entirely safe for them. Rather, the hero is the one who does what they think is right – reaching out to help another in their time of need – no matter how safe or unsafe this may be for them.[10]

The difference between a dead fool and a hero is not that the hero is smarter, it is simply that they have been fortunate enough to defy the odds and survive what could easily have killed them or harmed them in other ways.[11] In fact, it seems to me that even if it is not self-interest but rather a utilitarian concern for the greatest good that motivates the rational hero's decision not to attempt to save a person's life if there is little chance of them succeeding, they will still be deficient in goodness, or at least in a certain kind of goodness. Suppose our hero reasons as follows: 'If I try now to save that person's life, I will most likely be killed, which benefits nobody. But if I do nothing and make no attempt to prevent that person's death, then I will live to save the world some other day. I may for instance save five people tomorrow, which obviously I wouldn't be able to do if I died today. So by not (foolishly) trying to do *some* good today, I am (very wisely) making sure that I will be able to do *more* good in future. This does not make me any less good. On the contrary: because I am just as smart as I am good, I am simply waiting for a better opportunity to exercise my goodness, which makes me even better than I would otherwise be.' Now, while our rational hero, when he reasons thus, is no doubt committed to the good, there is still something wrong about this kind of reasoning – something disturbingly un-good – because the life that could possibly be saved today is considered dispensable. It is reduced to a mere number in a calculation. Goodness, however, doesn't only *not require* a calculation; it can easily get watered down by calculation – possibly even destroyed entirely.[12]

*

Alexander Badman-King: I agree that there's something wrong with Hero Hardy here and that Fool Hardy's unthinking goodness, for being unthinking, is all the more good. I like Bernard Williams's language of 'one thought too many' when it comes to problems of moral calculation; I do think Hero Hardy is indulging in one thought (or a few thoughts) too many.[13] Perhaps our souls ('minds', 'selves' etc.) have only so much room for virtues, and by indulging in calculation Hero Hardy is watering down, or elbowing out, the simple and immediate goodness.

But I think the kind of intellectual virtue that still concerns me – the possible kind of intelligence which might be crucial to a better kind of goodness than 'simple goodness' – is something that might be exercised in tandem with the immediate and compelling selflessness displayed by Fool Hardy. I imagine here that both characters, Fool and Hero, are compelled to help others in the same way, and both sacrifice themselves in the fire of battle, but thanks to the ability of Hero Hardy to survey a complex range of possibilities and weigh the risks and benefits of those possibilities very quickly, Hero saves thousands and Fool saves only one or two. The battle rages and bullets are flying . . . the artillery ceases and the whistle is blown. Over the top, amidst all the filth, blood and screams, two men throw themselves forward, side by side. They see two injured friends, stricken and in the line of an imminent machine gun assault. Fool Hardy grabs his friends and hauls them towards shelter. Hero Hardy sees the possibility of taking out the machine gun himself and hurtles towards the enemy trench. Both men die. One saves two, the other saves hundreds.

Maybe some souls have more room in them for virtues than others, maybe this vision of a Hero Hardy who is both good and clever is some-how inhuman, or maybe we should say that regardless of either man's cleverness both are equally good people. I am tempted by this third pos-sibility and I think it echoes your assessment: that while the simple good dog and the good mathematician have very different skillsets, both are equally good and their goodness is unaffected by other proficiencies. But I have a lingering suspicion that unlike mathematical proficiency, the intellectual virtue I have in mind here does still have a special modify-ing quality on goodness, and perhaps on badness also. Could it be a kind of 'moral entropy'? What I mean here is that (thinking back to the way other species' lack of intellect seems to mitigate our moral expectations of them) there is a kind of intelligence which creates possibilities for both virtue and vice, for good and evil, and that not only does the intel-ligent person have the capacity for doing greater good, they also have the capacity for its opposite. And the reason I say 'moral entropy' is that there seem to be lots of possibilities for acting in a way that is contrary to the selfless way – a complex, typically human kind of intelligence is likely to open a world of possibilities for self-preservation, hidden ways of being selfish where nobody will ever know.

A broad and sophisticated understanding of things also seems likely to make very apparent the cost of selfless behaviour: all the terrors of death and suffering. So, when the dog is violent, perhaps we are less inclined to judge the dog harshly because we have a sense that there wasn't much wiggle room for the dog, not much in the way of possibility to act otherwise, and, similarly, when the dog is gentle and loyal we might also have a weaker urge to heap praise upon that dog because this kind of simple virtue is only one of very few possibilities with which the dog is presented. Does the brave philosopher need to be braver than the brave pig; do all the demons visible to the sage and hidden from the beast give us reason to value them differently?

I suspect there is a danger here, with the sort of lauding of intellect in which I have been indulging, of failing to correctly identify both the extent and the complexities of non-linguistic, non-cerebral behaviour. I mean here something like the power of emotion, or something which might be called that. I don't just mean the counter-claim to this 'moral entropy' – that a lack of understanding can be and is a reason for heightened fear, pain, joy etc. (this would be the idea that because other animals cannot comprehend the possible benefits of a scary situation they will feel greater fear). I mean, rather, that it might be possible to identify varying 'richnesses' of goodness (and badness) independent of the cerebral domain of calculation. This is a difficult, nebulous sort of concept and, as with much of the moral psychology we have been discussing, we probably need to use a light touch to navigate it adequately; but I suspect that when we witness goodness or badness, we might also find that it comes in different sizes and flavours. I suspect these 'flavours' do map, somehow, onto some of the concepts and language we already use when discussing virtues. We have mentioned courage and kindness, and I wonder two things: what is the relationship between these flavours (are they all facets of one simple goodness which so far we have found mostly in a kind of selfless kindness), and how do we discern these qualities?

There might be some lingering sense in which we should address the epistemological question here since, although I began by stating my utter bemusement at those who find no compelling evidence for these occasions of goodness and badness, I wonder if the way in which we spend time with one another (we living things), the way we witness one another, can tell us something about goodness and badness. We see this goodness, we feel it (in an embrace, or just sitting on the sofa), we hear it in menacing tones and anxious breathing; is there a sense in which these qualities are somehow irreducibly mixed up with our living with one another? Can we discuss them and their depths without this sense of an irreducible 'thickness'?[14]

*

Michael Hauskeller: You are probably right to say that goodness comes in different sizes and flavours, and we would do well to remember that. There is not just one way of being good, and the ways in which a living being can be good also depend on what kind of being it is and what capacities of understanding and limitations it has.[15] The goodness we can reasonably expect from a human is different from the goodness we can reasonably expect from a dog, which in turn is different from the goodness we can reasonably expect from a cat. And perhaps there are some animals that are not capable of *any* degree or flavour of goodness because they just don't have what it takes to be good or, for that matter, bad – at least not in the same sense that humans, dogs and even cats can be perceived by us as being good or bad.

A dragonfly for example – which I imagine to be incapable of exhibiting any regard for others, of showing kindness or love – may be beautiful, but it cannot be good (in that still somewhat elusive sense we are trying to capture here).[16] This is not to say that the dragonfly may not be very good at being a dragonfly, having honed to perfection all the things that dragonflies can be good at, which suggests that there is a difference between being a good exemplar of one's kind and being good *simpliciter*. When I marvel at my dog Lottie's 'goodness', I am not making any judgement about her being or not being particularly good *as* a dog. And when I find some goodness even in my cats, it is not because they are good at being cats but because of their being capable of doing things that seem to transcend their nature, without being exactly *against* their nature either. It is as if when they show restraint and even tenderness towards each other and members of other species[17] (in this case dogs and humans, or more precisely *some* dogs and humans), and despite doing this in an undoubtedly cattish way, they become something more than just cats.

Perhaps we, too – when we overcome our usual cowardice and self-centredness, in ways only humans can – become more than just human, namely members of a larger biotic (or, more to the point, *symbiotic*) community that spreads across the species, based on some sort of mutual recognition. The dragonfly, on the other hand, is always wholly and completely a dragonfly, living in a myopic dragonfly world in which everything only appears as potential prey, a potential danger, or simply indifferent. But of course the dragonfly has beauty and to that extent also shares in goodness because beauty is, perhaps more than anything else, one of the ways in which we experience goodness.[18] When you initially introduced your dog Bleddyn into our conversation, you took care to point out that the goodness you witness there is not so much the perceived moral virtue of the dog himself, but rather a prominent quality of the whole *situation*. Similarly, we may look at the dragonfly darting across the pond and think (or rather feel) to ourselves, 'There is goodness here, something right and proper and wonderful.' And being able to see and appreciate that situational goodness is perhaps an essential part of what it is for us to be good in the narrower, moral sense. To be good in the narrow sense, then, means to be appreciative of goodness in the wider sense. It means recognising that something is valuable intrinsically, not because we can directly benefit from it, as a resource that we can use, but simply because it is what it is.

And it may well be that, just as different species have access to different levels and nuances of goodness, we humans also all differ from each other in terms of the degree and kinds of goodness we are capable of appreciating and practising. Just as the goodness of a cat is different from the goodness of a human, my capacity for goodness may be different from yours, not only in the sense that I might have less of it, but also in the sense that I might simply have *other* goodness-exemplifying capacities than you. I don't think Socrates got it right when he suggested (or even insisted) that all virtues are ultimately one[19] – that if you have one of them you have them all because in order to have one you need to be somehow connected to and enacting the 'Form of the Good' itself.[20] Perhaps there is no such form or idea – perhaps there is just a family resemblance between various instances of goodness, which we recognise as such because they all, each in their own way, make our life together better, helping us flourish, not in isolation, but as part of a larger, not yet fully formed and exceedingly fragile community.[21]

People are good in many different ways, as they are bad in many different ways, and most of us are indeed well versed in both goodness and badness. We are very much a mixed bag: there is some goodness in us, but we are not entirely good, not through and through. There are things we see and other things we are blind to, and there are times when we see and other times when we are blind.[22] We are a bit like the cats, who can be incredibly gentle one moment and ruthless killers the next. I suppose that most people are not capable of such extremes, but we can certainly be brave on some occasions and cowardly on others; compassionate and forgiving at times, and cold and vengeful at others. And perhaps we can be even worse than that, under the right (or wrong) circumstances. Perhaps our goodness is at least partly the product of a lack of opportunity for evil. Give us an environment that encourages our less kindly impulses, and we may gradually reveal or actualise a much darker side of us that we perhaps had no idea existed before it was unleashed.[23] Or perhaps some people are simply incapable of doing things that are really bad. They would never comply with evil, no matter what. But can we say for sure, without being tested, that we are one of them?

*

Alexander Badman-King: No, I suppose we can never have that kind of confidence in our own goodness. Or perhaps I should say that we *should* never have that kind of confidence in our own goodness. We are undoubtedly subject to the vagaries of life and the world of which we are a part; subject to the ebb and flow of the juices in our veins; subject to what tomorrow might bring. I think that, apart from anything else, a confidence in our own goodness, so as to suggest firm knowledge that we could not and would not do evil of any particular sort, claims knowledge which simply isn't possible. Equally, I suspect that there is something self-contradictory in expressing such confidence in one's own moral powers and dispositions. I wonder if inclinations and opportunities to do good are things for which we should feel some gratitude – that we should be grateful for not having been tested or broken. I am inclined to suggest that there's a humility mixed with the gratitude here which is an important part of being good, and it may also be related to the kind of forgiveness which is appropriate for those dogs who bark or cats who kill.[24] Perhaps such a stance suggests too much passivity, too much pious fawning over some kind of moral grace. Maybe this mixture of humility and gratitude competes with or diminishes a more direct responsibility for the kinds of capacities necessary for doing good or with incisive judgement of those who do wrong. I suspect there's a difficult balance to be achieved, again between different ways of being good, different sorts of virtues: on the one hand a tendency to be forgiving and on the other to be accurately judgemental.[25]

I like your use of the phrase 'reasonably expect'. Reasonable expectations do seem very important here and perhaps that is one way in which the power of reason can be helpful to being good. Intellect seems to grant a breadth of view which means that our judgements can be more accurate; when I know more about what is doggish, cattish and humanish I can temper my expectations accordingly. This might equally be said for when I have a clearer understanding of what is me-ish and what is you-ish. Perhaps this is part of the tragedy of philosophy: as our view broadens and our wisdom deepens we learn of the limits of all of these creatures, and again there is a kind of entropy. A process of reasoned investigation, of close and purposeful examination, reveals cracks that would otherwise go unseen. Where a path previously seemed free of problems, a more careful and incisive view shows where things might go wrong. It shows all the room for doubt. But this revelation as to how things can and might go wrong doesn't seem to preclude a hope that they might go right. While this wisdom makes forgiveness easier, a clearer view of possible failure also suggests a clearer view of possible success. When our view of one another and of ourselves is shorn of false certainties, the few remaining chances for goodness become sounder investments.

You may be right that Socrates' unifying virtue reaches too far, but perhaps the family resemblance is sufficient to do justice to that 'idea of the Good'. If we speak about goodness of the distinctly moral kind – that elusive regard for others which makes someone more than just a dog, or more than just a human, and then we speak about the beauty of the narrow-minded dragonfly in its environment, we may impose too much categorical order on these different ways of being good if we make them very distinct. Certainly, I would agree that the way we speak about moral goodness loses too much of its meaning if we apply it directly to the dragonfly – courage and compassion are the wrong words for that kind of creature – but is the nebulous sort of goodness, which I found in the initial scenario with Bleddyn and which we might also call 'beauty', only goodness by analogy? Are these senses of goodness so distinct from one another as to be merely a confusing use of language? I wonder if all of these various kinds of goodness are just different ways of being towards other things, kinds of living-with, and whether our own highly conscious, deliberate, linguistic way of being good is merely a very human and cerebral region of this otherwise continuous world of goodness.

I have no doubt that the dragonfly has such a different kind of mind from our own that it barely deserves to be spoken about as a 'mind' at all, but the dragonfly's rightness in its environment which radiates beauty might still be made sense of in a similar way to our own moral virtues. We are directed towards other things with a particularly human kind of psychology – we are creatures of complex memories and expectations, of categories and conversations – and so when we are beautiful in our own way it is through an exercise of these kinds of capacities. The relationships of which we are capable are those of courage and kindness, of diligence or intelligence, but perhaps there is enough continuity between these ways of being good and any and all ways of being good for us to be able to discern a kind of unity. The language of beauty may not entirely capture the goodness in an act of kindness, and the language of right and wrong might fail to clearly express the goodness of the dragonfly darting across the pond, but the application of 'goodness' to all these seems to draw on more than mere analogy. So perhaps the proficiency of the mathematician can, after all, find a place in this continuity of symbiosis.[26]

Perhaps, despite the continuity between goodnesses, there is a sense in which benevolence towards others, which is so clearly possible among humans and at least some other animals, is a richer sort of goodness. This needn't be a particularly strong value judgement, but the breadth of capacity which I previously mentioned as being grounds for expecting more of humans might speak of a certain kind of value quantity. If goodness is about living with other things in the right sort of way – about having a regard for the interests of others – then it seems that an ability to appreciate those interests in all their complexity and variety will grant a capacity for greater goodness. And this might still accommodate a sense of continuity with the dragonfly's non-conscious relationships with other organisms. I think the dragonfly is myopic in two ways: first, it barely has a mind at all (and so its behaviour hardly resembles 'awareness' in any sense we would recognise); second (and relatedly), the dragonfly has a narrow ecological role: its relationships in the network of its environment are sufficiently specialised that even its barely conscious reactions to the interests of other organisms are relatively restricted compared to, say, an old oak tree (which despite having even less of a mind than the dragonfly has a much broader range of symbiotic relationships).

It might be that using pseudo-biological language in this way stretches things too far and wanders dangerously close to an attempt to reduce 'goodness' to a biological mechanism. I think that would be a big mistake and should be avoided.[27] But I also believe that thinking in this way and using this language can help us understand the role of reasonable expectation in our moral thinking (to simultaneously include other living things in our moral considerations and, when appropriate, to forgive them and ourselves many of our weaknesses). I also think that this continuity of symbiosis can help us think of our own moral significance and how, like the old oak, our own many-branched moral psychologies have the capacity for great things. It needn't be that the wise, kind human is better than the good dog, or better than the dragonfly even, but the roots and canopy of that complex moral psychology can spread further in the world and exercise benevolence in so many places that would otherwise be unreachable to those other, narrower lives.

*

Michael Hauskeller: We humans indeed have a greater capacity and wider scope for benevolence (and, naturally, its opposite) than other animals, and that clearly is a function of our intellect. We have, or at least can have, a better understanding of the consequences and the reach of our actions and we can adjust our behaviour accordingly. (Whether we actually do this is of course another matter entirely.) That does not make us any better than other living things (as in more worthy and more entitled to enjoy life and the good that it has to offer). It does not justify our pride or our usual sense of superiority. Rather, it simply gives us a *responsibility* that nothing else in this world has.[28]

Our moral significance is one of duties rather than rights. In other words, there is a lot more that can reasonably be expected from us than from other animals. That said, I don't think we should demand *too* much of ourselves and each other. That we save the world or even make the world a better place *on the whole* is not something that can reasonably be expected from us, not only because we would be very unlikely to succeed (so far, the world has proven quite resistant to our efforts to improve it), but also because the attempt to do so might require heroic sacrifices from us that may undermine the very basis of our commitment to the good. Moral heroes are needed to ensure that as many people (and perhaps non-human animals) as possible can have a good life – a life that allows us to flourish both as the particular *kind* of beings that we are (be it human or dog or dragonfly) and as the particular *individuals* that we are, rich with (both lower and higher) pleasures as well as with love, with challenges and opportunities, with things to desire and strive for, to learn and be proud of. This is the good that needs protecting: it is both valuable and vulnerable, and there cannot be any moral goodness without an acute appreciation of all of this *as* good. The moral hero protects this good against whatever threatens to take it away from those who enjoy it, or attempts to secure it for those who have so far been prevented from enjoying it, but in order to do so, moral heroes sacrifice or at least risk their own enjoyment precisely of that good. Heroes are needed so that others can live their lives without having to be heroes.

We don't *all* have to be heroes, though; indeed, we *must* not be. If we were, always ready to sacrifice our own good for that of others, being a hero would be pointless because there would be nobody left to enjoy the good we were fighting to protect. That is why it is quite all right to occasionally take a 'moral holiday' (as William James called it),[29] let the world take care of itself, and simply enjoy life (and for instance engage in philosophical discussions about goodness), because that is what moral goodness is ultimately meant to protect: the ability to live a good, satisfying life. It is also why for most of us it may be enough to just 'take care of our garden' (as Voltaire's Candide suggested we do)[30] – that is, make sure, as best we can and in our own fashion, that our little part of the world – the part that we directly have a hand in shaping – is kept in good order. The hero's way is, after all, not the only and not even the primary way of protecting the good.

Another equally important way of doing that is simply to live a good life, provided we understand that a good life is not a selfish life, a life spent wholly in the pursuit of one's own narrow interests. Rather, a good life is a life shared with others in mutual recognition and appreciation of our respective needs; a life of shared joys and sufferings and in pursuit of something that we feel matters. It is, in other words, the kind, decent, but by no means entirely selfless life of an ordinarily decent human being – a life in which we carve out space, both for others and for ourselves, to flourish. And it may well be that in order to be such a decent human being we must not be too sure of our own goodness. There is, after all, a fine line between righteousness and self-righteousness,[31] and being overly confident of one's own goodness is a sure sign of its absence. Humility is indeed important.[32] It aids our understanding, and understanding is part of what constitutes our unique human way of being good.

I am reminded here of Leonard Cohen's famous lines in his song *Anthem*: 'There is a crack, a crack in everything. That's how the light gets in.'[33] Perfect goodness is neither achievable nor desirable. Without the cracks there would be no light, only darkness. We need to recognise and acknowledge our own cracks – our various weaknesses and character flaws – to be able to understand those of others and to remain alert to the various ways in which both goodness and badness manifest themselves. Not only to be able to forgive, but also to distinguish bad from worse, the forgivable from the unforgivable. Because that, too, is, as you rightly point out, part of our specifically human goodness, part of what we can reasonably be expected to do and to be good at and good for: having the ability and indeed the courage to make, when it really matters, a judgement and to declare, despite being fully aware of our own moral deficiencies and our general fallibility, that something or other is *wrong*, that we should not do it and should not tolerate it.

Notes

1. Bleddyn is one of two dogs that my wife and I adopted after they came from Romania to the UK following a nationwide cull of free-roaming dogs from 2013. Remus Creţan gives a good introduction to these culls and the support for animal rights and the dogs among the Romanian public in 'Mapping protests against dog culling in post-Communist Romania'.
2. Someone who has carried this Williamsesque insight (with a welcome dollop of Wittgenstein) into the realm of non-human animals and their moral characters is Raimond Gaita. Gaita reflects on the simple moral virtues of his dog Gypsy in *The Philosopher's Dog* (particularly 42–4).
3. This is perhaps a clumsy echo of Plato's reflection in the *Protagoras* on the possibility (or impossibility as Plato's Socrates would have it) of knowingly doing something wrong. Here Plato suggests the famously counterintuitive idea that 'none of the wise men thinks that any human being willingly makes a mistake or willingly does anything wrong or bad. They know very well that anyone who does anything wrong or bad does so involuntarily' (*Protagoras* 345d–e). I'm not going this far, but there does seem to be an inherent connection between goodness and motivation.
4. Martha Nussbaum has done extensive work in promoting 'flourishing' as a translation of the ancient Greek philosophical staple εὐδαιμονία ('eudaimonia'). In her *Therapy of Desire* Nussbaum explores this concept, and its relationship with happiness, in some detail (see 15). Nussbaum's is by no means the last word on this, but the kind of flourishing I'm talking about here draws a great deal on that tradition.
5. I have expanded upon some of these thoughts in *Living-With Wisdom*.
6. That non-human animals can also be moral subjects has been argued by Rowlands (*Can Animals be Moral?*). There is also plenty of empirical evidence that various species of animal frequently engage in altruistic and empathic behaviour. For an overview see Monso et al., 'Animal morality'.

7. I should note here the echo of Iris Murdoch's suggestion that 'it must be possible to do justice to both Socrates and the virtuous peasant' (*The Sovereignty of Good*, 2). Murdoch was very much concerned with the kinds of virtues which can be and are exhibited by those who are proficient not in specialist skills but instead only in a kind of well-meaningness.

8. Here I don't mean the same thing as Wittgenstein when he claims that ethical language is used as a kind of allegory or simile for instrumental value (or what Wittgenstein calls 'trivial sense' of 'good': 'A lecture on ethics', 9). However, there is some room here for accommodating an idea of similarity which might itself be similar to analogy. To go much further with that, however, would demand a fuller treatment of the nature of similarity itself. Suffice it to say that I would suggest that the goodness of kindness is conceptually prior to the goodness of proficiency (as opposed to Wittgenstein, who would have it the other way round), and that this is developed later in this discussion.

9. This is the view expressed by Aristotle through the virtue φρόνησις (phronesis). This is a kind of intelligence or even cleverness which is in addition to good intentions and motivations (*Nicomachean Ethics*, §VI, xiii, 1145a: 7–11).

10. According to Kirby in 'The hero and asymmetrical obligation', the hero is one 'who does what is right . . . even when it requires extreme sacrifice' (157).

11. It is, in other words, a question of *moral luck* whether one ends up a hero or a fool. While the discussion on 'moral luck', started by Bernard Williams and Thomas Nagel, focuses mainly on the blameworthiness of actions, it is generally understood that their praiseworthiness is also subject to luck. See the collection of papers in Statman, *Moral Luck*. More specifically, the luck that is needed to make the hero a hero has been analysed by Joel Deshaye: analysing Clint Eastwood's *Dirty Harry* films, Deshaye ('"Do I feel lucky?"', 24) remarks: 'Someone reckless who luckily saves the day is a hero, but someone reckless who only causes damage is not.'

12. For a devastating critique of a purely utilitarian approach to moral thinking see Maclean, *The Elimination of Morality*.

13. Williams, *Moral Luck*, 18.

14. The sense of 'thickness' here is a kind of cross between the ethical sense espoused by Bernard Williams and the cultural sense used by Clifford Geertz (Williams, *Ethics and the Limits of Philosophy*; Geertz, *The Interpretation of Cultures*, 6–9).

15. Mary Midgley writes: 'Human needs are multiple . . .; we have many sorts of goods because we have many wants' (*Beast and Man*, 190). Needs, however, she writes elsewhere, 'come as a set. They are intelligible only in the context of a whole way of life, which is in the first place that of a given species, and in the second that of a certain culture' (*Wickedness*, 144). 'Needs . . . are not entities on their own but aspects of people. And those sets are structured in a more or less familiar way, typical of the species' (*Wickedness*, 147).

16. Note that I am not claiming that insects are not conscious, although it is hard to say with any degree of certainty if and to what extent they are (see Allen-Hermanson, 'Insects and the problem of simple minds'). Nor would the fact that insects such as dragonflies are not moral subjects necessarily exclude them from moral consideration (see Carruthers, 'Invertebrate minds').

17. Which happens more frequently in animal interactions between different species than we normally care to acknowledge. See Willett, *Interspecies Ethics*.

18. For the various ways in which beauty grounds value experience and can serve as a guide to action, see Henning's Whitehead-based *The Ethics of Creativity*.

19. Socrates argues for the unity of virtues in Plato's *Protagoras* and other early dialogues. See also Vlastos, 'The unity of the virtues in the *Protagoras*'.

20. The 'Form of the Good' plays a key role in Plato's metaphysics and ethics. See Santas, 'The Form of the Good in Plato's *Republic*'.

21. See Midgley, *Utopia, Dolphins and Computers*, 124: 'Moral "pluralism" is correct in the sense that we really do have many distinct ideals. But of course we cannot just pursue them all at random. In trying to bring them together harmoniously, we need to have some sort of comprehensive world-picture, some vision of the whole within which we live and of our own relation to it.'

22. According to Iris Murdoch (*The Nice and the Good*, 191): 'We are not good people, and the best we can hope for is to be gentle, to forgive each other and to forgive the past, to be forgiven ourselves and to accept this forgiveness, and to return again to the beautiful unexpected strangeness of the world.'

23. Many examples of this process can be found in Minnich's *The Evil of Banality*.

24. While I might agree to some extent that Plato's Socrates was claiming too much through a total unity of goodness, I think there's plenty of room for thinking of virtues like humility as being far more central to goodness than others. I agree with Sharon Ryan when she suggests that the humility of Socrates (especially in the *Apology*) is foundational to what we might call wisdom ('What is wisdom?', 119).
25. This is, once again, a bit of Aristotle rearing its head, this time in the shape of the 'golden mean', or a mid-point between two extremes on a psychological or moral continuum (*Nicomachean Ethics*, §II, vi, 1106a–b).
26. Iris Murdoch expresses this idea when she says: 'It is so patently a good thing to take delight in flowers and animals that people who bring home potted plants and watch kestrels might even be surprised at the notion that these things have anything to do with virtue' (*The Sovereignty of Good*, 85).
27. I'm not offering a hard criticism of ethical naturalism here. In fact, there is a certain sense in which the view I am expressing has a great deal in common with Phillipa Foot's 'natural norms', by which all species have a set of characteristics which are natural to them and it is by these that we judge whether a member of that species is a 'good' example (*Natural Goodness*, 34–7). Of course, I am maintaining that the 'moral goodness' which Foot attributes to humans can also be exhibited by other non-human persons by dint of their being a person.
28. See Chapman and Huffman, 'Why do we want to think humans are different?'; Juergens, 'Human and nonhuman animals'.
29. James, *Pragmatism*, chapter 2.
30. Voltaire, *Candide*, 208.
31. For a philosophical analysis of self-righteousness, its relation to morality, and the 'temptation of moral certainty', see Bicknell, 'Self-righteousness as a moral problem'.
32. The epistemic, moral and practical value of humility is emphasised by Richards in 'Is humility a virtue?'.
33. 'Ring the bells that still can ring/ Forget your perfect offering/ There is a crack, a crack in everything/ That's how the light gets in.'

Bibliography

Allen-Hermanson, Sean. 'Insects and the problem of simple minds: are bees natural zombies?', *Journal of Philosophy* 105/8 (2008): 389–415.

Aristotle. *Nicomachean Ethics*, translated by H. Rackham. Cambridge, MA: Harvard University Press, 1934.

Badman-King, Alexander. *Living-With Wisdom: Permaculture and symbiotic ethics*. London: Routledge, 2021.

Bicknell, Jeanette. 'Self-righteousness as a moral problem', *The Journal of Value Inquiry* 44 (2010): 477–87.

Carruthers, Peter. 'Invertebrate minds: a challenge for ethical theory', *The Journal of Ethics* 11/3 (2007): 275–97.

Chapman, Colin A., and Michael A. Huffman. 'Why do we want to think humans are different?', *Animal Sentience* 23/1 (2018): 1–8.

Crețan, Remus, 'Mapping protests against dog culling in post-Communist Romania', *Area* 47/2 (2015): 155–65.

Deshaye, Joel. '"Do I feel lucky?": moral luck and the ethics of Eastwood's outlaw-lawman in *Coogan's Bluff* and the *Dirty Harry* films', *Film-Philosophy* 2/1 (2017): 20–36.

Foot, Phillipa. *Natural Goodness*. Oxford: Clarendon Press, 2001.

Gaita, Raimond. *The Philosopher's Dog*. London: Routledge, 2002.

Geertz, Clifford. *The Interpretation of Cultures*. New York: Basic Books, 1973.

Henning, Brian G. *The Ethics of Creativity: Beauty, morality, and nature in a processive cosmos*. Pittsburgh, KS: University of Pittsburgh Press, 2005.

James, William. *Pragmatism: A new name for some old ways of thinking*. New York: Longmans, Green and Co., 1907.

Juergens, Uta Maria. 'Human and nonhuman animals: equals in uniqueness', *Animal Sentience* 23/2 (2018): 2.

Kirby, Katherine E. 'The hero and asymmetrical obligation', *International Philosophical Quarterly* 50/2 (2010): 157–66.

Maclean, Anne. *The Elimination of Morality: Reflections on utilitarianism and bioethics.* London: Routledge, 1993.

Midgley, Mary. *Beast and Man: The roots of human nature.* Hassocks: The Harvester Press, 1978.

Midgley, Mary. *Wickedness: A philosophical essay.* London: Routledge & Kegan Paul, 1984.

Midgley, Mary. *Utopia, Dolphins and Computers.* London: Routledge, 1996.

Minnich, Elizabeth K. *The Evil of Banality: On the life and death importance of thinking.* Lanham, MD: Rowman & Littlefield, 2016.

Monso, Susana, Judith Benz-Schwarzburg and Annika Bremhorst. 'Animal morality: what it means and why it matters', *The Journal of Ethics* 22 (2018): 283–310.

Murdoch, Iris. *The Nice and the Good.* London: Chatto & Windus, 1970.

Murdoch, Iris. *The Sovereignty of Good.* London: Routledge, 1970.

Nussbaum, Martha. *Therapy of Desire: Theory and practice in Hellenistic ethics.* Princeton, NJ: Princeton University Press, 2004.

Plato. *Protagoras*, translated by Stanley Lombardo and Karen Bell. In *Plato: Complete Works*, edited by John M. Cooper. Cambridge, MA: Hackett, 1997.

Plato. *The Republic.* London: Penguin Classics, 2007.

Richards, Norvin. 'Is humility a virtue?', *American Philosophical Quarterly* 25/3 (1988): 253–9.

Rowlands, Mark. *Can Animals be Moral?* New York: Oxford University Press, 2012.

Ryan, Sharon. 'What is wisdom?', *Philosophical Studies: An international journal for philosophy in the analytic tradition* 93/2 (1999): 119–39.

Santas, Gerasimos. 'The form of the good in Plato's *Republic*', *Philosophical Inquiry* 2/1 (1980): 374–403.

Statman, Daniel (ed.). *Moral Luck.* Albany, NY: SUNY Press, 1993.

Vlastos, Gregory. 'The unity of the virtues in the *Protagoras*', *Review of Metaphysics* 25 (1972): 415–58.

Voltaire. *The Works of Voltaire: A contemporary version*, volume 1: *Candide*, translated by William F. Fleming. New York: E. R. DuMont, 1901.

Willett, Cynthia. *Interspecies Ethics.* New York: Columbia University Press, 2014.

Williams, Bernard. *Moral Luck: Philosophical papers 1973–1980.* Cambridge: Cambridge University Press, 1981.

Williams, Bernard. *Ethics and the Limits of Philosophy.* London: Routledge, 2006.

Wittgenstein, Ludwig. 'A lecture on ethics', *The Philosophical Review* 74/1 (1965): 3–12.

8
Evil

with Alexander Badman-King

Michael Hauskeller: Traditionally, the 'problem of evil' is the difficulty of holding on to the belief in an all-powerful, all-knowing and perfectly good God despite the fact that there are so many bad things happening in the world,[1] ranging from 'physical evils' such as diseases and natural disasters that do so much harm to innocent, good people, to 'moral evils' such as the various kinds of suffering we inflict on each other.[2] Here, 'evil' simply means bad, or bad for us. Obviously, if we no longer make the assumption that there is a God, and that this God can do anything, knows everything, and wants only the best for us, the problem of evil as it was originally conceived disappears because we can now easily explain the existence of all those evils. And yet, it seems to me that *evil*, in a narrower, more accentuated sense of the word, still poses a problem, even without God. Let me try to explain why.

First we need to distinguish between the common or garden variety of bad on the one hand and genuine evil on the other. The way I understand the word 'evil', which I believe is the way the word is commonly used, there are a lot of things that are bad without being evil, and that includes things that we regard as morally bad. Last winter, for instance, we provided food and shelter for a homeless woman. That turned out to be a mistake: she abused our trust and stole from us. We should have known better, of course, but still, we felt betrayed. The theft was bad enough, but the breach of trust was worse. She should not have done that. It was bad. Evil, however, it was not.

Most of us are quite capable of immoral acts, of doing things that are generally perceived to be morally wrong, even bad. We lie and we cheat, we break promises, disappoint those who rely on us, and hurt others to satisfy our own selfish desires. Whatever goodness we have in us, it clearly has its limits. We do of course condemn such behaviour, but we would not normally call any of these rather ordinary moral failures 'evil' (except perhaps in a religious context, where everything that runs counter to God's commands may be thought of as evil). Nor would we normally describe as evil many of the perhaps less ordinary acts that are punishable by law, such as tax evasion, dangerous driving, fraud or theft. We still think of such acts as wrong, and we may strongly disapprove of and even demand severe punishment for them. The attribute 'evil', however, we normally reserve for actions that we deem not just morally wrong,[3] but unacceptable in a different and more absolute way, as well as for the *people* who commit such acts.[4] Evil we call the mother who lets her children die of hunger as a punishment for their perceived sins, or the father who batters his children to death in one of his fits of rage. Evil we call the sex trafficker who forces vulnerable young people into prostitution for financial gain, and the serial killer who takes lives without remorse and enjoys the suffering he causes.

There is a strong connection here between what someone *does* and what they *are*.[5] An evil act, we tend to think, is the work of an evil person. Their actions define them because only someone who is evil would be capable of committing an evil act. Someone who is evil is rotten to the core. In contrast, bad (but not evil) things may be done by a (largely or in other respects) good person. We know we can do bad things out of weakness: because we are unable to resist temptation, because we let our (otherwise quite ordinary) desires get the better of us, because we don't think too much about the consequences of our actions. Evil, it seems to us, has a different source, and unless we are evil ourselves we feel incapable of doing things that are evil.

There is something about evil acts that defies our understanding.[6] This is what makes it a problem. We can understand the thief and the tax dodger as we can understand the liar and the adulterer. We understand why they are doing what they are doing. We understand their motives, what drives them. We understand them because those motives are not alien to us. We recognise them as our own even though we may choose not to act on them, perhaps because we have moral principles that we do not wish to violate or because we have enough imagination to realise how much hurt our actions will cause to others, but those we call evil we feel we cannot understand. We don't recognise us in them, or perhaps we refuse to. Deeply disturbed, we wonder how anyone can do such a thing to another human being, how such a thing is possible. We feel that it should be beyond what we are capable of doing, and yet those actions prove that it is not. Evil shatters the common human bond that we share with others, including many of those who transgress the law or the demands of morality. The bad we understand, but evil acts shock and disturb us. They shatter our confidence in the world. They make us doubt the very humanity of those who commit them. Evil acts are 'unspeakable' acts: acts that are so bad that we can hardly find words to describe them. They make us speechless. The bad we can forgive, but evil is unforgivable.[7]

*

Alexander Badman-King: I think you are right to draw this distinction between the 'common or garden variety of bad' and 'evil', and you are also right to locate this 'evil' in something deeply, consummately and unspeakably bad. But I also wonder if the 'problem of evil', which we still seem to retain even after disposing of any supposedly benevolent king of the universe, has something to do with this speechlessness which evil provokes, and whether we might find some continuity with both 'common bads' and the old problem of evil. What I mean here is that there seems to be something in this reaction to evil, something in this sense of speechlessness that reflects the way in which evil is somehow fundamentally alien to the world, that the way in which it shouldn't be is dramatic and, through this degree of dissonance, undermines our sense of the world in a piercing way. I wonder also if this violent disjunction from our normal world creates a sense of impotence, of being at a loss and in some way thrown into a scenario with something which is so different from the world we know that we are left adrift, powerless.[8]

I think this sense of shocking dissonance shares a great deal with the older problem of evil, and we can do without the cartoonish metaphysics of a cosmic lord and still retain this problem. We do need to be careful here about how we are using the word 'problem', because the traditional sense of 'problem of evil' uses 'problem' to mean 'logical inconsistency', and there is obviously nothing logically inconsistent in the kind of dissonance from which our speechlessness might stem: we are not speechless for having been caught out in a mistake in our argument.[9] But even before academics start to point out the philosophical problems which that religious account might have, we can reflect upon another kind of problem, something we might think of as almost pre-logical. Maybe this is still an issue of inconsistency, but it is a broader or more aesthetic sense of inconsistency, in the way that a bad note stands out in a piece of music, or the wrong word in a poem.[10] And I think we can reflect upon the way people tell themselves stories – stories they tell themselves every day just by living their lives. And even an everyday story without a god, a story well furnished with common or garden bad things, can be shattered by the introduction of events and characters so dark and terrible that they scramble the sense of meaning and continuity that our stories otherwise grant us. And I think that we should also recognise, in our use of the word 'problem', that some problems like these broken stories don't have solutions.

I also think that our 'godless' problem of evil has even more problems than the old problem (that's lots of problems), because we need to better understand the way in which it does or does not represent a continuity with the common or garden bad things. You are right to locate evil in those acts of extreme cruelty which you have given, and not in the many acts of neglect, selfishness, mischief or even malice that we witness very frequently, and you are also right to identify the evilness of these acts as closely related to the evilness of those who commit the acts. But I also think we might be dealing with a complex set of evils here, some of which might admit to greater continuity with our 'common bads', and some of which might be less to do with the evilness of the person committing them.

Maybe your four examples could be helpful again here: the punishing mother, raging father, greedy sex trafficker and sadistic murderer. Perhaps we would want to introduce the suggestion here that some, if not all, of these monsters admit to elements of continuity with our common bads. The raging father, as extreme and repugnant as his ferocious violence is, seems to be acting with a psychology which is common to many acts of violent anger. Is it then only the extremity of the act which means we can call it evil?[11] I suspect that the greedy sex trafficker might represent an even more plausible point of continuity, because we can imagine this character as rarely being directly involved in acts of violence, and their evil seems to stem from a willingness to turn a blind eye to the suffering of others in order that they might profit by that suffering. I don't think we need to look far for very mild instances of this kind of wilful neglect (any time we purchase a non-fairtrade coffee for instance). Perhaps one reason that instances of genocide evoke such horror in us is that we can see so many otherwise normal people co-operating in such obviously evil activities.[12] And I think this would be a fair use of the term 'evil': even if many of the participants seem to be normal sorts of people, the acts themselves might be described as evil.

Perhaps the sadistic murderer and the punishing mother give us something else. To my mind, there is something in these cases which represents a point of departure. When I imagine looking into the eyes of these people, seeing their faces at the moment of their heinous crimes, there is something there which seems, more than anything else, deserving of the name 'evil'. I am partly tempted to say that what we see there is an absence – a lack of something, a void of conscience, a void of common feeling for those they are harming – but actually I think there might be something else, something active: a presence. It is there most of all in that sadistic killer; unlike the raging father there is no heat in the motivation here. It is a cold, low, steady flame, but it delights in horror, in pain, in suffering, in that which it can recognise to be wrong. It does not act out of ignorance – indeed it is acutely aware of each and every detail of the damage it does, and it delights in that damage. At the deepest point of that cold flame there is, just like the old problem of evil, something contradictory: there is someone who recognises the evil of their act and it is that evil itself which motivates them; the wrongness is somehow the thing which drives them and, in being so driven, they invert the way motivation should work. Maybe this is, once again, a difference of degree, and still shares something with our common bads, or maybe this inversion of motivation does represent a dramatic disjunction from our usual stories, and it is some element of this cold flame which infects all that we call evil.

*

Michael Hauskeller: I have never seen this cold flame in somebody's eyes, this absence that is also a presence. I have never directly experienced evil in action, never met a person that I thought was evil. I have only ever read about acts that I would consider genuinely evil, or acts that somebody has denounced as evil, and I have of course seen photographs of people who are widely considered to be or have been evil. The 'Moors murderers', Myra Hindley and Ian Brady,[13] come to mind, which I suspect may have a lot to do with the fact that their well-known mugshots seem to capture their alleged evilness so perfectly. Looking at those pictures, at those eyes, you really feel as if you are looking into an abyss, as if there is nothing there that you could possibly connect with, only a chilling emptiness (and in Hindley's case perhaps also defiance). But I suppose that most of us could be made to look like psychopaths in the right circumstances.[14] A picture can be misleading. Even Hindley and Brady may look quite harmless in other photographs. It is also easy to project what we know about someone into their features. Then again, the American serial killer Ted Bundy,[15] who raped, killed and dismembered 30 women, keeping the heads of some of his victims as trophies, was by all accounts a very handsome and charming man, and looking at *his* picture, it is hard to believe that someone who looks so nice and so much like an all-American college boy could have been so depraved. Evil is not always written into people's faces. Often it is hidden away, cunningly waiting for the right opportunity to reveal itself.

Of course it may still be the case that the evil in question, even when it is not immediately visible, is something like your cold flame, which is both an absence and a presence. In a similar vein, St Augustine, wrestling with the traditional problem of evil, declared evil to be nothing, but his nothing was also a something, at least to the extent that people feel attracted to it.[16] Augustine worked on the premise that since everything has been created by God and God is good, everything that exists must be good too. So if there is something bad in the universe, it cannot be something, or at least not something positive. It must be an absence, namely the absence of being, which is nothing, or nothingness. And yet it is not nothingness itself that is evil, but the attraction that it has for us, or in other words the perversity of the human will. Evil comes into the world through our failure to love the right things: it is there every time we prefer what is less real to what is more real, every time we have a greater love for what is not than for what is.

Augustine thought that this perversion of the will that is the essence of evil was at work even in what we would probably see as minor infractions. In his *Confessions*[17] he describes how as a young boy he and some friends raided somebody else's pear tree, not because they were hungry or because the pears on that tree were particularly delicious, but for no good reason at all. In fact, most of what they stole they gave to the pigs because they had no other use for it. For Augustine, this is a paradigmatic case of evil precisely because the whole thing was so unnecessary. There was no benefit to the children except for the fun they were having stealing the fruit. But what they enjoyed about it was not the pears. What they enjoyed was the fact that they were *stealing* them – that, knowing quite well that it was wrong to do so, they did it anyway, not despite their knowledge that it was wrong, but *because* it was wrong. It was the transgression itself that they were attracted to.

Augustine's analysis of his own former self's actions as a paradigmatic case of evil chimes well with what you said earlier about the wrongness itself being a motivating factor (perhaps even the *primary* motivating factor) in what we tend to see as evil acts. And although I find it difficult to consider the young Augustine's actions evil, I can see how there might indeed be some continuity between our ordinary moral failures and what we call evil. Perhaps we have all, as Christian belief has it, fallen from grace – perhaps we all, to varying degrees, have this darkness in us, this emptiness, this nothingness, or some desire and longing for it.[18] Perhaps we all have the capacity to delight in destruction for the sake of destruction, in transgression for the sake of transgression, and while most of us manage to contain those darker nihilistic impulses, those we call evil simply give free rein to them.

I am wondering, though, whether evil always requires a sense of deliberate transgression: whether an evil act is always, at least in part, motivated by the knowledge that it *is* evil. Would it be wrong, then, to call an action that is driven entirely by, say, greed or lust or envy evil?[19] What if we do something really bad, not because it is bad, but because we regard it as necessary to get what we want, like perhaps the sex trafficker? What if we commit a heinous act because we are so enraged that we lose all control over ourselves, like perhaps the father who batters his child to death? What if it never occurs to us that what we are doing is wrong, like perhaps the mother who starves her children to punish them for their alleged misdeeds? There may be those who delight in evil for its own sake, but there are also those who do evil without being aware of it. Not all bad guys know that they are the bad guys, and some of the most evil acts may be committed by people who think of themselves as good.[20]

*

Alexander Badman-King: Perhaps a cold flame in the depths of the eyes is too dramatic and visual a way to imagine the flavour of this psychology, and I too am certainly fortunate enough never to have seen such demons in the flesh. And while I am also highly sympathetic to the Augustinian way of theorising evil as anything which is anti-good, I am more concerned that in that way of thinking we will lose the insight of your initial identification of something special in the way we use the word 'evil' to refer to certain extreme cases. Images, imagined or real, can certainly be misleading, but so can the temptation to have elegant and comprehensive theories.

I certainly think it is worth giving some room to the possibility that evil events or acts which are committed by people who are corrupt in a common or garden sense (the sex trafficker or even the dictator who thinks himself a saviour) do share something in common with the kind of evil which I have spoken of in terms of that cold flame – the evil which not only does wrong for the sake of doing wrong (which would need to include those childhood scrumpers), but which delights in the most extreme forms of wrongness. Maybe we are stretching things too far if we try to divorce this use of the term 'evil' from those children stealing fruit, and perhaps it is enough to find the core of the concept in just that motivation towards something bad for the reason that it is bad; Augustine might have done enough here. On the other hand, it is entirely possible that our temptation to use the term 'evil' to describe those 'cold-flame' cases and even extreme acts which are committed from other motivations (greed, rage, ill-conceived politics) is conceptually misleading.

Sensationalised images and elegant theories can lead us astray, but so too can the temptation to identify a moral concept with a use of language. It may be that the use of the term 'evil' amounts to not much more than saying something is 'very, very bad'. But I would hesitate to embrace this brand of explaining the problem away by identifying a potentially misleading use of language.[21] Identifying that kind of language problem might be helpful, but there may yet be something which the extreme cases (acts or motivations) share, something more than extremity, something conceptual which we might fairly identify as evil. And my temptation is to pursue the way in which both evil acts and evil motivations cause the kind of 'story breaking' which I previously mentioned. Can we find a way of talking (perhaps not in terms of 'story breaking' or 'cold flames') which allows us to identify and describe the common conceptual element beyond extremity?

There is a potential role here for very, very bad things which happen and which are not caused by people. We wouldn't call a volcano or a storm evil, and we would also struggle to describe the acts of other animals as evil.[22] We might even find it inappropriate to call climate change evil even when it is caused by humans, and it is hard to imagine anything more extremely bad than the destruction of entire ecosystems, species and millions or even billions of human lives. So what divides the concentration camp guards and the sex traffickers from those of us who drive the entire living world to destruction? Perhaps it is the way that the actions which seem to be driving climate change are, in some sense, 'natural', 'normal' or 'mundane': which is to say that, sadly, these actions (eating meat, driving cars, buying stuff and then some more stuff) and the motivations behind those actions seem natural to the human animal. Perhaps it is that these creatures are following appetites and inclinations which are themselves not extreme, and that it is only circumstances, technology and population that allow them to cause such destruction. Maybe this is why we won't describe the behaviour of the wolf or the volcano as evil (they are just doing what wolves and volcanos do). And is there a sense, then, that the concentration camp guards, and the sex trafficker, though individually driven by mundane or common motivations, are involved in something which has somehow gone wildly off-track, and perhaps this shares something with what we see in the 'cold flame' psychology (the motivation based on extreme badness) of the sadistic murderers? In all these cases it is not necessarily the extremity of the bad which makes them evil, but the combination of extreme badness and something uncannily alien to normal life.[23]

*

Michael Hauskeller: What defines normal life, though? Can evil not become frighteningly normal at certain periods in a country's history? Are those periods abnormal, then, and if yes, in relation to what? And is evil not natural to us in the sense that we, as humans, clearly have the capacity for it, in stark contrast to volcanoes and wolves?[24] Among all the things we know, living and non-living, it seems that only we humans have this capacity. Volcanoes cannot be evil because they have no will of their own. They don't even act: there is no 'they' that could act. Unlike living things, a volcano is not a distinct entity, something apart. Wolves on the other hand are, but we still don't normally consider them evil. However, I don't think this is because killing other living things comes naturally to them, because this is what they do, as the kind of beings that they are. Rather, wolves and other animal predators don't strike us as evil because there is no *malice* in what they do. They may destroy lives, but they don't *aim* at destruction. On the contrary, what they aim at (or what their actions aim at) is the preservation of life, primarily their own individual life, but also that of those who depend on them and ultimately their kind. Evil is, as Augustine said, a perversion (literally: a turning-about) of the will; it delights in destruction for the sake of destruction (the destruction of order, of beauty, of goodness), in dissonance, disruption and disjunction, in transforming something into nothing. It gains rapture out of rupture. It delights, if you will, in the breaking of stories, if stories are ways of making sense of what happens in life. Evil is senseless.

However, I fear that this conception of evil, compelling as it may be, may ultimately capture only one aspect or perhaps one particular kind of evil. It describes evil at its most conspicuous. Let us call this kind, for now, *primary evil*. Both the serial killer and the pear-stealing boy may partake in primary evil, and the difference between them is perhaps simply that what the killer is willing to destroy is of much greater value than what the boy destroys and while many of us are quite capable of wanton acts of destruction when it comes to things of minor value, only very few of us are prepared to go so far as to destroy what we regard as most valuable. It is those extreme forms of primary evil, where what is destroyed is of the greatest value, that we are most likely, in our ordinary discourse, to call evil. We may see this kind of evil as a problem because it so clearly is something that ought not to be, tearing, as it were, holes in the fabric of the world. But in another, more practical sense it is not such a huge problem for us because, fortunately, the more extreme forms of primary evil are rather rare: neither you nor I, we admitted, have ever knowingly come across it personally.

Yet there is another, derivative form of evil, which we may want to call *secondary evil* and which is much more common and for that reason perhaps also far more dangerous than the other sort. While primary evil is rooted in the will of people, secondary evil is structural. It is not tied to the will of any one individual. Rather, it survives and flourishes in certain institutions we create as well as in the failure to create certain other institutions.[25] It manifests in what we allow to happen – what we enable, what we do not care about enough to prevent – and in what we do ourselves without thinking too much about it and without intending any harm. It feeds on our indifference, inertia and complacency, our desire to stay on the winning side and to not get involved, our cowardice. We may thus find practices or institutions that are widely regarded – and rightly so – as profoundly evil even though none of those responsible for creating and upholding them would strike us as particularly bad, let alone evil. Think, if you wish, of the ongoing destruction of our environment or the rapid erosion of democratic structures and institutions that is currently taking place in the US and many parts of Europe. Think, if this makes it easier to contemplate the idea, of slavery, colonialism or racial discrimination. Aristotle thought slavery was part of the natural order of things,[26] Kipling cited the 'white man's burden' to justify British imperialism,[27] and Darwin thought that black people were, in terms of their evolutionary development, closer to the apes than to white Europeans.[28] Were they all evil? I don't think they were. But what they justified and to that extent also contributed to may well have been.

Quite often evil seems to be what we end up with when otherwise decent people don't care enough to put up a fight. Hannah Arendt, reporting from the Adolf Eichmann trial in Jerusalem in 1961, was struck by the 'banality of evil' that she found exemplified in Eichmann, a leading Nazi who organised the deportation of Jews to concentration camps in Eastern Europe during World War Two.[29] Whether Arendt was right about Eichmann is beside the point. The important insight here is that those who are responsible or co-responsible for the most evil deeds may turn out to be very unremarkable people who don't fit the image of a devil in human form that the rhetoric of evil tends to evoke in us. People who are not themselves evil can be agents of evil. They don't have to delight in destruction for destruction's sake. They don't even have to be particularly greedy, lecherous or irascible, or indulge in any other vices. They can help create and sustain evil simply by doing their job and wanting to do it well.[30]

*

Alexander Badman-King: Some philosophers have been tempted to describe these structures and collective systems to which you ascribe secondary evil in a way which is at least analogous to individuals, and maybe that is helpful.[31] What I mean here is that we might similarly be tempted to suggest that the reason evil seems to be a useful term in both collective systems and individuals is that a similar thing is happening in both situations. Is there something other than *very bad things* which both primary and secondary evils are doing? Is extremity of badness the only thing which these secondary and primary senses have in common?

You have suggested that a capacity for evil seems to be a uniquely human thing, and in both primary (individual) and secondary (systemic) evil this would hold true, but it is still tricky to see what is behind any distinction between volcanoes, wolves and the secondary sense of evil. Yes, humans are responsible for the secondary, systemic, social sense of evil: greed, cowardice, mistaken politics, and other small errors can accumulate to produce truly evil events and situations; but are we justified in our intuition that volcanoes and genocide are conceptually and morally distinct? Volcanoes might be the easy case here because, as you say, they are not persons – they have no will in the matter, and so we might suggest that evil cannot be attributed to the outcomes of inanimate processes. I would say, then, that it is more helpful to imagine a scenario involving a non-human predator: wolves, or maybe foxes or dogs.

Very often I am told stories about chicken massacres carried out by foxes (clearly, I move in peculiarly fowled circles). The reaction people have to these mass killings is, I think, quite revealing about the way people think about evil. These reports are offered to emphasise the fact that the fox did not kill just one chicken (because this would be almost forgivable) but killed *all* of the chickens and left their corpses behind. These conversations often turn to how this killing beyond need seems to bring the fox into the realm of evil, which should, we suppose, be an exclusively human preserve. As it happens, given half a chance foxes do often return for the corpses and then bury them for winter (they are usually scared away before they can finish the job) but it isn't a stretch of the imagination to conjure a scenario in which the actions of a non-human predator cannot be justified in terms of being aimed at self-preservation or the preservation of their kin.[32] Sadly, cases of dogs attacking sheep are not uncommon and there is no sense here in which these dogs are aiming at sustenance. In the heat of the moment I very much doubt that the dog (or the fox, or most other animals) is killing with any particular 'aim' at all: they are simply compelled to slaughter.

These animals are driven by inclinations, by juices in their veins, which are not very different from the sorts of motivations driving the humans in some of our cases of evil. I suspect that the raging father could certainly fit into this category, and all sorts of acts of murder and rape might belong in this category too, but even if true (cold-flame) malice is foreign to these creatures (and I think that is a fair assumption), our secondary evil still gives us problems. Mundane, banal motivations: cowardice, tribalism, greed – these lesser moral failures which collectively drive humans to secondary evil – don't seem to have any special quality which should separate them from the wild dog's unthinking slaughter. So is there anything else?

I think that perhaps Augustine's scrumping children might still have something more to offer here. They don't fit the special sense of evil with which we are working here (you have said already that your house guest's betrayal didn't fit the bill, and I think you're right), but you have suggested that they (and we might also imagine your guest) would only go so far. Perhaps the uniquely human thing about evil is that humans can have the capacity (we might say that they *should* have the capacity) to be sensitive to the extremity of badness. When the rampaging dog creates terrible carnage we cannot call it evil because we don't have any sense in which it has failed to be responsive to good and evil; but when a society fails to recognise the evil it is committing, even when it is composed entirely of people we would not describe as evil, we have a sense of a collective failure to be sensitive to something which is inherently compelling.[33] The extreme badness falls on deaf ears in the case of both the 'cold-flame' murderer and the genocidal prison guards. The scrumping children, like the murderer, are compelled by badness, but I think you are right to suggest that were the badness more extreme they would be repelled by it (not so the murderer). When we call the acts of a group of otherwise good people 'evil', when we talk about secondary evil, perhaps we have this same sense of failure to respond to extremity – a sense that our moral sensitivity is deficient.

I don't think I would necessarily want to reduce evil to this failure to be repelled by extreme badness. I suspect there is something complex happening with this phenomenon of evil which is probably a mixture of the failure to be repelled and the other possibilities we have touched on: the sheer extremity of the badness, Augustine's inclination to act for badness' sake and against goodness' sake, the story-breaking dissonance of unspeakable wrongs, images of cold-flame madness, and also, perhaps, the way in which our talking about these things uses language which tends to overlap in untidy ways that don't correspond precisely to concepts.

*

Michael Hauskeller: I suppose it is possible for non-human animals to be evil. We can easily imagine a dog that has been trained to be highly aggressive and a ruthless killer. A dog like this, a dog that has found its purpose in the destruction of other lives and that derives satisfaction from doing so, may rightly be called evil, at least as we commonly understand it. We do not normally think that evil can be found only where there is a clear understanding of the difference between right and wrong, good and bad, and a deliberate decision to pursue the latter rather than the former (Augustine's perversion of the will). Among all living beings that we have knowledge of, only humans seem to be capable of this particular perversion because only we have the conceptual resources for it. But evil (even what I earlier called 'primary evil') does not seem to require any of this if the way we commonly represent evil is anything to go by. We are, after all, used to depicting evil in non-human form as a kind of quasi-animal or 'beast' that is hell-bent on destroying us. We call such beasts 'monsters'.

Monsters are our preferred fictional incarnation of evil because not only *are* they evil, they also *look* the part, with their (typically) fiery eyes, razor-sharp claws and over-long teeth.[34] Yet the monster is a monster not because it has deliberately, in an act of free choice, turned its back on the good (notwithstanding the fact that this is precisely what the most famous monster in literature – Mary Shelley's monster of Frankenstein[35] – does; Shelley's so-called monster is not much of a monster as we understand it today). The most monstrous monster (representing the purest evil) is one that has no conception whatsoever of the good, one whose whole *being* is oriented towards wreaking havoc, maiming, hurting and killing. In the monster, the sheer will to destruction has become flesh, unhindered by reflection or by any possibility, however remote, of making a different choice and acting differently. 'I am the spirit that negates,' declares Mephistopheles in Goethe's *Faust*, 'and rightly so, for all that comes to be deserves to perish wretchedly.'[36] Total negation is the very essence of that spirit, which, for Goethe, is the spirit of evil.

Humans are not normally like this, and neither are non-human animals. We are certainly no strangers to malice, the desire to inflict harm on others – but we usually have a good reason, or think we do, and we are almost always motivated by other things as well. Those other motives make us less of a monster than we would otherwise be. And non-human animals are even less likely to be monsters in that way. They are less likely to be driven by pure malice. It is worth keeping in mind that the evil dog imagined above has been *turned* evil by human actions. It was not born that way. I suppose that in most cases evil animals are human creations. Predators are not normally evil; they simply do what they have to do in order to survive, without malice. As for the fox you mentioned, I don't know what drives him to kill more chickens than he can possibly eat. For all I know there is indeed some kind of murderous frenzy that overcomes him when he manages to get himself into a well-filled chicken run. But I still find it difficult to see the fox as evil, not because he has no clear conception of good and evil, but because he is not a monster, which is to say that he is not driven by malice, and malice is not what defines him. His intention is not to harm and inflict pain, to destroy what is good and beautiful – just as this is not our intention either when we have animals in their billions killed to provide food for us without worrying too much about how much is being wasted in the process, or how many of the deaths we cause are really not necessary at all. We are predators, too, ruthless and by and large uncaring, and the suffering and number of deaths caused by our predatory habits is immense. Yet because we mean no harm and just want to live our lives in peace and comfort we are not evil, at least not in the primary sense. In that sense, we are as innocent as non-human predators and can still think of ourselves as good people.

However, there is a difference between us and non-human animals, which is that we can actually see and understand the consequences of what we are doing. This is where secondary evil comes in. Secondary evil, as I understand it, does not consist directly in the damage done, even if there is a great amount of such damage. That is why there is no evil in the suffering and the deaths caused by natural disasters or by non-human animals. This is not to say that the suffering and the deaths in question should not concern us. They are no doubt bad. But the bad that has occurred on those occasions as a consequence of a certain kind of (non-human) behaviour has not been permitted to occur by someone who was able to foresee the consequences of their actions. None of the agents or quasi-agents involved knew any better, or even had the cognitive and moral capacity to do so. It is different for us. When we allow bad things to happen, we do know better, or at least could have known better.

We have what it takes to know better. We have the ability both to make a causal connection between what we do or fail to do and the bad that results from it, and to understand that what results from it is indeed bad. And if we don't act accordingly – if we still let it happen, if we choose to turn a blind eye and deafen our ears, not out of malice, but out of indifference, carelessness or negligence – then we are at least co-responsible for it. We are culpable because we choose to ignore what we, being what we are, *should* not ignore – because of our failure to be properly responsive to the bad that we allow to happen.[37] And it is this moral failure that transforms what would otherwise be merely bad into an evil.

*

Alexander Badman-King: It is perhaps ironic that we began this discussion by confronting a phenomenon which was, at least in part, defined as something which leaves us speechless; yet we have, after a fashion, spoken of it. Of course, 'speechless' needn't mean that we are doomed never to fathom this thing. It means that this thing, this evil, has a kind of dumbfounding impact, but I think we have shown how a process of philosophical discussion can lead to a kind of coming to terms with evil. It may be that evil does indeed display a complex array of characteristics which orbit around extreme badness, but I think that perhaps you and I have come to some agreement that an expected human capacity to correctly recognise the weight of badness in an event is particularly important for being able to call something evil.

I can't help but wonder if this raises yet another problem of evil. You speak of the way 'we', us humans, have – or at least should have – a capacity to correctly recognise and respond appropriately to extremity of badness. But I am left wondering who we should be including in this 'we'. Doubtless we are not including infants, or those who suffer from serious mental impairment, but what about the rest of us? Is there a threshold of sensitivity which enables us to belong to this group who are expected to recognise and respond to extreme badness?[38] You also offered a description of humans as being very much like other predatory animals and suggested that, for this reason, they should not be viewed as evil. I am inclined to agree, but is it only a lack of malice which means that the massive destruction of life by humans is not to be counted as evil (in the second, collective sense)? Perhaps the lack of responsiveness to extreme badness which we have identified as a core characteristic of both primary and secondary evil is also a reason for not labelling all of these people evil. In cases of human genocide we imagine that the plight of fellow humans being slaughtered should be sufficiently obvious to penetrate the moral awareness of almost everyone, but perhaps the plight of other living things is something which requires a greater sensitivity to evil. And if a sensitivity to the extremities of badness is something which comes in degrees, do those who have greater sensitivity also have a greater chance of being evil?[39]

Of course, one might suggest that the reason secondary evil is not applicable in cases of animal farming or environmental destruction is that these things are less extremely bad than genocide.[40] Let us suppose, though, that this massive destruction of non-human life does belong in the category of things bad enough to be called evil (I think that if we imagine an individual causing this destruction for the joy of it, we won't hesitate to describe them as evil in the primary sense, and that should be some justification).[41] Then why do we not expect every human to recognise and respond appropriately to this badness? Well, I suppose some of us do have such an expectation; many conservation charities or vegan activists probably would describe this human activity as evil, and perhaps they imagine that the badness here is so obvious that only a collective moral disease, a subconscious yet wilful social blindness, of the kind which infects genocidal or racist societies, could prevent humans from correctly recognising this badness. But maybe this blindness is not something foreign to humanity, not a disease, but simply the usual limit of its sight. Where would this leave those who can see further?

These thoughts are bleak, but I would suggest not terminally so. Perhaps it doesn't matter if this blindness is a malady or innate; it might be put right either way. And there may be some hope in the effort we have made here to speak of that which leaves us speechless. I've said that we have, in a sense, come to terms with evil, and I would like to imagine that doing so is part of something which might be described as progress. Certainly, I wouldn't want to suggest that societies inexorably (even if irregularly) grow more sensitive to evil – history seems to be too ready with evidence of frequent collapses for that to be true – but perhaps we humans are capable of at least brief pockets of moral progress. The past and present are replete with examples of collective evil being defeated, and although these victories may be local and limited, I am tempted to say that there is some truth in the idea that things like universal suffrage, the abolition of slavery, human rights and indeed animal rights show something like an improvement in our collective sensitivity to evil. And I think philosophy has a role to play in that process.[42]

I sometimes think that one of the main jobs of philosophy is to be sensitive to evil: to be vigilant, to stretch our minds out into the darkness and find the demons lurking there. It is tempting to imagine that then, like mad folk, we might have to go about the marketplace proclaiming doom, and calling for the wicked to renounce their evil ways (it may be that some vegan activism ends up a bit like this).[43] But a more moderate version might still have philosophy as a process of warning, whereby those in our societies who are sensitive to evil have an obligation to offer guidance, and to introduce the beginnings of change. Faust summons Mephistopheles for his own benefit,[44] but there might be ways that we can and should conjure demons for the greater good. To wrestle with unspeakable evil, to find the right words to describe it, to explore its possible forms and real manifestations, to find how deeply it suffuses our own souls, seem like important steps for illuminating that darkness which might otherwise go unnoticed. The first step towards defeating evil is to know its name.

Notes

1. For comprehensive critical discussions see for instance van Inwagen, *The Problem of Evil* and Tooley, *The Problem of Evil*.
2. Different ways of distinguishing moral and physical evil are discussed by Wallace, 'The problems of moral and physical evil'.
3. My view here clearly differs from the views of those who have argued that 'evil' just means something like 'very, very wrong'. See for instance Russell, 'Is evil action qualitatively distinct from ordinary wrongdoing?'. Among those who see evil as a distinct category, not to be captured by a particularly high degree of wrongness, are Garrard ('Evil as an explanatory concept'), Haybron ('Moral monsters and saints') and Calder ('Is evil just very wrong?').
4. See Barry, *Evil and Moral Psychology*.
5. See Singer, 'The concept of evil'.
6. That being said, we should still try to understand it as best we can because it is difficult to combat (and easy to glorify) that which we cannot make sense of. For the importance and possibility of understanding evil see Formosa, 'Understanding evil acts'.
7. For a critical discussion of this claim see Norlock, 'Evil and forgiveness'.
8. I'm certainly drawing here on many ideas which have been expressed in relation to acts of great evil. Perhaps most significant is Hannah Arendt's famous reflections on the trial of Adolf Eichmann. Of course, when Arendt reflects upon that final 'lesson of the fearsome, word-and-thought-defying banality of evil' she intends primarily to describe the way in which normal people can do vile things, but it is this contrast between normality and horror which grants this description of evil its power. That baffling dissonance is really what I am getting at here.
9. It is worth recognising that Paul Prescott ('The secular problem of evil') has gone to some lengths to argue that atheists suffer from a very similar (practically identical) problem of evil to theists. Prescott suggests that both theist and atheist alike must deny the existence of evil (or the badness of the world) to retain the cohesion of their worldview. And yet, not only is Prescott not focusing on the quite distinctly extreme kind of evil which we are focusing on (Prescott is concerned with a broader range of badness), he also hinges this thesis on a particular idea of a successful human being and a Camus-inspired 'enabling world' (110–12) – things which I am not willing to invoke.
10. It would certainly be fair to describe this as being a form of moral sentimentalism, though I would dispute any suggestion that this necessarily sets it against any and all forms of moral rationalism. Michael Gill ('Moral rationalism vs. moral sentimentalism', 22–5) gives a nice sense of the history of that dispute (drawing on the analogies of mathematics and beauty – which one is morality most like?), but my suggestion here is not meant to commit to an idea of morality as necessarily irrational.

11. It may be tempting to describe this not as 'extremity' but as 'pathology' and frame evil in terms of mental illness. For the purposes of what I am discussing here, that line of thought would be a distraction. I am inclined to agree with Mike Martin when he suggests that pathology does not absolve one who commits acts of evil (*Morality to Mental Health*, 121–2). Martin draws an analogy between the absolution of sociopathic violence and the absolution of lesser, common wrongdoing on the same biological basis (just less extreme). Why should the extremity alter the reasoning so dramatically? Aren't our own actions usually influenced heavily by biological factors beyond our control? And even to state this begs questions about control and 'free will' which stretch far beyond the remit of this conversation. Suffice to say that if anyone is to be held accountable for anything, there's a good deal of room to say that those guilty of extreme evil might be similarly judged.
12. Here is an even more explicit point of contact with Arendt's work on the 'banality of evil'.
13. https://en.wikipedia.org/wiki/Moors_murders (accessed 1 December 2021).
14. In a recently published interview in *Philosophy Now*, they used a photo of me that, as one reader commented, makes me look like a serial killer, which it does indeed. (Just in case there's any doubt, I'm not.)
15. https://www.biography.com/crime-figure/ted-bundy (accessed 1 December 2021).
16. See for instance *Confessions*, Book 7, chapters 11–13. For a comprehensive discussion of Augustine's conception of evil and its development see Evans, *Augustine on Evil*.
17. Augustine, *Confessions*, Book 2, chapters 9–14.
18. In support of this idea see for instance Kekes, *Facing Evil*, 126, and McGinn, *Ethics, Evil and Fiction*, 82. In opposition see Scarre, 'Can evil attract?'.
19. For a collection of readings that show how varied the sources and forms of evil actually are see Rorty, *The Many Faces of Evil*.
20. The claim that we all want what we want 'under the guise of the good' has been much discussed in the philosophical literature. I'm not convinced this is always the case – as discussed before, evil does seem to have its own attraction – but very often it is. See Anscombe, *Intention*, 70–1. For critical discussions of this view see Velleman, 'The guise of the good' and Orsi, 'guise of the good'.
21. Phillip Cole is a prominent sceptic when it comes to the usefulness of the concept of evil. In *The Myth of Evil* he suggests that, no matter whether it is in relation to people's characters (they are an evil person) or the consequences of actions (an evil set of events), the description of 'evil' 'doesn't seem to add anything to our understanding . . . or if it does, it seems to be some kind of mythological added factor that we can do without in our account' (7).
22. I am not denying the ability of non-human animals to do morally bad things, nor morally good things (Mark Rowlands argues for a form of non-human moral behaviour in *Can Animals be Moral?*).
23. My suggestions here mirror, in some ways, the suggestions of Paul Formosa in 'A conception of evil', where he asks 'why we should stop at just intention and motive. Might not other factors be relevant to our assessment of an evil act? There are indeed a number of factors that are relevant, but neither necessary nor sufficient, for judging an act to be evil. These factors include: the directedness of the perpetrator's intention; the type and strength of the motive; the effect the harmful action has on the perpetrator; the degree and nature of the harm intended; the nature of the situation in which the act was undertaken; and the details of the perpetrator's circumstances. While all these factors are relevant, they are not uniformly relevant in all cases. In different cases different sets of factors may be more or less relevant' (224). Ultimately there is a kind of Wittgensteinian family resemblance which I am using around the concept of evil whereby there are many possible things which contribute to something being evil, some more core to evilness than others (for Wittgenstein's seminal reflections on conceptual similarities see *Philosophical Investigations*, Part 1: 66–7).
24. That far from being the exception, evil is the normal (although pathological) state for humans has been argued by, among others, Bartlett, *The Pathology of Man*.
25. See Pleasants, 'Institutional wrongdoing and moral perception'.
26. Aristotle, *Politics*, 1254b, 16–21.
27. Kipling, 'The white man's burden'.
28. Darwin, *The Descent of Man*, 201.
29. Arendt, *Eichmann in Jerusalem*.
30. See Browning's classic case study *Ordinary Men*.

31. This personal-collective microcosm-macrocosm is as old as the hills, but as usual it can be traced to Plato's *Republic* (368d–369a).
32. Hans Kruuk's study of red foxes (*Vulpes vulpes*) killing gulls showed that while the foxes often hoarded the gulls' eggs, only very few of the actual birds killed were stored for later (meaning that the surplus killing was seemingly pointless). Kruuk makes similar observations of other predator species and their surplus killing in 'Surplus killing by carnivores', 234–5.
33. There's a significant extent to which this is drawing on Fischer and Ravizza's 'reasons-responsiveness' conception of moral responsibility (*Responsibility and Control*).
34. See Gilmore, *Monsters* for many examples.
35. Shelley, *Frankenstein*.
36. Goethe, *Faust*, 47.
37. See Smith, 'Culpable ignorance'.
38. I don't only mean biological variation here. It could also be variation caused by environmental factors. Susan Wolf's 'Jojo' (a child raised to be an evil tyrant) is an extreme thought experiment in this environmental mould ('Sanity and the metaphysics of responsibility').
39. Bendik-Keymer and Haufe apply Arendt's concept of banal evil directly to anthropogenic environmental destruction ('Anthropogenic mass extinction', 433).
40. Cora Diamond notably rejected any suggestion of the moral equivalence of human and non-human life, describing the arguments of Singer and Regan as being arguments for how 'knee-jerk liberals on racism and sexism ought to go knee-jerk about cows and guinea-pigs' ('Eating meat and eating people', 471).
41. It should also be noted that this environmental and climate destruction can also be described as the cause of massive loss of human life. It has been estimated that by 2030 climate change-related deaths will reach 700,000 (DARA, *Climate Vulnerability Monitor*).
42. By 'philosophy' I mean something similar to Pierre Hadot's 'philosophy as a way of life'. So this philosophy is not primarily an academic pursuit but, rather, a primarily ethical way of life more akin to a religion than to an academic discipline.
43. Maybe this reference to Nietzsche's Zarathustra is a bit unsophisticated and obvious, but there aren't many better 'mad men' in the history of philosophy; I am at least inclined to listen to those soapbox rants when they proclaim, 'I entreat you, my brothers, remain true to the earth, and do not believe those who speak to you of superterrestrial hopes!' (*Thus Spoke Zarathustra*, 42).
44. The definitive version of this classic tragedy is that of Goethe, and Goethe's Faust's tragic desire for knowledge makes it doubly appropriate here.

Bibliography

Anscombe, G. E. M. *Intention*. Cambridge, MA: Harvard University Press, 2000.
Arendt, Hannah. *Eichmann in Jerusalem: A report on the banality of evil*. Harmondsworth: Penguin, 1984.
Aristotle, *Politics*, translated by Ernest Barker. Oxford: Oxford University Press, 1995.
Augustine. *Confessions*, translated by Henry Chadwick. Oxford: Oxford University Press, 1991.
Barry, Peter Brian. *Evil and Moral Psychology*. London: Routledge, 2012.
Bartlett, Steven James. *The Pathology of Man: A study of human evil*. Springfield, IL: Charles C. Thomas, 2005.
Bendik-Keymer, Jeremy, and Chris Haufe. 'Anthropogenic mass extinction: the science, the ethics, and the civics'. In *The Oxford Handbook of Environmental Ethics*, edited by Stephen M. Gardiner and Allen Thompson, 427–37. Oxford: Oxford University Press, 2017.
Browning, Christopher R. *Ordinary Men. Reserve Police Battalion 101 and the Final Solution in Poland*. New York: Harper Perennial, revised edition 2017.
Calder, Todd. 'Is evil just very wrong?', *Philosophical Studies* 163 (2013): 177–96.
Cole, Phillip. *The Myth of Evil: Demonizing the enemy*. Westport, CT: Praeger, 2006.
DARA (Development Assistance Research Associates). *Climate Vulnerability Monitor*, 2nd edition 2012.
Darwin, Charles. *The Descent of Man*. London: John Murray, 1871.
Diamond, Cora. 'Eating meat and eating people', *Philosophy* 53/206 (1978): 465–79.
Evans, Gillian R. *Augustine on Evil*. Cambridge: Cambridge University Press, 1982.

Fischer, John Martin, and Mark Ravizza. *Responsibility and Control: A theory of moral responsibility.* Cambridge: Cambridge University Press, 1998.

Formosa, Paul. 'A conception of evil', *Journal of Value Inquiry* 42 (2008): 217–39.

Formosa, Paul. 'Understanding evil acts', *Human Studies* 30/2: 57–77.

Garrard, Eve. 'Evil as an explanatory concept', *The Monist* 85/2 (2002): 320–36.

Gill, Michael B. 'Moral rationalism vs. moral sentimentalism: is morality more like math or beauty?', *Philosophy Compass* 2 (2007): 16–30.

Gilmore, David D. *Monsters: Evil beings, mythical beasts, and all manner of imaginary terrors.* Philadelphia, PA: University of Pennsylvania Press, 2003.

Goethe, Johann Wolfgang von. *Faust.* Part One and sections from Part Two, translated by Walter Kaufmann. Garden City, NY: Anchor Books, 1963.

Hadot, Pierre. *Philosophy as a Way of Life*, translated by Michael Chase. Oxford: Blackwell, 1995.

Haybron, Daniel M. 'Moral monsters and saints', *The Monist* 85/2 (2002): 260–84.

Kekes, John. *Facing Evil.* Princeton, NJ: Princeton University Press, 1990.

Kipling, Rudyard. 'The white man's burden', *The Times*, 4 February 1899.

Kruuk, Hans. 'Surplus killing by carnivores', *Journal of Zoology* 166 (1972): 233–44.

McGinn, Colin. *Ethics, Evil and Fiction.* Oxford: Clarendon Press, 1997.

Martin, Mike. *Morality to Mental Health: Virtue and vice in a therapeutic culture.* Oxford: Oxford University Press, 2006.

Nietzsche, Friedrich. *Thus Spoke Zarathustra*, translated by R. J. Hollingdale. Harmondsworth: Penguin, 1967.

Norlock, Kathryn J. 'Evil and forgiveness'. In *The Routledge Handbook of the Philosophy of Evil*, edited by Thomas Nys and Stephen de Wijze, 282–93. New York: Routledge, 2019.

Orsi, Francesco. 'Guise of the good', *Philosophy Compass* 10/10 (2015): 714–24.

Plato. *Republic.* London: Harvard University Press, 2013.

Pleasants, Nigel. 'Institutional wrongdoing and moral perception', *Journal of Social Philosophy* 39/1 (2008): 96–115.

Precott, Paul. 'The secular problem of evil: an essay in analytic existentialism', *Religious Studies* 57/1 (2021): 101–19.

Rorty, Amelie (ed.). *The Many Faces of Evil: Historical perspectives.* London: Routledge, 2001.

Rowlands, Mark. *Can Animals Be Moral?* New York: Oxford University Press, 2012.

Russell, Luke. 'Is evil action qualitatively distinct from ordinary wrongdoing?', *Australasian Journal of Philosophy* 85/4 (2007): 659–77.

Scarre, Geoffrey. 'Can evil attract?', *Heythrop Journal* XLI (2000): 303–17.

Shelley, Mary. *Frankenstein.* London: Penguin Classics, 2003.

Singer, Marcus G. 'The concept of evil', *Philosophy* 79/2 (2004): 185–214.

Smith, Holly. 'Culpable ignorance', *The Philosophical Review* 92/4 (1983): 543–71.

Tooley, Michael. *The Problem of Evil.* Cambridge: Cambridge University Press, 2019.

van Inwagen, Peter. *The Problem of Evil. The Gifford Lectures delivered in the University of St Andrews in 2003.* Oxford: Oxford University Press, 2006.

Velleman, J. David. 'The guise of the good', *Noûs* 26/1 (1992): 3–26.

Wallace, G. 'The problems of moral and physical evil', *Philosophy* 46/178 (1971): 349–51.

Wittgenstein, Ludwig. *Philosophical Investigations*, translated by G. E. M. Anscombe. Oxford: Blackwell, 2001.

Wolf, Susan. 'Sanity and the metaphysics of responsibility'. In *Responsibility, Character, and the Emotions: New essays in moral psychology*, edited by Ferdinand David Schoeman, 46–62. Cambridge: Cambridge University Press, 1987.

9
Death

with Panayiota Vassilopoulou

Michael Hauskeller: When I was a little boy, I don't know how old exactly, perhaps five or six, there were many nights I couldn't sleep because I was so afraid of dying. I was also afraid that my parents might die (and eventually one of them did: my father, when I was nine), but that fear was of a different kind: it was the fear of being left alone in a world that I did not quite understand yet and that I felt unable to deal with by myself. I knew that something like that might happen, and it scared me quite a bit, but the fear that sometimes overcame me when I thought of my own death was much more intense and powerful. I was not just *afraid* of dying; I was *terrified*, so much so that I could hardly breathe, my chest being too tight and my heart beating too fast. I was in a panic, unable to sleep for hours. And it wasn't the *possibility* of dying that terrified me. I wasn't afraid that I might contract a deadly disease or get run over by a car, or for some other reason suffer a premature death. I didn't really expect to be dying anytime soon. What terrified me so much was the absolute *certainty* of my death – the fact that one day, however far in the future that day might be, I would cease to exist, and then never exist again. I don't know *how* I knew this. I guess that someone had told me that *everyone* dies, me included, but there must have been many other things I had been told that I was far less sure of. Yet for some reason, I never had any doubt that this particular bit of information was indeed correct and that there was not the slightest chance of me not dying. I simply *knew* that I was mortal, and I was overwhelmed and petrified by this knowledge.[1]

The terror that I felt had nothing to do with any views about what would happen to me after my death. My mother tried to raise me as a Catholic, making me study the Bible in Sunday school and regularly sending me to church to confess my sins, but none of this made much of an impression on me, except the claim that God sees everything – often repeated, for my personal benefit, by both my mother and the village priest who schooled me. This did not prevent me from doing things that I wasn't supposed to be doing, but it certainly instilled a sense of being watched in me. I may also have half-believed in heaven and hell, in the sense that I wasn't entirely sure that no such thing existed. My fear of death, however, was not affected by that. I did not fear ending up in hell. What I was terrified of was the idea of nothingness, for that is what I imagined death to be: the end of everything, an abyss that I would fall into, an eternal darkness swallowing me up, an emptiness so deep that there was no way I could possibly wrap my mind around it.[2] It was something that defied understanding, certainly *my* understanding – something that could not be, yet still was, a disturbing paradox at the heart of existence.[3]

This was a long time ago. Being much older now and therefore much closer to death, I no longer feel the same terror in the face of my own mortality. I have not exactly become indifferent to it, though what I feel now is not terror, but rather a mild trepidation, a discomfort, an unease. Whatever negative feelings I still have about my death, they are not the kind that keep me up at night. For the most part, I sleep comfortably. Yet it is far from obvious what has changed for me. The facts, after all, seem to be the same. I still believe that death is certain and that I will cease to exist when it comes. And I still find it impossible to understand it. I know that there was a time in the past when I did not exist. In fact, the time during which I did not exist exceeds the time that I have existed by billions of years. In that sense, my non-existence is far more natural, far more normal, than my existence. My existence is an anomaly. Yet for some reason the non-existence that lies behind me feels less of a problem than the non-existence that lies ahead of me.[4] I am not wondering all that much about how it is possible that there was a time when I did not exist. It certainly does not concern me. My future non-existence, however, both puzzles and concerns me. But perhaps it should concern me more. Perhaps the downright terror that I felt as a child was the more appropriate response to the fact of our mortality. Or perhaps I should, on the contrary, be even less concerned about it than I am. Perhaps I should not be concerned at all.

*

Panayiota Vassilopoulou: Non-existence does not scare me at all. Death, in my mind, is more related to suffering and most importantly to the suffering that one's death would cause to others. I do not want to die before my mother and I do not want to die after my daughter. The thought of my mother mourning my death is unbearable; this would devastate her, more than any other death, as the experience of my daughter's death would devastate me. For any parent the loss of their offspring seems to cause the most acute pain, the most intense suffering. And I say this having of course imagined these deaths in great detail. I have imagined – as I believe is the case with many of us, or so psychology tells us – the circumstances, the consequences, the grieving of the death of loved ones throughout my life from childhood to maturity: terrible thoughts, guilty thoughts, tormenting and yet so compelling. So why is it that nothingness does not concern me, and why is it that I am so troubled by suffering – perhaps as much attracted as I am averse to it? Isn't existence, being, life, that which we cherish most and, if so, shouldn't its extinction be the greatest loss, and invoke the greatest fear?

Let us imagine a situation where the world as we know it ceases to exist: people, cities, the universe, they all die, everything becomes nothing. What of it? If there were no one left to remember, to experience this nothingness and have to live with it, what would this have to do with any of us? What would concern me in such a situation is *how* this obliteration came about: was it the result of a war, of the destruction of the environment, of my own or other beings' thoughts and actions? These are the only questions, the only fears, that concern me and this is so because the answers they admit affect the life that I, and others, lead. But what of a partial destruction scenario, where there is indeed someone left to remember – someone or someones that are left behind?

In the anticipation of the death of others, especially loved ones, and of my own death, it is not death but life that seems invariably meaningless. It is not non-existence, the mere fact of absence, that is most painful and meaningless, but the experience of this absence, the present and future of a life in absentia. Van Gogh's paintings of peasants' shoes, a theme to which he often returned, portray this in an exemplary manner: a person dies, but their belongings, the books they read, the sheets they slept in, photographs, letters, images carved in memory – like a pair of worn-out shoes – are all left with the living.[5] Similarly of course with nature or culture: consider the destruction of Palmyra by Isis not long ago, which is reported as an atrocity that has 'ripped out the heart of the city'. The absence of the dead does not feel like nothingness or non-existence at all; on the contrary, there is no presence, no darkness more tangible, more unbearably visible, than a deeply felt absence. And now that I am older and have had actual experiences of the death of others, of dear ones, I can see how life goes on in the absence of those that died – without them, without any one of us. 'The world will live and die even without me,' I read in a novel when I was a teenager, and I have never forgotten it (although I have forgotten everything else about that book). Perhaps I have been rehearsing this idea all along, with reference to that or rather those who are more near and dear, as a way of coming to terms with the finality of life, with there being meaning in life in spite of death; but how about *because* of it?

The conception of philosophy as a study or 'cultivation' of death in Plato's *Phaedo* is intended as a mental process and practice through which we are to understand and become reconciled to our mortality.[6] The inevitability of death marks an end to one's life (at least earthly life), while birth (or conception) marks the beginning. Thus conceived, life unfolds in a linear fashion from a beginning towards an end, very much unlike the seasons or 'the clock whose hands are sweeping past the minutes of its face', as the song goes.[7] Of course Plato, in this dialogue and elsewhere, is arguing for immortality, in terms of the pre-existence of soul before birth and its existence after death: if philosophy is the study of death, immortality is the assessment of this study. And if successful, Plato's arguments would establish that death is a matter of the body, a mere fact holding for everything bodily and not the real death of 'us'.[8]

Note that immortality is not the same as everlastingness; it is not more of the same, as it were, but a life of a different kind, a life outside time, where being present before and absent after, or even existing as an individual before or after, makes no sense. Hence Christians talk not just of the immortality of the soul but more explicitly about resurrection: a new life, a totally other life that awaits 'us' – not just our soul but also our body – after death. But both agree that it is because of this other life that the embodied life, day after day, can make any sense, if at all: if life, *my* life, has a meaning, this is drawn from elsewhere – what Plato called the world of ideas, what Christians call God. That which matters is never lost and that which is lost never mattered. And yet, in the thought of an afterlife I find no consolation at all: devoted Platonists and Christians or not, we all cry when a loved one dies. It is this sadness, this emptiness, that I fear most.

*

Michael Hauskeller: Epicurus famously argued that death is simply non-existence and that non-existence is not to be feared. There are many things that can harm us when we are alive, but nothing can when we are dead. As long as we are, death is not, and as soon as death has come, we are not.[9] We only fear death because we confusedly imagine ourselves experiencing our own death: not the process of dying, but the condition of being dead. Yet when we are dead we are not aware of our condition, and what is more, there no longer is an I that can experience or for that matter *be* anything at all. The condition of being dead is not a condition we can ever be in. That is why, according to Epicurus, death should not concern us. But if death cannot harm the one who is dead, precisely because death is pure nothingness, why then do we mourn the dead? Why do we care when someone dies; why do we suffer if we believe that nothing bad has happened to them?[10] Yes, if a loved one dies, we feel their absence keenly and that absence does become a presence that overshadows and darkens our life. Their death is bad for us because it hurts us so. But again, *why* does it hurt us? Is it merely because we are now no longer able to spend time with them, talk to them, hear and see and touch them?

Imagine that your loved one, instead of dying, simply leaves, and you know there is little or no chance of you ever seeing them again. They are out of your life for good. No doubt you will find this very hard to accept. You will suffer from their absence; you may even find it unbearable. But is it as bad as if they had died? If you knew they had a good life somewhere else, living somewhere without you, but happy and fulfilled, could you not find solace in this knowledge? Could you not be happy for them? In contrast, when people die, they do more than just leave you. It is true that they are no longer in your presence, that they are absent from you and for you, but at the same time their absence is more than just an absence from you. It is an absence from the world. They have not just left you behind, they have left *everything* behind. They have fallen from the edge of the world. And isn't *that* what makes the death of a loved one so unbearable?

More than a hundred thousand people die every day. The vast majority of those deaths do not affect us. Which is a good thing: we wouldn't be able to live if they did. We would not, however, say that those deaths do not matter, even if they don't matter much to us. Of course, many of those who die are loved by someone. They will be mourned and missed by someone, just not by us. Yet there are also people out there who are loved by nobody. No one really cares if they live or die. Nobody will suffer from their absence; few may even notice that they are gone. In that case, would there be nothing bad about their death? Say there was an opportunity to painlessly kill somebody who, to the best of our knowledge, is not loved and will not be mourned or missed by anyone. Would it not still be wrong to do so? And wouldn't it be wrong precisely because it is bad for them to cease to exist or to enter a state of non-existence?[11]

Death is not bad because we suffer when it comes for those we love. Rather, we suffer because we feel that something terrible has happened to them: that they have been deprived of life; that something good and beautiful has been taken away from them. We may also feel that with their death something good and beautiful has been taken away from the world – that the world is poorer without them. For the same reason we may mourn the loss of great works of art or places of natural beauty: not because we can no longer *experience* them (or *we* can no longer experience them), but because they are gone and will never come back. They have not just been moved to a different place that we happen to no longer have access to. They have completely vanished from the universe. If death and destruction were bad only because of the suffering they cause (and only *if* they cause such suffering), then we could in principle overcome the evil of death (if it is indeed an evil) simply by changing the way we feel about it. That is precisely what Epicurus urged us to do: to understand that non-existence cannot harm us and is therefore neither to be feared when it happens to ourselves, nor to be deplored when it happens to others. We may feel sad when they die, but we really shouldn't. Our sadness about the death of others is owed just as much to a misconception of what death is as the fear we have of our own death.

But if that is so, why is that misconception so persistent?

*

Panayiota Vassilopoulou: We fear not only bad things but also good things – taking on a new, better job but with increased responsibility, becoming parents, performing in public, falling in love at the 'wrong moment'. In other words, we fear not only distraction, loss and pain; we also, or even mostly, fear the unknown. We fear change, uncertainty, consequences of our actions that we cannot foresee. The future, our future, unknown to each one of us, is as much desired as it is feared. What matters here, and in connection with Epicurus, is that we should not let fear – the fear of death most of all – lead our actions, thoughts and feelings; we should overcome our fears by rationalising them. Perhaps uniquely, death is not just an *unknown* – something that is unknown at a given moment but could be known in the future. It is *unknowable* because, as you have noted, no one who dies will actually ever experience their death since the one that one is will no longer be. So, for the Epicureans, the fear of death is irrational and unjustified: no one should fear one's own death because they will never be able to know what it is to die or to be dead. But this does not hold for the death of others.[12]

We do experience the death of others, and it may well be that this is the only way in which each one of us knows death at all; it may well be that this is the only thing there is to know about death. Wouldn't this make death knowable after all? If Epicurus is right, and by this I mean that there is no 'now', 'then' or 'after' for the one who is dead, anything we think (and imagine or fear) about our death is by analogy. If I am the only one alive, I will not know what it is to be dead (there will be no *I*); I will not know that I will die, and once dead I will not even know *that* I have died – that I no longer am when I will no longer be. And if this were the case, I would be, as far as I could tell, immortal. But I am not, and I know this because I am not the only one who is or has been alive. I can observe and experience other people's deaths; hence death, as far as I know it, and I do know this, is always the death of other people (and animals and plants, of course). This holds both for the deaths of those we love and for those we do not care about or even know at all. The affection is different in each case, but it is affection, a perception and feeling, nevertheless – even in cases where those that die are bad, seem to not deserve to live, or their death might seem, to them or others, better than the life they could have had.

In the Epicurean universe, the foundation of all knowledge is perception and it is from sense-experiences that we proceed to form pre-conceptions which, combined with feelings of pleasure and pain, allow us to form judgements about, and ultimately know, not only what is evident in the senses, but also what is not directly evident or is non-evident at all – like God, the void, justice. Although not explicitly mentioned in this context, isn't *my death* then, albeit non-evident to me, an example of the latter? And if indeed it is, then the misconception may be precisely this: we may mistakenly believe that dispelling the fear of death, *as a fear of non-existence*, not letting it be what drives us in life – as Epicurus and Lucretius advise in order to reach tranquility of mind – is *all* it takes to deal with death.[13] But it is not.

In Aeschylus's *Prometheus Bound*, Prometheus advises Io, Zeus's daughter, who is terrified and in great suffering, that not to know her future would be better than knowing it.[14] Indeed Prometheus's first gift to human beings was to cure us from the 'disease' of being able to foresee our death (which presumably we were able to do previously, and actually we are not too far from being able to do now) – not *that* we will die, i.e. that we are mortal, but how and when; more specifically, what kind of suffering our death will involve or cause. Prometheus's cure, as the Chorus prompts him to reveal, consists in planting 'blind hopes' in our hearts.[15] What do we, blindly, hope for? One way to think of this is to say we hope to *become* immortal, to extend our present life so that eventually, with the advancement of medicine and technology, we will not even have to die at all. Another would be to say that we hope there is an afterlife; that we will go to another place, where we will all meet again and live happily ever after. The afterlife will be *like* this life, only better; Paradise, the Elysian fields, the other place, will be just *like* this beautiful shore, these blooming fields, only better – without mosquitoes, as I heard a small child describe paradise at a storytelling gathering one hot summer evening on a Greek island. Plotinus's version is lovelier: a place that is no place, a time that is no time, a life where no one is born and no one dies, where everything is transparent to everything else, where I look into your eyes and know what you mean, and when you always mean all that you do not even say.[16] This is the life of Intellect – just *like* this life, only better.

   We know death by analogy and then analogies morph into myths. We need these myths in order to be persuaded that something is the case, over and above the philosophical arguments or scientific data that establish something as true or a fact. We need these myths not in order to survive, but in order to remain sane, to live well. Does this mean that we *will* to live our life *as if* we are immortal? Alarmingly, Tom Waits singing Brecht resounds in my head: 'mankind can keep alive thanks to its brilliance in keeping its humanity repressed'.[17] What if Prometheus was wrong? What if we were to decline his gift and live our life just as we are? What if, bluntly put, the only difference between those that left for pastures new and those dead is that the former are alive and the latter are not, precisely because I can no longer experience them, precisely because they will never come back to experience and be experienced?

   However unlikely, it is still possible, if we so wish, to meet with the living again in this life; to see how much they have changed, how they have been living, what they have become. Although not intersecting, our lives would still go on, develop. Separation is then as much *like* death as it is not. What if, really, to live as a mortal is nothing other than coming to terms with the fact, as a fact, that life is – in the words of Beaumont and Fletcher's Bellario in *Philaster* – a game 'that must be lost'?[18] And why then would it be better not to know when or how we will die? Why would the revelation of the circumstances of our death 'break our spirit' and drive us, like Io, to insanity? After all, when people are nowadays diagnosed with a life-limiting illness, medics predict and do tell patients how long they have left. But people react differently: for some, this is indeed hard to bear and causes them to fall into depression; but for others the prognosis acts as a motivating force, and the time they have left to live becomes the most creative, the most fulfilling of all. For what it's worth, when reading a new book I feel much better if I start at the last chapter.

*

Michael Hauskeller: We can only start with the last chapter of a book if and when the whole book has already been written and is ready for the reading. Yet the last chapter of our life has not been written yet. We don't know how and when we are going to die because there is nothing to know yet. Prometheus's gift is the openness of the future, without which the future wouldn't really be a future at all. Hope resides in this openness. If nothing is predetermined – if the future is not just a past in reversal, a past that we are still to experience as present – then there is always a chance, however slight, that things will turn out differently: that the doctors may be wrong after all and our supposedly deadly disease won't kill us within a year, that our execution will be put on hold, that we are miraculously saved from whatever threatens to end our existence at any given time. Perhaps it even leaves room for the hope that, however unlikely it may seem, we might somehow escape the fate that we share with all other living things and not die at all.

Our own death is, after all, an abstraction. It has no experiential reality. So we indeed know what dying is only from our experience with the death of other people. But what can we really learn from that experience? Somebody is there, a part of my world. They can be interacted with. They are fully real, a solid presence, until one day they aren't. One minute they are in this world, and the next minute they are gone for good. Not to a different place, but, as far as we know, to no place at all. There is a material change here, but it is more than just a change, and certainly more than just a *material* change. Something has happened that should have been impossible because it seems to defy the laws of nature: something has turned into nothing. It is like a conjurer's disappearing act, but in this case it is not an act. The thing in question, the person, really *does* disappear. They have not just disappeared from sight, hidden away through clever sleight of hand; they have *actually* vanished into thin air, leaving nothing behind but a body that quickly decomposes and loses its animal form. Only the hat is left, as it were; the rabbit is gone, and it won't come back, although other rabbits will pop out of different hats when new people, new living things, are born. This is just as mysterious, just as utterly incomprehensible as death, which only reverses the event of conception when something was created out of nothing. How can nothing become something? How can something become nothing?

What the death of other people teaches us is that death is real, at least as far as we are concerned. Whatever has happened to them, they are gone from our world. We may not be able to understand how this is possible, but we know it has happened. And it is not too difficult to imagine other people being gone from our world, because our world does not in any way depend on them. They are in this world, but they do not constitute it. Our own death is a very different matter and much harder, perhaps impossible, to understand or to understand the reality of. We can imagine the non-existence of others, but we cannot really imagine our own non-existence. When we try to do so, we always at the same time reaffirm our being, namely as an imagining subject.

I can imagine myself being deprived of all kinds of things – possessions, abilities and people – but I cannot imagine myself being deprived of myself. 'I am dead' is not a meaningful proposition, not even when it is uttered in the future tense. Death has no subject. For the same reason, 'You are dead' is not a meaningful proposition either. However, 'he is dead' and 'she is dead' *are* meaningful propositions, because the 'he' or 'she' in question is not a subject, but an object of my experience. They were part of my world, and now they are not. I myself, however, will always be part of my world, which is why trying to imagine one's own non-existence is the same as trying to imagine the end of the world. If I am no longer there, then the world is no longer there for me either. But for me, there is no other world than the world that is there for me, so if I cease to exist, that world will also cease to exist. From my perspective, there will never have been a world and there will never again be a world. But we know from the death of other people that when they die, the world continues to exist, which strongly suggests that when I die, the world will also continue to exist. But if the existence of the world (namely as an *object*) depends on the continued existence of its *subject*, then I will continue to exist as long as the world exists. Schopenhauer made that argument, insisting that the present cannot be lost,[19] which simply expands Epicurus's insight that when we are, death is not, and when death is, we are not. This would explain why we never *fully* believe in our own mortality.

*

Panayiota Vassilopoulou: It feels like this conversation is heading towards its final chapter. And perhaps this is why it has been so hard for me to write. To complete a conversation, a piece of writing, is in a certain sense the death of it – the admission that the end has come, an irreversible finality, about to turn the present into a past. But of course, if everything is left forever incomplete, nothing ever *is*, in this very sense in which philosophers have thought *being* to be superior, more real, more meaningful, than *becoming*. Schopenhauer was one of these philosophers. The world of becoming that he sees is a world of endless suffering and frustration – completely meaningless. Life, my life and yours, is but a dream, an illusion, and so too is my death and your death. The subject that keeps being (or the world as an object) in *real* existence is neither you nor I. It is an abstract, universal conception of a subject – a subject outside time, eternal and immortal, objectified into a set of timeless patterns much like the Platonic ideas.

Even if that subject (and its object) continued to exist, it wouldn't follow that you or I would continue to exist or that you or I ever really existed. The only evidence we have of the latter, for Schopenhauer, is that from our internal individual perspective we, and by analogy everything else, can get a glimpse of that non-individual and eternal real being, and that glimpse, *that present*, is what is real and as such can never be lost. True, one could look at a rose and see the 'ideal' – all the roses and all the flowers at once and none in particular – but not *this* rose, which I now hold in my hands; the rose that grew in my garden and will soon wither and die in my vase. Although equally true, one may find it harder to hold on to such a view when it comes to human beings. When I look at my mother, my daughter, my friend, I do not see just 'human being'; their lives and deaths are not just appearances of a being that is elsewhere, up above in some metaphysical sky or hidden in the depths of each one's individual, particular and as such illusory existence safeguarded merely by myself as a point from which they are viewed. Ultimately, one may deliberately want to resist viewing people, roses, the world and the present in such a way.

Not fully believing in one's own mortality seems to me to leave too open the horizon of a future at the expense of shrinking the present merely to a point of contact with the ever-spinning wheel of time. This may in fact resonate with the kind of present that Schopenhauer envisaged when he said that the present is not lost, but even so he too finds fault with the idea of living in anticipation of a never-ending future: such people, he says in the 'Aphorisms on the wisdom of life', 'go one living *ad interim*, until at last they die'.[20] The present I want to defend here is a different one: it is a lived presence, a stretched-out present, so to speak, paradoxically able to fit hours and days into its duration. The present can be lost. And it is *only* the present that can be lost; indeed, more often than not it *is* lost. The past has already been and the future is never really ours to lose or save. Habit, boredom, anxiety for the future, procrastination – these are all reasons why we may not be present in the present and thus turn the present all too quickly into a past.

We started this conversation from our fears about death: your fear of non-existence, my fear of the suffering caused by one's death to others. The fear of death, whatever form it may take, we agree, is what we need to overcome in order to live and die well. But how? The solution to this problem, if there is a solution, may not be one and the same for all and under every circumstance. In my view – and here we seem to disagree – the solution cannot be to live my life *as if* there will be no end and hope for some kind of miracle, either in terms of a treatment for a life-limiting illness or, more generally, in terms of the eternal life promised by religions and speculated by science. What I find more promising, albeit perhaps also more challenging, is the prospect of coming to terms with my death, being fully convinced that my death is as inevitable and as proximate at any given time as that of others.

Looking at my rose again: its certain death, the fleeting nature of its existence, makes it all the more beautiful and my paying attention to its image and smell, enjoying it as I write these lines, makes it all the more meaningful. We are not forever. We may find comfort in the idea that this may not be true. But we also tend to forget it, even if we do believe it to be true. We are at constant war with the human condition, at the core of which lies our mortality and temporal existence, and it is in this conflict that we often lose our present, the presence of ourselves and of others in the present. Perhaps we focus too much on the suffering and not enough on the abundance of life which is undeniably a compelling force everywhere around us; we fear death so much that we are all too eager to drown life in our desire for more and more. Starting from the last chapter, living one's life backwards that is, does not necessarily amount to a future that is lived as a past – especially a *given past* – in reverse. What is given in such a conception is that there is an end, a *given future* if you will, but precisely because of this the present is all that is at stake. There is no 'more' or 'less' in the present: all is here now and this is also why an absence may be so strongly felt. In 'The love song of J. Alfred Prufrock', T. S. Eliot writes:[21]

> There will be time, there will be time
> To prepare a face to meet the faces that you meet;
> There will be time to murder and create,
> And time for all the works and days of hands
> That lift and drop a question on your plate;

Time for you and time for me,
And time yet for a hundred indecisions,
And for a hundred visions and revisions,
Before the taking of a toast and tea.

'There *will* be time' . . . To live one's life backwards would be to change the future not to a past, but to a present tense.

*

Michael Hauskeller: There will be time, yes, but not necessarily for us, because our time can come to an end at any moment, unannounced and sudden. It may also last longer than we had expected, sometimes even longer than we desire.[22] Whatever we may think of the value of Prometheus's gift, it cannot be refused or returned. The human condition is, for better or worse, marked by both the certainty of death and the uncertainty of its occurrence in time. That it *will* happen is certain, but hardly ever *when*, unless it is imminent. But the lived present is indeed an extended one, incorporating change and all that is real in what we call the future and the past.

I am not sure, though, that your conception of that lived present is all that different from Schopenhauer's idea of an 'eternal present'. It is true that Schopenhauer, like many philosophers before and after him, thought of this ever-changing world, the 'world of becoming', as deficient and somehow not fully real in comparison to the 'world of being', which is supposed to be unchanging and for that very reason more real.[23] Personally, I have never understood that kind of intuition. The very distinction seems misguided. After all, the only world we know of is a world of becoming, where things constantly change and nothing lasts forever, including ourselves, so that becoming is in fact the only kind of being that we can experience or even imagine. Pure, change-free being is an abstraction and indistinguishable from nothingness. It does not exist and cannot exist. The desire to escape from the world of becoming is, then, ultimately a desire to escape from existence. Death is an integral part of life because life is change. But that also means that there are no endings – no *absolute* endings anyway – because every ending is also the beginning of something new. Endings are transitions. There are no final chapters. 'After the game is before the game.'[24]

Accordingly, Schopenhauer's eternal present should be understood not as a timeless present, but as one that lasts through time. It is not the moving image of an unmoving eternity, as Plato would have it,[25] but a moving, or lived, eternity. We take our present with us, through time. You may, however, be right that even in this sense the notion of an eternal present requires us to call into question the ultimate reality of the individual, or more precisely the ultimate reality of the *boundaries* that we commonly believe separate one individual from another. But perhaps that is not a bad thing. Perhaps it should be questioned. I understand why you would want to hold on to the idea that the individual is real and that there is nothing more real behind it – that the people we know and love and share our life with, and of course we ourselves, are not merely, as you put it, 'appearances of a being that is elsewhere'. I am inclined to agree. This rose is real, as real as it gets, and it is real precisely because it is here and now (having its place and its time) and because it will no longer be here tomorrow. Its reality depends on its being *this* rose and no other. The same goes for you and me. And because we are real, our death is real too. One day we will both be gone, and once we are gone, we are gone for good. This is what you recommend we fully accept and come to grips with lest we lose the present in a fruitless fight against mortality.

Yet you also suggest that we be less preoccupied with our own inescapable mortality and the suffering that comes with it, and focus more on 'the abundance of life which is undeniably everywhere around us a compelling force'. Now why would we do that? How does that help us to come to terms with death? Might not the reason be that we feel our own life extended and continued in all the other life that surrounds us, including the life that was there before us and that will continue to be there after we are gone?

There *will* be time, you said, and I added that there might not be for us. But perhaps that matters less than we commonly suppose. Life does indeed go on without us, but it *does* go on, and that may be precisely what makes the knowledge of death bearable for us, for the life that goes on is the same life that we find in ourselves. That life was never entirely disconnected from ours in the first place. Our life is shared with other people, other creatures.[26] We all live our own lives, but we also live in each other. The rose in your hand, you say, is beautiful and meaningful at least partly because it only lasts for a short while, and it is. But I wonder if our appreciation of its beauty may not also be informed by our recognition that this rose is one of many and when it dies roses will continue to bloom as they did before, long before this particular rose came into existence. There is discontinuity, but also continuity. What I am trying to get at is not reincarnation. It is more like shared presence or extended identity – a wider conception, or rather experience, of the self that transcends the customary but by no means compelling ontological separation between me and everything else. For those who find joy and solace in the existence of others, death has no (or much less) sting.

*

Panayiota Vassilopoulou: The present I tried to describe seems to me different from Schopenhauer's. For one thing, the present I talk about is not eternal: it is a present that can be lost. It is the present that one is aware can be lost; it is the present that, perhaps most likely in retrospect, one realises was lost. When I read a novel that I really enjoy, time passes so quickly and yet I manage to read so many pages in what seems to be such a short time. When I am bored, time passes slowly and after several hours I may realise that what I have read is but a few pages, and what is worse, that I remember none of it: I carry none of it in my present now. Reading a good novel or an engaging piece of philosophy, falling in love, being happy, experiencing beauty: these are not just present moments in time, but moments at which we are fully *present in the present* and our presence in that here and now is really intense. In such cases the present is not lost; it is experienced, enriched. Certainly, these are all just examples of gaining the present, gaining time; and boredom, as I have already mentioned, is just one reason among others for losing it. Another reason, which is what we have been concerned with here, is obviously death itself; but a yet further reason is the *fear* of death. We might not be able to do anything about the former, but there is a lot we can do about the latter.

'There *will* be time' might be a consolation – although I am not at all sure Eliot intended it that way – for those who read in it that there will be a future, be it an indefinite one or one stretching very far away, a broad 'horizon' as you previously said. But you are right to remark that it might not be very reassuring since this time may not be really in our future, or we may not even wish for it. My suggestion, however, was to change the future tense in that verse to the present, so that it reads: 'there *is* time'. And this time that *is* now, the present, is the time *to seize or lose*. Is my suggestion then Horace's all-pervasive *carpe diem*, seize (or pluck) the day? Yes, but combined with his equally well-known advice to remember that one is mortal: *memento mori*. Although the two do not appear together in the same context, their link is evident in *Ode* 1.11: the 'poet' Horace urges young Leuconoe to 'seize the day', precisely because this may be the 'last winter'.[27]

Carpe diem alerts us to the danger of losing the present in a futile attempt to gain the future and urges us to pay more attention to the present, to make the most of it. But without the constant reminder of our mortality as *memento mori* prescribes, we would be in danger of living too much in the present – being too frivolous even in Schopenhauer's book – living each day as if it were the first, a totally new day to be lived by a new-born self without a world, without a history, without a past. Horace's poem makes me think again of those whose death is imminent and for whom that limited time is the most creative or fulfilling they have ever had: what if we lived *as if* we were in that situation? What if we lived *as if* there were no future, as if there were no tomorrow, as if this day, every day, is not the first but the last? Within the mythological narrative of Prometheus, this would amount to a rejection of his gift.

But this is not an easy thing, and thinking this way may lead one to disengage from the world; to depression or insanity, as indeed has happened in some cases. It may also feel undesirable: too myopic, too restricted, a claustrophobic world with no room to project, set goals, plan out a life, as it were. Most importantly, even if one were willing to attempt it, to take these risks, would it be possible to live every day, every hour, as if there will be no other? In other words, would it be possible to live continuously present in the present? No. We do waste time; we also fall asleep literally and metaphorically. That this *must* happen is also part of the human condition. Being mortal and being in time and space are two sides of the same coin, but each creates limitations in two different directions. Coming to terms with our mortality would involve, on the one hand, living our life with the awareness that there is no indefinite future: that at some point in the *near* future we will cease to exist (at least in the way we know existence to be) and that today may very well be our last day. On the other hand, it would involve living our life with the awareness that we cannot consistently be in love, creative, happy, engaged, present in the present: this would be unrealistic, a misleading and tantalising expectation. We fall out of love, we experience pain and sorrow, we want to escape, hide away or rest. Keeping these periods of pain or recuperation intact is as important as keeping them at bay. Within this tension, to think that every crisis will be succeeded by better times, that after every night's sleep we will awaken to a fresh morning, that every end is also a new beginning, is indeed a consolation as well – especially for those who, like your younger self, fear non-existence. It does take a lot of strength to come to terms not only with the eventuality of death but also – and even more so, but in my opinion for good reason – with the finality of life at each of its stages.

Life is a game that must be lost. If life is such a game, it seems to be the only one. Why would one want to play a game that one knows for sure one will lose? One way to think about it would be precisely to admit that death has such a strong sting that we have made death 'the *oestrus* of life', as Andreas Embirikos, the Greek surrealist poet, put it.[28]

Or there may be an irreducible duality, like the one postulated by Freud, of the sexual instincts, which prompt us to survival, creativity and pro-creation, and the death instincts, which drive the living being back to an inorganic state.[29] The former may be momentarily triumphant; the latter will eventually be victorious, but while the duality lasts, the two could operate independently of each other, even if their effects appear com-bined. However, despite their appeal, psychoanalytic approaches never fully register with me.

Let us consider another way of making sense of it. That I am part of a greater whole – that this rose is one of many – is precisely the lively background (not an open horizon, but a beautifully framed landscape) against which I will to appreciate the meaning of my life or the beauty of the rose. Not so much, I think, because after death this life will continue somehow through others, as you have suggested, but because while we are alive our context, history, legacy and those 'others' are all alive too in this present. Take the person who is in love as an example: they don't just experience a connection with their self and the beloved; they experi-ence a connection with the whole world – 'being on top of the world' but looking down, seeing within the world. The self, the beloved, the world, they all are beautiful, meaningful, real, *now* in the present that one gains, amidst all the other presents that slip away.

Treating this day, today, as if it is the last prompts us to actively seek such a present, to be mindful of both its value and its precarious nature. Granted that this present cannot be experienced all the time, it can never-theless be experienced even under the most adverse circumstances, even in the hardest times. And when it is experienced – in different ways and for different reasons for each one of us – it seems to me to be invariably experienced as *being* rather than *becoming*, which perhaps gives this dis-tinction a different but more attractive meaning. For, ultimately, I believe this to be the reason why we play this game, life, despite knowing that we will lose in the end, despite knowing that *after this game is not before another*. As the saying goes, 'If you can't win a game, change the rules'; we can get it wrong of course, but winning that present, inscribing being onto becoming, may be what life is all about.

Notes

1. It is sometimes claimed that the young typically feel that they are immortal (see for instance Overall, *Aging, Death, and Human Longevity*, 3), but there is plenty of evidence that the fear of death I experienced as a child is not only quite common, but also tends to be more acute in young children before they have developed an adequate biological understanding of death. See Slaughter and Griffiths, 'Death understanding and fear of death in young children'.

2. That what makes death bad is not just the fact that it deprives us of many goods that we might have continued to enjoy if we had not died (Nagel, 'Death') or the fact that it frustrates our desire to stay alive in order to do certain things (Luper-Foy, 'Annihilation'; Williams, 'The Makropulos case'), but also the fact that we are simply no longer there – the very fact of our extinction – has been argued by for instance Benatar, *The Human Predicament* (102–10) and, in a more playful manner, Barnes, *Nothing to Be Frightened Of*.

3. For a critical discussion of this mystery (the unfathomability of one's own death) see Benn, 'My own death'.

4. Why our prenatal non-existence does not concern us while our postmortal non-existence does is not immediately obvious, and may appear to be irrational. Lucretius (*The Nature of Things*, 72–106) argued that our postmortal non-existence should concern us as little as our prenatal non-existence because non-existence is never to be feared. For a discussion of this kind of 'symmetry argument' see Kamm, 'Why is death bad and worse than pre-natal non-existence?'; Timmerman, 'If you want to die later, then why don't you want to have been born earlier?'; and Kaufman's response to Timmerman, 'Coming into and going out of existence'.

5. The most discussed of these paintings is undoubtedly *Shoes*, 1886, oil on canvas, Vincent Van Gogh Museum, Amsterdam; see, for example, Heidegger, 'The origin of the work of art', especially pp.13–14.

6. Plato, *Phaedo*, 67e.

7. *The Windmills of your Mind* (1968), music by Michel Legrand and English lyrics by Alan and Marilyn Bergman.

8. For a concise discussion of Plato's views on life and death with regard to the body and soul in the context of the argument for immortality in the *Phaedo*, see Michael Pakaluk, 'Degrees of separation in the *Phaedo*'.

9. Epicurus, 'Letter to Menoeceus', 67. For a critical discussion see Grey, 'Epicurus and the harm of death'.

10. A related question is: if death is not a harm, why is it bad, or wrong, to kill people? For a possible answer see Burley, 'Epicurus, death, and the wrongness of killing' and Burkhardt, 'Epicureanism and the wrongness of killing'.

11. And it may well be that this – the very ceasing to exist – is what we, or some of us, fear the most about death. In *Tragic Sense of Life* the Spanish philosopher Miguel de Unamuno wrote that, for him, 'nothingness was much more terrifying' than all the tortures of hell could ever be (44).

12. For a good discussion of these claims see Warren, *Facing Death*, 17–56.

13. Lucretius's forceful defence of the claim that the fear of death is unnecessary can be found in *The Nature of Things*, III, 830–1094 (including a brief discussion at 890–914 of mourning the death of others). See also Morrison, 'Nil igitur mors est ad nos?'.

14. Aeschylus, *Prometheus Bound*, 624.

15. Aeschylus, *Prometheus Bound*, 247–51.

16. Plotinus, *Ennead*, V.8[31], 4.

17. *What Keeps Mankind Alive?* in *The Threepenny Opera* (1928), music by Kurt Weill, lyrics by Bertolt Brecht. Sung by Tom Waits (1985) with English lyrics by Ralph Manheim and John Willett.

18. Bowers, *The Dramatic Works in the Beaumont and Fletcher Canon*, volume 1, *Philaster, or Love lies a Bleeding*, iii.1.

19. Schopenhauer, *Die Welt als Wille und Vorstellung*, 366: 'Nobody has ever lived in the past, and nobody will ever live in the future. The *present* alone is the form of all life, and it is also its certain possession, which cannot be snatched away from it. The present is always there, as is its content: both stand fast without fail, like the rainbow on the waterfall. For life is certain to the will, and the present to life' (my translation).

20. Schopenhauer, *Parerga and Paralipomena*, I, 44.

21. Eliot, *Collected Poems*, 4.

22. Or longer than is good for us. See Hauskeller, 'When death comes too late'.

23. A classic exposition of this view is Bradley's *Appearance and Reality*.

24. This quote, which is commonly attributed to the legendary German football coach Sepp Herberger, is, naturally, about football, but it also captures nicely a fundamental fact of life.

25. Plato, *Timaeus*, 37d.

26. For a more detailed discussion of this idea see Hauskeller, 'Killing death/sharing life'.

27. Horace, *Odes*, 1.11.4.

28. Embirikos, *Oktana*, 11.

29. See e.g. Freud, *Beyond the Pleasure Principle*, 24–33.

Bibliography

Aeschylus. *Prometheus Bound*, translated by Deborah H. Roberts. Indianapolis/Cambridge: Hackett, 2012.

Barnes, Julian. *Nothing to Be Frightened Of*. London: Virago, 2009.

Benatar, David. *The Human Predicament: A candid guide to life's biggest questions*. Oxford: Oxford University Press, 2017.

Benn, Piers. 'My own death', *The Monist* 76/2 (1993): 235–51.

Bowers, Fredson (ed.). *The Dramatic Works in the Beaumont and Fletcher Canon*, volume 1. Cambridge: Cambridge University Press, 1966.

Bradley, Francis Herbert. *Appearance and Reality*. London: Swan Sonnenschein, 1893.

Burkhardt, Tim. 'Epicureanism and the wrongness of killing', *The Journal of Ethics* 24/2 (2020): 177–92.

Burley, Mikel. 'Epicurus, death, and the wrongness of killing', *Inquiry* 53/1 (2010): 68–86.

Eliot, T. S. *Collected Poems 1909–1962*. New York: Harcourt, Brace & World, 1963.

Embirikos, Andreas. *Oktana*. Athens: Ikaros, 1980 [in Greek].

Epicurus. 'Letter to Menoeceus'. In *Exploring the Philosophy of Death and Dying: Classical and contemporary perspectives*, edited by Michael Cholbi and Travis Timmerman, 67–9. London: Routledge, 2021.

Freud, Sigmund. *Beyond the Pleasure Principle*. In *The Standard Edition of the Complete Psychological Works of Sigmund Freud*, volume 18, translated under the general editorship of James Strachey, in collaboration with Anna Freud. London: Hogarth Press, 1953–74.

Grey, William. 'Epicurus and the harm of death', *Australasian Journal of Philosophy* 77/3 (1999): 358–64.

Hauskeller, Michael. 'Killing death/ sharing life', *Tropos* 9/2 (2016): 47–58.

Hauskeller, Michael. 'When death comes too late: radical life extension and the Makropulos case'. In *Death and Meaning*, edited by Michael Hauskeller. Cambridge: Cambridge University Press, 2021.

Heidegger, Martin. 'The origin of the work of art'. In *Off the Beaten Track*, edited and translated by Julian Young and Kenneth Haynes. Cambridge: Cambridge University Press, 2002.

Horace. *Odes and Epodes*, edited and translated by Niall Rudd. Cambridge, MA: Harvard University Press, 2004.

Kamm, F. M. 'Why is death bad and worse than pre-natal non-existence?', *Pacific Philosophical Quarterly* 69/2 (1988): 161–4.

Kaufman, Frederik. 'Coming into and going out of existence'. In *Exploring the Philosophy of Death and Dying: Classical and contemporary perspectives*, edited by Michael Cholbi and Travis Timmerman, 112–18. London: Routledge, 2021.

Lucretius. *The Nature of Things*, translated by A. E. Stallings. London: Penguin Classics, 2007.

Luper-Foy, Steven. 'Annihilation', *The Philosophical Quarterly* 37/148 (1987): 233–52.

Morrison, A. D. 'Nil igitur mors est ad nos? Iphianassa, the Athenian plague, and Epicurean views of death'. In *Lucretius: Poetry, philosophy, science*, edited by D. Lehoux, A. D. Morrison and A. Sharrock, 211–32. Oxford: Oxford University Press, 2013.

Nagel, Thomas. 'Death', *Noûs* 4/1 (1970): 73–80.

Overall, Christine. *Aging, Death, and Human Longevity: A philosophical inquiry*. Berkeley, CA: University of California Press, 2003.

Pakaluk, Michael. 'Degrees of separation in the *Phaedo*', *Phronesis* 48 (2003): 89–115.

Plato. *Timaeus*, translated by Benjamin Jowett. London: Macmillan, 1959.

Plato. *Phaedo*, translated by David Gallop. Oxford: Clarendon Press, 1975.

Plotinus. *The Enneads*, translated by G. Boys-Stones, J. M. Dillon, L. P. Gerson, R. A. H. King, A. Smith and J. Wilberding. Cambridge: Cambridge University Press, 2018.

Schopenhauer, Arthur. *Parerga and Paralipomena*, 2 volumes, translated by E. F. J. Payne. Oxford: Clarendon Press, 1974.

Schopenhauer, Arthur. *Die Welt als Wille und Vorstellung*, edited by Lutger Lütkehaus. Zurich: Haffmans, 1988.

Slaughter, Virginia, and Maya Griffiths. 'Death understanding and fear of death in young children', *Clinical Child Psychology and Psychiatry* 12/4 (2007): 525–35.

Timmerman, Travis. 'If you want to die later, then why don't you want to have been born earlier?' In *Exploring the Philosophy of Death and Dying: Classical and contemporary perspectives*, edited by Michael Cholbi and Travis Timmerman, 104–11. London: Routledge, 2021.

Unamuno, Miguel de. *Tragic Sense of Life*. New York: Dover Publications, 1954.

Warren, James. *Facing Death: Epicurus and his critics*. Oxford: Clarendon Press, 2004.

Williams, Bernard. 'The Makropulos case: reflections on the tedium of immortality'. In *Problems of the Self*, 82–100. Cambridge: Cambridge University Press 1973.

10
Birth

with Alison Stone

Alison Stone: We all die, and we are all born. Yet philosophers both in the past and today have said little about birth and much more about death. A possible explanation is that death lies in one's future, and is a source of anxiety,[1] or a bad thing that one has grounds to fear, whereas one's birth lies in the past, so that one has no grounds to fear it.[2] Another explanation might be that we are born of women, and women's voices and experiences have been neglected within the history of philosophy.[3] Whatever explanation we adopt, though, the neglect of birth is unfortunate, because our existence is shaped by the fact that we are born as well as by our mortality. We are not only mortals, but also *natals* – beings who are born. Our condition is one of *natality* as well as mortality.[4]

How does birth shape our existence? To answer this question, we first need to clarify what it is to be born. Sometimes we say that someone is born just when they exit their mother's womb. But I prefer to understand birth more broadly than that, so that we can better appreciate its bearing on our whole condition and mode of existence. On the wider understanding that I favour, to be born is, first, to *begin* to exist at a certain point in time.[5] And, second, our beginning to exist itself occurs in a *process* by which we are conceived and gestated in, and then leave, someone else's womb.[6] Above I said that we are born of women, which suggests that this 'someone else' must always be a woman or mother. But this should be qualified, now that growing numbers of trans men are bearing babies. What matters is coming from a womb, not necessarily a maternal womb. Third, to be born is to come into the world with – or rather as – a particular body, and in a given place, set of relationships with other people, and situation with regard to society, culture and history.

How do these facts shape our existence? Let me speak here about just a few ways: dependency, relationality, situatedness and givenness. To start with dependency, to be born is to begin life as a baby, and human babies and infants are acutely helpless at first, utterly dependent on the older people who care for them physically and emotionally. Indeed it has been said that human babies remain foetuses outside the womb for most of their first year of life.[7] Essentially, human babies are so helpless because of the 'obstetric dilemma'.[8] Once early hominids became bipedal, their pelvises narrowed while, simultaneously, their brains enlarged. As a result babies had to start passing out of the birth canal much earlier in their development than they had before – and much earlier than the young of our nearest primate neighbours do.[9]

Moreover, human babies are not just profoundly helpless at birth; human children and the young also remain dependent on adult care and education for a long time compared to the young of other species – often right into adolescence and beyond. This is because we require so much education and enculturation to achieve maturity and become full social participants. And this too is an indirect consequence of our unformed and open-ended nature as infants, which means that culture becomes constitutive in our entire formation.[10] In sum, to be born is to be dependent on others before one ever becomes independent.[11] And because dependency is our more basic condition, we achieve independence – to whatever extent we do – against a background of ongoing and persistent dependency on others.

Because we depend so heavily on our first care-givers, our relationships with them influence us hugely. These relationships are intensely emotionally charged and affecting, as we depend on them for everything. Also, having left the womb so early in their development, human infants are very unformed and immature physically and mentally, which gives their first relationships particular power to mould and shape them. But, again because we are so unformed in infancy, we have yet to form a sense of self or any sort of organised personality. Putting these points together, the impact of our earliest relationships is such that they come to structure our most basic sense of self as well as our personalities.[12] This may be easier to see in the latter case: our earliest relationships shape our basic dispositions, habits, traits, patterns of emotional reaction, and the organised patternings of these that constitute personalities. But arguably, also, one's more fundamental sense of having a self at all is formed on the model of the others who surround one during one's earliest years.[13] Thus, to be born is to have a relational self – a self that is constituted the way it is by one's relationships.

In being born one arrives not only in a specific set of relationships with care-givers but also, more broadly, in a situation: a place within certain historical, social, ethnic, geographical and generational circumstances.[14] One's initial situation affects every subsequent situation one comes to be in, so that all one's situations flow down through one's life from one's birth. I don't mean to say that the course of someone's entire life is already set at birth. At every step along life's way we respond to our situations, making sense of them and finding possibilities of action in them; these responses bring us into new situations to which we respond in turn. Nonetheless, my whole series of situations is the particular series it is because of how it descends from the initial situation into which I was born. This is the more so as my ways of responding to successive situations are themselves shaped by my initial natal situation. That situation gives rise not only to the series of circumstances I have to respond to but also to how I make sense of these circumstances drawing upon the culture, history, relationships, etc. into which I was born and by which I have been influenced.

As we are born, our initial situations are given to us, not chosen. I did not ask or choose to be born; nor did I choose where, when, and in what circumstances and culture I was born. And as soon as one is born one begins to imbibe the culture around one, at a stage when one is very unformed with no capacities to question any of the ideas one is imbibing. So, first and foremost, we *receive* and inherit culture and history. What is given to us comes before what we make, and we make what we do on the basis of what we have already been given. This does not mean that we cannot change, criticise or reject our cultural inheritances; it means that we can only learn to do this having already received those inheritances in the first place.[15]

*

Michael Hauskeller: Indeed, we are all born, and we all die. 'All' includes non-human animals, for we share both our mortality and our natality with them. Unlike non-human animals, however, humans *know* that they are going to die and *know* that they have been born, which is to say they know that quite soon they will cease to exist, that not long ago they did not yet exist, and that their existence is, consequently, just a brief interlude between two eternities of non-existence. There is no indication that any other animal has this kind of understanding.[16] Non-human animals might be dimly aware of the possibility (though not the necessity) of death because many of them spend much of their life warding off threats to their continued existence, but it strikes me as very unlikely that they have any idea that they were born and that once they did not exist. Since they won't be able to remember their being born, let alone coming into existence, it must seem to them as if they have always been around. It is true that we do not remember our birth or conception either, but we have others who teach us (and the mental capacities to understand) that we, like everyone else, only came into existence a short while ago, which is almost as unfathomable, although perhaps less frightening, as the fact that we will soon, once again, not exist.

However, the fact that we are aware of our natality just as much as we are aware of our mortality is not the only aspect of our own natal situation that is specific to our human condition. There are of course many other animals that come into the world we share with others just as unformed, helpless and dependent as we do, although it usually takes them less time to grow out of that state of dependency. Yet there are also countless animals, including some mammals, which enter this world fully formed and ready for action, equipped with all the abilities and skills they need to survive in a hostile environment with little or no support or protection from others. And yet, these animals are born too.

Being born, therefore, is not the same as being born helpless and dependent, unless what we mean by 'being born' is our being conceived, in which case we are indeed all initially helpless and dependent, since nothing can bring about its own existence, and a certain amount of development always needs to take place to generate something as complex as a living organism. Yet there is still a difference between our being *conceived* helpless and dependent and our being *born* (in the narrow sense) helpless and dependent, because the latter is consciously experienced while the former is not. It is also likely to affect what you call our relationality in different ways because only if we are *born* helpless and dependent are we dependent not only on certain biological processes taking place undisturbed, but also on other people (or animals) and what they choose to do or not to do.

In any case, it seems to me that when we try to understand how our natality shapes our existence, we need to carefully distinguish between the fact that we *came into existence* at some point in time, the fact that we *know* we did, and the fact that we came into existence *in a particular way*, namely in the way humans traditionally come into existence, with nine months of gestation in the maternal womb, followed by a sudden expulsion from this comparatively safe place into a shared and, in contrast to us, fully formed world for which we are ill equipped when we are forced to enter it and in which we can only survive for many years to come with the support and care of others. Each of these facts may shape our existence, in terms of both the way we are and the way we understand ourselves in our relation to the world in which we find ourselves. However, they may well shape our existence in different ways.

To find out how exactly those facts shape us, let us imagine things are different than they are. There are at least three scenarios to consider. First, what would change for us if our existence had no beginning? Is that even conceivable?[17] And would an existence with no beginning also necessarily have to be an existence with no end? Is there, then, a (logical or ontological?) connection between our natality (in this sense) and our mortality? Second, what would change if our existence had a beginning, but one that was very different from what it is now? Let's say we didn't slowly grow into this world, but started our existence fully formed, with all the physical and mental abilities that an adult human typically enjoys, like the androids or 'simulacra' in Philip K. Dick's novel *We Can Build You*[18] who come into (conscious) existence abruptly with no extended transition period during which nothing (or almost nothing) gradually becomes something. What would that be like? How would it shape our experience of the world?[19] And finally, what if we came into existence the way that humans have always come into existence, but had no awareness of it at all? Would we then be different than we are now?

*

Alison Stone: You are absolutely right to point out that unlike other animals we are aware that we will die and have been born. This is important for considering how birth shapes our existence, for the following reasons. When philosophers say that our 'mortality' shapes our existence, 'mortality' encompasses both the fact that we will die and our awareness of the same. For it is only through that awareness that we will die that this fact comes to shape our whole existence. If we weren't aware that we will die, but just in fact did when the time came, then that fact would have no bearing on our whole way of leading our lives up to the point of death.

So the question arises whether something parallel holds for birth. Does birth, too, affect the shape of our lives only through our awareness that we were born? There seems to me to be an asymmetry between death and birth here. Birth leads to the helplessness and dependency of human babies and infants, which in turn shapes the relationality of our selves. But that helplessness and dependency obtains without babies and infants yet being aware that they have been born – they only learn this later, from older human beings. Thus birth begins to shape our existence straight away, before we yet have any understanding of it. Birth also has immediate shaping effect because being born places one immediately into a particular situation in the world. This, again, happens and begins to affect one's life before one is at all aware of having been born. This asymmetry between birth and death is a consequence of their temporal asymmetry. Because my birth is in my past – it has already happened by the time I am in existence – it has already begun to have effects on me by the time I form the mental capacities to be aware of it. Conversely, because my death is in the future, and hasn't yet happened, it can only affect my existence through my anticipation of it.

You are also quite right that, as the case of 'precocial'[20] animal species shows, a being can be born, i.e. gestated and expelled from a parent's womb, without that necessarily resulting in the level of helplessness and dependency we see in human infants. I should have been clearer: when I offered a definition earlier of what being born consists in, I took this to be what being born consists in for human beings. Moreover, in the human case, we are conceived and gestated in someone else's womb and then expelled from that womb at a relatively early point in our development compared to our nearest primate neighbours, who are precocial – that is, establish a significant degree of independence very quickly after leaving the womb. This relative 'earliness' on our part is why we begin extra-uterine life so helpless and dependent.

I completely agree with you that being born has a number of components that are usefully distinguished, each with different ramifications for our existence. As you say, a first component is coming into existence at a given point in time – and a given place in space – while a second component is coming into existence in the particular way we do as human beings, through nine months of intra-uterine gestation terminating in a prolonged period of postnatal infantile helplessness. The first component means, for one thing, that we have beginnings, hence that certain events come first in our lives; for another, it means that we are situated in time and space and, in consequence, with respect to other variables such as nationality, ethnicity and history. Meanwhile, the second component shapes our dependency and helplessness. And these sets of consequences in turn interact: for example, being situated and dependent means that we start off situated in a particular set of relationships with the other human beings on whom we at first depend.

I must confess that I struggle with counter-factual scenarios about birth. I'm interested by your point that the simulacra in Dick's novel come into existence very differently from ordinary human beings. Once switched on, the simulacra come straight into fully formed, adult, conscious and cognitively complex experience. They experience deep horror at having sprung suddenly in the world with its overwhelming presence and richness, and also at the magnitude of the transition they have just made.[21] It is because the simulacra have come straight into fully formed, conscious adult existence that they become immediately aware of having made that transition, and of how mysterious and mind-boggling it is.

I had previously thought that the simulacra's plight was suggestive about the potentially traumatic nature of being born generally – given the magnitude of the transition both from non-existence to existence and from conception through gestation into extra-uterine existence. But perhaps instead the simulacra's plight illuminates the contrast with human birth. We shade into existence gradually, during gestation, which makes the transition into existence correspondingly less stark and absolute. And we already have experience before leaving our parent's womb so that, abrupt and overwhelming as exiting the womb may be, it is much less abrupt and overwhelming than what happens to the simulacra. And unlike them, we have years to develop cognitively and acquire adult mental capacities at the same time as we gradually get to grips with the world around us.

*

Michael Hauskeller: We 'shade into existence gradually' – I like that. It captures very nicely the fact that being born (that is, coming into existence for a living being) is not an event but a process. Existence does not come as a surprise to us: once we realise that we exist, we have already got used to it. Death, on the other hand, seems to be sudden: an event, not a process. One moment we exist, the next moment we are gone. Although perhaps that is not always true. Just as, at the beginning of our life, we go through a process of physical and cognitive development that eases our way from non-existence into existence, we can also undergo a comparable process of physical and cognitive decline at the end of our life that may help us get to grips with the approach of non-existence. In that case, death also becomes a process, mirroring the process of birth: a gradual shading, or fading, out of existence that makes the dying of the light[22] more tolerable.[23]

Perhaps, then, there is less asymmetry between birth and death than we thought. You have pointed out that while birth shapes us directly, death can only shape us by being anticipated because it still lies ahead of us, while our birth has already happened. We are born, but we have not died yet. That is true of course, but I am wondering whether death really needs to be anticipated to have an effect on us. Is it only the *knowledge* of death rather than death itself, or more precisely the fact of our mortality, that shapes our existence? We identified helplessness and dependency as direct effects of our being born (the way humans are). But what do we mean by that? Are we not helpless and dependent on others precisely because we do not have the means yet to keep ourselves alive? For a newborn child, death is just around the corner, and the only thing that stands between the child and death is other people who are willing and able to come to the rescue and, to the best of their abilities, protect it from dying. And even then their existence is still precarious.[24]

Our extreme helplessness and dependency at the beginning of our life is therefore just as much a function of our mortality, that is, our being able to die (which is a fact whether or not we are aware of it), as it is a function of our natality, our having been born. So maybe there is indeed a strong connection between our natality and our mortality, which are not so much opposites but rather two sides of the same ontological coin.

Yet however that may be, the fact remains that we are born, and that we are born helpless and dependent. That state of dependency is our original position, our starting point in life, but also our default position. We remain dependent throughout our lives, not only on other people, but also on our environment in general, for our survival and flourishing. Not necessarily to the same extent as we do in early childhood, but some degree of dependency is always there, and it often increases again considerably when we approach the end of our lives. But as you have made quite clear, and rightly so, we are dependent on other people and on there being a fully formed world not only because without it we would not be able to last very long and would perish almost immediately after arriving in it, but also because we would not be able to *make sense* of the world. Indeed, we would not even be able to make sense of ourselves.

Because we are new to this world when we get here, we rely, like an amnesic traveller who suddenly finds herself stranded in a foreign land about which she knows nothing and whose language she does not speak, on the land's native inhabitants to guide us and show us the way. Without them we would be lost, and so we have no choice but to trust them.[25] We learn their language and do as they do until we have become one of them. That is the situatedness and givenness that comes with our natality. When we enter this world, everything is new to us, even we ourselves. But the world we enter is not new. It is an old world, with people who arrived before us and who already know their way around and can teach us how things work around here. Learning from them, we complete our transition from non-existence to existence. We become someone, a *particular* someone, by absorbing what is already there and using it for the formation of ourselves. We can only become who and what we are with the help of a world that is already in place. The new needs the old.

The old, however, may also need the new, and I think we should talk about this too. We have already acknowledged that our having been born shapes our existence in various ways. But how does the fact that people *keep* being born – that after we have arrived on the scene other people arrive, and that they will continue to arrive even after we have left it – shape our existence?[26] Just as we are affected not only by our own mortality, but also by the mortality of other people (most acutely by those that are dear to us), we may also be affected by other people's natality. When we enter the world we are new and the world is old. But then, after a while, we become part of that old world, and others arrive as the *new* new ones. We teach them our ways as we have been taught by others. But perhaps there is also something that they can teach us, something that we, the old, rely on them for. Perhaps the dependency that defines our existence is not as one-sided as it initially appeared. Perhaps the old needs the new just as much as the new needs the old.[27]

*

Alison Stone: I agree that death, like birth, is a process – at least for the majority of us in industrial societies who live long enough to die through gradual decline, loss of capacities, illness and ageing. Moreover, during these processes of dying, of going gradually out of existence, we are liable to become very heavily dependent on care from others once again, as we were in infancy and childhood. So it can be helpful to consider death in relation to birth, with an eye to their parallels. Doing so brings out features of death that have been rather sidelined in the philosophical discussion of death, which has mainly focused on being dead, i.e. non-existence.

If it is helpful to view death in connection with birth, then should we also, when considering natality, keep its interaction with mortality in constant view? Perhaps so, given for instance that our infantile dependency is shaped by our mortality as well as our natality, as you rightly observe. Yes, we are born helpless; but this means that we cannot satisfy our basic physical needs through our own efforts, and so are vulnerable to suffering and, in the end, dying in the absence of help from others. Mortality is likewise at work in our dependency on others more generally, throughout adulthood. I cannot meet my physical needs through my own efforts alone; I am dependent on others through networks of production, distribution, exchange and communication which, among other things, keep shops supplied with food. I also depend on others – as the coronavirus pandemic has made clear – to use these networks in a considerate way, say by not buying up all the pasta in the supermarket. Adult dependency has continuities with infantile dependency, for in both cases we cannot meet our physical needs unaided. Thus adult dependency is connected both with natality, through its continuities with infantile dependency, and with mortality, in that if our needs go unmet what we are vulnerable to, ultimately, is dying.

As you also point out, in infancy and early childhood our mortality affects our dependency, and so our existence, without us having any awareness of death – so I moved too hastily in saying that mortality only affects our lives through our anticipation of it. Perhaps we can say the following. While we are vulnerable and dependent through our lives, we are especially so in infancy and early childhood. But while the very young are especially vulnerable to dying, they are not yet aware of death. From later childhood onwards we become less vulnerable – we become ordinarily rather than especially vulnerable – but now we are aware of death, and once acquired this awareness inevitably mediates how we treat our ongoing vulnerability and dependency.

From all this, does it follow that natality ought always to be addressed in connection with mortality?[28] I hesitate to say 'yes', for two reasons. First, our philosophical reflection on death is so much better developed that it tends to crowd birth out as soon as death is brought onstage. Second, only once we have begun to grasp how natality structures our existence can we start to see how these natally shaped structures are simultaneously shaped by mortality. But to reach that point, we first need an account of natality, and getting it into initial view is most easily done by tackling it in its own right. We need, as it were, a two-part account: part one concerning natality in its own right, and part two reconsidering natality in its connection with mortality.

As you say, to be born is to come as a newcomer into a world that is already old. One aspect of this, which I take from Hannah Arendt, is that the arrival of new people is a source of hope for those already there in the world.[29] Being new, these people carry the promise that they will do new things, renewing and refreshing the world – not ploughing the same old furrows but swerving aside and thereby making things better. Being born unformed and open-ended, the newcomers are full of possibilities, hence again giving hope. Yet newcomers must take on the traditions that hold in the parts of the world into which they are born. Without these traditions of meaning-making and interpretation we would have no way of making sense of the world at all.

This combination of novelty and tradition can be handled in many ways. From a conservative and traditionalist standpoint, one might be hopeful that newcomers will inherit existing traditions, keep them alive, and carry them forwards. From a more revolutionary perspective, one might hope that they will overthrow outworn traditions. Or one might hope that the newcomers will do things that at last fulfil the previously thwarted hopes of past generations. Alternatively again, one might view the arrival of newcomers more bleakly, thinking that inevitably over time these individuals will imbibe more and more tradition, accrue more and more of the past, until they are so weighted down with history that all the open-ended possibilities are crushed out of them. Perhaps here a responsibility arises for older people relative to each generation of newcomers: that we don't so overburden the young with the weight of tradition that they become unable to fulfil their promise of bringing renewal.

*

Michael Hauskeller: The arrival of new people in the world can indeed be, and often is, a source of hope for those who are already in it. The promise of renewal, but also of continuity, of the world and (human) life not ending when my life and *my* world come to an end, is, for many of us, a strong incentive to seek, support and promote the continued arrival of new people. This is why the birth of a new person is, every time it happens, generally experienced as such a momentous event by those who are involved in it or witness it. There is mystery here, and great wonder, because what we are witnessing is not a mere transformation of matter, but the coming-into-existence of something genuinely new, something that was not there before, not even in a different form: where there used to be nothing, now there is something. This is both very ordinary, because it happens all the time, and, in its utter incomprehensibility, absolutely extraordinary, and its being so common makes it even more extraordinary. It is the closest we get to a miracle, with the possible exception of death, which is equally miraculous in that it reverses the situation: where there used to be something, now there is nothing. We pop into existence like a rabbit out of a conjuror's empty hat, and then, after hopping about for a while, we vanish again (or are vanished) into thin air. But unlike death, and despite the pain and hardship that the process of giving birth usually involves for the mother, the birth of a new person is generally seen as a cause for celebration. Not always, of course, because there are circumstances that may turn the arrival of a new person into a misfortune, but in most cases we tend to see birth, the appearance of a new person in our midst, as a happy occasion.

However, this welcoming attitude towards birth is far from universal. For some, the arrival of new people in the world is a source not of hope but of despair, or something close to it. You mentioned the promise that new people carry, and they do. Yet what we may see as a promise, others may see as a threat, since a threat is simply the promising of something that the one to whom the promise is made would much prefer not to come to pass ('I promise, you will regret this!'). New people carry the threat that they will soon push us, the old, aside, staking a claim to what we, through luck or hard work, have managed to secure for ourselves. They serve as a potent reminder of our ephemerality, as if the birth of others tolls the death knell for us.

This negative attitude towards birth, or at any rate the birth of others, is particularly prominent among transhumanists and generally those who think of death, and especially their own death, as 'the greatest evil', and who consequently urge us to do everything in our power to rid ourselves of the scourge of ageing as soon as possible so that our lives can be extended indefinitely, before it is too late and we are forever deprived of our existence.[30] Once we have achieved this goal, we no longer have to concern ourselves with bringing new people into existence to carry the torch of humanity into the future. Once death is no longer inevitable and becomes increasingly rare, the exception rather than the rule, we may have to severely restrict the number of births, but that would be okay and pose no major problem because, it is argued, we would no longer *need* new people.[31] If renewal is needed or desired, we can always take care of it ourselves, with the help of a presumably never-ending supply of new technologies and thus opportunities for transformative experience.

This professed indifference towards renewal through birth (the continued coming-into-existence of new people) masks an underlying resentment that, I think it is fair to say, is also palpable in the anti-natalist movement promoted by philosophers like David Benatar who try to convince us that it would have been much better for us if we had never been born, or, more precisely, had never come into existence.[32] This is supposedly so even if our lives happen to be really quite wonderful. According to Benatar, even the happiest and luckiest among us would have been better off if they had never existed. The fact that no life is *completely* without pain or suffering is believed to be enough to tip the balance against existence.[33] Crucially, we are not meant to infer from this – as it would seem quite natural to do – that it would *also* be better for us if we died as soon as possible, because even though it would not have been bad for us never to have existed, it allegedly *is* bad for us to stop existing. This is rather convenient for those who profess to believe that it would have been better for us never to have existed because it allows them to keep living their lives comfortably instead of having, for consistency's sake, to commit suicide. Birth, they claim, is an evil, but so is death.[34]

Obviously, however, while it is possible for us to stop existing, it is *not* possible for us never to have existed. Our birth has already happened, while our death has not. This means that the only practical conclusion we can draw from all of this is that, for one thing, we should stop letting new people come into existence, and, for another, we should try to hold on to our *own* existence as long as possible. Anti-natalism thus provides a moral justification for making sure that we stay in charge and that the old get older still.

*

Alison Stone: I am intrigued by what I take to be your suggestion that transhumanism and anti-natalism are bedfellows, united in part as ways of propping up the privileges of the old. I am sympathetic; I do think that Western societies are becoming increasingly gerontocratic – the recent crop of US presidential candidates being one reflection of that. My sense is that you are not much taken with either anti-natalism or transhumanism. I have doubts about them too.

Beginning with Benatar's philosophical anti-natalism, he argues that for each of us it would always have been better had we not come into existence. Existing always involves at least some pain, which is bad, whereas non-existence involves the absence of pain, which is good. This is non-existence here not in the sense of being dead but in the sense of never having come into existence in the first place. To be sure, existence always involves at least some pleasure as well, which is good; but non-existence involves the absence of pleasure, which is neither good nor bad. Thus the net balance of pains and pleasures favours non-existence, for Benatar, so that it is always wrong to bring someone into existence through procreation.

I am not convinced. If the absence of pain is good (for someone, the one who would otherwise have existed), then correlatively the absence of pleasure must be bad for them rather than neither-good-nor-bad. Still, this would only level existence and non-existence – although even that presumably entails that one may bring a new person into existence by procreating. We could go further, though, to say that positive pleasures – taking these to encompass the various goods of human life – weigh more heavily in the balance than mere absences of pain. Along such lines we might conclude that, other things being equal, it is better to come into existence than not, and that it is a good thing for someone to exist.[35]

Popular anti-natalism often has an environmentalist aspect. The thought is that we ought to avoid populating the world with yet more human beings who will pollute it, deplete its resources, contribute to habitat loss and species destruction, continue habits of over-consumption, and so on. I wonder whether this form of anti-natalism, by depriving possible future people of the good of existence, makes future generations pay the price for the environmentally damaging activities of those currently in existence. One might object that until someone has come into existence they are not there to be deprived of its goods. But if someone can be benefited by not ever coming into existence – as per Benatar's reasoning – then conversely someone can be deprived by not ever being brought into existence.

Still, an environmentalist anti-natalist could say that what good there is in existing, for any individual human being who comes into existence, is outweighed by the environmentally harmful consequences of that person existing. That is, whereas for Benatar existing is primarily bad for the human individual who exists, for the environmentalist anti-natalist it is primarily bad for the rest of the natural environment. I find this an unnecessarily pessimistic view. We could regard the birth of new human beings optimistically, thinking that some of these people will grow up – as Greta Thunberg has done – to challenge environmentally harmful practices, to demand change to these practices, to come up with alternatives, and to inspire and motivate others to change. But instead the anti-natalist view is that the overwhelming environmental harmfulness of these future people existing outweighs all the positive and hopeful possibilities those people might come up with. Implicitly, then, the further thought seems to be that human beings cannot possibly change our ways of life and learn to live in ways that allow the rest of the planet to flourish as well. Thus, given that we cannot change, it is better for us to remove ourselves – or rather remove our future successors – from the scene. I like to have more hope and trust in new and future generations than this.

Finally – transhumanism and the project of making existing human beings immortal. I find it plausible that death is a bad thing, because it deprives us of the goods of existence. But I am also open to the idea that, bad as death is, immortality would be worse.[36] By 'immortality' I mean actually living forever, as distinct from living for a few hundred years or so. Simone de Beauvoir, for one, suggests that if I were immortal I would never face any real choices. Since I would know that in the future I could come back to every option and possibility, there is nothing at stake now when I decide among them.[37] With a mortal life, when I make choices, I am making a real commitment through which I come to be one sort of person rather than another, and end up leading just this one life rather than any other. The options I decide not to take are ones that thereby become closed off to me forever. Were this not the case, none of the courses of action I 'decide' upon would carry any real meaning for me, as I would have nothing invested in them; my 'choices' would be weightless.

Beauvoir's thought, then, is that even though death is bad because it deprives me of those things I value in my life, immortality would be worse. Death, at least, deprives me of those things only when I die, while the prospect of my death enhances these things' value to me as long as I remain alive; indeed, arguably, my mortality is necessary to their having meaning and value at all. Immortality, on the other hand, would strip these things of meaning and value while I am (endlessly) alive. So whereas as a mortal I enjoy meaning and value for a limited time, as an immortal I would never enjoy any meaning and value at all.

I take it that you are raising a different concern about transhumanism, though. Namely, that if those of us already in existence became immortal, then we would no longer have any reason for procreating and giving birth. Even if we still did so, the meaning of new births would be completely changed, and the balance between old and new generations would have been disrupted. It is not clear how newcomers could bring any renewal into the world, as the old with their pre-existing meanings and habits would never be going out of it. Once again, this seems to point to the interdependence of natality and mortality, such that eliminating the latter would deprive us of the former as well.

*

Michael Hauskeller: You are right that, like you, I am not buying the transhumanist glorification of lives that never end, and neither am I buying the anti-natalist vilification of existence. Existing is neither better nor worse than not existing. The dead are not worse off than the living, nor are they better off; nor are those who have never lived better or worse off than those who have lived, mostly because non-existence is not a state one can be in.[38] Even though we are used to talking that way, there is not really anyone who *is* dead, just as there is not anyone who has not come into existence (yet or ever). Assertions that he or she doesn't exist have no referent. 'Good' and 'bad', however, are predicates of being. Nothing is good or bad for us before we come into existence, or after we have ceased to exist. There are only ever better and worse ways of existing. Some lives are better than others, not only in terms of the net balance of pleasure over pain, but also because they are richer, more connected, more lived perhaps. Life, and lives, must be judged on their own terms, including lives that are so bad that they appear no longer worth living.

Every (individual) life has a beginning and an end. You and I have been talking a lot about death. We emphasised connections between natality and mortality. But one aspect that we have not yet mentioned is the radical *contingency* of our existence, and at first glance at least this is an aspect that is based more firmly in our having being born than in our having to die. There is a real difference here, in that while each of us, at least for the time being, *must* die one day, it seems that none of us had to be born. Death has always been a necessary part of human existence, and it probably always will be. In contrast, there is, for all we know, nothing necessary about our birth. On the contrary, for each of us it was, before it came to pass, extremely unlikely that we were going to exist. If the slightest thing had gone differently than it did, we would not be here today. If your parents hadn't met, if they hadn't fallen in love and hadn't had intercourse, if they hadn't had it at that particular time and a different sperm had fused with a different egg, you would not exist. It is true, your parents might have had a child and that child may have been given your name, in which case someone bearing your name would still exist, but that someone would not be you, just as your brother or your sister is not you, unless we want to assume that, before we are born, there already exists a (not yet embodied and possibly eternal) soul waiting for its opportunity to be born, and then seizing it eventually, using any genetic makeup that happens to become available to it. In that case, however, what we take to be the beginning of our existence would not really be that at all. Birth would be a transition to a new form of existence, which is very different kind of thing; perhaps a new beginning of sorts, but not a *radical* new beginning. It is a new bottle, but still the old wine. If, however, there is no such thing as a pre-existing soul and we truly come into existence when we seem to – new wine in a new bottle – then there is no necessity to our existence, which is owed to pure chance. Each of us has made the transition from non-existence to existence against all the odds.

Once again, this aspect of our being born informs our entire existence. We are contingent beings, not only in the sense that we could easily not have existed, but also in the sense that we can just as easily cease to exist at any time. We usually feel quite secure in our existence, as if we couldn't possibly not be, but we also know very well, in an abstract kind of way, that one day it will all be over and, more importantly, that we cannot be certain that that day is not today. For all we know, today may be the last day of our lives, and that is because nothing in this world makes it necessary for us to be here. These days we can quickly be propelled back into non-existence if we happen to come too close to someone who, unknown to us, is carrying a virus, or if we happen to touch something that they touched earlier. That is all it takes. One day we are fit and healthy, a couple of days later we are in intensive care and dead shortly after. Once again, then, the fact and the circumstances of our being born, in this case its contingent nature, prefigure a life that is characterised by the possibility of ending at any given time.

Yet the contingency of our birth is not only a permanent feature of our being there in the first place. It also extends to the circumstances into which we are born and that shape our existence, first relating to *that* we are, but then also to *what* we are and *how* we are. We are contingent beings not only in the sense that we could just as well not be, but also because we could conceivably be very different from the way we are, namely if we had been born into other circumstances. I could be speaking a different language and be raised in a different tradition and belief system. As a consequence, I could have developed different interests, different culinary preferences and different moral convictions. The interests, preferences and convictions that I in fact have make me who I am, but it is by accident of birth that I have become the person that I am now. It is also by accident of birth, at least partly, that my life has turned out the way it has. We don't all enjoy the same starting conditions. Some are born with a silver spoon in their mouth, others with a plastic spoon, and some with no spoon at all. In this respect, some are luckier than others. If death is the great equaliser, birth is the great differentiator.

I like to think that realising this, the radical contingency of our being born at a particular time and place and in a particular (cultural, social, political, religious, familial, etc.) situation, may make people more tolerant and understanding, more open to other ways of life and other ways of looking at the world. We have all, after all, been thrown into our existence[39] without being asked, randomly and apparently without any particular purpose. We did not choose to be born and we had no say in the where and when of it. We don't know why we are here, where we come from or where we are going. Yet we have been born, and we are not dead yet. Necessary or not, we do exist, and we have the potential to shape the world, as we have been shaped by it. And that is no small thing.

Notes

1. For example, Françoise Dastur claims that '[t]he question of the origin of things is indeed a source of disquietude for our understanding, but the question of their end constitutes the torment of our entire being' (*Death*, 36). Likewise, for many existentialist philosophers there are structural connections among anxiety, mortality and the future (for instance Heidegger, *Being and Time*).
2. On fear as properly directed towards the future see Svendsen, *A Philosophy of Fear*, 39, 43, who refers in support of his argument to Aristotle's *Rhetoric*, where the latter defines fear as pain arising from the expectation of a coming evil.
3. For this explanation for philosophers' neglect of birth, see particularly Cavarero, *In Spite of Plato*.
4. The concept of *natality* goes back to Hannah Arendt, *The Human Condition*, although in her view natality has only an ambiguous link with physical birth.
5. Again, Arendt emphasises 'the new beginning inherent in birth' (*The Human Condition*, 9).
6. Cavarero stresses, partly against Arendt, that one is always born *from* someone, in whose womb one is generated, so that intra-uterine gestation is part of birth in the broader sense (*In Spite of Plato*, 59).
7. Montagu, *Touching*, 54–7.
8. Recently some zoologists such as Dunsworth have challenged the widely accepted idea that the obstetric dilemma accounts for the helplessness of human young (Dunsworth et al., 'Metabolic hypothesis for human altriciality'). Nonetheless, explanatory appeal to the obstetric dilemma remains standard.
9. According to zoologist Adolf Portmann (*Biologische Fragmente zu einer Lehre vom Menschen*), human babies would have to be born at 18 to 21 months if they were to have the level of independence on leaving the womb of the young of our nearest primate neighbours – chimpanzees, orangutans and bonobos.
10. See Gehlen, *Man*, 24, who argues that because of our unformed nature on leaving the womb we are especially open-ended, 'undetermined', 'world-open' beings.
11. The extent of our dependency has also been highlighted by Kittay (*Love's Labor*) and, in her wake, MacIntyre (*Dependent Rational Animals*). Kittay makes the point that dependency is prior to independence.
12. As Brison ('Relational selves and personal identity', 218) has put it, 'selves exist only in relation to other selves, that is, that they are fundamentally relational entities. On this view, persons or selves . . . are what Annette Baier has called "second persons".'
13. For this distinction between one's basic sense of self (or 'core self') and one's concrete personality structure see Stern, *The Interpersonal World of the Infant*.
14. Situatedness has been discussed in two main bodies of philosophical writing: first, in work by Sartre, Heidegger and other existentialists and phenomenologists, where my situation is understood as the background against and out of which I engage in making sense of the world; and second, in work by feminist philosophers, especially epistemologists, foregrounding how our social locations with respect to various axes of power affect what we can know.
15. On the idea that we can only criticise power relations and social arrangements from within them, not outside them, see for one Butler, *The Psychic Life of Power*.
16. Note that I am not assuming here that non-human animals could not possibly have a concept of death, as is often claimed. There is now in fact ample empirical evidence that many social animals do have some understanding of what the death of others means and that it is irreversible. For a brief overview of the evidence see Anderson, 'Comparative thanatology'. Perhaps some species can even, as Monso has argued ('How to tell if animals can understand death'), understand that they are mortal in the sense that they themselves *can* die. However, to understand that one *must* die sooner or later requires not only a level of abstraction but also a knowledge of history and biology that seems to go far beyond the abilities of even the most social of non-human animals. The same is true for the knowledge that one was born.
17. O'Byrne (*Natality and Finitude*) has argued that our having been born is just as relevant, if not more so, for our experience and our understanding of finitude as the knowledge that we are going to die, not least because it highlights the importance of our relations to others for our lives.
18. Dick, *We Can Build You*.
19. I have analysed this situation with reference to Dick in 'What is it like to be a bot?'.
20. The distinction between 'altricial' and 'precocial' species is between those that are helpless at birth and those that are more independent. Human beings are 'secondarily altricial': having

earlier in our evolutionary history been precocial, the developments that resulted in the obstetric dilemma led to our being born 'early' and thus becoming altricial. See Gould, *Ever Since Darwin*, chapter 8.

21. Dick, *We Can Build You*, 77–8.

22. Dylan Thomas: 'Do not go gentle into that good night./ Rage, rage against the dying of the light' (*The Poems of Dylan Thomas*, 239).

23. This is what Leon Kass ('L'Chaim and its limits'), raising concerns about the wisdom of radical life extension, has suggested: 'Who would not want to avoid senility, crippling arthritis, the need for hearing aids and dentures, and the degrading dependencies of old age? But, in the absence of these degenerations, would we remain content to spurn longer life? Would we not become even more disinclined to exit? Would not death become even more of an affront? Would not the fear and loathing of death increase in the absence of its harbingers?'

24. According to Hans Jonas (*The Phenomenon of Life*, 83), it is precisely this precarious balance between being and non-being and the resulting need to stave off non-being at every turn that constitutes the very essence of life. Life and death, then, are inextricably intertwined. This is particularly evident in the newborn child, whose existence unites 'the self-accrediting force of being already there and the demanding impotence of being-not-yet' and thus has to be understood as a 'suspension of helpless being over not-being, which must be bridged by another causality' (*The Imperative of Responsibility*, 134). Compare my own 'The ontological ethics of Hans Jonas'.

25. See Harris, *Trusting What You're Told*.

26. In *Death and the Afterlife*, Samuel Scheffler speculates that the prospect of humanity's imminent extinction shortly after our own death ('doomsday') would affect us more than the knowledge of our own mortality currently does. If we knew that all human life would disappear from the face of the earth 30 days after we die, this would render much of what we do today meaningless.

27. As Jantzen (*Foundations of Violence*, 38) puts it: 'with each new infant, new possibilities are born, new freedom and creativity, the potential that this child will help make the world better. Freedom, creativity, and the potential for a fresh start are central to every human life and are ours in virtue of the fact that we are natals.'

28. It is worth noting that whereas some feminist philosophers such as Cavarero and Jantzen have favoured giving centrality to birth and not death, reversing the traditional order of priorities, other feminist philosophers have disagreed, advocating re-balancing rather than reversing the importance of birth and death. See Clack, *Sex and Death*, and Heinämaa, 'Phenomenologies of mortality and generativity'.

29. Arendt, *The Human Condition*, 177–8, 247.

30. See for instance Bostrom, 'The fable of the dragon tyrant'. From a transhumanist perspective, bringing new people into the world is at best unnecessary and at worst a threat to one's own supposed right to immortality. Brent Waters (*This Mortal Flesh*, 109–10), drawing a connection between natality and mortality, argues that transhumanists have no interest in natality because 'the birth of a child serves as a reminder of necessity's death and decay'. For a concise summary of the transhumanist attitude to continuing procreation see Cruz, 'Transhumanism and the fate of natality'.

31. Grey, 'Aging, childlessness or overpopulation'.

32. Benatar, *Better Never to Have Been*; Benatar and Wasserman, *Debating Procreation*; Benatar, *The Human Predicament*.

33. Benatar, *Better Never to Have Been*, 48: '[A] life filled with good and containing only the most minute quantity of bad – a life of utter bliss adulterated only by the pain of a single pin-prick – is worse than no life at all.'

34. Benatar, *The Human Predicament*, 110: '[D]eath is an evil and thus part of the human predicament.'

35. I am informed by, among other critics of Benatar, Harman's 'Critical study: David Benatar, better never to have been', and McLean's 'What's so good about non-existence?'.

36. This is, of course, argued by Bernard Williams in 'The Makropulos case: reflections on the tedium of immortality'. A similar argument was made by Beauvoir in fictional form, in her 1946 novel *All Men are Mortal*.

37. See Schott, who states Beauvoir's view in these terms (*Birth, Death and Femininity*, 3–6).

38. See Johansson, 'Two arguments for Epicureanism' and Taylor, 'Why death is not bad for the one who dies'.

39. The concept of 'thrownness' was introduced and developed by Heidegger in *Being and Time*.

Bibliography

Anderson, James R. 'Comparative thanatology', *Current Biology* 26/13 (2016): R553–R556.

Arendt, Hannah. *The Human Condition*. Chicago: University of Chicago Press, 1958.

Beauvoir, Simone de. *All Men are Mortal*, translated by E. Cameron. London: Virago, 1995.

Benatar, David. *Better Never to Have Been: The harm of coming into existence*. Oxford: Oxford University Press, 2006.

Benatar, David. *The Human Predicament*. Oxford: Oxford University Press, 2017.

Benatar, David, and David Wasserman. *Debating Procreation: Is it wrong to reproduce?* Oxford: Oxford University Press, 2015.

Bostrom, Nick. 'The fable of the dragon tyrant', *Journal of Medical Ethics* 31 (2005): 273–7.

Brison, Susan. 'Relational selves and personal identity'. In *The Routledge Companion to Feminist Philosophy*, edited by Ann Garry, Serene J. Khader and Alison Stone, 218–30. New York: Routledge, 2017.

Butler, Judith. *The Psychic Life of Power*. Stanford, CA: Stanford University Press, 1997.

Cavarero, Adriana. *In Spite of Plato*, translated by Serena Anderlini-d'Onofrio and Áine O'Healy. Cambridge: Polity Press, 1995.

Clack, Beverley. *Sex and Death*. Cambridge: Polity Press, 2002.

Cruz, Eduardo R. 'Transhumanism and the fate of natality: an introduction', *Zygon* 48/4 (2013): 916–35.

Dastur, Françoise. *Death: An essay on finitude*, translated by John Llewellyn. London: Athlone, 1996.

Dick, Philip K. *We Can Build You*. New York: Harper, 2008.

Dunsworth, Holly M., Anna G. Warrener, Terrence Deacon, Peter T. Ellison and Herman Pontzer. 'Metabolic hypothesis for human altriciality', *Proceedings of the National Academy of Sciences of the United States of America* 109/38 (2012): 15212–16.

Gehlen, Arnold. *Man: His nature and place in the world*. New York: Columbia University Press, 1988.

Gould, Stephen Jay. *Ever Since Darwin*. New York: Norton, 1977.

Grey, Aubrey de. 'Aging, childlessness or overpopulation: the future's right to choose', *Rejuvenation Research* 7 (2004): 237–8.

Harman, Elizabeth. 'Critical study: David Benatar, better never to have been', *Noûs* 43/4 (2009): 776–85.

Harris, Paul. *Trusting What You're Told: How children learn from others*. Cambridge, MA: Harvard University Press, 2012.

Hauskeller, Michael. 'The ontological ethics of Hans Jonas'. In *Medicine and Society: New perspectives in continental philosophy*, edited by Darian Meacham, 39–56. New York: Springer, 2015.

Hauskeller, Michael. 'What is it like to be a bot? SF and the morality of intelligent machines'. In *Minding the Future*, edited by Barry Dainton, Will Slocombe and Attila Tanyi. New York: Springer, 2021.

Heidegger, Martin. *Being and Time*, translated by John Macquarrie and Edward Robinson. Oxford: Blackwell, 1962.

Heinämäa, Sara. 'Phenomenologies of mortality and generativity'. In *Feminist Philosophies of Birth, Death and Embodiment*, edited by Robin May Schott, 73–153. Bloomington, IN: Indiana University Press, 2010.

Jantzen, Grace. *Foundations of Violence*. London: Routledge, 2004.

Johansson, Jens. 'Two arguments for Epicureanism'. In *Exploring the Philosophy of Death and Dying*, edited by Michael Cholbi and Travis Timmerman, 70–77. London: Routledge, 2021.

Jonas, Hans. *The Phenomenon of Life*. New York: Harper & Row, 1966.

Jonas, Hans. *The Imperative of Responsibility*. Chicago: University of Chicago Press, 1985.

Kass, Leon. 'L'Chaim and its limits: why not immortality?', *First Things* 113 (May 2001): 17–24.

Kittay, Eva Feder. *Love's Labor: Essays on women, equality, and dependency*. New York: Routledge, 1999.

MacIntyre, Alasdair. *Dependent Rational Animals*. London: Duckworth, 1999.

McLean, Brian. 'What's so good about non-existence?', *Journal of Value Inquiry* 49/1–2 (2015): 81–94.

Monso, Susana. 'How to tell if animals can understand death', *Erkenntnis* (2019). https://doi.org/10.1007/s10670-019-00187-2.

Montagu, Ashley. *Touching: The human significance of the skin*. 3rd edition. New York: Harper and Row, 1986.

O'Byrne, Anne. *Natality and Finitude*. Bloomington, IN: Indiana University Press, 2010.

Portmann, Adolf. *Biologische Fragmente zu einer Lehre vom Menschen*. 3rd edition. Basel: Schwabe, 1969.

Scheffler, Samuel. *Death and the Afterlife*. Oxford: Oxford University Press, 2013.

Schott, Robin May. *Birth, Death and Femininity*. Bloomington, IN: Indiana University Press, 2010.

Svendsen, Lars. *A Philosophy of Fear*, translated by John Irons. London: Reaktion, 2007.

Stern, Daniel. *The Interpersonal World of the Infant*. London: Karnac, 1988.

Taylor, James Stacey. 'Why death is not bad for the one who dies'. In *Exploring the Philosophy of Death and Dying*, edited by Michael Cholbi and Travis Timmerman, 78–84. London: Routledge, 2021.

Thomas, Dylan. *The Poems of Dylan Thomas*, edited by Daniel Jones. New York: New Directions, 2003.

Waters, Brent. *This Mortal Flesh: Incarnation and bioethics*. Grand Rapids, MI: Brazos Press, 2009.

Williams, Bernard. 'The Makropulos case: reflections on the tedium of immortality'. In *Problems of the Self*, 82–100. Cambridge: Cambridge University Press, 1973.

11
Love

with Troy Jollimore

Troy Jollimore: People sometimes say to me, of course love is interesting, but why is it interesting to philosophers? I am always amused by the presupposition lying behind such remarks: that philosophers are not interested in the things that interest ordinary people. I suppose it might be worth thinking about how we have gained that reputation. At any rate, over the years I have found love to be philosophically fascinating – an inexhaustible source of questions and puzzles.

Any conversation about love will be shaped by our assumptions about just what the word means. For my part, I have mostly been interested in 'personal' love – love of persons, love between persons. Romantic love, love for friends, love for family members, those are the paradigm cases. The word gets used in many other ways, of course. And love for things that are not persons shares at least some common ground with personal love. Loving nature, or the practice of medicine, or the music of The Beatles, or early twentieth-century painting – any of these, like love for a person, can provide a sense of purpose, help to give one's life a shape, and help to constitute the lover's identity.[1] You don't really know a person unless you know what they love; from which it follows that you don't really know yourself unless you know what you love.[2]

But while this is as true of love for persons as of any other form, love for persons also seems distinctive in certain ways that make it especially important, and especially interesting. A person, unlike the practice of medicine or the music of The Beatles, might love you back. Or they might not.[3] They might have all sorts of attitudes toward you. Early twentieth-century painting will never know that you love it, or care; your loving it will not affect how it develops, or influence its experience of the world; and its changing attitudes toward you, and your attitudes toward it, will not affect your experience or alter in any way the course of the development of your attitudes. Loving is a little like speech, I think. You can speak *to*, or *at*, all sorts of things, but you can only speak *with* another entity that also possesses the concept of speech and the relevant communicative abilities. It is only with another speaker that you can have a conversation. And to me, love is most interesting when, in this way, it resembles a conversation.

A lot of the philosophical discussion about love clusters around the core question of whether we have reasons to love the people we love.[4] Much of our talk suggests that we do, sometimes if not always. (But if it were only sometimes, and not always, this in itself would be somewhat mysterious.) We are often able to identify many of the features that draw us to someone, to say what we find attractive. On the other hand, we almost never feel that we can give the complete account; if we are foolish enough to try to say everything, it nearly always feels that something is still missing from our list. And philosophers have been ingenious in generating counterintuitive implications from the idea that we have reasons to love our beloveds. For instance, if this were true, then wouldn't you have just as much reason to love an exact replica of your beloved?[5] Or wouldn't it be rationally required that you replace your partner with someone who had all the same attractive qualities plus one additional attractive quality, should the opportunity come along?[6] I suspect that a lot of these objections are based on false presumptions about what reasons are and how they must work (and at the end of the day, I do think we have reasons to love the people we love). Indeed, thinking carefully about love might be a very good way of coming to a better understanding of how reasons in general work.

One of the objections that tends to strike people most forcefully, here, is based on the idea of love at first sight. If we love for reasons, the argument goes, then love at first sight cannot exist, since we cannot know, on first meeting someone, what our reasons for loving them are.[7] Now, obviously we could get around this objection just by claiming that love at first sight does not exist. But that option is not available to me because I happen to think that love at first sight probably does exist, at least in some cases. Not only romantic cases, by the way; in fact, even people who are sceptical about specifically *romantic* love at first sight will likely admit that it happens in other sorts of cases – for instance, parents of newborns.[8] Many such people will say that they started to love their babies at birth, or perhaps even before birth. Now, we could say that this is not really love, but that seems to me an unattractive option.

So I have had to do a lot of thinking about what to say about such cases, and what has become clear to me is that the key is to correctly understand certain things about the relation between love and time. Parents who say, not only sincerely but I think truly, that they love their newborn infants are simply drawing on the fact that they know that these infants *will* develop lovable qualities as they grow older. They do not, of course, know *which* particular qualities they will develop; but in a sense that does not matter, because the nature of the parent–child relationship is such that there is a kind of commitment inherent in it to loving the person for *whatever* qualities make themselves available. It is something like the way in which, in romantic love, once you really fall in love with someone you end up loving all sorts of things about them, including some things that at the beginning would have struck you as quite trivial, or perhaps even unattractive, or weren't noticeable at all. But the difference is that in the parent–child case these things you come to love really do come to function as reasons, whereas in the romantic case they often do not; they are things you have a positive feeling about, given that they are attached to the person you yourself are now attached (in a different sense) to. I am thinking, for instance, of the list that Harry gives Sally at the end of the film *When Harry Met Sally*, of all the silly things he now loves about her, now that he loves her: the way she orders food, the way she crinkles her nose, that kind of thing.[9]

These aren't the reasons why he fell in love with her, and indeed I don't think they are reasons at all, because his valuing of them is entirely posterior to his valuing of her, not only chronologically but normatively. But other such features may become reasons. This is part of love's transformative power: it can prompt us, or teach us, to see and appreciate values we were blind to before. After you come to love someone, you might love the fact that they are assertive and confident, whereas before such behaviour would have struck you as irritatingly aggressive and brash. Or you might love their commitment to their moral ideals, which in a different context would have seemed to you a kind of irritating self-righteousness. And so on.

*

Michael Hauskeller: The love that parents commonly feel for their children right from the start is indeed interesting because it suggests that at least in this case it is not any particular qualities that the other person possesses that makes us love them. Instead, we seem to be predisposed to find and cherish whatever lovable qualities they may end up developing, thus supplying our love with the objective grounding that it needs in order to appear justified in our own eyes as well as in the eyes of others. However, while you are right that once we love someone even rather mundane and perhaps not particularly remarkable qualities may come to strike us as endearing and make those we love (even more) lovable to us, we do not usually seem to fall in love with someone for no reason whatsoever. Unlike Titania in Shakespeare's *A Midsummer Night's Dream*, who falls madly in love with a donkey-headed weaver just because he is the first person she sees after unknowingly being treated with a love potion in her sleep,[10] our choice of romantic partner is normally not entirely arbitrary. It is a particular person with particular observable qualities that we fall in love with, and the qualities that we observe in them (while no doubt still being ignorant about many others they also possess) are part of the reason why we start loving them.

The way reasons enter into the love parents tend to feel for their children is perhaps more akin to the love that sometimes develops between partners in arranged marriages. Here considerations other than love have brought two people together; if they are lucky, they subsequently discover what is lovable about the other, thus giving rise to affection, which may eventually deepen into love.[11] In both cases the connection precedes the emotional involvement: parents love their children primarily *because* they happen to be their children, and partners in arranged marriages may love their spouses primarily *because* they happen to be married to them.[12] There is of course no guarantee that this will happen, and I do not mean to suggest that love in arranged marriages is just as likely to develop as it is in parent–child relationships. The predisposition to love one's children just because they are our children is clearly much stronger than the predisposition to love one's partner just because they are our partner. What favours love in both cases, however, is that if we don't really have much choice in the matter and we are bound to spend decades of our life with someone, it is much easier to do so if we love them.

But what about those cases in which we actually seem to have a choice? We cannot choose our children (unless we adopt them or genetically engineer them),[13] but we can, in modern Western societies, choose our lovers and life partners, and that choice is normally governed not by considerations of expediency (i.e. by what the other can do for us, although that is not unheard of either) but by considerations of love. Most people would not want to commit to spending their life with someone they do not love or at least someone they think they could grow to love. So why do we start loving people that no prior biological or social connection compels or prompts us to love? Surely there is something about *them* that makes us love them (in addition to whatever it is in *us* that makes us love them). But it is indeed very difficult to say what exactly it is that attracts us to certain people and inspires our love for them. When our partner asks us why we love them we may tell them that we love them because they are beautiful, smart and funny. Yet although those qualities certainly seem rather lovable and therefore seem to provide us with good reasons for loving someone – we would not expect to love someone for being ugly, dumb and dreary, though we may love them *despite* being all that[14] – clearly there are lots of other people who are also beautiful, smart and funny, so could we just as well love those others?

I suppose we could have loved some of them just as well if circumstances had been different and we had met them first (time and history are relevant here: being in the right place at the right time for instance), but it is still a fact that we do not love everyone who is beautiful, smart and funny. This would suggest that if we love people for a reason, we love them not because they have those (fairly general) qualities, but because they have those qualities in their own particular way.[15] People are not just assemblages of abstract qualities; they are *concrete* and unique individuals, each different from the others, which also means that there are no two people who are beautiful, smart and funny in exactly the same way.

In real life, there are no exact replicas of anyone. Even identical twins are anything but identical.[16] At the very least they have different histories with different experiences. Yet what we love is not those thoroughly individualised (and therefore indescribable) qualities as such, but the person who reveals themselves through them. If that were not so, then it would not be possible for us to continue loving someone even after they have lost some of those qualities that initially attracted us to them. Yet that is exactly what happens. If those we love, over time, lose their beauty and perhaps even become less smart and funny, we may still go on loving them. And if we do not, one might conclude that we did not really love them in the first place.[17]

*

Troy Jollimore: People do tend to lose certain attractive qualities over time – particularly in terms of physical beauty – but the good news is that we often tend to compensate by developing new ones, especially if we manage to remain active and engaged with life.[18] Our culture tends to under-emphasise wisdom, richness of experience, acuity of judgement, curiosity, and various other virtues that frequently increase over time, but they are significant, and I think that element of compensation is part of the story about why love does not, in fact, and indeed should not, fade as physical beauty and other attractions of youth fade. At the same time, it is quite right to say, as you do, that one's fundamental attachment has to be to the person, not to the qualities. The right sort of direct attachment to the person puts one in a position to look out for, and appreciate, those new, good qualities when they come along; they will strike you in a way that they almost certainly would not if they were exhibited by a stranger, someone to whom you had no such attachment.

And in fact, since love tends to change us over time, what typically happens is that a relationship with an individual helps make me the sort of person who is especially likely to appreciate the sorts of virtues and attractions that that individual has developed or is going to develop.[19] When love is going well, these processes are simultaneous: your lover develops certain virtues, and you develop the ability to perceive and appreciate these virtues. And of course the same thing is happening in the opposite direction. (This is presumably a version of something that happens with respect to self-love as well, though of course in that context developing a virtue and developing the capacity to appreciate that virtue are so tightly bound up that we tend not to notice that they are separate at all.)

There is another part of the constancy story that is important, and again it goes back to the idea of being attached to a person rather than their qualities. As I see it, part of what this involves is that we value a person as a temporally extended being – precisely *not* the way, that is, that we value a tool.[20] Take a pocket knife. If it is just a tool, what matters is that it is sharp, because that is what a good knife needs to be; and if it loses its edge, and for some reason cannot be made sharp again, the tool has no more value and needs to be replaced. The fact that it once was sharp means nothing – it is not going to help you cut through anything now. But if the value I place on my knife is not instrumental but rather sentimental, a species of what philosophers call *final* value – if, for instance, I value the knife because it used to belong to my grandfather – it won't matter so much, and maybe won't matter at all, if it is no longer sharp. It is what it *was*, the story of the knife and its history, that matters to me.[21] So past qualities, in this context, continue to matter, and those are qualities that cannot be lost. The knife will always be the knife that used to belong to my grandfather. And this, of course, is how we value persons when we actually love them. If my lover was once beautiful, it will always be true that she was beautiful. All the meaningful stories about how we met, and the things we did together, and the support we gave each other, and so on, will always be true.[22] Some of these can be thought of in terms of qualities – like beauty – whereas others seem to have a narrative significance.

But a number of philosophers have assumed that if we make an appeal to the past, then we have to throw out qualities altogether, and *only* talk about narrative matters: a shared history, or something like that. And this does not seem to me to be true. After all, you can admire someone, or for that matter despise them, for an act they committed even before you knew them! So part of the reason love continues even when a person loses their qualities is that their past possession of those qualities is still part of who they are, at least when they are viewed in the way that is proper to love. It is like the old Gershwin song *They Can't Take That Away from Me*, which, I think, gets it exactly right. Assuming the lawyers let me get away with it, I'm going to quote two stanzas:

> There are many many crazy things
> That will keep me loving you
> And with your permission
> May I list a few
>
> The way you wear your hat
> The way you sip your tea
> The memory of all that
> No, no they can't take that away from me

It is striking that the kinds of qualities mentioned here are not general qualities – beauty, charm, etc. – but particular, quirky, idiosyncratic ones. Which goes back to your suggestion that we love people, at least at first, because 'they have those qualities in their own particular way'. It seems to me that appreciating the kinds of general qualities that are relevant here is a kind of achievement: there might be many beautiful people, just as there are many beautiful paintings, but it does not follow that you are going to be able to see every one *as* beautiful.

General properties, in a way, render people *eligible* for love.[23] But whether you actually fall in love in any given case – or even feel strongly attracted to someone, for that matter – depends on all sorts of largely contingent and arbitrary matters: who you are, what kind of situation you are meeting this person in, what is going on in your life at that moment, whether you are already pursuing a relationship with someone else, what your last relationship was like, and so forth. Reasons are present, here, in the explanatory sense, but *justifying* reasons barely enter into it at all: you don't have, or need to have, a good reason for falling in love with Mary rather than Eliza, or for not falling in love with anyone at a particular moment. A person might just leave you cold, as a piece of music might. Or a particular performance of that piece. But when they don't leave you cold – when you do become attracted – then things start to happen. You look more closely, and open yourself to that person – they arrest your attention – and all sorts of trivial and odd things become connected, in your mind, with the person you have begun to develop an attachment to, and their other qualities. And you begin to see those little things as manifesting or expressing the deeper, more general qualities and, whatever precisely this means, the person herself.[24] And you start to think, I really do like the way she sips her tea, or the way he wears his hat. And of course this can easily be bound up with all sorts of fantasies and crazy thoughts; so even as, on the one hand, infatuation-love of this sort encourages close, attentive perception, it can also act as an impediment to that very thing.[25]

Thinking about the beginnings of relationships, and what draws us into them, brings us back to the fascinating topic of arranged marriages. Really, you know, every marriage is an arranged marriage. What we usually mean by that term is a marriage that is arranged for you by someone else, as opposed to what we think of as the more usual case – a marriage that you and your partner arrange for yourselves. But really, these are just as much arranged marriages as the others, because in every case you need to learn – or at the very least, re-learn – to love the person you are married to. You either hope that the love arises and develops, or you hope that it continues, that it survives. Because no matter how strong the initial attraction, you do change, over time. And so does your lover. We do not fall in love with, or marry, a fully formed, fixed-identity object.[26] And some of the reasons why you are attracted to someone, or develop feelings for them, or choose to get married, will not be the same reasons that end up sustaining the love over the decades one hopes are to come. With arranged marriages it is more obvious: because someone else is doing the arranging, there is no pretence that you are committing yourself to this person because you have been spontaneously seized with an overwhelming and irresistible desire for them. But really, there is an element of this in every long-term romantic relationship. You want to be with this person now, and you also have an intimation that you are still going to want to be with them 10, 30, 50 years from now. And on the basis of this intimation you take a risk – the tremendous, life-altering risk that marriage is.

*

Michael Hauskeller: What you said earlier on would suggest that it cannot really be explained why we start loving a particular person – why Mary rather than Eliza. If I love Mary not because of, say, her beauty and wit (because there are lots of others who are also beautiful and witty), but because of the particular *way* in which she is beautiful and witty (not to mention the way she sips her tea), and you love Eliza because of the particular way in which *she* is beautiful and witty (and the way *she* sips her tea), while presumably remaining unaffected by Mary's charms and virtues and her peculiar tea-sipping habits, the reasons we have for loving them seem at best idiosyncratic. They are reasons just for *us*, and that means they are not really reasons at all because they fail to make anyone (ourselves included) understand why we love them rather than someone else.[27] Ultimately, all we can say here is that we love them because they are who they are (or perhaps who they appear to be when we start loving them) and because we are who we are, and somehow that is enough to get us going.[28]

In Plato's *Symposium*, the comic playwright Aristophanes explains the nature of romantic love and especially partner selection through a curious and rather charming myth that is worth remembering here, because it highlights some of the most interesting and puzzling features of love.[29] According to that myth, humans originally had a spherical shape, possessing four arms, four legs and four ears, two noses, two pairs of eyes and, most importantly, a set of sexual organs on each side, some of them female on both sides, some of them male, and some male on one side and female on the other. They were enormously powerful and dangerous, and when they threatened to attack the gods, the gods decided to cut them in half to weaken them. From that day on, we have all been desperately trying to reunite with our lost half, searching for it among those that are of the same sex as the one we lost. If we are lucky enough to find it, we become happy and fulfilled, seeking to melt into each other, never wanting to be separated from them again, and doing everything we can to spend the rest of our lives with them, without having any clear idea of *why* we feel that way.

This Platonic myth suggests that, for one thing, our sexual orientation is innate, part of our very essence as a particular individual, and for another, that there is one and only one person out there that is a perfect match for us, able to restore us to our original (perfect) condition and literally completing us. Love, then, is what happens when our natural desire to become one with ourselves has finally been satisfied.[30] This would explain why it is so difficult to identify the reasons why we love someone romantically: we love them not because they have particular qualities that others do not have, but simply because they happen to be the only person that once *was* us (or part of us), which is why they *belong* to us like nobody else does. Love for another person is in this respect very much like self-love: we don't usually love ourselves (or at least care deeply about our own interests) because we are particularly brilliant or virtuous; we do so simply because we are we, *whatever* we are.[31]

While the myth may be fanciful, it reflects very nicely the way we often experience romantic love. When we really love someone, we tend to feel that he or she is 'the one', the one we have been waiting for all our lives and the only one that matters: our 'soulmate'. But of course this is most likely an illusion: if there were only one person for us to love, it would be virtually impossible to find them (unless we had some secret tracking system that steered us towards them, or some higher power were pulling the strings of our love life). There are just too many people in the world for this to be plausible. And yet, it is true that for love to be successful and reciprocal, the lovers need to be compatible, like two puzzle pieces that fit together. It is also true that we are often *looking* for love, almost as if we were loving already, and when the right person comes along our love has found its target and becomes fully actualised. It could have been somebody else, but it wasn't, so that *this* person is now, as a matter of fact, the one who completes us and who appears uniquely suitable for the role of our beloved. And if our initial love lasts and develops, then our beloved becomes, through our shared history and the merging and co-shaping of our lives, increasingly a part of us and thus irreplaceable, so that it no longer matters that we were not *actually* made for each other, because we are now engaging in the process of making ourselves for each other. Chance thus transforms into destiny.

If we are lucky, that is. Once love has started, commitment kicks in (the arranged marriage aspect of it).[32] We may then discover new qualities and learn to cherish the ones that are already there, and in this way love is sustained. But of course that does not always happen. People also stop loving each other. We may become 'seeing' through love, but we may also become, over time, blind to the good that is there, and what once struck us as a very lovable quality in the other ceases to do so. Compensation does not always work, and though we will always be, as you say, the ones who had certain qualities, we are also the ones who have lost them, and it appears that the loss of at least some of those qualities cannot be compensated. Even if we were once compatible, since we change we may also become, over time, incompatible.[33] If that were not so, marriage would not be the 'tremendous' risk that it is.

When we commit to a relationship, we are taking a chance on someone. And while some changes may not affect our love, there are others that can destroy it. Even if we love the person and not their qualities, we cannot completely detach the person from their qualities. If for instance my beloved suddenly started wearing MAGA hats and proclaimed Donald Trump to be a great man and president, then I suspect my love for her might not survive that particular transformation or revelation.[34] We may sometimes acquire new virtues in the course of our development, but we also acquire new vices, or discover them in the course of a relationship, and the virtues we saw initially may have been more imagined than real. There are limits to the changes that love can accommodate.[35] The question is, what exactly defines those limits?

*

Troy Jollimore: There are indeed limits to the changes that love can accommodate. And I would also say that there are limits to the changes love should accommodate. So an initial answer to the question of what defines those limits – which I think is plausible, but incomplete – is that they are defined by morality.[36] Assuming that you are a basically decent moral person, for instance, you could not, to take your example, accommodate being with a person who, after four years of the Trump presidency, somehow still supported him.[37] Of course, what one perceives as their moral limits will vary from person to person, but that isn't particular to love; there is plenty of disagreement about what morality requires, and just as much disagreement about how much we are permitted to disagree about that – that is, how much my own personal value code might differ from yours without it being the case that one of us must be deeply morally wrong. Also, as in so many areas, we human beings are quite bad at predicting how we will actually react. I might *think*, in the abstract, that certain changes in my partners would be tolerable (or intolerable), and then discover, when they come about, that in fact I *can't* tolerate them (or that, to my own surprise, I *can*).

So morality seems to me part of the answer, but surely not all of it. Other values likely matter too, as long as they are central to who you are, or who you think you are. Could you, as a philosopher, be with a committed anti-intellectual? Could an artist be with someone who had no aesthetic sense? Could someone with a modicum of intelligence and aesthetic sensitivity love someone who made reality TV for a living? In fact, we can find examples of all of these; and people often point to such examples as showing that there is no essential connection. But all it really shows is that the world is complicated. The counterexamples are odd, and call out for explanation; what is more, they often end badly. The far more common cases of couples sharing values and outlooks on the world, at least to a considerable extent, strike us as natural and sensible.

Surely this accounts to some degree for the popularity of Aristophanes' myth. Sharing (enough) values with someone is normally part of what makes it feel like they 'fit' you. Of course, I agree with you that Aristophanes' version of the 'soulmates' story, and for that matter any version of it, is obviously false and absurd. But a more moderate version of it gets something right: there is presumably a limited number of people with whom you could form a successful romantic relationship. It is an open question what that number is, just as it is an open question how many people actually manage to find a fitting partner; knowing what we know about people's desire to be happy and fulfilled, and to *seem* happy and fulfilled (including to themselves), and their proclivity for spinning tales that show themselves, and their lives, in the best possible light, we must surely suspect that a significant number of people *claim* to have found an astonishingly ideal fit – maybe even 'the one' – when in fact they have not. (In the words of the old Stephen Stills song, 'If you can't be with the one you love, honey, love the one you're with'.)[38] And again, people sometimes grow together over time. After a decade, or two, or more, a couple who did not fit much at all at the beginning but who stayed together for other reasons – perhaps they are simply obstinate – might end up fitting quite snugly.

I am not at all convinced, by the way, that we are unable to say *anything* to explain why we fit with some people better than others, or are attracted to certain people, and so on. Maybe we just have a different conception of what counts as an 'explanation'. I certainly take Wittgenstein's point that explanation must come to an end somewhere, but people can often be quite articulate in describing what attracts them to their lovers. Of course, not everyone is, but that is likely a fact about particular people – that they are not very articulate, or don't have a lot of self-insight, etc. – rather than a general fact about love. That said, we must acknowledge that grasping the explanation doesn't necessarily require that I then have the same emotional response – it is not like maths, where, if I understand the proof of the theorem, now I have to believe the theorem. The Beatles exaggerated (though they did it beautifully) in *And I Love Her* when they sang, 'And if you saw my love, you'd love her too'. In fact, and fortunately, it doesn't work that way at all. But I resist the conclusion that, as you write, 'the reasons we have for loving [people] seem at best idiosyncratic. They are reasons just for *us*, and that means they are not really reasons at all, because they fail to make anyone (ourselves included) understand why we love them rather than someone else.'[39]

The full story about why I resist this conclusion is somewhat complex. But let me say, first, that I reject the claim that your reason for loving Mary is a reason just for you. It is true that not *everyone* will be moved by the way she is beautiful and witty, and sips her tea, and all that; or even that literally *everyone* will acknowledge that there is something here to be moved by. But another person *might* be so moved, if they are able to see in it what you see in it; and they might also be able to see it to an extent without actually being moved themselves. (I think I understand what people enjoy in basketball – I am not utterly mystified by their claim to enjoy it – even though I happen not to enjoy it myself.) And after all, there are many people around who are widely acknowledged as beautiful, and whose beauty is visible to lots of people, not just to their romantic partners. (So again, I think it often *is* possible to explain to others – who can perhaps already see it for themselves anyway – why I love a particular person; but getting them to see this, or grasp it, does not usually result in their falling in love themselves.) And there is a fair bit of agreement about who is witty and who isn't witty – though again, not everyone agrees.

One might, of course, insist that to be a reason, a consideration has to be convincing to everyone; it must be universally persuasive. But this condition is unacceptable. Andrew Wiles's proof of Fermat's Last Theorem is, I take it, convincing, but it won't convince most people; it only convinces those with the necessary mathematical expertise to understand it. Similarly, people who think Cézanne's paintings are extraordinary works of art are right, but not everyone can see it; they leave some people cold. The question of whether some consideration is a reason is not a question of whether it persuades everyone, but one of whether it persuades everyone who can understand it, or grasp it, or who can see things in the right way – it isn't obvious, actually, precisely how we ought to cash out this notion, but I suspect that the right way of doing so will leave it open that reasons for loving individuals do, in fact, count as legitimate reasons.

It is easy to get confused here, I think, because many of the reasons that might explain why I have come to love a particular person – reasons *why* I love A – are not the same as reasons *for* loving A; and if we focus on the wrong sort of reason, they can strike us as sheerly arbitrary, nothing but matters of chance. (The question 'Why do you love Mary, as opposed to someone else?' has two components: first, why, out of all the people in the world, only some were such as to be eligible lovers for you – that is, people to whom you might be attracted and form a relationship with, under the right circumstances; and second, why, out of all those eligible persons, it was Mary you ended up forming a relationship with.) Suppose Svetlana is an art expert, and she loves the work of Cézanne. And we ask, why does Svetlana love Cézanne's paintings? You could answer this in terms of her biography: when she was an undergraduate she had a gifted and exciting art professor, Professor C, who inspired her to change her major from Economics to Art History. And then, through a series of further events, she ended up focusing on Cézanne.

In one sense, this is a true answer to the question about why Svetlana loves Cézanne, because if not for Professor C she would never have got deeply into Cézanne. But when a person asks a question like 'Why does Svetlana love Cézanne's paintings?' they often want a very different kind of answer; they mean something more like 'What is it that Svetlana loves about Cézanne's paintings?'. Now we are being asked not simply how she got to be the sort of person who can love Cézanne's paintings – and thus, who can be moved by whatever reasons there are for us to love them – but about those reasons themselves. These, obviously, are a very different sort of reason from the explanatory reasons offered in the first story.

The point is that many of these reasons do not seem arbitrary, or mere matters of chance. That a person happened to take a course from Professor C during a certain semester, or that two people happened to be at the same party one summer evening, or that A bumped into B when he was feeling particularly lonely and B was feeling particularly flirtatious, etc., are all arbitrary matters of chance. But the beauty of a painting by Cézanne, A's entertaining way of telling a story, B's vivaciousness, intelligence and compassion – these are not arbitrary factors. These are things that *explain* why one might find a person attractive and, potentially, come to love them. For most people, they help to *make sense* of the fact that someone is loved. Again, not for everyone; reasons need not be universally persuasive. Some people might find A's stories boring, or see B as pretentious rather than smart, or place no value on any species of compassion. But again, some people don't find Cézanne's paintings beautiful, either. Some people don't see anything wrong with murder. Whatever the right test is for detecting reasons, it has to allow for a lot of diversity in human responses to them.

*

Michael Hauskeller: I suppose you are right. We do seem to have reasons for loving the ones we love, even though those reasons may not be accessible to everyone and are not the kind of reasons that make love inevitable once they have been recognised, because apparently we can acknowledge and 'see' a person's lovable qualities without actually loving that person. There is a gap here between the acknowledgement of lovability and the event of falling in love, which I think can be explained by the fact that it takes two for love to take place. Love is a relation between two people, the one who loves and the one who is loved, and in order to love a particular person we need to be who we are, and also need to be ready for them (that is, be at a stage in our lives at which it is possible for us to love that person), just as they need to be ready for us in order to love us back.

Earlier on you said that love, or more precisely personal love, resembles a conversation, which would suggest that love is not really love if it is not returned. Presumably, if love for people is like a conversation, we require some sort of response to keep it going. If I talk and you stay silent, then clearly the conversation is over, or indeed never properly started in the first place. So is it not possible then to love someone who does not love us back?[40]

At first glance, the very suggestion that love needs to be returned in order to exist would appear preposterous. Seeing that our literature, our films and our popular music, not to mention our own personal histories, feature plenty of stories of unrequited love, it certainly does seem possible for us to love someone who does not love us back. Yet if unrequited love is still love, it resembles more the love we have for things than that which we have for (or with) people, except that we do not commonly wish for those things to return our love, whereas we most certainly do when we love people.

You pointed out previously that the difference between loving things and loving people is that people 'might love you back', but if that is all, then the love itself might not be all that different. It seems to me that, phenomenologically, an essential part of our love for people (or perhaps more generally for sentient beings) is that it comes with a strong *desire* that the other return our love, and if it is not returned, something essential is missing. If we love the music of The Beatles, we don't expect them (or their music) to love us back, nor does it bother us that they don't, but if a person we love does not love us, we tend to be deeply unhappy. Unrequited love is like a broken promise, or a gift carelessly rejected. It is not yet what it clearly hopes and strives to be, which I think is an opening-up towards each other, a kind of merging of bodies and souls, a covenant of mutual trust, a lasting communion.

Perhaps this becomes clearer (and more convincing) when we consider what love actually is. We have not really addressed that fundamental question yet. People often talk as if love is an emotion, a kind of strong positive feeling for someone, like a warm glow in our heart or belly that occurs whenever we think of the person we love. And yet, while this might be a more or less accurate (if incomplete) description of what happens to us when we fall in love with someone, mature love – the kind of love that our falling in love may grow into if we are lucky and do not quickly fall out of love again – seems to be both more and less than that. For one thing, we commonly distinguish categorically between *loving* someone and *liking* someone, in such a way that not even liking someone very, very much amounts to loving them. (And perhaps that is what distinguishes love for people from love for things: 'loving' the music of The Beatles *is* in fact the same as liking it very, very much.) And for another, we seem to be able to love someone even while having acute negative feelings towards them. There may for instance be times when we are very angry with the person we love, or long periods when we don't actually feel much at all. And yet we would not normally think that we have stopped loving them during the period that we are angry with them or while we do not experience any sort of warm glow. Our love for a person somehow persists through various emotional changes and the ups and downs of ordinary life, and it does not seem to be something that we actually, at any given moment, need to *feel* in order for it to exist. Yet if love is not a feeling or emotion, what exactly is it?

It seems to me that at least part of the answer must be a strong commitment to be there for each other, in good times and in bad, in sickness and in health. Isn't that what we are really saying when we are confirming our love for someone? And isn't that what we really want to know when we ask someone whether they love us? A declaration of love, then, is not an articulation of how we feel, but a promise, and love itself is not an emotion, but a practice.[41]

*

Troy Jollimore: Love has so many different components or aspects – volitional aspects, emotional aspects, perceptual aspects and so on – that I don't want to say that it's 'exactly' anything. It is not as if the word *love* is a noun that stands for some sort of well-defined object. Better to think that there is a substantial linguistic territory we can refer to as 'love-talk', that describes, refers to and to some degree constitutes a large and varied set of practices, arrangements, behaviours and psychological phenomena. Within this territory there are a lot of things we can truly say, in various contexts, and some of those things make love out to be a kind of entity or object; but again, we should be careful not to take the idea that love is any sort of *thing* too literally. I trust the word *love* more when used as a verb, because clearly loving is something we do, or as an adjective or adverb, because some actions, and ways of behaving, and so on, clearly are loving, while others are not. But all of these admit of various interpretations. If a person asks, did my parents love me?, this is a very different sort of question than if she asks, do I still love my husband? Both of them might be very difficult to answer, and there can be disagreements about what would determine a true answer; but whatever the accounts are, they need to be sensitive to the differences between the distinct cases.

I agree with you that *liking* someone is very different from *loving* them. *Liking* seems to be more of a third-personal assessment; you can like someone very much while being completely detached from them. Loving, on the other hand, seems to involve some kind of identification: the person is important to you in some way – they are part of your life.[42] Perhaps this gets at the kind of mutually acknowledged relationship you mention above. Which is, in its own way, an interesting question. I suppose I am willing to admit to the existence of some emotion or passion that might merit the label 'unrequited love', but I fully agree with you that such a thing is very different from romantic love in the full-fledged sense, which involves a relationship in which one is loved in return; and I agree with you, too, that wanting to be loved in return is one of the things we want when we love.

Whereas, as you say, if you love the music of The Beatles – and I certainly do – I do not want the music to love me back. So is this really just a case of intense liking, a purely third-personal appraisal? The appraisal is certainly part of it, perhaps even the core. But here, it seems, I have another desire, too, connected to my love for Beatles music, which is to make connections with others who love that music – to be part of that community. This is one of the reasons, I think, people go to concerts: they go not just to see the band and experience a live performance of the music they love; they also go for the communal experience, to be with others of their kind. So even this sort of love, I think, involves certain feelings directed toward people that I hope will be reciprocated. Here, as elsewhere, love brings people together, and leads to the building of communities.[43]

I don't want to say that we cannot imagine a person who loved some work of art and did not feel this desire; someone, even, who preferred that he be the only person who loved that artwork, or the only one who knew about it. All I want to say is that this is far from the typical case, in which the appreciation of beauty seems to give rise to a desire to be with and engage with others who share that appreciation. We can perhaps also imagine someone who loves another person but does not want that love to be reciprocated. But this, too, is highly unusual.

Love directed toward artworks, or other beautiful things, may by its nature tend to be less jealous and possessive than love of persons. I may want to be my lover's only lover, and even with friends – a relationship that tends to be less exclusive than romantic love – I want to be special in the eyes of my friends. I wouldn't really want to be a 'friend' to someone who considered *everyone* their friend. I don't want to share my lovers and friends, then; or at least, there are limits. But I don't seem to mind in the same way sharing beautiful works of art. The fact that there are millions of people who love Beatles music does not make it, or my relationship with it, less special or meaningful to me; and in wanting to be part of that community I don't need to be a leader of that community, or at the centre of it – whatever that might mean. I just want to be part of it, to have some contact with like-minded human beings who can share this experience with me. (That said, it might also be that I am glad that not all of my passions are as widely shared as my love for The Beatles. I think I need to think more about this.)

How different is this from our experience of romantic love? Here, too, the desire for shared experience seems to be significant. However, here our attention is focused not on some third thing – the artwork, whatever – but on each other; though we should not overlook the importance of the various interests and passions for things other than ourselves that we presumably do share. (If we don't, our relationship is surely doomed.) And we also should not ignore the fact that, while the core community is a community of two – myself and my romantic partner – there may also be a larger community, something like that which exists in the case of art. Maybe part of loving that person is a desire to be around others who like and admire her, who appreciate what is valuable in her, and who also appreciate and endorse the fact that I respond in such ways – that is, people who value our relationship, just as we in turn may value the relationships they form. The idea of marriage as a social institution, in part, expresses this: you make a commitment to a person in front of a community, and the presence of that community in some sense establishes it, makes it real. In getting married, or enacting a similar sort of ritual, you are in a sense performing your love in front of an audience. In doing so you make visible, for a moment, two things that are ordinarily somewhat more abstract: the love itself, and the community that coalesces around it. Which might help explain the tremendous symbolic value we have tended to invest in such rituals.

*

Michael Hauskeller: I am sympathetic to your suggestion that loving something or someone also typically involves the desire to build a community of the like-minded around that love, or integrating that love into a community, and that, consequently, love tends to, as you say, bring people together. However, there is also a very real sense in which love, especially romantic love, takes us *out* of already existing communities.[44] The friend you used to hang out with is suddenly no longer available because they are now in a relationship and prefer to spend their time with the person they love rather than with you, and things that used to be very important to them suddenly no longer matter all that much. When we fall in love with someone, the other person all but becomes our world. We tend to have eyes only for them, and everything (and everyone) else suddenly takes a back seat. This may change and become less exclusive over time, but if the love persists, so does, to a greater or lesser extent, the exclusion of others, especially since, as you also noted, romantic love often comes with the expectation that the one we love not only loves us back, but also loves nobody but us, at least not in the way (and with the same kind of intensity) they love us.

In romantic love, jealousy and a certain degree of possessiveness are not aberrations, but very common, almost defining features, which distinguish the love we have for our partners from the love we have for, say, our children, or our parents.[45] On occasion there may be some jealousy in those relationships too, but it is far less pronounced, and we don't find it odd, let alone improper, if a parent loves more than one of their children, and loves them all equally, or a child loves both of their parents. I don't expect my children to feel love only for me, and I am not jealous of their love for my wife. Romantic love is different, although it is not at all obvious why it has to be. If it is possible to love more than one parent and more than one child, why should it not be possible to love more than one romantic partner? And yet, genuinely open relationships are rare and often lead to misery and heartbreak. We may want to be open and tolerant and non-possessive, but our psychological makeup, for whatever reason, is such that we find it difficult if not impossible to actually be that way.

In that sense, love is selfish. It involves staking a claim on the other. And when we marry someone, it is primarily that claim that becomes officially sanctioned and publicly accepted. I am yours and you are mine, we declare. This is not necessarily a bad thing. The freedom we lose by binding ourselves in this way – the freedom to love whomever we want whenever we want – is ultimately not worth having because the price we have to pay for it is high. To love and be loved, not just today, but also tomorrow (what Etta James called a 'Sunday kind of love'), and not just as one among many, but as the chosen one, the one that matters above all others, fulfils a basic human need. If we have that kind of love, we know that there is at least one person in this world we can always rely on, who is always there for us. And knowing that we are that person for them, that they can always rely on us to be there for them, gives a meaning and a significance to our life that is hard to come by any other way.

Notes

1. On love for things that are not persons see Shpall, 'Love's objects' and Singer, *The Pursuit of Love*, 31–44. On love for nature specifically see Furtak, 'On the love of nature'. In general, philosophers who view love primarily as caring, and who focus on the role that love tends to play in the psychology of the agent, tend to place less significance on the distinction between love for persons and love for other sorts of things (including, of course, *humans* who are not *persons*). See for instance Frankfurt, 'Autonomy, necessity, and love' and *The Reasons of Love*, and Jaworska and Wonderly, 'Love and caring'. Philosophers who place as much or more importance on the nature of the love object (as in my *Love's Vision*, for instance) tend to view love for persons as something distinct from, and perhaps more interesting than, love for non-persons. Angelika Krebs, for example, advances a 'dialogical model' of love which sees it as, fundamentally, a kind of sharing (of feelings, practical commitments and endeavours). Since such things cannot be shared with non-persons, it follows that 'according to the dialogical model, interpersonal love is different from the "love" a person feels for things or ideas' ('Between I and thou', 7).
2. As Susan Wolf writes, 'Who and what I love says something about me that distinguishes me from other people . . . Indeed, it is sometimes said that who and what we love defines us; our loves are closely bound up with and partly constitutive of our identities' ('The importance of love', 189–90).
3. A few writers have built into their definition of love that it must be reciprocal, and so exclude unrequited love by definition. Robert Ehman writes that '[w]hile reciprocity is not a condition of our desiring a person . . . it is nevertheless a condition of genuine love' ('Personal love', 123). Others who hold that love must be reciprocal to be genuine include Karol Wojtyla, who writes that unrequited love 'lacks the objective fullness which reciprocity would give it'(*Love and Responsibility*, 84), and Angelika Krebs, who identifies love with a kind of sharing (of feelings, commitments and lives) and writes that 'Where the lovers' desire to share is frustrated because of external constraints, we may still talk about love, but not in the full-fledged sense' ('Between I and thou', 22). Alan Soble takes the other side, holding that 'the thesis that love is by nature reciprocal seems supportable neither by observation nor by theory' (*The Structure of Love*, 239). Sara Protasi, in 'Loving people for who they are', uses the claim that unrequited love is clearly a real phenomenon as a premise of her argument. On the more moderate view that love necessarily involves the *desire* that it be reciprocated, see note 41.
4. There is a large philosophical literature on the question of whether we have reasons for loving and, if so, what their role and nature might be. I defend a moderate form of the view that we have reasons to love those we love in *Love's Vision*, 'The importance of whom we care about' and 'Love as "something in between"'. Other contributions to this debate (I make no pretence of being comprehensive here) include Abramson and Leite, 'Love as a reactive emotion'; Calhoun, 'Reasons of love'; Delaney, 'Romantic love and loving commitment'; Frankfurt, *The Reasons of Love*; Helm, 'Emotions as evaluative feelings'; Howard, 'Fitting love and reasons for loving'; Hurka, 'Love and reasons'; Keller, 'How do I love thee?'; Kolodny, 'Love as valuing a relationship'; Kraut, 'Love de re'; Kroeker, 'Reasons for love'; Martin, 'Love, incorporated'; Smuts, 'Normative reasons for love'; Soble, *The Structure of Love* and 'Love and value, yet *again*'; Solomon, *About Love*; Stump, 'Love, by all accounts'; Velleman, 'Love as a moral emotion'; Whiting, 'Impersonal friends'; and Zangwill, 'Love: gloriously amoral and arational'.

5. Versions of this argument are discussed in Bernstein, 'Love, particularity, and selfhood'; Delaney, 'Romantic love and loving commitment', 346; Fisher, 'Reason, emotion, and love'; Grau, 'Irreplaceability and unique value'; Kolodny, 'Love as valuing a relationship'; Milligan, 'The duplication of love's reasons' and *Love*; Parfit, *Reasons and Persons*; Protasi, 'Loving people for who they are'; Smuts, 'Normative reasons for love'; Soble, *The Structure of Love*; and Young, 'Love reveals persons as irreplaceable'.

6. For discussions of the idea that our lovers are irreplaceable see (in addition to works cited in the previous note) Abramson and Leite, 'Love as a reactive emotion'; Grau, 'Irreplaceability and unique value' and 'Love and history'; Helm, *Love, Friendship, and the Self*, 175–210; Howard, 'Fitting love and reasons for loving'; Kolodny, 'Love as valuing a relationship'; Matthes, 'History, value, and irreplaceability'; Moller, 'Love and death'; Soble, *The Structure of Love*; and Wonderly, 'On being attached'.

7. Ronald de Sousa writes that love 'has an essentially temporal structure, insofar as it is the result of a process of attachment and therefore distinct from merely immediate attraction. Love at first sight is a contradiction in terms' ('Emotions, education, and time', 442). Christian Maurer echoes de Sousa's view: 'It is a mistake . . . to think that what is experienced "at first sight" is love, or that love proper can be there "at first sight"' ('On love at first sight', 168). Diane Jeske (*Rationality and Moral Theory*, 59) and Sara Protasi ('Loving people for who they are', 232 n44) take similarly sceptical views regarding love at first sight, holding that it is impossible to know on the basis of a brief acquaintance whether someone would be a good or appropriate love partner. The possibility of love at first sight is defended or asserted in my 'Love and the past'; Solomon, *About Love*, 44–5; Smith, 'The "what" and "why" of love's reasons'; and Ben-Ze'ev, *The Subtlety of Emotions*, 419.

8. I discuss this case in particular in 'The importance of whom we care about'. For other discussions of love for very young persons see Harcourt, 'Attachment, autonomy, and the evaluative variety of love'; Hurka, 'Love and reasons', 168–9; Kroeker, 'Reasons for love', 283; and Wonderly, 'Early relationships, pathologies of attachment, and the capacity to love'.

9. David Velleman ('Love as a moral emotion', 370) holds that such idiosyncratic features (see also the Gershwin song quoted later) are relevant to love inasmuch as they express one's fundamental value as persons – a value which, on Velleman's Kantian account, all human beings express equally. To be valued for those features, and not for that more fundamental and universal value, would be inappropriate and objectionable: 'Someone who loved you for your quirks would have to be a quirk-lover, on the way to being a fetishist.' I discuss this aspect of Velleman's view in *Love's Vision*, 134–5.

10. William Shakespeare, *A Midsummer Night's Dream*, Act 3, Scene 1.

11. See Nelson and Jankowiak, 'Love's ethnographic record', especially section 3.2.1.

12. The description of the parent–child case seems to fit Niko Kolodny's view that 'one's reason for loving a person is one's relationship to her' ('Love as valuing a relationship', 135–6). The arranged marriage case may or may not fit as well, depending on whether we take it that the primary reason for love is the marriage itself, or whether we see the marriage as an opportunity for the participants to discover what is (independently) lovable about their partners.

13. For obvious reasons, the idea of choosing one's children is controversial, but has found support from some philosophers and ethicists. See for instance Glover, *Choosing Children*.

14. On the idea of loving someone in spite of their flaws see Matthes, 'Love in spite of'.

15. Compare Velleman, 'Love as a moral emotion', 371–2: 'The desire to be valued in this way is not a desire to be valued on the basis of one's distinctive features. It is rather a desire that one's own rendition of humanity, however distinctive, should succeed in communicating a value that is perfectly universal.'

16. See Claridge et al., *Personality Differences and Biological Variations*. For criticisms of the idea that this sort of fact about 'empirical' uniqueness could matter to our reasons for loving, see Young, 'Love reveals persons as irreplaceable' and Grau, 'Irreplaceability and unique value'.

17. A sentiment expressed in the famous statement from Shakespeare's Sonnet 116: 'Love is not love/ Which alters when it alteration finds.' For a statement to the contrary see Rorty, 'The historicity of psychological attitudes', 404: '[E]ven a true historical love might end in dissolution and separation. That it did end would not prove that it had not existed, or that either its permeability or its dynamism were defective. On the contrary, it might be just these that establish . . . that it was indeed Ella that Louis loved, and that he did indeed love rather than swoon.'

18. See my *Love's Vision*, 138–9. One might also follow Delaney in holding that as our qualities change, the nature of our commitment also changes, from romantic love to something more enduring and stable (if less exciting): a 'loving commitment' ('Romantic love and loving commitment', 348–53). Rorty ('The historicity of psychological attitudes') is very insightful on how love changes as people and their qualities change.

19. See my *Love's Vision*, 138–9. Dean Cocking and Jennette Kennett ('Friendship and moral danger') have defended what they call a 'drawing view of love', which holds that lovers display a profound 'receptivity to direction and interpretation', influencing each other and at the same time allowing themselves to be influenced by the other's values, beliefs and desires. As Michael Smith writes, on the drawing view, 'the underlying receptivity to direction guarantees that the lover and beloved are, quite literally, made for each other' ('The "what" and the "why" of love's reasons', 154). Related views are discussed by Nehamas in *On Friendship*, Millgram in 'Aristotle on making other selves', and Rorty in 'The historicity of psychological attitudes'.

20. The following discussion draws on my 'Love and the past (and present, and future)'.

21. On this kind of final/sentimental value see, for example, Fletcher, 'Sentimental value', Hatzimoysis, 'Sentimental value', and Tenen, 'An account of extrinsic final value'. The idea that sentimentally valued items have final value is criticised by Tucker in 'The pen, the dress, and the coat'.

22. This is related to Neil Delaney's point that 'among the [properties] figuring into the lover's grounds [for love] will be historical-relational properties involving *you*, say the property of having been her dance partner at the USO social in '44, or having been the one who proposed to her on the Champs-Elysées. It is precisely the accumulation of these historical-relational properties that largely accounts for love's strongly individuative character' ('Romantic love and loving commitment', 346). On the relevance of historical properties see also Hurka, 'Love and reasons', 166–9 and Rorty, 'The historicity of psychological attitudes', 403–4.

23. See my 'Love as "something in between"'.

24. Again, this is a main theme of Velleman's 'Love as a moral emotion', though he puts a particularly universalistic and Kantian spin on what it means for qualities to represent 'the person herself'.

25. On the idea that love involves projecting one's ideas and ideals onto the beloved, thus preventing us from seeing him accurately, see Stendhal, *Love*. Stendhal famously refers to the process as 'crystallization', comparing the lover's fantasies to the crystals that would accumulate on boughs in the Salzburg salt mines. Iris Murdoch emphasises both the role of love and loving attention in seeing people truly and justly (see her famous example of M and her daughter-in-law, D, in *The Sovereignty of Good*, 17–18) and the way that ego-based fantasies can obscure our view of reality: 'The chief enemy of excellence in morality (and also in art) is personal fantasy: the tissue of self-aggrandizing and consoling wishes and dreams which prevents one from seeing what is there outside one' (*The Sovereignty of Good*, 59).

26. Rorty writes that love is one of a set of psychological attitudes that 'arise from, and are shaped by, dynamic interactions between a subject and an object . . . Not only are such relational psychological attitudes individuated by their objects, but also the trajectory of the subject's life – the subject's further individuation – is affected by this relational attitude, this activity' ('The historicity of psychological attitudes', 399–400).

27. Ronald de Sousa writes, 'it is the very essence of reason to be universally applicable: a reason for you must be a reason for anyone' (*Love*, 56–7), and takes this to suggest that the fact that a person is beautiful, or witty, etc., cannot be a genuine reason. Troy Jollimore responds to de Sousa's argument in 'Love as "something in between"'.

28. A classic statement of the idea that we love our beloveds 'because they are who they are' is found in Montaigne, who wrote in his essays that the only explanation he could offer his friend Etienne de La Boétie for his lover was that he loved him '[b]ecause it was he, because it was I' (*The Complete Works*, 169). Alexander Nehamas's *On Friendship* is in large part an exploration of and elaboration on Montaigne's claim.

29. Plato, *The Symposium*, 189c–193e.

30. Here again the literature is quite sizeable. Pre-modern writers who seem to advance union views of love include Montaigne ('On friendship' in *The Complete Works*, 164–77), Kierkegaard (*Stages on Life's Way*, 56) and Hegel ('On love' in *On Christianity*, 304–5). More recently, Mark Fisher has claimed that lovers of long standing share beliefs and desires, see the world through each other's eyes, and cannot tell their thoughts apart (*Personal Love*, 26–8, 103). Margaret Gilbert claims that love relationships involve a kind of 'fusion' in which 'parties come

continuously jointly to accept numerous beliefs, values, and principles of action' ('Fusion', 266–7). Robert Nozick writes that loving involves the desire to form a '*we*', and seems to take it that love is fully achieved when such a *we* is formed ('Love's bond'). And Roger Scruton writes that love begins to exist 'just so soon as reciprocity becomes community: that is, just so soon as all distinction between my interests and your interests is overcome' (*Sexual Desire*, 230). Alan Soble, who is sceptical about union views ('Aristophanes cannot be right that what lovers want more than anything else is to be welded together'), offers a helpful survey and critique of them in 'Union, autonomy, and concern', 90. See also Singer, *The Nature of Love*, 406 ff.

31. Compare Frankfurt, *Taking Ourselves Seriously and Getting It Right*, 35–6.

32. It is common to think of love relationships as passing through various somewhat uniform and predictable stages – in particular, from an initial infatuation stage to a more settled and stable committed stage. In addition to Delaney's 'Romantic love and loving commitment' see McKeever, 'Love', 215, and Halwani, 'Love and sex', 2.

33. Here again, see Rorty, 'The historicity of psychological attitudes', 403–4.

34. See my *Love's Vision*, 142. On the worry that such accounts render love excessively moralistic see Pacovská, 'Love and the pitfall of moralism'.

35. Compare Protasi, 'Loving people for who they are', 224: 'If, for instance, the beloved is not recognizable as the person we fell in love with, it is appropriate that our attitude tracks that change . . . People who develop drug addiction or depression or who experience a traumatic or life-changing event (such as going to war or religious conversion) may change radically and suddenly.' Delaney claims, plausibly, that what we desire is not an unconditional commitment that would persist through all changes, but a flexible commitment that would survive many, in particular the kinds of ordinary changes one expects human beings to undergo ('Romantic love and loving commitment', 348–9).

36. As Aristotle writes in his *Nicomachean Ethics*, 'what is evil neither can nor should be loved' (*Complete Works*, 1842). See May's *Love* (184–9) for an argument against Aristotle's claim.

37. But of course, since our friends and lovers change us, and since change happens incrementally, and possibly imperceptibly, there is always the chance that in such cases we ourselves might be so altered by love that we, too, become bad people, turning against the good and toward our lovers rather than the other way round. That this risk exists is a central point of Cocking and Kennett's 'Friendship and moral danger' and is also emphasised by Nehamas in *On Friendship*.

38. See Kierkegaard, *Works of Love*, 173: 'The emphasis is not on loving the perfections one sees in a person, but the emphasis in on loving the person one sees.' John Armstrong seems to endorse this Kierkegaardian thesis, writing that many people 'imagine that when they do find the right person love will be easy, will flower spontaneously and survive of its own accord. The main thrust of this book is in the opposing direction . . . The problem is not in finding the person but in finding the resources and capacities in oneself to care for another person – to love them. Searching for the right "object" diverts attention from finding the right attitude' (*Conditions of Love*, 35).

39. See my 'Love as "something in between" '.

40. Those who defend the view that love necessarily involves a *desire* for reciprocation include Baier, 'The ambiguous limits of desire', 55, Nozick, 'Love's bond', 70, and Delaney, 'Romantic love and loving commitment', 340. This view is rejected by philosophers including Fisher, 'Reason, emotion, and love', 197, and Newton-Smith, 'A conceptual investigation of love', 126–7.

41. One can draw clear connections here to Kant's distinction between pathological love, which is a matter of feeling (and seems to have, for Kant, no moral value), and practical love, which is a matter of will and which we have a duty to manifest. For commentary see Fahmy, 'Kantian practical love'. For a contemporary account of love that is largely grounded in, and elaborates on, Kant's distinction see Ebbels-Duggan, 'Against beneficence'.

42. There are many ways of understanding the kind of identification involved in love. Obviously union views incorporate identification in a very strong sense. For a somewhat different version see Helm, *Love, Friendship, and the Self*, especially 145–74.

43. Compare Ted Cohen's remarks on art in 'The very idea of art', 12, and Alexander Nehamas's related remarks on aesthetic qualities including humour and beauty in *Only a Promise of Happiness*, 80–4.

44. As Iris Murdoch wrote in her novel *A Word Child*, 'The assertion made by a happy marriage often alienates, and often is at least half intended to alienate, the excluded spectator' (cited in Wilson, *Iris Murdoch as I Knew Her*, xi). Martha Nussbaum acknowledges that '[i]ntense attachments to particular individuals, especially when they are of an erotic or romantic sort,

[often] call attention away from the world of general concern' (*Upheavals of Thought*, 461). One might also mention Elizabeth Bennett's rhetorical question in Jane Austen's *Pride and Prejudice*: 'Is not general incivility the very essence of love?'

45. On the role of jealousy, possessiveness and exclusivity in romantic love (and their putative role in *defining* romantic love) see, for instance, Farrell, 'Jealousy and desire'; Jenkins, 'Modal monogamy'; Lockhart, 'The normative potency of sexually exclusive love'; McKeever, 'Is the requirement of sexual exclusivity consistent with romantic love?; and McMullin, 'Love and entitlement'.

Bibliography

Abramson, Kate, and Adam Leite. 'Love as a reactive emotion', *Philosophical Quarterly* 61/245 (2011): 673–99.

Aristotle. *The Complete Works of Aristotle*, volume 2, edited by Jonathan Barnes. Princeton, NJ: Princeton University Press, 1984.

Armstrong, John. *Conditions of Love*. New York: W. W. Norton, 2003.

Baier, Annette. 'The ambiguous limits of desire'. In *The Ways of Desire*, edited by Joel Marks, 39–61. Chicago, IL: Precedent, 1986.

Ben-Ze'ev, Aaron. *The Subtlety of Emotions*. Cambridge, MA: MIT Press, 2000.

Bernstein, Mark. 'Love, particularity, and selfhood', *Southern Journal of Philosophy* 23 (1986): 287–93.

Calhoun, Cheshire. 'Reasons of love', *Foundations of Science* 21/2 (2016): 275–7.

Claridge, Gordon, Sandra Canter and W. I. Hume. *Personality Differences and Biological Variations: A study of twins*. Oxford: Pergamon Press, 1973.

Cocking, Dean, and Jennette Kennett. 'Friendship and moral danger', *The Journal of Philosophy* 97 (2000): 278–96.

Cohen, Ted. 'The very idea of art', *National Council on Education for the Ceramic Arts Journal* 9 (1988): 7–14.

Delaney, Neil. 'Romantic love and loving commitment: articulating a modern ideal', *American Philosophical Quarterly* 33/4 (1996): 339–56.

Ebbels-Duggan, Kyla. 'Against beneficence: a normative account of love', *Ethics* 119 (2008): 142–70.

Ehman, Robert. 'Personal love', *The Personalist* 49 (1968): 116–41.

Fahmy, Melissa. 'Kantian practical love', *Pacific Philosophical Quarterly* 91 (2010): 313–31.

Farrell, Daniel. 'Jealousy and desire'. In *Love Analyzed*, edited by Roger Lamb, 165–88. Boulder, CO: Westview Press, 1997.

Fisher, Mark. *Personal Love*. London: Duckworth, 1990.

Fisher, Mark. 'Reason, emotion, and love', *Inquiry* 20 (1977): 189–203.

Fletcher, Guy. 'Sentimental value', *Journal of Value Inquiry* 43/1 (2009): 55–65.

Frankfurt, Harry G. 'Autonomy, necessity, and love'. In *Necessity, Volition, and Love*, 129–41. Cambridge: Cambridge University Press, 1998.

Frankfurt, Harry G. *Taking Ourselves Seriously and Getting It Right*. Stanford, CA: Stanford University Press, 2006.

Frankfurt, Harry G. *The Reasons of Love*. Princeton, NJ: Princeton University Press, 2014.

Furtak, Rick. 'On the love of nature'. In *The Routledge Handbook of Love in Philosophy*, edited by Adrienne M. Martin, 205–14. London: Routledge, 2020.

Gilbert, Margaret. 'Fusion: sketch of a "contractual" model.' In *Joint Commitment: How we make the social world*. Oxford: Oxford University Press, 2015.

Glover, Jonathan. *Choosing Children: Genes, disability, and design*. Oxford: Clarendon Press, 2006.

Grau, Christopher. 'Irreplaceability and unique value', *Philosophical Topics 32* (2004): 111–29.

Grau, Christopher. 'Love and history', *Southern Journal of Philosophy* 48/3 (2010): 246–71.

Halwani, Raj. 'Love and sex'. In *The Oxford Handbook of Philosophy of Love*, edited by Christopher Grau and Aaron Smuts. Oxford: Oxford University Press, 2017. DOI: 10.1093/oxfordhb/9780199395729.013.29.

Harcourt, Edward. 'Attachment, autonomy, and the evaluative variety of love'. In *Love, Reason and Morality*, edited by Esther Engels Kroeker and Katrien Schaubroeck, 39–56. London: Routledge, 2017.

Hatzimoysis, Anthony. 'Sentimental value', *Philosophical Quarterly* 53/212 (July 2003): 373–9.

Hegel, Georg Wilhelm Friedrich. *On Christianity: Early theological writings*, translated by T. M. Knox. New York: Harper and Bros., 1948.

Helm, Bennett. 'Emotions as evaluative feelings', *Emotion Review* 1 (2009): 1–12.

Helm, Bennett. *Love, Friendship, and the Self: Intimacy, identification, and the social nature of persons*. Oxford: Oxford University Press, 2010.

Howard, Christopher. 'Fitting love and reasons for loving', *Oxford Studies in Normative Ethics* 9 (2019): 116–37.

Hurka, Thomas. 'Love and reasons: the many relationships'. In *Love, Reason and Morality*, edited by Esther Engels Kroeker and Katrien Schaubroeck, 166–9. London: Routledge, 2017.

Jaworska, Agnieszka, and Monique Wonderly. 'Love and caring'. In *The Oxford Handbook of Philosophy of Love*, edited by Christopher Grau and Aaron Smuts. Oxford: Oxford University Press. 2017. DOI: 10.1093/oxfordhb/9780199395729.013.29.

Jenkins, C. S. I. 'Modal monogamy', *Ergo* 2/8 (2015): 175–94.

Jeske, Diane. *Rationality and Moral Theory: How intimacy generates reasons*. New York: Routledge, 2008.

Jollimore, Troy. *Love's Vision*. Princeton, NJ: Princeton University Press, 2011.

Jollimore, Troy. 'The importance of whom we care about'. In *Love, Reason and Will: Kierkegaard after Frankfurt*, edited by Anthony Rudd and John Davenport, 47–72. London: Bloomsbury, 2015.

Jollimore, Troy. 'Love as "something in between"'. In *The Oxford Handbook of Philosophy of Love*, edited by Christopher Grau and Aaron Smuts. Oxford: Oxford University Press, 2017. DOI: 10.1093/oxfordhb/9780199395729.013.29.

Jollimore, Troy. 'Love and the past (and present, and future)'. In *Philosophy of Love in the Past, Present, and Future*, edited by Andre Grahle, Natasha McKeever and Joe Saunders. London: Routledge, 2022.

Keller, Simon. 'How do I love thee? Let me count the properties', *American Philosophical Quarterly* 37/2 (2000): 163–73.

Kierkegaard, Søren. *Stages on Life's Way*. Princeton, NJ: Princeton University Press, 1945.

Kierkegaard, Søren. *Works of Love*, translated by Edward Hong and Edna Hong. Princeton, NJ: Princeton University Press, 1995.

Kolodny, Niko. 'Love as valuing a relationship', *The Philosophical Review* 112/2 (2003): 135–89.

Kraut, Robert. 'Love de re', *Midwest Studies in Philosophy* 10 (1986): 413–30.

Krebs, Angelika. 'Between I and thou – on the dialogical nature of love'. In *Love and its Objects: What can we care for?*, edited by Christian Maurer, Tony Milligan and Kamila Pacovská, 7–24. London: Palgrave Macmillan, 2014.

Kroeker, Esther Engels. 'Reasons for love'. In *The Routledge Handbook of Love in Philosophy*, edited by Adrienne M. Martin, 277–87. London: Routledge, 2020.

Lockhart, Jennifer. 'The normative potency of sexually exclusive love'. In *The Routledge Handbook of Love in Philosophy*, edited by Adrienne M. Martin, 83–92. London: Routledge, 2020.

McKeever, Natasha. 'Love: what's sex got to do with it?', *International Journal of Applied Philosophy* 30/2 (2016): 201–18.

McKeever, Natasha. 'Is the requirement of sexual exclusivity consistent with romantic love?', *Journal of Applied Philosophy* 34/3 (2017): 353–69.

McMullin, Irene. 'Love and entitlement: Sartre and Beauvoir on the nature of jealousy', *Hypatia: A journal of feminist philosophy* 26/1 (2011): 102–22.

Martin, Adrienne M. 'Love, incorporated', *Ethical Theory and Moral Practice* 18/4 (2015): 691–702.

Matthes, Erich. 'History, value, and irreplaceability', *Ethics* 124/1 (2013): 35–64.

Matthes, Erich. 'Love in spite of', *Oxford Studies in Normative Ethics* 6 (2016): 241–62.

Maurer, Christian. 'On love at first sight'. In *Love and its Objects: What can we care for?*, edited by Christian Maurer, Tony Milligan and Kamila Pacovská, 160–74. London: Palgrave Macmillan, 2014.

May, Simon. *Love: A new understanding of an ancient emotion*. Oxford: Oxford University Press, 2019.

Millgram, Elijah. 'Aristotle on making other selves', *Canadian Journal of Philosophy* 17/2 (1987): 361–76.

Milligan, Tony. *Love*. London: Routledge, 2011.

Milligan, Tony. 'The duplication of love's reasons', *Philosophical Explorations* 16 (2013): 315–23.

Moller, Dan. 'Love and death', *Journal of Philosophy* 104/6 (2007): 301–16.

Montaigne, Michel de. *The Complete Works*, translated by Donald M. Frame. New York: Everyman's Library, 2003.

Murdoch, Iris. *The Sovereignty of Good*. London: Routledge and Kegan Paul, 1970.

Nehamas, Alexander. *Only a Promise of Happiness: The place of beauty in a world of art*. Princeton, NJ: Princeton University Press, 2007.

Nehamas, Alexander. *On Friendship*. New York: Basic Books, 2016.

Nelson, Alex J., and William Jankowiak. 'Love's ethnographic record: beyond the love/arranged marriage dichotomy and other false essentialisms'. In *International Handbook of Love*, edited by Claude-Hélène Mayer and Elisabeth Vanderheiden. Cham: Springer 2021. Online first: https://doi.org/10.1007/978-3-030-45996-3_3.

Newton-Smith, W. 'A conceptual investigation of love'. In *Philosophy and Personal Relations*, edited by Alan Montefiore, 113–36. Montreal: McGill-Queen's University Press, 1973.

Nozick, Robert. 'Love's bond'. In *The Philosophy of (Erotic) Love*, edited by Robert C. Solomon and Kathleen M. Higgins, 417–32. Lawrence, KS: University Press of Kansas, 1991.

Nussbaum, Martha. *Upheavals of Thought*. Cambridge: Cambridge University Press, 2001.

Pacovská, Kamila. 'Love and the pitfall of moralism', *Philosophy* 93 (2018): 231–49.

Parfit, Derek. *Reasons and Persons*. Oxford: Oxford University Press, 1984.

Plato. *The Symposium*. London: Penguin, 1999.

Protasi, Sara. 'Loving people for who they are (even when they don't love you back)', *European Journal of Philosophy* 24/1 (2014): 214–34.

Rorty, Amelie Oksenberg. 'The historicity of psychological attitudes: love is not love which alters not when it alteration finds', *Midwest Studies in Philosophy* 10 (1986): 399–412.

Scruton, Roger. *Sexual Desire: A moral philosophy of the erotic*. New York: Free Press, 1986.

Shpall, Sam. 'Love's objects'. In *Love, Reason and Morality*, edited by Esther Engels Kroeker and Katrien Schaubroeck, 57–74. London: Routledge, 2017.

Singer, Irving. *The Nature of Love*, volume 3: *The Modern World*. Chicago, IL: University of Chicago Press, 1997.

Singer, Irving. *The Pursuit of Love*. Baltimore: Johns Hopkins University Press, 1994.

Smith, Michael. 'The "what" and "why" of love's reasons'. In *Love, Reason and Morality*, edited by Esther Engels Kroeker and Katrien Schaubroeck, 145–62. London: Routledge, 2017.

Smuts, Aaron. 'Normative reasons for love, parts 1 and 2', *Philosophy Compass* 9/8 (2014): 507–26.

Soble, Alan. *The Structure of Love*. New Haven, NJ: Yale University Press, 1990.

Soble, Alan. 'Union, autonomy, and concern'. In *Love Analyzed*, edited by Roger Lamb, 65–92. Boulder, CO: Westview Press, 1997.

Soble, Alan. 'Love and value, yet *again*'. In *Love, Reason, and Will: Kierkegaard after Frankfurt*, edited by Anthony Rudd and John Davenport, 25–46. London: Bloomsbury Academic, 2015.

Solomon, Robert. *About Love: Reinventing romance for our time*. Indianapolis, IN: Hackett, 2006.

Sousa, Ronald de. 'Emotions, education, and time', *Metaphilosophy* 21/4 (1990): 434–46.

Sousa, Ronald de. *Love: A very short introduction*. Oxford: Oxford University Press, 2015.

Stendhal. *Love*, translated by Gilbert and Suzanne Sale. Harmondsworth: Penguin, 1975.

Stump, Eleanore. 'Love, by all accounts', *Proceedings and Addresses of the American Philosophical Association* 80/2 (2006): 25–43.

Tenen, Levi. 'An account of extrinsic final value', *Journal of Value Inquiry* 54/3 (2020): 479–92.

Tucker, Miles. 'The pen, the dress, and the coat: a confusion in goodness', *Philosophical Studies* 173/7 (July 2016): 1911–22.

Velleman, David. 'Love as a moral emotion', *Ethics* 109 (1999): 338–74.

Whiting, Jennifer. 'Impersonal friends', *The Monist* 74/1 (1991): 3–29.

Wilson, A. N. *Iris Murdoch as I Knew Her*. London: Hutchinson, 2003.

Wojtyla, Karol. *Love and Responsibility*. New York: Farrar, Straus and Giroux, 1981.

Wolf, Susan. 'The importance of love'. In *The Variety of Values*. Oxford: Oxford University Press, 2015.

Wonderly, Monique. 'Early relationships, pathologies of attachment, and the capacity to love'. In *The Routledge Handbook of Love in Philosophy*, edited by Adrienne M. Martin, 23–34. London: Routledge, 2019.

Wonderly, Monique. 'On being attached', *Philosophical Studies* 173/1 (2016): 223–42.

Young, Elizabeth Drummond. 'Love reveals persons as irreplaceable'. In *Love and its Objects: What can we care for?*, edited by Christian Maurer, Tony Milligan, and Kamila Pacovská, 177–91. London: Palgrave Macmillan, 2014.

Zangwill, Nick. 'Love: gloriously amoral and arational', *Philosophical Explorations* 16/3 (2013): 298–314.

12
Faith
with Brian Treanor

Brian Treanor: Today, there is a very strong tendency to associate faith with religion. This is especially true in the United States, where I live. Whether or not that association is strictly accurate is something worth investigating, and turns, I think, on just what one means by 'religion'.[1] However, I think it is a serious error to confine 'faith' to its expression in churches, synagogues, mosques and temples, although those expressions are, of course, examples of faith.

In general, even thoughtful people tend to think of faith in terms that are either too narrow or too broad. We think of faith too narrowly when we restrict it to a particular type of (discrete, denominational, traditionally religious) belief. On this view, faith is something unique to 'religious' people, and it is often disparaged by 'non-religious' folk not merely as irrational but as fundamentally anti-rational. We think of faith too broadly when we use it simply as a synonym for belief, so that a belief in String Theory or a belief that Charlemagne was crowned Holy Roman Emperor on Christmas Day, 800 AD, has the same epistemic status or existential worth as the belief in transmigration of souls or that Christ rose on the third day. But I think both the narrow view and the broad view of faith miss the mark in various ways, and that faith is, in fact, both something widely distributed among people (contradicting the narrow view of faith) and something substantially different from simple opinion or belief (contradicting the overly broad view of faith).

To my mind, a good working definition of faith starts with a distinction between 'faith that . . .' and 'faith in . . .'.[2] 'Faith that . . .' is something like belief; it is an assertion that something or some state of affairs obtains. Like other beliefs, it tends to concern itself with making claims about some particular thing – past, present or future. 'Faith in . . .', in contrast, has to do with one's fidelity to and trust in a certain reality. To have faith in something is to recognise and affirm its worth. Of course, these two forms of faith can be, and often are, found mixed together. However, the less faith is occupied with specific claims about states-of-affairs (faith that . . .) and the more it is concerned with a relationship I have with reality (faith in . . .), the closer it is to the essence of faith.

There are other important qualifiers that distinguish faith from belief (and from knowledge), and perhaps we will have time to talk about some of them in our conversation. Faith requires a 'leap' beyond certitude or what is confirmable.[3] Therefore, all faith is 'undecidable' – it cannot ultimately be safeguarded or assured; it is always open to doubt, and it can fail. But if faith is a 'leap', it is also a 'wager'; and the measure of faith is just what we are willing to put on the table as our stake. In its clearest and most compelling expressions, faith is the willingness to stake one's life. Because faith is a type of existential wager, it will always alter our behaviour or way of being. This means, in the Catholic sense, 'faith without works is dead'; but it also means that faith is, in a sense, never fully accomplished. It must be perpetually renewed to remain faith. When it comes to facts, it may be true, as Charles Sanders Peirce says, that there are things we can no longer doubt, no matter how hard we try; but when it comes to faith, every day is a new test.[4] True, some days may be easier than others, but faith is something that must be affirmed again and again. When two people stand before each other and say, 'I do . . . till death do us part', they are making a leap of faith. And whether that faith will be sustained will depend on how each of them acts over the course of their lives. We cannot know that they were 'right' to affirm that faith until one or the other dies, having been faithful to each other. Truth, in this instance, is less like an idea that corresponds to a certain state of affairs and more like remaining faithful to a reality. Truth as troth.

A useful paradigm for faith is 'a commitment to first principles about what is meaningful'. Because such principles have to do with what is ultimately meaningful, they inform and shape one's 'way of life'; and because they are first principles, we argue *from* these commitments rather than, or at least before, arguing *for* them. To state this even more plainly: we all have commitments, especially commitments about meaning and value, that form the bedrock of our worldview; and these fundamental commitments are, and to some degree must remain, simply given. There is no proving them.

The idea that things are meaningful is so widely shared that if we take it as an example of faith – that is, a commitment to a first principle that shapes one's way of being – then *everyone is a person of faith*. Of course, an obvious objection is that some people, including some very clever people, claim that nothing is meaningful – that meaning is a human fantasy drawn over the meaningless chaos of the real. There is quite a bit to say about such claims; but, as a first response, let me point out that no one, not even the self-proclaimed nihilist, actually lives as a nihilist. William James says that any actual, meaningful belief will change the way someone lives in the world.[5] And so, if a person *says* nihilism is true but, when put to the pins, *behaves* as if the world and her actions are meaningful, we must, at the very least, view her avowed nihilism with scepticism. I suspect nihilism is a dark night of the soul through which every intelligent and reflective person struggles; but I also suspect that no one lives in that darkness. So, we have all got faith in this basic sense: we wager our lives on the belief that the world is meaningful. We take this as a given, without trying to establish it; and it shapes our worldviews and frames our projects.

*

Michael Hauskeller: Faith, you say, is a 'type of existential wager': when we have faith in something, for instance the meaningfulness of the world, we stake our lives on something we do not and cannot know to be true. While I appreciate your suggestion that faith is much more common than narrowly defined religious belief, but is still different from ordinary belief in what we take to be facts, and I agree with most of what you say about the nature or essence of faith, I am rather wary of comparing faith to a wager because it reminds me uncomfortably of Blaise Pascal's famous wager.[6] We should believe in God and live as if God exists, Pascal argued, because if God exists, the costs of not believing in him will be immense (we will lose an eternity in heaven), while the costs of believing in him if he does not are marginal (perhaps a few earthly pleasures that we have to forgo). Therefore, since there is a lot to gain and very little to lose, we should place all our bets on the existence of God. Far from being irrational, Pascal insists, this is in fact the most rational choice to make when there is no way to know whether or not God exists.

I don't know whether anyone has ever started believing in God (or anything else for that matter) because they have analysed the costs and benefits of doing so in such a cool and detached manner. I find this difficult to imagine. However, even if that were psychologically possible, it would still seem appallingly calculating and transactional, and I like to think that faith is not really like that at all – that it is more intuitive, disinterested and foundational, in the sense that, as you put it, we do not usually have to argue *for* our faith, because we always already argue *from* our faith. This would also suggest that faith is not deliberately chosen. Then again, when I think about it, it would seem that sometimes we *do* choose to have faith in something or someone, namely when we 'put our faith in' certain things or (mostly, I suppose) people. The marriage vow is a good example, as here we solemnly promise to another person that we will be and will remain 'faithful' to them – that is, have faith in them and preserve that faith no matter what (and also, of course, honour the faith the other has in us and prove ourselves worthy of it). This seems like a deliberate decision (although probably in most cases based on some prior faith in that person), one by which we *commit* to something rather than merely *express* such commitment.

But the faith that you cited as a paradigm case of widespread (and perhaps universal) non-religious faith, namely faith in the meaningfulness and value of the things we do and pursue (the sheer *mattering* of things), strikes me as different from that, because it is not really *optional*. It comes naturally to us, very much like the basic assumption we make whenever we do anything in this world, which is that such a world really exists, namely as an external, material reality whose existence does not depend on our perception of it, or like the basic assumption you and I make when we converse with each other, namely that the other is not a machine, but a conscious, thinking being.

Are those basic assumptions – which I hesitate to call 'beliefs' – also examples of faith? They are certainly similar, in that we build our lives around them even though it is impossible to prove that they are true. Yet we usually also find it impossible to doubt them, except in a very theoretical way that has no impact on the way we actually live our lives. (David Hume comes to mind here: he cannot reason himself out of his sceptical conclusions, but finds himself immediately cured when he joins his friends for a meal, a chat and a game of backgammon.[7]) In contrast, while we also do not usually doubt that what we do is meaningful – that it matters – once that doubt is raised it is much harder to ignore it.

The possibility that our value assumptions are mistaken and that it does not really matter what we do or do not do is more than just a rather far-fetched theoretical possibility. Not only can it severely affect our lives, causing indifference and depression; it is also much more plausible. While it is theoretically possible, but for various reasons rather unlikely, that there is no external world and no other minds, it is, based on what we know (or think we know) about the world, not at all unlikely that our values are merely human projections and not rooted in objective reality. In other words, what we can reasonably *believe* about the world in which we find ourselves does not (at least not in any obvious way) support our value commitments, and it is precisely that gap between what we have *reason* to believe (i.e., that ultimately nothing matters) and what we *feel* is the case (i.e., that what we do *does* matter) that is bridged by faith, which does not consist in quenching our doubts, or in arguing them away, but in suspending them and refusing to let our lives and pursuits be governed by them. Therefore there can be no faith where there is no doubt – and I don't mean *grounds* for doubt, but actual doubt – which is why a firm belief in the existence of something, be it objective values or the existence of a benevolent God who has a plan and who protects us, is not so much faith as it is the *rationalisation* of faith, and also as such its abdication.

*

Brian Treanor: I think your concern that 'wager' implies something like 'hedging one's bets' is well founded. William James quips that 'if we were ourselves in the place of the Deity, we should probably take particular pleasure in cutting off believers of this pattern from their infinite reward', which always gives me a chuckle.[8] But the deeper point is, as you suggest, that 'faith' based in such mechanical and transactional calculations would lack the spirit that I tend to associate with faith – the idea that faith animates or vivifies one's life, perspective, choices and actions, rather than merely disinterestedly directing them. For this reason, I generally prefer the language of a 'leap of faith' over a 'wager', since leap suggests to me a kind of activity and committed choice. Nevertheless, 'wager' does have the virtue of reminding us that *something is at stake* – that something may be won or lost – and that faith matters in some significant way.

I also think that you put your finger on something essential when you point out that faith and doubt are inextricably linked. Clearly, there are some things we cannot know or verify, but which we also cannot really doubt in a meaningful sense. The example of the existence of the external world is a good one. But, while the bare meaningfulness or mattering of things is more or less universally affirmed, it is also, unlike the existence of an external world, open to quite profound and disturbing doubt. Moreover, once the shadow of doubt falls on faith, it can be quite hard to shake.

It seems right to say that faith must, by definition, be open to the possibility of doubt – that faith is an assertion made in the context of a question about which doubt is still possible. But, as your examples suggest, the theoretical possibility of doubt and the existential experience of doubt are two different things. And I would be inclined to agree that faith is something that is inextricably tied to the latter. Faith is a disposition we have in the context of questions in which doubt is still a 'live' option and a real danger.

It seems to me that any mature faith – whether it is faith in the meaningfulness of things, or in one's spouse, or in the existence of God – experiences and wrestles with moments of doubt. The 'dark night of the soul' is more than a poetic trope; it is an essential part of the experience of faith itself. Put another way, faith is always troubled by doubt, by the nagging possibility that it might be in error. This does not mean a faithful person is disturbed by doubt at each moment, that her days are an anxious maelstrom of uncertainty; it means, rather, that faith is a process and a struggle, and that it will never be completely free of doubt. Because of this I am disinclined to hold up the 'childlike' model of faith as a paradigm. It is true that faith is characterised by a certain naiveté, but it ought not be the unquestioning, credulous naiveté of a child. That kind of faith can only be maintained by failing to question things and requires insulating oneself from new experiences that might raise questions. But the naiveté of a child is not the only option on offer.

Paul Ricoeur speaks of a 'second naiveté' that can be recovered after the dark night of the soul, a naiveté that is 'chosen again', in light of all the reasons to doubt and without dismissing them.[9] On this model, faith is – and *ought to be* – challenged by difference, critique or doubt. However, such challenges do not so much end faith as transform it. In my initial reflection I said that no one is free from commitments to unproven and unproveable first principles that shape their way of being in the world. Doubt can push us off our foundation, but over the long run it does not remove the necessity of having a foundation of some sort. No one lives in permanent doubt about things, especially where meaning or purpose is concerned. Eventually we choose a perspective and get on with life. It might be that we lose the faith we have and adopt some different way of looking at things; it might be that we return to our faith in a new way. Thus, a theist who experiences a crisis of faith might become an atheist, become a different sort of theist (adopting a new denominational affiliation or even a different religion), or return to their existing faith in a new light. Likewise, the faith we have in another person can be tested – say, by a crisis in a marriage; and that crisis could end in a loss of faith in the marriage or end in a new and different commitment to it. Seen in this light, faith and doubt are in an ongoing dialogue in which faith asserts something and doubt questions it, only to give rise to a new expression of faith.[10]

Faith is a process, not an achievement. And questioning, critique, and even doubt are not the enemies of faith or cause for its failure, but rather essential elements in its evolution and maturation. Of course, I don't want to trivialise the dark night of the soul or suggest that it is not dangerous to faith. Faith *can* fail in a variety of ways. Which is why, when I claimed that an overly narrow view of faith runs the risk of missing all sorts of 'non-religious' expressions of faith, I also maintained that an overly broad view of faith – one that suggests too easily that 'everyone is a person of faith' – runs the risk of making faith a meaningless signifier. We have got to maintain a distinction between, on the one hand, a person whose first principles operate at a kind of subconscious level, and require little other than that she not despair (e.g. the mere mattering of things), and, on the other hand, a person who is more reflective about those principles, what they require and how they animate their way of being in the world.

*

Michael Hauskeller: If I understand you correctly, what you are saying here is that a reflective approach to the world and one's own being in it is not only compatible with faith, but actually an essential part of it (or at least an essential part of any true or 'mature' faith). This seems to be at odds with the common understanding (or misunderstanding?) of 'faith' as being opposed to a commitment to science and reason.

Poincaré once remarked that to 'doubt everything or to believe everything are two equally convenient solutions; both dispense with the necessity of reflection'.[11] This is a point well made. It is indeed just as easy to believe nothing as it is to believe everything, precisely because neither requires reflection, or at least not the sort that involves any kind of critical judgement. Employing critical judgement means that we think about what *deserves* to be believed and what does *not* deserve to be believed, and doing this can be hard work. Today, in post-truth times, it seems that fewer and fewer people are willing to put in that work, preferring instead to put their faith in 'rabid partisans or empty quacks'[12] that 'make a great noise in the world',[13] and to stubbornly keep that faith even when all the evidence shows that it is not at all deserved. But do those who are not willing to do the reflective work and who blithely ignore reality really show faith (in an idea, a worldview or a person), or are they just lazy thinkers?

Of course, some might say that there is no difference – that faith and lazy thinking are actually one and the same. In contrast, what we have suggested in our discussion so far is something different, almost the opposite: namely that faith and critical reflection are not mutually exclusive, that one can both believe and question and doubt, and not alternately (first believing, then doubting, then believing again and so on), but more or less simultaneously, with doubt being an integral and indeed indispensable part of faith. If faith means remaining open to possibilities, including the possibility that we might be completely wrong in what we believe, then faith and doubt are indeed two sides of the same existential coin. But is that really what faith is – as it were, the very essence of faith? Or is it just something that happens to be an integral part of *some* people's faith?

At the beginning of our conversation, you made a distinction between 'faith that' and 'faith in', maintaining that 'faith in' – which you defined as 'one's fidelity to and trust in a certain reality' whereby we 'recognise and affirm its worth' – is closer to the essence of faith than any particular beliefs about that reality we may or may not have. Perhaps we should give some more thought to what that actually means. Let us start by asking ourselves what this fidelity and trust that you identified as the essence of faith is based on. I think it is based on concrete *experience*. Often, when people try to articulate their religious faith and explain *why* they have faith, they don't resort to listing things that they believe. They say nothing or little about the existence and nature of God or other more specific doctrines that they hold to be true. Instead, they tend to describe experiences that are marked by a strong sense of presence. It seems to be the feeling that something is there, something powerful that cannot be accounted for in naturalistic terms, some kind of superior alien force that is aware of us just as we are aware of it, greater than anything we know or we can ever hope to understand. This feeling is undeniable and commanding, yet enigmatic. It is opaque in the sense that it does not tell us much, if anything, about what kind of entity it is that we feel to be present, what it wants or for that matter if it wants anything at all. In this way, it is very much like the experience of what Rudolf Otto used to call the numinous, which we encounter as a 'terrifying and fascinating mystery'.[14]

Because of the indefinite or opaque nature of the experience, there is indeed plenty of room for doubt here, and that includes the doubt that the presence we seem to be feeling is merely a projection, that we are deceiving ourselves, that where we feel something there is, in reality, nothing. And yet the experience itself is undoubtedly real and even incontrovertible, and it is this experiential incontrovertibility that first awakens our faith and then sustains it through all the doubts that as thinking, reflective beings we cannot fail to have. Religious faith, then, is not only faith in some kind of transcendent reality – something other than ourselves and other than the physical entities that we are familiar with from our ordinary interactions with the world – but also faith in ourselves, in the trustworthiness and reliability of our own experience, a faith that is perhaps akin to the faith we naturally have in what we have 'seen with our own eyes' or what we 'remember clearly and distinctly'. Even though we know very well that there are such things as false memories (when people 'remember' things that in fact never happened)[15] and hallucinations (when people 'see' things that are not really there),[16] we still find it very hard not to believe what we saw or remember. Similarly, even though we know, theoretically, that when we experience what we take to be a transcendent power we might be mistaken about the nature of our experience, in practice the experience is persuasive and difficult to shake.

*

Brian Treanor: You are correct that faith is not, on my view, opposed to reason.[17] In fact, reason can help to sort out the experiences that you suggest ground faith. And, as I have said, this does not just mean that reason can play devil's advocate, undermining faith in favour of some alternative, sceptical account; reason can also help to make clear the experiences that are the ground for faith, and to make the foundation of faith stronger. In general, I would say that reason is one of the tools for exercising the 'critical judgement' you call for – what others might call 'discernment'.[18] We merely need to remember that while reason is an essential tool, one of our most useful, it is not the only tool at our disposal, nor is it the best tool for every job.

However, you raise a very important point for consideration when you ask: 'If faith means remaining open to possibilities, including the possibility that we might be completely wrong in what we believe, then faith and doubt are indeed two sides of the same existential coin. But is that really what faith is – as it were, the very essence of faith? Or is it just something that happens to be an integral part of *some* people's faith?' I often criticise at least some of the thinkers grouped under the banner of 'new atheism' for levelling attacks against religion that are really attacks against certain forms of literalism and fundamentalism in religion.[19] That is to say, for suggesting that a certain kind of faith – a kind of faith I also find problematic – is somehow normative or representative of faith *tout court*. For example, while both are Christian, Jerry Falwell was a radically different thinker from Rowan Williams (to say nothing of 'postmodern' philosophers of religion like Richard Kearney, John D. Caputo and Merold Westphal);[20] and I would venture that someone who conflates them or lumps them, undifferentiated, under the same banner needs to reassess just how 'disinterestedly' and 'objectively' their own reason is operating.

But, if that is the case, I need to be just as careful not to suggest that the particular form of faith I am describing here is the only form that faith can take. The influence of Jerry Falwell and others of his ilk is, obviously, significant, and it should not be ignored. There are people who resist thinking critically about their faith, whose epistemic goals are more oriented toward sectarian triumphalism than deeper understanding. The former is often an exercise in aggression, as well as ossification, while the later requires the critical engagement and reflection that you rightly emphasise.

We must remember that undue epistemic confidence and resistance to correction are not unique to expressions of faith; they are all too common in reasoning as well, as attending any academic conference will make abundantly clear. It is no use saying that 'reason is structurally open to correction and modification' and 'faith is structurally closed to correction or modification', because it begs the question. It excuses poor reasoning in matters 'outside of faith' by suggesting that it is somehow 'not actually reason(able)', while vilifying unreflective faith as the essence of faith itself. Instead, I think we should recognise that both reason and faith are subject to certain misuses or abuses (some of which they share, and some of which are unique to one or the other). An appropriate epistemic humility ought to dispose us such that both reason and faith remain open to correction and evolution. This and similar epistemic virtues should help us maintain a position that concedes that, no matter how confidently we 'know' or 'believe' something at the moment, we would, given sufficient new data, insight or experience, be open to the evolution of our understanding.[21]

Finally, I think you strike upon something important when you stress the value of experience and presence. Antoine de Saint-Exupéry observed that 'truth is not that which is demonstrable, but that which is ineluctable'.[22] We take something to be true when it is a truth we cannot avoid; no matter what adjustments we make, what epistemic or existential contortions we undergo, we find ourselves confronted with something that we cannot, if we remain honest and have integrity, deny. This truth could be, for example, the heliocentric model of the solar system. Here the naked-eye observations of Copernicus – and, later, Galileo's use of the telescope and advances in physics – make ineluctable the reality that the earth revolves around the sun. However, ineluctability is manifest in different, more experiential ways in the example of 'I love Madeline' (or, indeed, 'I no longer love Madeline'). And, in both instances – the Copernican overthrow of the Ptolemaic system and the falling-out-of-love-with-Madeline – correction is a perennially open option for any honest inquirer. Demonstration is one way in which we make the ineluctable evident; it is not, however, ineluctability itself. Thus, your example of an 'experience we cannot deny' cuts to the very heart of not only faith, but truth itself.

So, I think you are right to observe that 'incontrovertible' experiences – which I have called 'ineluctable' – both awaken and sustain faith. Those events may be concrete personal experiences, novel experiments, rational arguments or something else, although I think you are right to stress the significance of concrete personal experience in matters of faith. And if experience both awakens and sustains faith, we see again how faith is, or can be, significantly less inflexible and dogmatic than common caricature. In my example above, my love for Madeline – my faith *in her*, and my faith *in myself* and *in my love for her* – can fail. Experience can fail to sustain that reality. I could come to realise that the incontrovertible truth of the feeling I once had for her is now, in fact, quite dubitable.

Similarly, a person's experience can cause them, over time, to doubt their theism, or to doubt their militant anti-theism (reductive materialism itself is a form of faith). Some people have found themselves dragged, kicking and screaming as it were, either from or to faith of one kind or another. C. S. Lewis describes himself as the 'most dejected and reluctant convert in all of England' on the night he first accepts theism.[23] Thomas Merton, Augustine and other converts describe the slow, painful, reluctant process of accepting what was, for them, a new – and at first unwelcome – faith.[24] They give accounts of myriad ways in which they turned to escape, like animals caught in a trap, and the reluctance (at least initially) with which they realised the ineluctability of what would become their new faith. Of course, as you suggest, the seemingly irresistible force of reality that brought each of them to theism was no sure guarantee of sustaining it, as Lewis's crisis of faith after his wife's death makes evident.[25] The critique or doubt that remains structurally present in faith can lead us either to a second naiveté that renews our faith in a new form, or to a different faith, or to the loss of faith. The leap of 'faith in' must be made again and again; it is never accomplished for good. Its success depends on the experiences we have (that is, what the world reveals to, or demands of or imposes on us), our trust in ourselves (that is, the way we employ critical judgement or engage in discernment), and our commitment to that truth (that is, fidelity, truth as troth).

*

Michael Hauskeller: I agree with you that the common rationalist assumption that faith is blind, biased, mostly wishful thinking, and ultimately a force of darkness, while reason is open-eyed, objective, oriented towards truth, and as such a force of light, is an oversimplification and a self-serving distortion of the organic connection and interplay between reason and faith that our understanding requires to do full justice to our experience of the world. Critical thinking is important, but it needs to be applied also to reason, so that we can realise its limits and its shortcomings and do not grossly overestimate its power and reach. The great Gilbert Keith Chesterton once wrote: 'The madman is not the man who has lost his reason. The madman is the man who has lost everything except his reason.'[26] Faith complements reason, keeps it grounded in experiential reality, and makes it sensible. It ensures that we don't reason ourselves out of love and friendship, decency and compassion, beauty and meaning. Reason is a tool that needs to be applied wisely because it is indeed, as you say, 'not the best tool for every job', and it can easily lead us astray.

Then again, so can faith when it becomes detached from reason. In fact, isn't that precisely what is wrong with a strong commitment to any comprehensive rationalism: that we put too much faith in our own ability to discern the truth, too much faith in reason to provide the answers to all important questions, too much faith in science to find solutions to all emerging problems? Epistemic humility, it seems, would consist in having a little less faith in all these things and a more reasonable attitude towards reason itself. Clearly, we need to have some faith in reason, and it is reasonable to do so, but *how much* faith we should have in it is open to debate, which leads us to the more general question of what exactly we should have faith in and how strong, resilient and impervious our faith should be, because surely not every faith is justified and not every faith deserves to be maintained. If faith is trust in a certain reality and an affirmation of its worth, we should expect that there are instances of faith where the reality in which one trusts does not exist or lacks the worth that one attributes to it.

The leap of faith, you said earlier, *must* be made again and again. I take this to be a hypothetical imperative, not a categorical one. In other words, we must make that leap of faith again and again *if* we wish to sustain our faith in the face of the challenges it may (and most likely will) encounter in the course of a life lived with honesty and integrity. The big question, however, is why and in what circumstances we should do so. Why, when confronted with evidence that our faith in some reality or other and our affirmation of its worth may possibly be misplaced, should we hold on to it? What distinguishes justified from unjustified faith? If 'life's a piece of shit when you look at it', as the British comedy troupe Monty Python memorably quipped in *The Life of Brian*, and we *have* actually looked at it, should we then still turn our eyes away and continue to 'always look on the bright side of life'? Should we still hold on to our faith in the power and goodness of God if we can no longer deny that the world is full of evils, taking recourse in reason and putting it to the service of our faith by coming up with an explanation that allows us to get rid of the cognitive dissonance? Or should we simply give up our faith?

As I am writing this, Joe Biden has just been declared the winner of the 2020 US presidential election. A few days ago, on election night, when it still looked as if Donald Trump might be re-elected, Biden addressed his supporters with some encouraging words: 'Keep the faith, guys. We're gonna win this!'[27] As it turned out, he was right. But for all he and his supporters knew at the time, it could have gone the other way. He could have lost, in which case their faith would have been misplaced. Meanwhile, Trump's supporters were also 'keeping the faith', telling reporters that 'President Trump was appointed and anointed by God to get our nation back on the right path' and following the example of the president's spiritual advisor Paula White by publicly praying to God to secure Trump's victory and to strike down all his enemies.[28] Now that the race is lost, many supporters have found a means to maintain and justify their faith (in God, Trump and victory) by alleging foul play, while the incumbent claims that in actual fact he *did* win the election. Given what we know about Trump, this is not surprising. What is surprising and indeed utterly incomprehensible to me is that more than 70 million Americans have kept their faith in Trump after four miserable years of his presidency, which may well have required a great number of repeated leaps of faith that were greatly facilitated by a widespread willingness to embrace alternative facts. Or is that not faith?

*

Brian Treanor: Your desire to get down to the brass tacks of what faith looks like in the world is, I think, appropriate as we approach the end of our conversation. Faith has a chequered history to say the least, a survey of which makes clear the importance of the 'big question' you rightly put before us: in what should we have faith, and on what grounds?

Here I think I would be inclined to begin with the distinction I made above between 'faith that . . .' and 'faith in . . .'. When it comes to 'faith that . . .', what we are really talking about is a kind of belief in specific claims about the way the world is. In such cases, the grounds for justifying faith are reasonably well understood and widely shared. For example, if I have 'faith that' my cancer has been cured, I might form that belief on the basis of what my physician has told me after treatment. After all, there is value to her training, expertise and years of experience. I might be even more convinced of my belief if I receive a second expert opinion that concurs with the assessment of my physician. Now, this 'faith' or belief could still prove to be wrong, and cancer could be lurking in my body. Nevertheless, I have good grounds for my 'faith that' I have been cured. In contrast, it seems straightforward to say that my faith that I have been cured is not well justified if it is based on the opinion of my car mechanic or grocer, even if they turn out to be correct. Of course, it is all too clear that some people do have faith that, for example, wildly implausible, internally contradictory, social media-driven conspiracy theories are true. Nevertheless, there are many quite well-understood and commonsensical guidelines for when and how to form beliefs (faith that . . .) and how strongly we should be committed to them.

The case is somewhat different when it comes to examples of 'faith in . . .', which I have asserted is more the essence of faith. Here we are not speaking of some empirical reality that could be confirmed or disconfirmed; rather we are speaking of our willingness to affirm the value of and remain faithful to something. Or, perhaps more often, 'someone', without limiting that category to human beings. It might be better to say that 'faith in' is often concerned with a reality with which we can be in a kind of 'personal' – that is, individual, intimate, experiential – relationship. Earlier in our conversation you mentioned the importance of *presence*, which I think cuts right to the heart of what I am getting at here.[29]

Thus, for example, we can speak of faith in another person – a spouse, a close friend, a mentor. Such faith is a recognition of their intrinsic value, their meaningfulness, their worthiness based on experiences I have had with them – that is, on a relationship I have experienced. Of course, like 'faith that' something is the case, 'faith in' a person can be tested, and it can fail. Perhaps one's spouse is unfaithful, or succumbs to addiction, or commits a serious crime that harms someone else. In such instances a person is going to be faced with the question of whether her faith in her spouse, friend or mentor is still possible. Perhaps she may come to wonder if it was ever warranted in the first place, or if it was all a monstrous error. But it seems to me that such challenges to 'faith in' can play out in a variety of different ways. A questioning person might give up faith in a friend who has betrayed her. But it is also possible that she decides to remain faithful – that her faith in the friend is tested but, rather than breaking, is transformed. A new relationship emerges. On the other side of the doubt that troubles faith, there can be a new faith.

Gabriel Marcel speaks of 'creative fidelity', a commitment to remaining flexible and adaptable in the face of tests and trials that we cannot predict.[30] When a person stands before a lover – whether the ceremony is religious or secular – and says some version of 'I do . . . till death do us part', she is making a commitment that is, on the face of it, absurd. A great many marriages end in divorce, so the odds alone are not as good as the vow suggests. Moreover, she is, in a sense, *committing herself to a person she has never met*: the future self of her lover. What on earth could justify such faith? Nothing, other than a love so audacious that it is willing to commit itself to something, or someone, whatever may come. And Marcel suggests that when such faith is tested – *and it will be* – it is able to survive not by wishing reality was different (for instance, I wish my spouse had not failed us in some particular way), but rather by making oneself different (for instance, by transforming oneself to meet the demands of fidelity to – that is, faith in – the other). Of course, sometimes even 'faith in . . .' *should* fail. Perhaps the clearest example is the case of abusive relationships. It would be obscene to suggest that the way to respond to a disrupted 'faith in' a newly abusive partner is to learn to tolerate the abuse. Not every challenge to faith leads, after the dark night of the soul, to renewed faith. Sometimes we do, and should, lose faith.

However, is God – or reality – an abusive partner? Certainly, there are abundant reasons to suspect this is the case. We might remember that even Christ was tempted to despair on the cross: 'My God, my God, why have you forsaken me?'[31] Despair is certainly a legitimate, even rational, possibility when surveying the world and the human condition. But, bracketing for the moment the excellent humour of Monty Python, is it really so implausible to imagine someone on death's door, even someone who lived a very difficult life, thinking at the end:

> Malgré tout je vous dis que cette vie fut telle
> Qu'à qui voudra m'entendre à qui je parle ici,
> N'ayant plus sur la lèvre un seul mot que merci,
> Je dirai malgré tout que cette vie fut belle.[32]

> Despite everything, I tell you that this life was such
> That to those who will listen, those I speak to,
> No word on my lips other than thank you,
> I will say, despite everything, that this life was beautiful.

This kind of faith in the meaningfulness of the world and the value of life does not require that we turn a blind eye to or minimise the horror ('*despite* everything . . .'); rather, it claims that, in the midst of the confusion, suffering, loss and death, there were nevertheless experiences of wonder, joy, grace or love. That the darkness of the world is never total; and that, for each of us, at the end of our life and our world, the ledger will record more than unceasing loss.

*

Michael Hauskeller: I really like Aragon's poem, not least, I suppose, because like him (and you, I think) I strongly believe that life is, despite all the pain and nastiness, beautiful and very much worth living. Yet it would probably not have occurred to me to call this appreciative attitude towards life 'faith'. This is because such a sustained focus on what is beautiful and good in one's life rather than on what is ugly and bad (without denying that there is a lot of that too), and the determination not to submit to the latter and to rebel (in Camus' sense)[33] against it by refusing to let it control and shape one's attitude to life, seems to be, on the face of it, not really a *belief* of any kind, nor does it show *trust* in something that we cannot be certain of, both of which we would normally expect to be involved in instances of faith (whether it be 'faith that' or 'faith in'). The attitude expressed in the lines you quote from Aragon's poem seems predominantly if not exclusively *backward*-looking: approaching the end of life, we judge that, all things considered, it was worth it. It seems like a case of selective perception, rather than one of belief or trust. After all, the good things that happened in my life, to which I now choose to give much greater weight than to the bad things, undoubtedly existed. They were, and are, just as real as the bad things.

Then again, reading the whole poem, the picture changes somewhat. A different interpretation suggests itself when Aragon earlier on speaks of the 'stupid belief in the clear blue sky' (*sa croyance imbécile à l'azur*) that he or his poetic persona has held on to, and *wanted* to hold on to, all his life. Why would that belief be 'stupid' if it were justified, if it were simply the recognition of an existing reality? There must be something not quite rational about it, something that goes beyond the evaluative choices we all make when we decide what is important for us and in what way and to what extent.

What lies underneath, it seems to me, is not the kind of innocuous optimism that declares the same glass to be half full that the pessimist thinks of as half empty – which would merely indicate a difference of perspective and perhaps temperament, but not necessarily a fundamental disagreement about the nature of reality. Because clearly, a glass that is half full is in fact also half empty. Faith enters the equation only when we (not exactly believe, but) feel that, contrary to what our senses and all publicly available and communicable knowledge tell us, the glass that appears only half full is in fact, somehow, *more* than just half full and what appears to be empty space is not empty at all. In other words, it is felt that all the bad that happens in our lives can never cancel out the good because the good is, in some undefinable and perhaps quite unfathomable way, more *real* than the bad. All faith in a reality is faith both in the *goodness* of that reality and the reality (i.e. causal power and endurance) of that goodness as well as the comparative irreality (weakness and ultimate inefficiency) of whatever appears bad about it.

If we have, like Aragon, an enduring faith (*croyance*) in the 'clear blue sky' we do not merely choose to pay more attention to it than to the clouds that frequently cover and conceal it. Rather, we trust that the sky is *still* clear and blue behind the clouds, that it will remain so no matter how many clouds go by, and that it will eventually reveal itself again in all its glory and splendour. This is faith precisely because it is *not* well-founded. It is not knowledge, nor is it even justified belief. I readily acknowledge that some kind of experience must (or at least in many instances does) precede or inspire our faith, but that experience falls short of providing us with 'good grounds' for our faith in the way that you suggested earlier when you cited the case of a man who believes his cancer has been cured because the experts – those who are in a position to know – assure him that it is gone. Faith is not grounded in expert opinion.

My belief that the earth is spherical rather than flat is not faith, precisely because there is no or very little room for reasonable doubt here. Uncertainty, or rather unknowability, the impossibility of being *sure*, is the essence of faith. This is why your example of the marriage vow is such a good one. With that vow, you said, we commit ourselves to a person *we have never met*: the *future* self of our lover. It is true that in this case our decision to commit ourselves is normally based on our previous experience with our partner. We think we know them well enough to make such a momentous lifelong commitment. However, it is also true that our experience here is necessarily very limited and incomplete. We don't know what the future will bring, what challenges we will encounter, and how we and our partner may change over time. For all we know, we may not make it. So we are indeed taking a leap of faith here, trusting, despite all the statistics that suggest a high probability of failure, that things will turn out well because fundamentally they already *are* well. And that trust, I think, is what faith is all about.

Notes

1. See Caputo, *The Prayers and Tears of Jacques Derrida*; Caputo, *The Insistence of God*; Caputo, *Cross and Cosmos*; Kearney, *Anatheism;* Kearney and Zimmerman, *Reimaging the Sacred*.
2. This is a theme I explore in greater depth in *Melancholic Joy*, based on distinctions made by Gabriel Marcel. See especially 'On the ontological mystery' and *Homo Viator*.
3. In philosophy, the leap of faith is perhaps most famously associated with Søren Kierkegaard. See, for example, his *Concluding Unscientific Postscript*. Other figures who speak about the leap of faith in one way or another include William James, *The Will to Believe* and Richard Kearney, *Anatheism*.
4. 'Let us not pretend to doubt in philosophy what we do not doubt in our hearts,' writes Peirce in 'Questions concerning certain faculties claimed for man', 86–7. Peirce's point is that there are certain things that we cannot, in fact, doubt. We can say 'I doubt that I am reading this book', but *saying* it and *believing* it – or even entertaining it as a possibility – are two very different things. And Peirce argues that if what we mean by 'doubting' is nothing more than saying the words 'I doubt that X', our doubt is a trivial thing and not worth much philosophical scrutiny.
5. 'There can be no difference anywhere that does not make a difference somewhere – no difference in abstract truth that doesn't express itself in a difference in concrete fact and in conduct consequent on that fact' (James, *Pragmatism*, 45).
6. Pascal's *Pensées*, section 233.
7. Hume, *A Treatise on Human Nature*, Book 1, part 4, section 7: 'Most fortunately it happens, that since reason is incapable of dispelling these clouds, nature herself suffices to that purpose, and cures me of this philosophical melancholy and delirium, either by relaxing this bent of mind, or by some avocation, and lively impression of my senses, which obliterate all these chimeras. I dine, I play a game of backgammon, I converse, and am merry with my friends; and when after three or four hours' amusement, I would return to these speculations, they appear so cold, and strained, and ridiculous, that I cannot find in my heart to enter into them any farther.'
8. James, *The Will to Believe*, 5.
9. Ricoeur, *The Symbolism of Evil*.
10. See Ricoeur, *Critique and Conviction*.
11. Poincaré, *La Science et l'hypothèse*, 2: 'Douter de tout ou tout croire, ce sont deux solutions également commodes, qui l'une et l'autre nous dispensent de réfléchir.'
12. James, *Memories and Studies*, 58: 'The deadliest enemies of nations are not their foreign foes, they always dwell within their borders. And from these internal enemies civilisation is always in need of being saved. The nation blest above all nations is she in whom the civic genius of the people does the saving day by day, by acts without external picturesqueness; by speaking, writing, voting reasonably; by the people knowing true men when they see them, and preferring them as leaders to rabid partisans or empty quacks.'
13. Nietzsche, *Also sprach Zarathustra*, 'On the flies of the market' (my translation): 'In the world even the best things are worthless without someone who performs them: those performers the people call great men. Little do the people understand what is great, namely that which creates. But they have a taste for all performers and actors of great things. Around the inventors of new values the world revolves, invisibly it revolves. But around the actors revolve the people and fame: such is the way of the world. Spirit has the actor, but little conscience of the spirit. He believes always in that which makes people believe most strongly – in *him*! Tomorrow he has a new belief, and the day after, one still newer. Quick of perception is he, like the people, and his moods change. To upset is what he means by "prove". To madden is what he means by "convince". And blood he deems to be the best of all reasons. A truth which only slips into subtle ears he calls a lie and a nothing. He indeed believes only in gods that make a great noise in the world!'
14. Otto, *The Idea of the Holy*.
15. See Marsh et al., 'False memories'.
16. See Oliver Sacks, *Hallucinations*.
17. Different thinkers – Aristotle, Thomas Aquinas, John Locke, William James, John Henry Newman and many others – develop different accounts of the relationship between faith and reason. And while some thinkers, Kierkegaard for example, stress the irrationality of faith, there are many others who develop a framework in which they are compatible or complementary.

18. We must distinguish between 'a blind leap of faith and a wise one' (Kearney, *Anatheism*, 44). The possibility of the former remains a perpetual danger for religion; and there are obviously countless instances of people who have followed religious impulses to their detriment or, worse, to murderous ends. Nevertheless, the possibility of leaps or wagers toward destructive ends does not itself occlude the possibility, and historical fact, of people who made similar leaps toward the most selfless and admirable ends.
19. To be clear, many atheist critiques of religion – and especially of religious excesses – are appropriate and even salutary. However, it is a mistake to reduce all forms of religious expression to extreme forms of anti-scientific irrationalism.
20. Caputo's and Kearney's works are cited above. Among Westphal's numerous books, see *Overcoming Onto-Theology*. Falwell and Williams also clearly have quite different views of the relationship between faith in God and facts about the world, for example, climate change. In February 2007, Falwell preached a sermon in which he insisted that climate change is essentially a myth and that, in any case, 'God has it all under control'. Williams, in contrast, insisted in a 2009 lecture: 'I think that to suggest that God might intervene to protect us from the corporate folly of our practices is as unchristian and unbiblical as to suggest that he protects us from the results of our individual folly or sin.' Consequently, 'God's faithfulness stands, assuring us that even in the most appalling disaster love will not let us go – but it will not be a safety net that guarantees a happy ending in this world'.
21. This is the view of pragmatism and, on my account of things, hermeneutics; it is also the view of science.
22. Saint-Exupéry, *Wind, Sand and Stars*, 218.
23. Lewis, *Surprised by Joy*, 228–9.
24. See Merton, *The Seven Story Mountain* and Augustine, *Confessions*.
25. Lewis, *A Grief Observed*.
26. Chesterton, *Orthodoxy*, 32.
27. https://www.youtube.com/watch?v=q17TNeeoJKU (accessed 1 December 2021).
28. https://www.huffingtonpost.co.uk/entry/donald-trump-spiritual-advisor-holds-hysterical-prayer-service_uk_5fa3c748c5b6b35537e3ff7e (accessed 1 December 2021).
29. On presence see Marcel, *The Mystery of Being*, volumes 1 and 2.
30. Marcel, *Creative Fidelity*.
31. Matthew 27:46.
32. Aragon, 'Que la vie en vaut la peine'.
33. Camus, *The Rebel*, 19.

Bibliography

Aragon, Louis. 'Que la vie en vaut la peine'. In *Les Yeux et la mémoire*. Paris: Gallimard, 1954.
Augustine. *Confessions*, translated by Henry Chadwick. Oxford: Oxford University Press, 2009.
Camus, Albert. *The Rebel*, translated by Anthony Bower. Harmondsworth: Penguin, 1962.
Caputo, John D. *The Prayers and Tears of Jacques Derrida: Religion without religion*. Bloomington, IN: Indiana University Press, 1997.
Caputo, John D. *The Insistence of God: A theology of perhaps*. Bloomington, IN: Indiana University Press, 2012.
Caputo, John D. *Cross and Cosmos: A theology of difficult glory*. Bloomington, IN: Indiana University Press, 2019.
Chesterton, Gilbert Keith. *Orthodoxy*. New York: John Lane, 1909.
Hume, David. *A Treatise on Human Nature*, edited by L. A. Selby-Bigge, 2nd edn revised by P. H. Nidditch. Oxford: Clarendon Press, 1975.
James, William. *Memories and Studies*. New York: Longmans, Green and Co., 1911.
James, William. *Pragmatism*. Mineola, NY: Dover, 1995.
James, William. *The Will to Believe*. Mineola, NY: Dover, 1960.
Kearney, Richard. *Anatheism: Returning to God after God*. New York: Columbia University Press, 2011.
Kearney, Richard, and Jens Zimmerman. *Reimaging the Sacred*. New York: Columbia University Press, 2015.

Kierkegaard, Søren. *Concluding Unscientific Postscript*, translated by Howard V. Hong and Edna H. Hong. Princeton, NJ: Princeton University Press, 1992.

Lewis, C. S. *A Grief Observed*. London: Harper, 1961.

Lewis, C. S. *Surprised by Joy*, London: Harvest Books, 1995.

Marcel, Gabriel. *Creative Fidelity*, translated by Robert Rosthal. New York: Farrar, Straus and Giroux, 1964.

Marcel, Gabriel. *The Mystery of Being*, volume 1: *Reflection and Mystery*, translated by G. S. Fraser. London: The Harvill Press, 1951.

Marcel, Gabriel. *The Mystery of Being*, volume 2: *Faith and Reality*, translated by Rene Hague. London: The Harvill Press, 1951.

Marcel, Gabriel. *Homo Viator*, translated by Emma Crawford. New York: Harper Torchbooks, 1962.

Marcel, Gabriel. 'On the ontological mystery'. In *The Philosophy of Existentialism*, translated by Manya Harari. New York: Citadel Press, 1995.

Marsh, E. J., A. N. Eslick and L. K. Fazio. 'False memories'. In *Learning and Memory: A comprehensive reference*, volume 2: *Cognitive Psychology of Memory*, edited by H. L. Roediger, III, 221–38. Oxford: Elsevier, 2008.

Merton, Thomas. *The Seven Story Mountain*. Boston: Mariner Books, 1999.

Nietzsche, Friedrich. *Also sprach Zarathustra*. Munich: Hanser, 1966.

Otto, Rudolf. *The Idea of the Holy*. Oxford: Oxford University Press, 1923.

Pascal, Blaise. *Pensées*. New York: E. P. Dutton & Co., 1958.

Peirce, Charles Sanders. 'Questions concerning certain faculties claimed for man'. In *The Essential Writings*. Lanham, MD: Prometheus, 1998.

Poincaré, Henri. *La Science et l'hypothèse*. Paris: Ernest Flammarion, 1902.

Ricoeur, Paul. *Critique and Conviction*, translated by Kathleen Blamey. New York: Columbia University Press, 1998.

Ricoeur, Paul. *The Symbolism of Evil*, translated by Emerson Buchanan. Boston, MA: Beacon Press, 1967.

Sacks, Oliver. *Hallucinations*. New York: Alfred J. Knopf, 2012.

Saint-Exupéry, Antoine de. *Wind, Sand and Stars*, translated by Lewis Glanatière. London: Harvest, 1939.

Treanor, Brian. *Melancholic Joy: On life worth living*. London: Bloomsbury, 2021.

Westphal, Merold. *Overcoming Onto-Theology*. New York: Fordham University Press, 2001.

13
Beauty
with Elaine Scarry

Michael Hauskeller: In one of his most influential essays, the transhumanist philosopher Nick Bostrom predicts that in the future, when we will all be radically enhanced and thoroughly posthumanised, we are going to enjoy music that is, due to our vastly refined senses and cognitive capacities, 'to Mozart what Mozart is to bad Muzak'.[1] While Bostrom apparently cannot wait to get to that stage, I, for one, find the prospect of Mozart sounding like bad muzak rather off-putting. Why would anyone wish that what now has tremendous value for us over time lose all its value? Why would we wish for the beautiful – Mozart – to be transformed into something ugly or at least indifferent – bad muzak? And how likely is that anyway? What would beauty have to *be* for such a transformation to be possible?

Naturally, this is not about Mozart and whether we find his music beautiful or not. 'Mozart', in Bostrom's analogy, clearly stands for anything we currently hold in high regard not because it is particularly useful, but largely if not solely because it is experienced as beautiful by many people. *Whatever* we regard as beautiful today, Bostrom suggests, strikes us as beautiful *only* because, for one thing, we have not come across anything significantly better yet, and for another, because our senses are not sufficiently developed to perceive its many flaws and imperfections. If we had better music, better paintings, better poems, or altogether better ways of expressing ourselves, if we had better sunsets and spring meadows, as well as a more discerning ear and eye, we would immediately realise how unworthy of our attention and love all the things that we now find beautiful really are. A posthuman poet would no longer feel, when looking at an ancient statue of a Greek god, that he needs to change his life,[2] and his heart would no longer be dancing with the daffodils that he once saw beside a lake,[3] because – being fully aware of their inferiority – he would have paid no attention to them in the first place. He would have moved on from Greek statues and daffodils.

Yet for this whole scenario to be plausible, we would have to accept certain assumptions about the nature of beauty. Most importantly, we would have to correctly assume that beauty is, by its very nature, *comparative*, in the sense that a beautiful thing (whether it is a material object or something else, perhaps an action or a moment in time, a constellation of things or a situation) is always, unless it is the most beautiful thing that could possibly exist, *more or less* beautiful. This means that for anything that is beautiful, not only can we always find (or at least conceive of) other things that are less beautiful than it and things that are more beautiful, but the things that are less beautiful are also *ugly* (that is, aesthetically worthless) in comparison to it, as the beautiful thing itself is ugly in comparison to all the things that are more beautiful than it. The beauty of a particular thing or event is thus located on a scale that reaches from the ugliest, or least beautiful, to the most beautiful, or least ugly. In this respect, then, beauty would be very much like size. We know that things are not 'large' or 'small' in themselves, but only ever in relation to other things that are, respectively, smaller or larger, and perhaps beauty is just like that. Declaring that something is beautiful would then just be a convenient shorthand for saying that it is more beautiful than most things we know, just as we call things 'large' without qualification when they are larger than we are (say, an elephant) or larger than a thing of that particular kind normally is (a large elephant). But is beauty really like that?

It is no doubt true that we occasionally talk as if it is possible to compare things in terms of their beauty, especially people. Jane is beautiful, but Mary is even more beautiful. The evil queen is the fairest in the land, but Snow White is 'a thousand times more beautiful' than she. We may even feel inclined to compare our beloved to a summer's day and find her more lovely and more temperate.[4] But do such comparisons truly do justice to the phenomenon of beauty? It seems to me that as soon as we start comparing the beauty of one thing or person to that of another we have already lost sight of the beauty that is equally present in both of them. When we look at a beautiful object or listen to a beautiful melody, and become fully *aware* of their beauty, everything else disappears or fades into the background, all other beautiful things included. It is as if nothing else existed. The beauty of that one object fills the entire world, allowing for no comparison and ruling out any possibility of improvement. The beautiful thing is, in its beauty and while we are aware of it, perfect, which is why, just as there can be no grades of perfection (because the less perfect would not be perfect), there can be no

248   THE THINGS THAT REALLY MATTER

grades of beauty either. The beautiful thing, and that goes for *every* beautiful thing, is literally beyond compare. It is, in a Kantian sense, priceless because its value is absolute, not relative to the value of other things.[5] If that were not so, Mozart's music and other beautiful things would have a very uncertain future.

*

Elaine Scarry: Is it possible that the human species might bring about – or be the recipients of – a transformation in the direction of the good that would be as extreme as the negative transformations we can imagine (annihilation by nuclear weapons, loss of collective culture due to climate catastrophe, subjugation to an array of super-intelligent computers) are bad? Something like this question might have been what initially motivated Nick Bostrom's claims about beauty. If so, his starting point seems entirely right even though his conclusion seems almost entirely wrong. His starting point would be this: the greatest imaginable good that could come to us would have to have something to do with beauty. His conclusion is this: it would be a degree of beauty or a form of beauty that made Mozart by comparison sound grating and coarse. Let me respond to each in turn.

Is it correct to believe that an extreme transformation to humanity in the positive direction would necessarily involve beauty? There does not appear to be a better candidate. Although alternatives can be formulated, almost all of them lead back to beauty. For example, a good that is as good as the imaginably bad is bad might be for all human beings to have greater aliveness – either for all to have longer lives or to have, throughout their lives (regardless of duration), a more fully felt experience of their own aliveness, so much so that they 'live' the equivalent of many lifetimes. But 'greater aliveness' has for many centuries and in many geographies (by ordinary people as well as by theologians, philosophers and poets) been designated almost a synonym for the experience of coming into the presence of the beautiful.

This may be because the beautiful person or tree or mathematical theorem or sunrise brings about a higher level of attention that raises the bar for what counts as perceptual acuity, helping to establish in the perceiver a higher capacity for attention that can then in turn be given to other perceptual objects that previously seemed unremarkable. Or because the beautiful person or thing elicits the desire to protect and preserve it, engaging us in the work of prolonging its survival, whether because it is actually alive, as in the case of a child or a brook, or because, though not technically alive, it has the quality and claim of 'aliveness', as when one wishes to pass on a poem to successive generations of students or when people all over the world suddenly become alarmed that a canvas stolen from a museum will suffer harm, as though its surface were woundable live tissue rather than inanimate pigment on linen. Or because it affirms not the survival of the beautiful thing but the perceiver's own survival: what exactly is the peculiarly intense pleasure, the sudden bright electric conviction one feels when experiencing beauty if not the heightened assurance that life is good and *must* continue, as in Augustine's description of music as a life-saving plank in the midst of the ocean?[6] In all three explanations, beauty acts as a life pact between the perceiver and the thing perceived.

Another outcome that would be as extreme a transformation in the positive direction as an existential catastrophe would be extreme in the negative direction would be the creation of just relations among all people of the world – a symmetry among family members, neighbours, citizens, nations. But here again we arrive at a vision long recognised as inseparable from beauty, so much so that isolated pockets of beauty in our own imperfect world are often taken to be tokens or promises of our ability to bring about a more just world than we inhabit at present, as when the rainbow is taken as a harbinger of peace,[7] or as when Bertrand Russell speaks of the heavens that lovers and poets have sometimes created as a rehearsal for, or promissory note that we might one day create, an international realm of equal beauty, despite the species' current record of nearly uninterrupted cruelty.[8] If such a state of symmetry and fairness among the world's people were not immediately perceptible as beautiful, or if such symmetry could only be achieved by destroying the natural beauty of earth (eliminating all trees, for example), it would hardly count as a good whose extremity matched the bad extremes presented by the possible nuclear, climate and technological catastrophes.

While it seems clear that any extreme prosperity that came to humanity would have to be bound up with beauty, that prosperity provides no reason why Mozart's music would cease to be regarded as beautiful. Our greater aliveness – and the more just relations we might then go on to achieve as a result of our heightened sensory powers and enlarged brains – would be likely to increase the pleasure of listening to Mozart since, back here in our untransformed world, his compositional genius already enlists us into the very Olympian feats of perception that we hope to achieve, in a more abiding way, in our future state. The fact that he seems to catapult us forward into those future capabilities is part of what we mean when we use the word 'genius' to describe him, just as we call

Shakespeare a genius because one experiences the temporary expansion of one's own intelligence in the very act of hearing his lines.

Although this transformed world will no doubt present us with new objects of beauty, present objects of beauty are unlikely to be eclipsed. Nick Bostrom speaks as though beauty is a drawer of finite dimensions that can only fit a limited number of items. But the hunger for beauty, as Kant says, is inexhaustible and can never be full. Sappho does not cease to be revered when, 25 centuries later, the odes of John Keats become audible or when, 26 centuries later, the compositions of jazz suddenly break across our ears. Even if one of Saturn's rings suddenly migrated to our own planet, it does not seem our bond with the moon, a bond many millennia long, would be severed, just as there are no reports suggesting that the dazzling photographs of other galaxies emerging in recent years have diminished people's ardour for this shady glade or that sun-drenched grove on earth. The destruction of beautiful objects will be the outcome not of positive transformations to humanity but instead of existential catastrophes: even the single most enduring and widely shared object of beauty – the sun – may cease to be regarded as beautiful if the earth reaches burning temperatures; and although climate change may bring many other catastrophes, the potential disappearance of the sun as an object of beauty accurately summarises the scale of the tragedy.

*

Michael Hauskeller: You may be giving too much credit to the transhumanist vision of the wonderful future that supposedly awaits us if only we are bold and determined enough to make some radical changes to our nature. What is valued in that vision is not so much beauty as pleasure, and beauty, if it is recognised at all, is of importance only to the extent that it provides us with pleasurable experiences. Here, beauty is a means, not an end. Yet while being in the presence of beauty can certainly give us great pleasure, there is surely much more to it than that. It is not the fact that it pleases us that *makes* it beautiful, just as it is not the pleasure and appreciation we feel when we witness (or read or hear about) someone doing something really kind for others that makes what they do good. Rather, as with the good, the beautiful provides us with a *reason* to feel pleasure. We feel pleasure *because* there is beauty, and our becoming *aware* of that beauty is what gives us pleasure.

But what exactly is it that we become aware of here? Is it, as you put it, that 'life is good and *must* continue'? (Is it really, and must it?) Does all beauty speak to us of the preciousness of life, or of 'aliveness'? And what exactly does that mean – 'aliveness'? What we become aware of in beautiful things is certainly something of value, something we strongly feel is worth protecting and preserving. There is a moral imperative here that is an integral part of the experience of beauty. While there is no indication of this ethical dimension in the English word 'beautiful', which originally meant little more than being pleasing to the senses, its German equivalent, the adjective *schön*, initially also meant kind and considerate, and one of the words derived from it is the verb *schonen*, which means to not harm, or in other words to protect and preserve. Incidentally, it is also related to the English noun 'sheen' (radiance, shine), which has on occasion been used as an adjective, at a time when it meant beautiful.

Because experiencing something as beautiful means experiencing it as worthy of our protection, even demanding it, many of us feel a keen sense of loss when a beautiful thing is destroyed, and we are appalled and even morally outraged when this happens. The wanton destruction of beauty is intuitively understood to be an evil. There is thus indeed a perceived connection between the beautiful and the good. At the same time, however, we find it rather difficult to make rational sense of this connection. We tend to think of beauty as a surface phenomenon, as mere appearance. We think of it as something that does not necessarily reflect the reality of things – the true, largely invisible substance of the world. The beautiful can be a distraction; it can serve to conceal the bad, the ugliness beneath. We know that simply because something or someone *looks* good, it doesn't mean they *are* good. We are warned not to judge a book by its cover, not only because the book might actually be a lot better than its tattered and unsightly cover suggests, but also because it might be a lot worse than we are led to believe by its attractive outward appearance. A person can possess an exquisite face and yet have a cruel or treacherous heart, and the magnificent landscape we adore may, on closer inspection, reveal a nature that is red in tooth and claw. It would seem, then, that not everything that is beautiful is also good.[9]

And yet, if that is so, why is beauty so important to us? Because it clearly *is* important. In fact, it seems to me – and I'm sure many would agree – that a world entirely devoid of beauty would not, no matter what it was like in other respects, be a world worth living in. This is what you suggest too. But why is that so? Are we so superficial that we cannot see below the surface, so deluded that we attach more value to the mere appearance of things than to what they truly are? In what sense can beauty, as music was for Augustine, be said to be a 'life-saving plank in the midst of the ocean', when we all know that in any real ocean only real planks, made from something more solid than mere sounds, would be able to save us? Famously, the band on the Titanic kept playing when the ship began to sink, and there is no doubt beauty in that, but all their playing obviously did not prevent the ship from sinking, nor did it save anyone from drowning. So what, we may wonder, is beauty actually *good* for?

Then again, when we ask that question, we already take it for granted that there is a fundamental difference between the good and the beautiful. It strikes me, though, that you are quite right to suggest that any form of goodness that is lacking in beauty is also lacking in goodness, and vice versa – that any form of beauty that exists *solely* on the surface is deficient not in something else but in *beauty*. 'Beauty' without goodness is not beauty, and 'goodness' without beauty is not goodness.[10] Both are like broken promises, and neither can satisfy us because they fail to be what they claim or strive to be and what we need them to be. (This is what Schiller got right and Kant got wrong.[11]) I said earlier that the beautiful can serve to conceal the 'ugliness beneath'. This is not just a metaphor. There are beautiful and ugly thoughts, feelings and actions just as much as there are beautiful and ugly sounds, images and bodies. The kind act is beautiful, and it is beautiful in its kindness. In calling a deed beautiful we recognise that it goes beyond what we are supposedly morally required to do, perhaps also that it has a different source than a mere sense of duty. That does not make it any less good. If anything, it makes it *more* good, more *comprehensively* good.

But again, what is beauty, what does it *have* to be, if without it life would no longer be worth living and the good would be less good or perhaps not even good at all? The Ancient Greeks, especially the Pythagoreans, saw the world's beauty as a clear indication that it was a *kosmos*: not a random, chaotic conglomeration of things, but an ordered whole, governed by reason, united by harmony and symmetry.[12] Plotinus later claimed that the good radiates beauty, which envelops it like a veil, or an aura of light, indicating that beauty is not surface, that something good and precious shines (or sheens) through it, making itself visible in many different forms and ways.[13]

*

Elaine Scarry: The astonishing plentitude of beautiful things – the ever-increasing plentitude across any individual's lifetime – is indeed a feature not often enough acknowledged. In this it perhaps resembles colour vision. John Dewey says, accurately I believe, that it takes a child several years of actively dealing with the world to be able reliably to discern 'such gross discriminations as black, white, red, green';[14] yet current neuroscientists tell us that the average adult can distinguish 26,000 colours (and millions if grey tones are included).[15] Over a long lifetime, assuming one is not in pain or surrounded by a damaged environment, more and more moments of the day are interrupted by small explosions of the beautiful.

Like colour, beauty is something we learn to see. Perhaps in childhood it takes work to recognise the first seven instances, but after many years the number may be closer to 26,000, and just as in the realm of colour a painter may, by endless practice, go way beyond the ordinary to become a virtuoso colourist, so those whose everyday practice requires their attention to beauty – say, gardeners, cloud watchers and those who draw – may acquire a virtuoso ability. What's important here are not the numbers (one can add to or subtract zeros from the number given above) but the recognition that beauty – far from demanding that we continually whittle down candidates until we can get to just one – hones our minds to enable us to see ever more instances.

The fact that many beautiful things are 'universally' – or at least 'widely' – shared misleads us into thinking that universality, whether in fact or theory, is a necessary feature. The realm of beautiful objects includes not only those that are widely and enduringly shared across centuries and geographies – such as sky – but things that are specific to small groups of people and to single observers. This plurality or variability in the objects of beauty is another of its benign features: it would be unfortunate if everyone chose the same mate; it would even be unfortunate if everyone chose exactly the same house design. Beauty plays a part in deciding the partner with whom and the room in which one lives. Both shared and unshared objects of beauty, both those that endure across millenia and those that are short lived (the position of a fallen leaf on the sidewalk), work together to affirm the life pact and to push us in the direction of a greater regard for just relations. They together carry out the foundational work of beauty.

Now, when I say beauty is a life pact I understand myself to be speaking literally, as is signalled (but not exhausted) by the three explanations I gave: that beauty provokes a greater acuity of perception, that it provokes in us the care to extend the life of the beautiful thing, and that it affirms our own wish to be alive (as you acknowledge when you say that without it life might not seem worth living). What helps to obscure this key feature is the fact that beauty is often misdescribed – or at least unhelpfully described – as having 'ugliness' as its opposite. Because the word 'ugly' does not for me have an easily graspable meaning in everyday life, it is not one I ordinarily use. A more accurate word for the state that is opposite to beauty seems to be 'injury'.

This opposition was visible a few moments ago when looking at the large frame of human possibility: the alternative for a future humanity between catastrophe (whether brought about by nuclear peril, climate change or runaway artificial intelligence) or instead a transformed realm of greater aliveness and more just relations is surely a stark choice between injury on the one hand and beauty on the other. This same opposition is equally discernible in everyday practice, whether we are contemplating a river, or a person, or a maths theorem, or a painting. It can seem harsh to conclude that any one of these locations is, if badly injured, somehow outside the realm of beauty, as in the case of a polluted river or a soldier whose face has been terribly defaced by an explosion or a painting that is torn. Along the way, the opposition often confronts us with painful consequences that we have to wrestle with and in any given instance may have to overcome. But overall, it is not too much to say the opposition is life-saving.

Part of the work of beauty is to make us unequivocally opposed to injury – to make us not just rationally but irrationally and intuitively opposed. If that were not the case – if we started to persuade ourselves that an injured face or injured tree limb or shattered stained glass window or error-ridden mathematical proof were as beautiful as a noninjured face, tree, window or proof – what would stop us from inflicting injuries on people, windows and trees, and lying about the solution to a maths problem? Community rules? But how did we arrive at those? Our first, visceral instinct when we see someone being injured is to stop it; our first, visceral instinct if we see an injury is to repair it. If a friend ceases to be able to walk, our first obligation is to see if his legs can be repaired, not to persuade him and oneself that his condition is acceptable and lovely. If repair to his body is not possible, we will repair the city by introducing ramps and lifts so that not being able to walk ceases to be an injury.

Beauty is not some ornamental or optional habit of mind: it keeps intact our deep aversion to injury (an aversion to inflicting it; a sense that where it exists, it must be eliminated) and again returns us to and affirms Augustine's beauty as a 'life-saving plank in the midst of the ocean'. You say that in the midst of a roiling ocean only a literal plank – or let's say a sturdy raft or small skiff or a compassionate dolphin – would be life-saving. But surely you don't doubt that the skiff or the dolphin or the sleek and simple plank would appear beautiful to anyone at that moment. I remember a distressful moment when a surgeon was preparing to close a wound on my face; as he hovered over me, studying it, he murmured to himself, 'I see just how to do this'. As I heard him speak I was, though not fully conscious, aware of perceiving his words as one of the most beautiful sentences I had ever heard.

This basic distinction might make someone say: oh, if injury is the opposite of beauty, then is someone one does not perceive as beautiful 'injured'? No. This would be like saying there is a north pole and a south pole, so if something is not at the north pole it must be at the south pole, when in reality it is simply in New York (or any one of thousands of other locations). There can be opposite poles without a gradual ascent and descent between them.

Without even necessarily being aware of it, the existence of beauty keeps intact our aversion to injury. You point out that a beautiful person or landscape might have hidden perils, but there is no claim here that any instance of the beautiful at that moment in time and space is directly linked to an ethical aversion to harm on a one-to-one scale; the workings are diffuse and take place over time and fortunately are assisted by the fact that the world is so full of beauty. It is as much the species as the individual person that is being given an increased chance of surviving (think of the way the beauty of a mate often inspires in the perceiver the desire to have children and so literally keep the species going).

*

Michael Hauskeller: If the opposite of beauty is injury, could we not also start at the other end and say that the opposite of ugliness is (something like) intactness or integrity? I don't quite understand why you think we should avoid talking about ugliness altogether. Isn't it precisely the *ugliness* of the environmental devastation and other forms of destruction you describe – of the polluted river, the torn painting, the injured face – that makes us realise, viscerally, without the need to think about it first, that something has gone badly wrong here? That we need to do something about it, or, better still, make sure things like this don't happen in the first place? If beauty does indeed provoke and keep alive, as you say, a 'deep aversion to injury', doesn't ugliness do this too?

The experience of beauty stimulates the desire to keep the beautiful thing alive and intact, while the experience of ugliness repels us and makes us wish for something different. And just like beauty, ugliness is a positive, absolute quality that we immediately experience as such. Being beautiful or ugly is not just a matter of degree. There may be many things that are neither beautiful nor ugly, but ugliness is not just a lesser degree of beauty, just as evil is not just a lesser degree of goodness. They are not on the same scale. This is what Bostrom gets wrong. Plato, incidentally, makes the same mistake in his *Greater Hippias* when he has his Socrates insist that there must be one single property, beauty, that all beautiful things have in common, but which they possess in different degrees: the most beautiful pot is, he says, ugly in comparison with a beautiful girl, and the beautiful girl is ugly in comparison with a goddess.[16] What he fails to realise (in contrast to Socrates' seemingly naïve opponent Hippias, who seems incapable of making the mental leap from the concrete to the abstract, the particular to the universal, that Socrates demands) is that those things are very different in nature, which is why their beauty – that which makes them beautiful – is also very different in each case, and accordingly also what makes them ugly. There is not one scale for all.

This does not necessarily mean that we do not all have the same standards of beauty (although different ones for different kinds of things) or that beauty is, as they say, in the 'eye of the beholder', which is what you seem to be suggesting when you say that beauty is not universal in the sense that there are things that are beautiful only for a few or perhaps even for one person only. To use your examples, why is this person, or this house, beautiful to me, but not beautiful to you – why does is make me feel more alive, but not you – if their beauty is a quality that they truly possess rather than one that either of us may or may not attribute to an object, depending solely on our individual circumstances and predispositions? Of course, one of us may be wrong, and blind to the beauty that is actually there, while the other is open to it, so that beauty would be something that is *revealed* to the attentive observer rather than merely projected onto things.

I am not sure this is what you mean, though. You say that the plank in the ocean is likely to appear beautiful to anyone whose life depends on it, which would suggest that beauty is, at least in this instance, situational, perhaps even utilitarian. The plank appears beautiful to the drowning man not because of what it is, but because of what it can do for him. It is beautiful not because it is 'sleek and simple', but because it can save his life. (I suppose a plank that is *not* sleek and simple will be just as beautiful to him as long as it is up to the job of saving him.) So presumably if I were not in that kind of situation, if my life did not depend on it, then I might very well not find it beautiful at all. And the same goes for the skiff or the dolphin.

Yet if the beauty of an object does indeed depend on who encounters it and in what circumstances they do so, then is it not possible, for some, to find beauty precisely in injury? I am thinking of people like Lord John Talbot who in Shakespeare's *Henry VI* swears to revenge himself on the French, vowing to, as Nero is supposed to have done, 'play on the lute, beholding the towns burn',[17] or the Italian poet Filippo Marinetti who in his *Futurist Manifesto*, written in 1909, celebrates the beauty of aggression, violence and destruction, glorifying war and 'the beautiful ideas which kill' and wishing for a 'strong healthy injustice' and more cruelty and hatred, and all of this apparently for the sake of achieving greater aliveness. It would seem, then, that some people's life pact is quite compatible with the injuring of others.

*

Elaine Scarry: The extreme of pluralism you assign to me – a kind of free-for-all without constraint – is far from my view. In saying that beauty is the opposite of injury – that it prohibits us from inflicting it and presses us to repair it – I place a constraint on what constitutes the beautiful. I can object to the Italian Futurist's will to injure (as can even the radical aesthetic pluralist) and I can equally object to his mis-recognition of beauty. During recent decades, when humanists – in literature, art history, architecture, painting – were cultivating the practice of indifference to beauty, they sometimes attributed their repudiation to the fact that Hitler was beauty-loving. This startling phenomenon may be the last vestige of Hitler's ability to get others to carry out his will: he describes himself as a beauty lover and 70 years later some sprinkling of people in the United States and on the European continent continue to accept his self-description. Imagine if a man were to break the legs of a thousand dancers while holding up a postcard of a Degas dancer and shouting out his commitment to ballet. Should we hold our heads and ponder the puzzle of how a ballet lover could inflict such cruelty, or should we instead recognise the simple emptiness of his claim to love ballet?

If beauty works to diminish injury, should we, you ask, say it is utilitarian? If by utilitarian you mean that a given phenomenon has a consequence, that the consequence entails increased happiness, and that the increased happiness can potentially be distributed across the earth, then yes, beauty is utilitarian. The term would then also apply to most historical accounts of beauty. If the beautiful causes wings to sprout from our shoulder blades and incites us to remember the immortality of the soul, as Socrates claims in *Phaedrus*,[18] that would be utilitarian; if the beautiful brings 'pleasure in the realm of hearing and seeing that is beneficial', as Socrates eventually concludes in *Greater Hippias*,[19] that would be utilitarian; if the integrity, proportion and *claritas* of the face of Jesus give Christian believers a greater access to God and the Holy Spirit, as Aquinas counsels in *Summa Theologica*,[20] that would be, for that community of believers, utilitarian; if beauty brings about an 'unselfing' as I – following Simone Weil and Iris Murdoch[21] – hold, that would be utilitarian.

The work of beauty to diminish injury, to diminish the near synonym injustice, is a cause–effect dyad that drifts across populations and
centuries rather than something like a light-switch that one can without
fail point to in any solitary perceiver. At the same time, there are countless moments when the straightforward light-switch is apprehensible,
as one may feel on one's own pulse. An experiment that took place in
Sweden in 1984 showed that hospital patients whose rooms looked out
onto a grove of trees recovered from their operations more quickly and
required less pain medication than those whose windows faced a brick
wall;[22] in 2012, one journal reported that 1,200 subsequent medical
studies had confirmed this outcome.[23] This consequence has in turn had
another major consequence: a greatly intensified focus on architectural
beauty in the design of new hospitals. Both architectural and medical
magazines now often feature articles with titles such as 'Ten most beautiful hospitals in the country'.

The healing in all these studies was physical, but a kindred possibility of repair may take place in the realm of the psyche. Architectural
designs for some new European prisons now stress ample window light
and gardens. Recently, a researcher at Berkeley observed what happened
when he dropped a box of pens on the sidewalk after asking one group of
students to look up into the high canopy of eucalyptus trees and another
group of students to look at the wall of a building; those in the first group
more often sprang to his assistance in collecting the spilled pens.[24]

You question my resistance to the word 'ugly'. You used the word
a moment ago – providing contexts in which it was almost a synonym
for injury – and to this I have no objection. But often the word is used in
everyday conversation in a way that is misleading – literally: it leads the
speaker down a path where he may falsify himself and the object he a
moment ago was looking at. When he describes someone or something
as 'ugly', he distances himself from what he is describing by pronouncing
himself superior to it; whereas when he describes someone or something
as 'injured', he distances himself from the wound but not from the site of
the wound, whether it is a person or a tree. Whenever Socrates in *Greater
Hippias* pronounces a maiden or a horse or a pot 'ugly', my classicist colleague Greg Nagy gives the alternative translation 'repulsive'. That visceral word is implicit in the word 'ugly'.[25] What is beautiful attracts – we
wish to prolong our stay with it; what is ugly repels – it makes us want
to get away as quickly as possible. Both 'injury' and 'ugliness' elicit in us
the feeling of aversion, but only in the second case do we run away (and
adopt the posture of disdain while running). If instead of a maiden or a
horse or a pot we are speaking about a moral action – an act of cruelty,

for example – then I am more likely to agree to use the word 'ugly' in describing it; now flight and self-preservation seem appropriate (though even here, I may be succumbing to the self-congratulatory pleasure of judgemental disdain).

In resisting the word 'ugly', I do not suppose that it will fall out of use, since it is a time-honoured word for designating whatever is far from the realm of beauty. When in our conversation I first rejected the word, I only wished to note that it seldom has meaning for me. When Socrates says the beautiful pot once placed in the company of a beautiful maiden will now appear ugly, what does this mean? I remember a large, two-handled Attic wine cup in the Berlin State Museum; on it, a satyr pushes a maiden on a swing, and there is an inscription: 'Oh, Beautiful'.[26] Now I bring to mind a particular living woman who, whenever I see her, without fail strikes me as extraordinary in her beauty. I now place the wine cup in her presence; even if my attention is more caught up in the countenance of the living woman, I don't know what it means to say that the cup now appears ugly, just as when I imagine the woman standing by the side of Thetis, the flashing light of the goddess may rivet my attention, but the woman's appearance hasn't altered in a way that the word 'ugly' assists me in grasping.

Perhaps *Greater Hippias* provides too easy an example of the vacancy of the word (and we do not know for certain that Plato is the author). However, there are many other works where sentences containing the word 'ugly' make little concrete sense until, as one presses on, one comes to see that injury or diminished aliveness is entailed, as when Plato allies the word with other adjectives – 'ugly, sick, and weak' – or when Plotinus speaks of ugliness as 'torn', 'encrusted', 'perishable'.[27] If Plato in *Greater Hippias* had said the pot that seemed so alive now next to the maiden looks unalive, as the maiden next to the flashing goddess looks unalive, we could begin to follow what might be at stake. As Diotima counsels, that which is beautiful quickens; that which is at a far remove from beauty does not.[28]

*

Michael Hauskeller: Yes, no doubt the experience of beauty can have that effect on people. It can indeed be health- and sanity-restoring. In his book *At the Will of the Body*, Arthur Frank, reflecting on his battle with cancer and with the pain that came with it, remembers how, in a moment of utter despair, beauty came to the rescue: 'Making my way upstairs,' he writes, 'I was stopped on the landing by the sight – the vision really – of a window. Outside the window I saw a tree, and the streetlight just beyond was casting the tree's reflection on the frosted glass. Here suddenly was beauty, found in the middle of a night that seemed to be only darkness and pain. Where we see the face of beauty, we are in our proper place, and all becomes coherent.'[29] While the pain he was in threatened to undermine the coherence of his life, that sudden, unexpected encounter with beauty restored, at least for a while, that coherence, and not, as he writes, 'because I dissociated myself from my body, but rather because I associated myself beyond my body'.[30] His pain was still there, but it mattered less because his encounter with beauty made him care again for things and people other than himself. Beauty, then, became indeed, as Iris Murdoch would have said,[31] an occasion for unselfing that, paradoxically, gives the one who experiences it a reason to want to go on living.

I want to believe that this is what beauty is and does. And yet, it seems that some people (perhaps a lot more than we would like) are 'quickened' and made to feel more alive by violence and destruction. Why else would they seek it out? Why would so many of us delight in watching it or reading about it, and fewer but still too many delight in causing it? This is why earlier on I cited Marinetti's glorification of war and mechanisation, which you attribute to a mis-recognition of beauty, meaning that when he and others talk about the beauty of violence, destruction and dehumanisation, we should not take them at their word because these things are *in fact* not beautiful at all. But why can they not be? Should we deny that they can make anyone feel more alive? That is precisely what they seem to do. You are right, of course, that the actions of someone who claims to love something but destroys it anyway (as in your example of the man who claims to 'love' ballet and yet breaks the legs of ballet dancers) is putting the lie to his words. What he does seems to blatantly contradict what he says. But Marinetti does not claim to love the things he wants to see violated and destroyed. Rather, he claims to love violence and destruction itself. And *that* is also what he thinks and feels is beautiful. So if there is a contradiction here, it is not the contradiction of the hypocrite. What is it, then?

You suggest that calling a mass murderer like Hitler a lover of beauty is somehow conceptually incoherent – that someone who was able to instigate and condone so much horror and human misery cannot *possibly* have loved beauty, and perhaps you are right. But what does that mean exactly? We can easily imagine Hitler or someone like him greatly enjoying and admiring the sight of the Alps or the music of, say, Wagner or Beethoven, or other things that many people would agree really *are* beautiful.[32] Surely, this is not out of the question. And again, if there is a contradiction here, it is not the contradiction of someone who claims to love what they destroy. Perhaps Hitler only destroyed the things and people he didn't love and didn't find beautiful. It seems to me that if we want to insist that despite appearing to love some beautiful things he did not *really* love beauty, we need to assume, contrary to what I suggested in my previous response, that all beauty is connected and shares a common essence, so that our sense of it cannot be limited to particular incarnations of it. Accordingly, if someone has what it takes to appreciate beauty, they will appreciate it *wherever and in whatever form* it appears, and if they don't, we can be sure that whatever they experience is not the experience of beauty.

If for instance you see beauty in an art form such as ballet and love it because it is beautiful, it would not only make no sense for you to disable the dancers, because you cannot have the one without the other; doing so would also demonstrate your failure to understand that the beauty of the dance *is*, at least in part, the beauty of the dancers, so you cannot value the one without also valuing the other. And if you value it, you cannot possibly want to destroy or damage it. Similarly, if the experience of beauty makes us discover and affirm the value of life and aliveness, then we should expect that our appreciation extends to *all* life and would not be consistent with its selective destruction.

Perhaps this is why when Marinetti praises the beauty of destruction, we suspect a linguistic perversion: the destruction that he praises and professes to love is ultimately the destruction of beauty or of beautiful things. What he voices in his *Futurist Manifesto*, then, is not his love of beauty at all, but on the contrary his hatred of it, which of course would suggest that we can experience beauty without necessarily loving it. We are odd creatures, quite capable of hating and wishing to destroy what we know we ought to love, cherish and protect. 'Oft, in a garden seeking rest/', writes Baudelaire in his *Les Fleurs du Mal*:

> I dragged my sluggish atony,
> And felt the bitter irony
> Of Sunlight tearing at my breast;
>
> And springtime's green magnificence
> Cast such despair upon my heart
> That on a flower I, did impart
> Revenge for Nature's insolence.[33]

*

Elaine Scarry: Baudelaire's poem 'To one who is too gay' illuminates the pathology you seek to diagnose. The speaker in the poem candidly tells us he is a 'coward'. He 'creeps' through the world, 'dragging' his slack body. He kills the beautiful flower not only because it is itself so alive – 'verdant' and full of 'springtime' – but because it threatens to awaken him. So, too, he wishes to whip, rape and 'infuse with venom' the woman whose limbs glow and whose dress flows with colour because the sight of her alive-ness threatens to 'dazzle' him into new life. Given the essential grounding of beauty in the life pact, it is not clear to me how we can increase our comprehension of its nature by focusing – as you ask us to do – on those who choose to bring about death or who keep themselves in a near-death state by eliminating from the face of the earth the very things that call out on behalf of life, such as lovely flowers and persons, and all the things Marinetti enumerates in the Tenth Article of his *Futurist Manifesto*: 'We want to demolish museums and libraries, fight morality and feminism.'

Can we comprehend X (beauty) by tracking those who flaunt their indifference to X or who parade their commitment to not-X? We can surely learn something from them. But what? Perhaps the extremes to which human beings will go to prove that they are free of both cultural and natural constraints: to violate a rule or a custom, there may be only modest freedom in that; to flaunt one's disregard for the call of beauty and aliveness – surely to accomplish that, they may reason, would be the triumph of the will!

I do not contest the importance of thinking about Hitler and Marinetti, only the importance of thinking about them as a path toward understanding beauty. My book *The Body in Pain* dedicates many pages to trying to understand how one person can stand in the presence of another person in pain and not know it, not know it so completely that the person himself inflicts the pain and then luxuriates in that infliction. The incontestable reality of the injured human body can be lifted away from the hurt person and – in part because it shuts down an onlooker's capacity to think – can be attached to a regime or idea or claim at that moment so feeble it lacks any form of legitimate substantiation. One may hold up a placard that says 'here is beauty' and the vivid spectacle of gore may seem to confirm the very thing it clearly contradicts, just as to the eyes of the torturer the terribly hurt body of the prisoner certifies how important the regime and its questions are, even when it is precisely because the regime has so little support that it has resorted to torture. So, too, the postcard of Degas waved over the fallen dancers may seem to confirm what a clear-thinking person can see it contradicts, just as a kite inscribed with the words 'we love Beethoven' and flown over a concentration camp may lead the aghast onlooker to mistake the undeniable reality of the injury for the undeniable truth of the paper-thin proclamation. Even fairytales counsel us that the overpowering reality of a naked body (not now a wounded body but merely one unclothed) can be used to confer the spectre of validation on a false claim: thus the crowd applauds the emperor's finely spun clothes at the very moment he appears before them wearing nothing.[34] This phenomenon of analogical verification deserves a conversation but not our conversation about beauty.

Beauty has an essential structure. It recruits the perceiver into a life pact, and stands with the perceiver in opposition to injury. It is this structure that is universal across geographies and centuries, not the objects of beauty. These in contrast are variable, plastic, often changing even in the field of vision of a single individual. The plurality of beautiful things is one I believe we agreed to (though a moment ago you seemed briefly to countenance the idea that universal agreement may be required). The fact that some beautiful things *are* universally shared – as I argued earlier – misleads us into thinking that such universality is a requirement.

The more something is tied up with the literal fact of survival the more likely it is to be a universally esteemed object of beauty. Is there anyone in any century who has failed to be astonished by the beauty of water, whether in a brook or a waterfall, a mist lying in a mountain valley or lifted into high white clouds, a snowflake on one's sleeve, beads of rain on the leaves of Lady's Mantle? Is there anyone who has not remarked on the beauty of air as it becomes visible in the lift of someone's hair or scarf, or moves through meadow grass or tree canopy, or becomes audible in a flute or a baby's breathing or the downward double-noted spiral of a veery's song? Every person on earth at some point stands spellbound to watch the sun rise or set on the horizon. People salute its beauty even in their final moments of life, as my mother did, suddenly pointing to sun-cast shadows of leaves on her bedroom wall and faintly exclaiming 'Look! Look!' – just as centuries ago a dying Oedipus said, 'O sunlight . . . This is the last my flesh will feel of you'[35] and the young girl Polyxena described the path to her execution as her small remaining corridor of sunlight.[36]

Does something have to be allied with survival to be universally saluted for its beauty? Can a human-made object elicit or deserve universal acknowledgment? Shakespeare is far from universally revered but at least his work provides the idea of plausible universality. Perhaps the widespread adulation he elicits means we can elevate to the status of a life principle something that strictly speaking is not needed to survive, or perhaps it means that it *is* needed to survive: that we need to find among the plural objects those we can work to agree to, and that, in the end, our survival will depend on heightening our ability to agree. Perhaps Shakespeare and other widely revered artworks give us practice at entering into collective agreements – not in the end a signed covenant to love *A Midsummer Night's Dream* but to dismantle the world's nuclear architecture and the practices that are causing the earth to warm. Without such universal accords, we almost certainly will not survive.

As for the plural objects of beauty – let us call them the Myriad Variables after the Cepheid Variables that enabled astronomers to measure the distance from earth to stars – two questions remain unanswered. First, the one you have twice raised: what if a person's or landscape's outer beauty is unmatched by its inner beauty? Does that mean that the outer beauty is itself false, deceptive, cruel? I think the answer is certainly no. A young man's physical beauty may alert a person to her demand for inner beauty – that is a gift even if the young man himself cannot satisfy that demand. She may not even have realised she was looking for a just person until she saw his physical beauty, and then felt disappointed not to discover moral beauty at the same location. Perhaps she will eventually find someone with both outer and inner beauty, or perhaps she will find someone with inner beauty and an unremarkable exterior that might have led her to overlook the person, had the physically beautiful scoundrel not awakened her to her hunger for inner beauty. So, too, with the earth. If a field of wildflowers or a city avenue of sycamore trees hides landmines, its countenance is not at fault for the landmines and, along with all the other beautiful places on earth, it helps us to recognise the deep horror of such objects as well as all other genres of cruelty.

The second question about the plurality of beautiful objects concerns their strange conflation of self and selflessness. The sudden rush of pleasure one feels when confronted with someone or something beautiful – which is the way the daily re-signing of the life pact is felt on one's pulse – can be highly individualised. We saw this with the fact that we each choose a different mate or house, but even the leaf on the sidewalk need not, either in practice or theory, arrest the attention of every passerby because the intricate network of experiences of plants and trees, shapes and colours, things above one's head and beneath one's feet have made this particular person eligible to hear this one leaf ring the bell; their coming together may be as finely honed as a lock and key, or a space capsule docking at a space station. But now if a Myriad Variable can be so specific to a single person's psyche (or to the people of a single region), is it strange that it simultaneously brings about an unselfing? Does it unweave the very self it so carefully and intricately matched? Perhaps it (at least for a moment) disperses just the cluttered and irrelevant part of the self and addresses the part that is on course to stay alive, or perhaps it (again, at least for a moment) unweaves even this essential self, so the possibility of being open, renewed and differently woven is a possibility.

It may be that the universal objects of beauty should also be given a name, such as the M Constants, as a way of acknowledging that – though unvarying and unexceptional – they still, like the Myriad Variables, arrive in a way that seems marvellous or miraculous, accompanied by the never-before-in-the-history-of-the-world feeling we acknowledged at the outset.

Notes

1. Bostrom, 'Why I want to be posthuman when I grow up', 112.
2. Rilke's 'Archaic torso of Apollo' (*Selected Poems*, 92–3) ends, famously, with the line: 'You must change your life.'
3. This is how Wordsworth (*Poems*, 49–50) ends his poem 'I wandered lonely as a cloud': 'And then my heart with pleasure fills,/ And dances with the daffodils.'
4. William Shakespeare, Sonnet 18: 'Shall I compare thee to a summer's day?/ Thou art more lovely and more temperate.'
5. According to Kant (*Foundations*, 60), human beings have dignity, which he defined as an absolute, non-comparative value, in contrast to all other things (and other living beings), which only have a relative value, that is to say, a price: 'Whatever has a price can be replaced by seomthing else as its equivalent.'
6. *De Musica* xiv, 46. For an English translation see Augustine, *Selections from 'De Musica'*, 196. For the Latin see Augustinus, *De Musica*, 226. A more recent philosopher allying beauty and aliveness is Kant. Rudolf A. Makkreel shows Kant's under-recognised stress on the association in *Imagination and Interpretation in Kant*, 11–12n7, 87, 89, 92, 100, 101–4.
7. Genesis 9:13–15.
8. Russell, *Has Man a Future?*, 14.
9. For a discusson of the conjunction of beauty and evil in art see, for instance, Devereaux, 'Beauty and evil'.
10. For an interesting attempt to connect beauty and goodness, featuring a 'moral theory of beauty' and a corresponding 'aesthetic theory of virtue', see McGinn, *Ethics, Evil, and Fiction*.
11. See Tauber, 'Aesthetic education for morality'.
12. See Horky, *Cosmos in the Ancient World*.
13. Plotinus, *Enneads*, 1.6.
14. Dewey, *Human Nature and Conduct*, 31. On the child's early difficulty in grasping colours see also Dewey, *How We Think*, 275–6.
15. Linhares et al., 'The number of discernible colors in natural scenes'.
16. Plato, *Greater Hippias*, 289b.
17. William Shakespeare, *Henry VI*, Act 1, Scene 4.
18. Plato, *Phaedrus*, 251bcd, 58.
19. Plato, *Greater Hippias*, 295, 298a, 302e, 303e, 1548–58.
20. Aquinas, *Summa Theologica*, I.Q39.8, 201, 202.
21. See Weil, 'Love of the order of the world', 180, and Murdoch, *The Sovereignty of Good*, 2.
22. Ulrich, 'View through a window'.
23. Stall, 'Private rooms'.
24. See Study 5 in Piff et al., 'Awe, the small self, and prosocial behavior'.
25. Nagy, translation of selected passages from *Greater Hippias*.
26. Written on the rim of the drinking cup (F 2589 in the Collection of Antiquities at the Berlin State Museum) is '*eia o eia kale*'. The location of the inscription on the vessel's rim means that the words may touch the person's lips as he drinks, as though the cry is taken into his own mouth; or if his lips are on the edge opposite to the inscription, it will be seen by him as he drinks.

27. See Plotinus, *Enneads*, I.6.5, and Plato's *Laws*, Book I, 646b, containing a phrase which Malcolm Schofield translates as 'emaciation, ugliness, debility', Benjamin Jowett translates as 'leanness, ugliness, decrepitude', and G. B. Bury translates as 'leanness or ugliness or impotence'. It should be noted that in addition to being bound up with diminished aliveness, the ugly, for both philosophers, is of course elaborately bound up with the vocabulary of the immoral and the unjust.
28. Plato, *The Symposium*, 206b, 86–87.
29. Frank, *At the Will of the Body*, 33.
30. Frank, *At the Will of the Body*, 35.
31. E.g. Murdoch, *Existentialists and Mystics*, 353, 369.
32. Hitler clearly saw himself as a lover and promoter of beauty: 'Mankind', he proclaimed, 'has a natural drive to discover beauty. How rich the world will be for him who uses his senses. Futhermore, nature has instilled in everyone the desire to share with others everything beautiful that one encounters. The beautiful should reign over humans; the beautiful itself wants to retain its power.' Quoted in Spotts, *Hitler and the Power of Aesthetics*, 119.
33. Baudelaire, *The Flowers of Evil*, 77. The lines are from poem called 'À Celle qui est trop gaie' (To one who is too gay). In its original French, the lines I cited read: 'Quelquefois dans un beau jardin/ Où je traînais mon atonie,/ J'ai senti, comme une ironie,/ Le soleil déchirer mon sein,/ Et le printemps et la verdure/ Ont tant humilié mon coeur,/ Que j'ai puni sur une fleur/ L'insolence de la Nature.'
34. Here I adapt Hans Christian Andersen's *The Emperor's New Clothes* (1837) by providing an alternative to his own explanation of why all who see the king – the crowd, the king's retinue, the king himself – 'bear witness' to what they are told to see.
35. Sophocles, *Oedipus at Colonus*, 86.
36. Polyxena says, 'O light! I still can say that word; but all the light/ That now belongs to me is what remains between/ This moment and the sword beside Achilles' tomb.' Euripides, *Hecabe*, ll. 435–7, 76.

Bibliography

Aquinas, Thomas. *Summa Theologica*, volume 1, translated by Fathers of the English Dominican Province. New York: Benziger Brothers, Inc., 1947.
Augustine. *Selections from 'De Musica'*, translated by W. F. Jackson Knight. In *Philosophies of Art and Beauty: Selected readings in aesthetics from Plato to Heidegger*, edited by Albert Hofstadter and Richard Kuhns, 185–202. Chicago, IL: Chicago University Press, 1964.
Augustinus. *De Musica*, edited by Martin Jacobson. Berlin: Walter de Gruyter, 2017.
Baudelaire, Charles. *The Flowers of Evil*, translated by John E. Tidball. Bishopston Editions, 2018. *The Flowers of Evil, Les Fleur du Mal*, translated by William Aggeler. Stilwell, 2015.
Bostrom, Nick. 'Why I want to be posthuman when I grow up'. In *Moral Enhancement and Posthumanity*, edited by Bert Gordijn and Ruth Chadwick, 107–37. New York: Springer, 2008.
Devereaux, Mary. 'Beauty and evil: the case of Leni Riefenstahl's "Triumph of the Will"'. In *Aesthetics and Ethics: Essays at the intersection*, edited by Jerrold Levinson, 227–56. Cambridge: Cambridge University Press, 1998.
Dewey, John. *Human Nature and Conduct: An introduction to social psychology*. New York: Henry Holt, 1922.
Dewey, John. *How We Think*. In *The Middle Works of John Dewey 1899–1924*, volume 6, edited by Jo Ann Boydston, 177–356. Carbondale, IL: Southern Illinois Press, 1985.
Euripides, *Hecabe*. In *Medea and Other Plays*, translated by Philip Vellacott. Harmondsworth: Penguin, 1963.
Frank, Arthur. *At the Will of the Body: Reflections on illness*. New York: Mariner Books, 2002.
Horky, Phillip Sidney (ed.). *Cosmos in the Ancient World*. Cambridge: Cambridge University Press, 2019.
Kant, Immanuel. *Foundations of the Metaphysics of Morals with Critical Essays*, translated by Lewis White Beck and edited by Robert Paul Wolff. Indianapolis, IN: Bobbs-Merrill Co., 1969.
Linhares, João Manuel Maciel, Paul Daniel Pinto and Sergio Nascimento. 'The number of discernible colors in natural scenes', *Journal of the Optical Society of America* 25/12 (2008): 2918–24.

McGinn, Colin. *Ethics, Evil, and Fiction*. Oxford: Clarendon Press, 1997.

Makkreel, Rudolf A. *Imagination and Interpretation in Kant: The hermeneutical import of the Critique of Judgment*. Chicago, IL: University of Chicago Press, 1990.

Marinetti, Filippo Tommaso. *The Futurist Manifesto*. https://www.societyforasianart.org/sites/default/files/manifesto_futurista.pdf (accessed 1 December 2021).

Murdoch, Iris. *The Sovereignty of Good over Other Concepts: The Leslie Stephen Lecture*. Cambridge: Cambridge University Press, 1967.

Murdoch, Iris. *Existentialists and Mystics: Writings on philosophy and literature*. New York: Penguin, 1999.

Nagy, Greg. *Greater Hippias*, translation of selected passages (unpublished manuscript).

Piff, Paul, Pia Dietze, Matthew Feinberg, Daniel M. Stancato and Dacher Keltner. 'Awe, the small self, and prosocial behavior', *Journal of Personality and Social Psychology* 108/6 (2015): 883–99.

Plato. *Plato in Twelve Volumes*, volume 9, translated by W. R. M. Lamb. Cambridge, MA: Harvard University Press, 1925.

Plato. *The Symposium*, translated by Walter Hamilton. Harmondsworth: Penguin, 1951.

Plato. *Greater Hippias*, translated by Benjamin Jowett. In *Collected Dialogues of Plato including the Letters,* edited by Edith Hamilton and Huntington Cairns. Princeton, NJ: Princeton University Press (Bollingen Series LXXI), 1961.

Plato, *Phaedrus, and the Seventh and Eighth Letters*, translated by Walter Hamilton. Harmondsworth: Penguin, 1973.

Plotinus. *Enneads*, edited by Lloyd P. Gerson. Cambridge: Cambridge University Press, 2019.

Rilke, Rainer Maria. *Selected Poems*, translated by C. F. MacIntyre, Berkeley, CA: University of California Press, 1957.

Russell, Bertrand. *Has Man a Future?* New York: Simon and Schuster, 1962.

Scarry, Elaine. *The Body in Pain: The making and unmaking of the world*. New York: Oxford University Press, 1985.

Sophocles. *Oedipus at Colonus*, translated by Robert Fitzgerald. London: Faber & Faber, 1957.

Spotts, Frederic. *Hitler and the Power of Aesthetics*. New York: Overlook, 2003.

Stall, Nathan. 'Private rooms: evidence-based design in hospitals', *Canadian Medical Association Journal* 184/2 (7 February 2012): 162–3.

Tauber, Zvi. 'Aesthetic education for morality: Schiller and Kant', *The Journal of Aesthetic Education* 40/3 (2006): 22–47.

Ulrich, R. S. 'View through a window may influence recovery from surgery', *Science* 224/4647 (27 April 1984): 420–1.

Weil, Simone. 'Love of the order of the world' in *Waiting for God*, translated by Emma Craufurd. New York: Harper and Row, 1951.

Wordsworth, William. *Poems in Two Volumes*. London: Longman, Hurst, Rees, Orme and Browne, 1807.

14
Sacredness

with Drew Chastain

Drew Chastain: What does it mean for something to be sacred? Is this a purely religious concept, or is the concept accessible to secularists as well? What does something's being sacred normatively demand of us? Can anything be sacred, or do only some things qualify? I come into this conversation having some ideas about how to respond to these and related questions about the sacred, but I don't want to start off the conversation with too many assertions. Instead, let's start with examples.

I imagine that the first examples that come to the minds of most are religious. All religions have their sacred things: sacred progenitors, such as Buddha, Lao Tzu, Jesus, Muhammad or the Lakota's White Buffalo Calf Woman; sacred beliefs pertaining to the origin of things and the physical and moral order of things; sacred places, including places of worship, places in nature that seem to carry a special power or presence, and places where important things have happened; sacred times, like the time of the week set aside for worship, the time of the day set aside for prayer and the time of the year to conduct important transitions or to contemplate special themes; and also sacred objects, like the holy relics, holy water and holy cross of the Catholic religion, and the sacred pipes, sacred bundles and sacred feathers among the Lakota. To my mind, the English word 'holy' is especially suited to capture a more purely religious connotation of the word 'sacred'. The designation 'holy' puts something in a category both divine and moral, transcendently set apart from the unholy, profane and mundane. But is the category of the sacred limited to the religious category of the holy?

To think this through, consider another case of appeal to the sacred, originating in recent political strife in the United States – an example also involving the Lakota (obviously, I have a special interest in the Lakota people). The recent and ongoing controversy concerns the construction of the Dakota Access Pipeline (DAPL) through the Standing Rock Lakota reservation, which at one point passes under the Missouri River.[1] One problem the Lakota and their allies have with the pipeline is that it disrupts sacred sites and burial grounds, which can perhaps be understood as a kind of religious concern. But the bigger call to action is the Missouri River's high risk of exposure to oil spills. To express their deep dismay, protesters calling themselves 'water protectors' shout the slogans on their signboards and banners: 'Water Is Life', 'Water Is Sacred', 'Defend the Sacred'. Some go much further than carrying signs: the more activist core of the resistance have been motivated enough to risk their lives sabotaging pipeline construction. Standing in front of a bulldozer, one water protector declares, 'We do this for the next seven generations. We do this for unborn children that are coming to this world. We're protecting the water. Our water is life. We will not let it get desecrated.'[2]

Is this appeal to the sacredness of water a religious one? Is this just like what Catholics have in mind when they deem a basin of water in a cathedral holy? I don't think so (and here my assertions begin!). When a priest blesses water, this is supposed to bestow upon that particular volume of water a divine quality and a moral purpose. But the DAPL resistance is saying that all water is sacred because water is a source of life, not just because a particular religion decides that water is sacred. In the media, the association of the DAPL resistance to the protection of sacred Lakota sites has led the general public to believe that an argument about religious rights is being made, as when a bakery refuses to make a wedding cake for a gay couple based on a sensitivity to what the owners consider to be the 'sanctity of marriage'.[3] Granted, it may be difficult to pry apart these two kinds of cases – protecting water as sacred and protecting heterosexual marriage as sacred – but I think the first kind of case has a secular justification, while the second must rely on a religious one.

I believe that other examples help us to see that there is such a thing as a secular, or non-religious, appeal to the quality of the sacred. Going back to US politics, the words and actions of the 45th president inspired numerous calls for protection of what is sacred or hallowed, but what needs protecting in this case is the secular institutions of American democratic government, like the Department of Justice or the Capitol Building, not religious institutions. Similarly, House Speaker Nancy Pelosi said in a tweeted response to President Donald Trump that 'The memory of 9/11 is sacred ground, and any discussion of it must be done with reverence.'[4] But I think we can also look to our own everyday lives to find examples of the non-religiously sacred. Don't we view our homes and our closest relationships with family and friends as having a sacred quality, regardless of whether one subscribes to any particular religion? Doesn't art have a sacred quality, and certain places in nature, even if the art has no religious content and even if we approach our experience of nature with no religious framework?[5]

So is there really a non-religious sacred, or does all appeal to the sacred access an ineliminably religious sensibility? What more can we say about the quality of the sacred? What makes something sacred and what does its being sacred require of us? And, to make explicit one more question which we can address now or later in the discussion, is this sacred quality really in things 'objectively', or is the sacred found only in the eye (or the soul) of the beholder?

*

Michael Hauskeller: Somebody once told me that her morning coffee was sacred to her. It is not unusual for people to use the term 'sacred' in connection with things and activities that are decidedly profane. And we normally don't think twice about it. We understand what they mean, and what they mean is clearly not that what they are describing as sacred has a special connection to God or is in other ways religiously significant. Someone who tells us that their morning coffee is sacred to them does not thereby declare herself to be a faithful member of the religious sect of coffee worshippers. Are they, then, perhaps misunderstanding and misusing the term 'sacred', falsely applying it to something that it cannot meaningfully be applied to? I don't think so. We don't just grudgingly tolerate the profane usage of the word 'sacred' (namely as inappropriate but too widely used to be worth protesting against). Rather, we treat it (especially if we do *not* have any particular religious commitments) as perfectly acceptable.

And you are right that we have a different attitude towards the word 'holy': if someone told me their morning coffee was holy to them, I would be rather puzzled because what they are saying doesn't seem to make any sense, or rather it would only make sense if they indeed belonged to a sect of coffee worshippers. This – the fact that the word 'sacred' can be used in a non-religious sense, whereas the word 'holy' cannot – appears to have nothing to do with the etymology of these words. In German, for instance, the word *sakral* (which corresponds to the English 'sacred') can be meaningfully used *only* in a religious context, and the word *heilig* (corresponding to the English word 'holy') can be used both in a religious and a non-religious context. Accordingly, you cannot say 'Mein Morgenkaffee ist mir sakral' (My morning coffee is sacred to me), but you *can* say 'Mein Morgenkaffee ist mir heilig' (My morning coffee is holy to me).

Now, what do we mean when we say something like that? It seems to me that we are, perhaps more than anything else, expressing a strong commitment to an object or an activity. 'My morning coffee is sacred to me' means more than just 'I *like* drinking coffee in the morning' or 'I much *prefer* drinking coffee in the morning to drinking something else or nothing at all'. Rather, what we are saying is that we do not intend to let anything come between us and our morning coffee – that we intend to have it no matter what, to protect it against everyone and everything that threatens to prevent us from having it. The statement is meant to convey the unconditionality of our commitment. Of course we are rarely ever entirely serious when we make such a claim. Even someone who declares her morning coffee to be sacred to her may occasionally, when required, agree not to have it. And we know this of course already when she says it, which is part of the reason why we accept such statements in the first place. If we believed that the person who tells us their morning coffee is sacred to them really meant it, if we believed that they would literally do *anything* to make sure they can enjoy a coffee in the morning, we would consider them quite mad. Nonetheless, it is precisely this willingness to protect their habit under *any* circumstances that the word 'sacred' is meant to convey here.

Your example of the DAPL and the rhetoric employed by those who protest against it is different from the morning coffee example in one important respect: the claim made here is not about something being sacred *to someone* (me, or us, or someone else), but about something being sacred, period, which shifts the attention away from the subject of experience to the object as the source of one's commitment. What is sacred to me may or may not be sacred to you. When I assert that something is sacred to me, I affirm an unconditional commitment to it, but I do not expect, let alone demand, that you share my commitment. In contrast, when I assert that something is sacred, without qualification, then I affirm not only my own unconditional commitment to it, but I also affirm your, and indeed everyone's, *obligation* to be unconditionally committed to it, too. What is sacred *must* be sacred not only to me, but also to you.

The Missouri water protectors' assertion that 'water is sacred' functions as a call to arms.[6] The assertion is in fact a demand: that water be protected against misuse and pollution, that those who engage in misusing it abstain from doing so in future, and that those who allow it to happen rise against it and make sure it will happen no longer. But it is also suggested that the source of the unconditional commitment that is demanded from everyone is the water itself, something about it that puts both me and you and everybody else under the strong obligation to protect it no matter what. Claims that certain political institutions are sacred as well as Pelosi's claim that the memory of 9/11 is sacred contain similar demands for unconditional commitment and similar assertions that the source of the obligation is not the one who makes the claim (their personal preferences and interests) but the object or activity which is claimed to be sacred. A mere (subjective) demand thus transforms into an (objective) command.

It is not immediately obvious what makes all these things sacred in the eyes of the ones who claim such a status for them, except for the unconditional commitment that they command. Such commitment is necessitated by a great value that the sacred thing is thought or perceived to possess. This value is not relative, but absolute in Kant's sense, meaning that the value the thing in question has is of a kind that cannot be measured and calculated.[7] There is nothing that is of greater value because its value is not of the sort that a thing can have more or less of (as for instance monetary value). In that sense it is irreplaceable: there is nothing that can take its place without loss. What is sacred is inviolable: it *can* be violated, but it *ought* not under any circumstances. That is why human life is often said to be sacred: because we want to make it clear and remind ourselves and others that nothing, no gain in the world, can justify its wilful destruction.

*

Drew Chastain: I think that there might actually be something a bit tongue-in-cheek, or not wholly genuine, about saying that my morning coffee is sacred. It would depend upon what the person making this statement has in mind. So let me try to sort this out. I would like to make a distinction between stronger and weaker uses of the word 'sacred' (or its equivalents in other languages). It is not that the weakest uses of the word are misuses, but that something of the gravity of the concept of the sacred is left out. I don't think we are accessing the fullness of the concept of sacredness if we are using it to mean only that a sacred thing is something very important, even if the level of importance imputed to the sacred thing approximates an unconditional commitment. The developers of the DAPL may have a very deep commitment to mining and distributing oil, or to money, and it could be said because of this that the leaders of the oil industry hold oil or money sacred. But I think this would be a weaker, or less genuine, use of the concept. If so, why is that? What is missing?

Well, I think that there might be more than one element left out of an account of the sacred that focuses exclusively on how important, valuable, irreplaceable, etc. the sacred thing is. One missing element is what could be called the 'ego-checking function' of the sacred. Genuine sensitivity to the sacred involves not only taking something to be important, but also being able to relax one's own inflated sense of self-importance. This is why I think there's something superficial in saying that oil or money is sacred to someone in the oil industry. In the present day context of climate change and ecological spoliation, it's known that expansion of the oil industry makes things worse for life on earth, so pursuit of pipeline construction indicates a prioritisation of self-interest over the greater good.[8] In one sense, in something more like a figurative sense, the high prioritisation of oil and money is like taking something to be sacred, but in a deeper sense it indicates a lack of sensitivity to the sacred, because it shows an inability to check the ego.

For a similar reason, taking one's morning coffee to be sacred could also be a somewhat superficial case of holding sacred – again, depending on context. If it really is just addiction that drives the need for morning coffee, then this same overwhelming need for self-stimulation could lead one to neglect other things that should be held more important than getting a fix, like helping one's children get ready for school. I don't think that a coffee habit leads to such dire consequences all on its own, but imagine someone saying that my morning heroin or cocaine is sacred. Given the destructive nature of these addictive substances, treating them as sacred would seem to reveal a deeper general lack of sensitivity to the sacred, because their habitual use tends to make one more and more self-regarding (even if perversely so) and less and less other-regarding.

Since coffee does not tend to be destructively addictive like this, I think there is a way in which coffee can be more than superficially sacred, similar to the way in which psychoactive drugs like marijuana and psychedelic mushrooms attract attributions of sacrality.[9] Genuine sensitivity to the sacred also seems to involve an openness to experiences of meditation, contemplation, purification, harmony, unity, connection, wonder, etc., which could all be loosely categorised as spiritual experiences.[10] If my morning coffee is sacred, not just because I have a need for it or because I judge coffee to be highly valuable, but also because morning coffee is part of my way of being centred, balanced or focused, or of getting in touch with myself or regaining my connection with the world and others, then I think that is a deeper reason for calling it sacred, and I wouldn't be surprised if this is part of what your friend means in calling her morning coffee sacred.

As a point of clarification about spiritual experience, and going back to the religion question, I don't think openness to spiritual experience requires religiosity, if religiosity means commitment to the institutions or practices of a given religion, and/or commitment to a supernatural or transcendent reality.[11] I think that there can be spirituality without religion, and that sensitivity to the sacred is at the core of spirituality, to which religion adds further commitments. So, it makes sense that sensitivity to the sacred would be closely associated with religion, because religion's central function is spiritual, but then the reason why deeper sensitivity to the sacred does not require religion is because spirituality does not require religion. In fact, I am willing to take this a step further. I think it is possible that religion can lead us astray spiritually, by warping our understanding of what we should be viewing as sacred. Just as the oil industry can place too much importance on oil or money, a religion can place too much importance on its holy fetishes or on a transcendent vision of reality which eclipses appreciation of the immanent value of life on earth.

There is more that I want to get to in response to what you said, but for now let me note that we seem to be agreeing that attributions of the sacred fall along a subjective/objective spectrum. If by 'subjective' we mean that something is sacred personally, but without expectation that it would be sacred for everyone, I don't think that this would always be the less genuine or shallower attribution of the sacred. If the reasoning I gave earlier makes sense, then taking coffee to be sacred can have depth even if it is not expected that everyone would view it as sacred. But, on the flip-side, I do think that if one does not acknowledge the sacrality of things that show up on the objective end of the spectrum, this would indicate a shallow sensitivity to the sacred. The question is then, how do things show up on the objective end such that perhaps everyone should view these things as sacred?

Let me stop here with a suggestion for how water ends up on the objective end, though I don't know that this explanation accounts for everything that is objectively sacred. All life depends on clean water for its flourishing, water being both an origin and a sustainer of life. Being at the root of our existence, water merits our deepest respect for its life-supporting power. For much that is objectively sacred, I think this would be why something is objectively sacred, because our life or our physical, psychological or spiritual flourishing fundamentally, and perhaps irreplaceably, depends on it.

*

Michael Hauskeller: I am not sure about this. There are a lot of things that our life depends on. Water is certainly one of them, but there is also oxygen, food, a certain temperature, gravity, certain microorganisms in our body, and many other features of our environment and our own physical constitution that we cannot live without. This certainly makes all these things extremely valuable to us, and indeed *objectively* valuable in the sense that their value is not merely imagined or based on a personal preference. We really *will* die without them. And precisely because these things are objectively valuable in this sense, it would be very unwise for us to neglect them. But surely those who protest the DAPL with the battle cry that 'water is sacred' do not merely mean to say that we cannot live without water and should therefore, if we are smart, protect it. Their appeal is not an appeal to people's self-interest. Rather, what is being suggested is that water is somehow beyond our legitimate reach. It is not at our disposal. We can use it, not in any way we see fit, but only as it is meant to be used, namely to sustain life. That is how far our permission to use it extends. To go beyond that, it is suggested, is not only unwise, it is also an infraction, a breach of the order of the universe. We may of course disagree with this assessment or sentiment. We may think that water is just water, simply a resource, perhaps something we cannot do without, just like oxygen, but its value is strictly instrumental. It is good *for us*, and that's all there is to it. There is no *immanent* value here that needs to be appreciated – nothing that merits, as you say, our respect, except in a very pragmatic, utilitarian sort of way.

And yet there is something about water that can indeed command our respect in a way that oxygen (or for that matter, coffee), despite its crucial role for our survival, cannot, although 'respect' is perhaps not quite the right word because it indicates a rational assessment of merit, which I don't think we engage in when something strikes us as sacred. *Awe*, or even *reverence*, seems more fitting: an immediate, emotional reaction firmly embedded in an experience, raw and unfiltered by the intellect. There is beauty in the sacred, but not the cuddly kind. It is, rather, the German poet Rilke's menacing beauty, which 'is nothing but the beginning of terror which we are barely able to endure, and it amazes us so, because it serenely disdains to destroy us'.[12] Water has this kind of beauty (which Burke, Kant and others called 'the sublime'[13] and Rudolf Otto 'the numinous'[14]), not as a chemical substance (as H_2O), but as a presence in our lifeworld,[15] as we encounter it in many of its concrete instantiations, namely as rivers and lakes and oceans, which are equally life-giving as they are life-destroying or at least life-threatening.

The sacred is not, in the first instance, a concept, but an experience (although of course our knowledge of what water is and does informs that experience) and it is as much an experience of absolute (non-instrumental) value, commanding unconditional commitment, as it is an experience of a power that makes our own interests and concerns appear quite trivial, indeed greatly deflating our sense of self-importance. It is, however, an odd sort of power because it is compatible with weakness or vulnerability: the sacred demands that we leave it alone and that we not spoil it, which would be unnecessary and indeed pointless if it were powerful enough to look out for itself. The inviolable can but must not be violated. Its power is normative: it is authority. In any case, when we encounter the sacred we encounter something that is, or that we perceive to be (in some undefined and perhaps undefinable way), greater than us. So it has indeed, as you say, an ego-checking function, but not in the way that it reminds us that we are not alone in the world and that there are other people out there whose interests deserve to be taken seriously too. Rather, what it strongly suggests to us is that the world does not revolve around us – or at any rate not around *me* specifically – and that there are layers to this world that we can't even begin to fathom, let alone control. The imperative that constitutes the sacred is not necessarily a *moral* imperative and perhaps not a religious one either. Clearly, there is no transcendent vision of reality at work here, because the experience of the sacred is not really a vision of anything, but it still seems to involve an awareness (however vague and dim) of something more than meets the eye. Although, in its own way it does of course meet the eye, or at least it meets us *through* the eye, through our senses. We don't *think* the sacred, we *see* it.

*

Drew Chastain: It seems to me that when the life-supporting function of air is threatened in the way that water's life-supporting function is threatened by oil spills, we are just as inclined to consider air sacred. If we developed ways of disrupting gravity that threatened life, we would have good reason to consider gravity sacred, and I think the same goes for the endangerment of life-supporting micro-organisms in our body. Even if these things are not threatened, we have good reason to view them as sacred owing to the part they play in maintaining life and making life possible.

Also, for those who are open to the idea that everything is sacred (pansacramentalism),[16] I think that one reason why this makes sense is that everything is in some way a part of the interconnected and interdependent marvel of life. Now, I don't think that pansacramentalism entails that everything merits serious respect in the way that water does, because not everything is as vital to life as water. But, in an exploration of the nature of the sacred, I believe that something else an account of the sacred must explain is the possibility of pansacramentalism. Even if not everyone who appreciates the value of the sacred would agree with pansacramentalism (perhaps on the logic that if some things are sacred, others must be profane),[17] the idea seems plausible to me, or at the very least I think that pansacramentalism is an admirable aspiration with some kind of discoverable meaning that an account of the sacred should make room for.

You suggest that water can be viewed as sacred, unlike some other things, partly because of how we experience water, in particular because of a certain kind of experience of awe. Perhaps you are right that we can have such an experience in relation to water but not things like air, gravity, etc. (although that is not clear to me), but I am resistant to tracing sensitivity to the sacred exclusively to a kind of experience rather than to a kind of thought, as if our relation to the sacred is largely non-rational. Instead, I think there is a kind of experience and a kind of thought that go together in the normativity of sacrality, without the experience or the thought being more fundamental, so that talk of thought-based 'respect' for the sacred does make sense.

When it comes to our experience of the sacred, I also don't think that awe, as a kind of experience that makes me feel small and vulnerable, is the only kind of experience of the sacred we can have. Sensitivity to the sacred can also thrive within an experience of connection that makes me feel, well, connected and supported, rather than fragile and overwhelmed. Relating this to the normativity of the sacred, I think we can see that both kinds of experience can be ego-checking, in the sense that both kinds of experience can help us realise that life and reality are not all about me. Awe leads me to see that there are greater, more powerful things. Connectedness leads me to see that I do not exist independently and that the value of my life is inextricably linked to the value of other things and of life in general. These are the kinds of ego-checking thoughts that are present in experiences of the sacred.

In your response, you express the concern that tracing the normativity of the sacred to acknowledgement of our dependence might imply that our attitudes toward the sacred are more self-interested and instrumentalist than is appropriate for genuine sensitivity to the sacred. But I think what is really going on is that, in the kind of sensitivity to the sacred that gets cultivated in connection-based spiritual experience, the atomistic distinction between self and other collapses. Intrinsic value is found in oneself and in other things while the relational value of the interconnection and interdependence of things is also made manifest. Connection-based experience leads us to take stock of intrinsic values and relational values all at once, without conditioning the value of other things on the value of self. Going back to our main example, to say that water is sacred isn't just to say something about the value of water, nor is it just to say something about the value of those who depend on water; it is to say both, and it also says something about the reality and value of interconnectedness.

Before I hand the talking stick back to you, I should say one more thing about inviolability, which has come to be seen as a key characteristic of the sacred (Ronald Dworkin, for one, explicitly equates 'sacred' and 'inviolable').[18] At the risk of sounding endlessly contrarian, I don't think that 'inviolability' is an apt term to express the kind of protection merited by all things genuinely sacred. I see at least two problems with it. First, it is a negative expression rather than a positive one, meaning that it tells us what we should not do rather than what we should do, as if respect for the sacred is all about prohibition.[19] The sacred inspires a call to respectful attitude and action – gratitude, appreciation, preservation[20] – even when what is sacred is not threatened. A declaration of inviolability calls up a political context in which we are standing by our deepest commitments, and respect for the sacred does indeed inspire taking such a stand when there is a threat, but mere negative inviolability does not capture all of what normativity of the sacred involves.

Second, inviolability ends up having rather different meanings for different sacred things, such as persons, artworks, nature and religious items, to name a few general categories. Reference to inviolability can involve a prohibition against a number of different kinds of things, such as a prohibition against killing, modifying, acting against consent, degrading value, betraying a principle, and so on. Again, the problem is that the language of inviolability doesn't take our insight very far and may even be misleading. I am not sure it is even the right word for some of these prohibitions, and, what is more, I am not sure that genuine sensitivity to the sacred requires the kind of absolutism implied by the word 'inviolability'. If one takes human life to be sacred, and also takes embryonic homo sapiens life to be human, does a decision to abort indicate a failure of one's sensitivity to the sacred? Or might it be the case that genuine concern for the sacred can sometimes be trumped by other considerations? To my mind, having respect for the sacred isn't the same thing as being a moral absolutist, but talk of inviolability seems to imply that.

*

Michael Hauskeller: Okay, so let us try not to be moral absolutists and still make sense of people's claims that (in their view) certain things (you mentioned a few: persons, artworks, nature, religious items) are sacred. If by calling something sacred we do *not* mean that it should never be violated, what exactly *do* we mean? What is the thought that you insist we are having when we call something sacred?

You are right, I think, that inviolable or 'not to be violated' may well mean different things for different objects (and perhaps also different things for the same objects in different situations). What we think constitutes a violation of, say, the memory of 9/11 is not what we think constitutes a violation of water, which in turn is not what we think constitutes a violation of human life. Also, what *I* think constitutes a violation of the memory of 9/11 is not necessarily what *you* think constitutes such a violation. What constitutes a violation of a thing depends on its nature, on what kind of thing it is, and it may also depend on who perceives it. There is a lot of room for interpretation. However, the same can be said, and with equal justification, about the sacred: that the memory of 9/11 is sacred in a different way than water or life is sacred, in the sense that the sacredness of these things requires us to behave in different ways towards them, namely always in a way that is appropriate to and appreciative of them and appropriate to and appreciative of what it is about them that we think is valuable and worth protecting. In terms of what we are supposed to do with it or not do with it, calling something sacred does not provide us with any clear directions, and even less so if we think that something may well be understood as sacred without being understood as inviolable, in which case there would be no contradiction between calling something sacred and allowing it to be violated under certain (still to be determined) circumstances.

And yet it seems undeniable to me that people who use the language of the sacred normally do so in order to make an absolutist claim of inviolability, even though they may choose to apply that claim rather selectively. If someone tells you that for them 'human life is sacred', you can be pretty sure that they are 'pro-life' and against abortion and probably also against assisted suicide.[21] They are also likely to think that abortion is wrong under almost any circumstances – that even if a woman has been raped or if her child is going to suffer from a severe disability it is still wrong for her to abort[22] – and that assisted suicide is wrong under any circumstances, even for someone who is in severe pain and has nothing left to live for.[23] Yet even if they are willing to allow for exceptions (and there aren't too many self-declared pro-lifers who would do that), they will still insist that in all other cases abortion and assisted suicide are definitely wrong and should not be allowed. For them, the term 'sacred' spells prohibition and the rejection of compromise.

The strange thing is of course that, especially in the United States, many of those who claim to be 'pro-life' on the grounds that 'human life is sacred' are also in favour of the death penalty and against stricter gun laws (and seem to believe that a man to whom nothing whatsoever seems to be sacred was a great president). It is tempting to see this as inconsistent and hypocritical, and perhaps it is, but I suppose those who think that way would disagree. They might argue (if they cared enough to try to make sense of their position) that the death penalty is only for people who have through their own actions forfeited the right to life: their life is no longer sacred because *they* have desecrated it. Executing those offenders would then amount not to a violation but to a *restoration* of the sanctity of life.[24] Also (they might say), everyone has the right to defend their life and the lives of their loved ones against aggressors precisely *because* life is sacred, and without easy access to guns they cannot really do that. Protecting one's own life must have priority over everything else because it is itself a 'sacred responsibility':[25] the heightened risk for aggressors can of course be discounted (because they have desecrated life through their aggression) and the heightened risk for all others of being shot dead by some lunatic with a gun is no doubt regrettable but a price that has to be paid for the protection of the sanctity of life.

What should we make of such an argument? Can we say with confidence that whoever argues like this is wrong or insincere? How do we know what is sacred and what is not? You spoke earlier of the 'genuinely sacred', which 'merits protection', which suggests that there are also things that only *appear* to be sacred (to someone) without actually *being* sacred. But again, how do we know which is which? Is there a test we can apply, and if so what test would that be? And perhaps more importantly, what follows, practically speaking, from our belief or the assertion that a certain thing, say human life, is sacred? Can we both believe that human life is sacred, but draw very different practical conclusions from it? And if that is possible, what exactly is it that we believe when we believe something is sacred?

*

Drew Chastain: Let me take one more example from Lakota culture to set up various closing observations: the case of holding the buffalo sacred. John Fire Lame Deer says, 'The buffalo is very sacred to us. You can't understand . . . the feeling we have toward it, unless you understand how close we were to the buffalo. That animal was almost like a part of ourselves, part of our souls. The buffalo gave us everything we needed. Without it we were nothing. Our tipis were made of his skin. His hide was our bed, our blanket, our winter coat. It was our drum, throbbing through the night, alive, holy. Out of his skin we made our water bags. His flesh strengthened us, became flesh of our flesh. Not the smallest part of it was wasted.'[26]

On the question whether sacred means inviolable, the Lakota holding the buffalo sacred is an interesting case to consider. This is a case not only of using something sacred instrumentally, like we do water, but also of killing innocent sentient beings for that purpose. Now, I do believe the Lakota can still be understood as viewing the buffalo as inviolable, even with the killing and the using. For one, the Lakota can see all non-human animals as people and, working within this framework, they also tend to view the slaughtered buffalo as having offered itself willingly, so that buffaloes' deaths are not against their consent.[27] But then, if the aspect of the buffalo that the Lakota are not violating is their consent, there can be respect for consent on purely contractarian grounds, so there is still the question of what qualifies respect for the buffalo as respect for the sacred, rather than just 'respect for persons'.

Lame Deer emphasises existential dependence and spiritual connection, and the Lakota's normative response to this is best expressed as 'not wasting' (or 'preserving value') rather than 'not violating'. Yes, some idea of something being inviolable – in some way or other, and to some degree or other – may be present in all respect for the sacred, but I don't think this gives us the meaning of the sacred. To put it another way, we can arrive at conclusions of inviolability by way of sacred reasoning and also by way of non-sacred reasoning. My concern is that by treating all cases of perceived inviolability as respect for the sacred, we are failing to distinguish the special normative domain of spiritual reasoning around the sacred from independent moral reasoning processes. Talk of the sacred weakens, losing touch with genuine spiritual resources.

What about the idea that human life is sacred? As you laid out, this declaration has been used among conservatives to express some absolutist views against the destruction of homo sapiens life. Moral arguments and religious arguments can be marshalled in support of such a claim against violation, but, importantly, that still leaves open whether any genuine spiritual sensitivity is at work. A common argument made against destruction in this context – which I do take to be a spiritual, ego-checking kind of argument – is that, when it comes to humans, such matters of life and death are not up to us, but should instead be left up to natural processes or divine decision. But I have two frustrations with treating the idea that human life is sacred as a paradigm that guides public consciousness and academic theory. First, in the reasoning just given, the emphasis on non-destruction because it is not up to us is negatively guiding, whereas respect for the sacred is more deeply a matter of continual preservation of value, which is very much up to us. I think that a more spiritually robust declaration that human life is sacred would instead emphasise preservation of the value of humanity's existential interdependence and spiritual connection. Even if those emphasising the negative would also appreciate the positive, the notion of inviolability does not point us in the positive direction.

Second, treating human life as a paradigm and perhaps best case of a category of being that everyone should view as sacred presents a model that is heavily informed by moral reasoning of a Kantian or a contractarian sort, or else by the Western religious reasoning that we are made in the image of God.[28] But this can obscure how spiritual reasoning is distinct from such moral or religious reasoning and how spiritual reasoning applies much more broadly. I would agree that there is a very strong prima facie moral case against destroying human life and using human life without consent, but if these moral norms guiding our human comportment toward one another are taken to be the essential hallmarks of respect for the sacred, then we are at risk of becoming blind to what it means to respect non-human life and nature. We become prone to thinking that, if it is permissible to destroy and use what is non-human, that must mean that non-human categories of being are not sacred. We lose sight of our sacred commitment to preserve the value of what is non-human, ignoring the intrinsic value and our interdependence and interconnection with what is non-human. If absorption with our sacred commitment to our own species, or even to the transcendently divine, eclipses our sacred commitment to the immanently non-human, then I think we are insufficiently sensitive to the sacred.

*

Michael Hauskeller: The sacred buffalo case is indeed interesting because it suggests that holding something sacred is fully compatible with using it and even destroying it. I suppose that in this case the preservation of value that you argue is the response that the sacred demands from us consists in making sure that the buffalo, once killed, is put to good use and that nothing is wasted, and that only as many buffaloes are killed as is necessary to sustain the lives of those who depend on them for food, shelter, clothing, etc. (as well as those who will depend on them in future), thus making sure that there will always be more buffaloes, so that even though *this* buffalo might now be dead, *the* buffalo remains very much alive. The value that is then to be preserved here is not tied to the life of the individual animal, whose killing is clearly not seen as a violation of the sacred. Instead, it is seen as a *sacrifice*, which is the exact opposite of a violation of the sacred.

Sacrifice means 'making sacred', which suggests that it is through the act of killing that the animal *becomes* sacred, and it does so because it is precisely through its death that it contributes most to the preservation of value, which is not the value of any particular buffalo (or for that matter, any particular Lakota), but the value of the situation as a whole. That situation involves the Lakota, the buffalo, and a specific way of living (and dying) that binds them together, in such a way that the buffalo is no longer an ontologically distinct entity, but part of the Lakota's very 'soul' – an integral, essential part of who and what they are. Sensitivity to the sacred is then indeed a recognition and appreciation of the interconnectedness of things that is also 'ego-checking' insofar as it puts the lie to our usual presumption that there exists a strict ontological divide between us and the world we inhabit. Perhaps that is the key insight to be gained from an acute sensitivity to the sacred, or what you call a 'spiritual' outlook on the world.

So are there things that are 'genuinely' or 'objectively' sacred, or does the sacred exist merely in the eye of the beholder, as you put it at the beginning of our conversation? I share your concerns about using the presumed sanctity of human life as the guiding paradigm for our understanding of what sacredness actually is or means because, as you rightly point out, this may make it easier for us to perceive and treat non-human life and nature as *not* worthy of our respect. From experience we know that this worry is well-founded. I am, however, wary of the implications when you talk about our 'sacred commitment' to preserve the value of what is non-human and about our being 'insufficiently sensitive to the sacred', which seems to suggest that being sacred is a property that certain things have whether or not they are respected or recognised as sacred. On the face of it, this seems rather unlikely.

Take the example of the buffalo. It is easy to see how buffaloes can be sacred to the Lakota. They play a crucial role for a particular form of life, which, for the Lakota, presumably is *the* form of life, perhaps the only one that is available to them or perhaps the only one that they would consider worth having, but in any case the one that defines who they are. Without the buffalo there would be no Lakota. For me and you, however, the situation is clearly different. We are not Lakota and our lives in no way depend on buffaloes. Accordingly, we have no reason to think of buffaloes as sacred, and it would be fairly ridiculous if either of us made such a claim. Indeed, it would make no sense for me to declare that 'buffaloes are sacred'. Yet if things may be sacred to one group of people without being sacred to another group of people, then sacredness cannot be a property that they possess no matter what (or absolutely, independent of the currently existing circumstances and relations). That does not mean that it is *subjective* in the sense that whether something is sacred or not depends entirely on whether or not someone *sees* it as sacred. Sacredness is not in the eye of the beholder, but it may well be in the *life* of the beholder. The connections and the interdependence are real; they are not just imagined. And if that is what sacredness picks up on, it is objective in that sense (though at the same time also relational rather than absolute).

Perhaps it is this kind of objectivity that makes pansacramentalism a viable option even for the secularist. Buffaloes play virtually no role in our life, but there are plenty of other things that do. Not only are there many things we could literally not live without, there are even more things that are an integral part of us in the sense that they define who and what we are, and they all hang together. Moreover, precisely because all these things are part of us – of our human 'soul' – what is valuable about them is precisely what is valuable about us. Their goodness is our goodness, and in preserving the values we find outside of us we protect ourselves, or at any rate our particular form of life. So perhaps this is what being sensitive to the sacred means: cultivating our awareness of the multitude of connections that form the basic constituents of our life, cherishing all the good in our life that results from them and then acting in such a way that none of it is ever lost, so that it keeps being there to be cherished by whoever comes after us.

Notes

1. A trove of scholarly information about this issue from the perspective of those resisting the pipeline can be found on the Standing Rock Syllabus webpage: https://nycstandswithstand ingrock.wordpress.com/standingrocksyllabus/ (accessed 1 December 2021).
2. Quoted from the documentary film *Black Snake Killaz: A #NoDAPL story* (2017), 16:58–17:12, produced by Unicorn Riot. https://www.youtube.com/watch?v=4dWeg_jHdK0 (accessed 1 December 2021).
3. In the end, the Supreme Court ruled in favour of the baker, despite there being an interest in protecting both free speech and gay rights, emphasising that the prior 'Civil Rights Commission's ruling against the baker, Jack Phillips, had been infected by religious animus' (Liptak, 'In narrow decision, Supreme Court sides with baker').

4. Tweeted by Nancy Pelosi (@SpeakerPelosi) on 13 April 2019: https://twitter.com/SpeakerPel osi/status/1117024802403840000 (accessed 1 December 2021).

5. The stimulating collection of essays *Is Nothing Sacred?* (ed. Rogers) explores whether art, nature, life and liberty can be considered sacred in a secular context. Some of the writers argue in the affirmative, including Alan Holland, Matthew Kieran, Suzanne Uniacke, Simon Blackburn, Richard Dawkins and Ronald Dworkin.

6. It is, in other words, what since Austin (*How to Do Things with Words*) has commonly been called a 'speech act', in recognition of the insight that what is being *said* is one thing, while what people *do* and intend to achieve by saying it may often be quite another. Accordingly, when something is being said that appears to be a description of a presumed reality (e.g. 'this is sacred'), the purpose of saying it may well not be to inform the listener about what the speaker thinks is the case, but to get them to act in a certain way (i.e. to protect what the speaker has declared to be sacred).

7. Kant distinguishes the absolute inner value, or dignity, that rational beings are supposed to have from the merely relative external value, or price, that everything else has, including non-human animals. Dignity is defined as 'an unconditional, incomparable worth' (Kant, *Groundwork of the Metaphysics of Morals*, 43), meaning that it is not possible for a thing to have less or more of it than any other thing. It is, in that sense, above all price, or priceless.

8. See Watts, 'Oil and gas firms "have had far worse climate impact than thought"'.

9. These are just the first two that occurred to me, based on their pervasiveness in US culture; the travel website Matador Network provides a casual but informative list of numerous sacred plants, with my suggestions both appearing on the list (well, cannabis more generally, and the kinds of mushrooms containing psilocybin and psilocin, although mushrooms, of course, are really plant-like fungi). The 13 other sacred plants are African dream root, peyote, San Pedro, henbane, Salvia divinorum, tobacco, blue lily, ayahuasca, Syrian rue, jurema, jimson weed, kava and yopo (Brown, '15 sacred plants from cultures around the world'). Perhaps a longer list would include the various plant sources of caffeine.

10. Much more could be said about spiritual experience or religious experience, a topic greatly shaped over a century ago by the psychological analysis of William James (*The Varieties of Religious Experience*) and the phenomenological analysis of Rudolf Otto (*The Idea of the Holy*). These two theorists of rather different styles agree that religious experience is of primary importance in understanding the significance of religion (James, 19; Otto, 4). However, while Otto insists that religious experience requires an encounter with a radically mysterious and numinous (so, supernatural) other (28), James is less insistent. James himself prefers a theistic interpretation of religious experience (439–44) but allows that the intensity and oddity of religious experience could have an entirely naturalistic explanation and yet retain all its value nonetheless, because it is the fruits, or effects, of religious experience that matter, not the origin (211). Somewhat in the spirit of James's secular side, I believe that spiritual experiences (sans metaphysical suppositions) actually provide us with an understanding of spirituality and also our deep understanding of the sacred, and then religious traditions come out of that. I lay this out with more nuance in a forthcoming paper, 'Faith, meaning and spirituality without religion'.

11. Of course, the word 'religion' itself is contested, as is the supposed distinction between the religious and the secular. Charles Taylor's *A Secular Age* provides a richly historically informed and deeply reflective assessment of the multiplicity of conceptual frameworks at work here. Just as Taylor unpacks a tripartite ambiguity in the idea of secularity (1–4), Lois Lee's *Recognizing the Non-Religious* cautions against lumping all secularists together as having a singular 'non-religious' identity. Bruce Ellis Benson ('Is there such a thing as religion?') reminds us that the idea of religion as an institution organised around certain kinds of belief developed in the West over many centuries, and then Christianity used itself as a model for religion which it then attempted to impose on others. This is helpful context, but I would say that we now have this common idea of religion as a loosely defined communal tradition of beliefs and practices, and my view is that there can be spirituality without that – a view Benson appears to share, although I think that his focus on the experience of awe as a basis for non-religious spirituality provides too thin an analysis of spiritual experience (701–3). What is lacking, I think, is a deep sense of connection.

12. Rilke, *Duineser Elegien*, 7: 'Denn das Schöne ist nichts als des Schrecklichen Anfang, den wir noch grade ertragen, und wir bewundern es so, weil es gelassen verschmäht, uns zu zerstören.'

13. Burke, *A Philosophical Inquiry into the Origin of Our Ideas of the Sublime and the Beautiful*; Kant, *Critique of Judgment*. For a more general exploration of the history of the concept and its significance for contemporary environmental aesthetics see Brady, *The Sublime in Modern Philosophy*.

14. Otto, *The Idea of the Holy*.
15. For an intriguing analysis of the various roles that water plays in our lifeworld as well as its mythological aspects and symbolic significance, see Illich, *H₂O and the Waters of Forgetfulness*.
16. A doctrinal example of this can be found in Jainism, in which it is held that there are souls (*jivas*) in everything, even inanimate objects, earning all things the respect of *ahimsa*, or non-injury (Huntington, 'Jainism and ethics', 190–1, 194–5). The challenge of viewing all things as sacred in this starkly moral way, so that everything is, in a way, inviolable, leads to complex ontological and ethical reasoning among Jains. Albert Schweitzer was greatly inspired by the moral inclusivity of Jainism, which produced in him a deep frustration with the necessity of killing, for instance, mosquitoes (Barsam, 'Albert Schweitzer, Jainism, and reverence for life'). However, as will come out later in our dialogue, I don't believe that imputing sacrality always entails avoiding destruction.
17. Emile Durkheim, a most influential sociological theorist of the sacred, is often held up as declaring that there cannot be the sacred without the profane. In his studies of aboriginal peoples of Australia, Durkheim supposes this distinction to arise when people collectively gather in 'effervescent' rituals which contrast greatly with the everyday humdrum of ordinary life (so it should also be noted that, for Durkheim, the sense of the sacred emerges within spiritual experience, of a communal sort): 'In one world he languidly carries on his daily life; the other is one that he cannot enter without abruptly entering into relations with extraordinary powers that excite him to the point of frenzy. The first is the profane world and the second, the world of sacred things' (*The Elementary Forms of Religious Life*, 220). Yet it should also be noted that, in Durkheim's discussion of the contagiousness of sacred force (*mana, wakan*, etc.) that allows this spiritual energy to spread from one thing to another, there really isn't anything that can't have this religious force superadded to it (327). So, Durkheim is really only insisting that we must live with a conceptual contrast, or that we must experience the sacred and the profane separately (312–13). Even if we accept this, he's not saying that, ontologically, some particular things are necessarily profane and others sacred, meaning that his framework still allows that, in principle, anything could be viewed as sacred.
18. Dworkin, *Life's Dominion*, 73–4.
19. Once again, Durkheim is influential here, emphasising the idea that something being sacred involves extensive prohibition, primarily to separate the profane from the sacred. See especially *The Elementary Forms of Religious Life*, Book 3, chapter 1. We shouldn't be convinced by all of Durkheim's reasoning, but I won't deny that setting apart and prohibition are part of the complex family of phenomena relating to the sacred. Still, these negative comportments should not be treated as absolutely definitional.
20. For more on how gratitude as a spiritual attitude makes sense in a secular context see Chastain, 'Gifts without givers'; Lacewing, 'Can non-theists appropriately feel existential gratitude?'; Solomon, *Spirituality for the Skeptic*, 103–6.
21. See for instance May's 'The sacredness of life'. Taking his cue from Pope John Paul II's encyclical letter *Evangelium Vitae*, May confidently asserts that 'every person of good will' must 'recognize the dignity, indeed sanctity, of human life from its inception', 'defend it from the vicious . . . attacks launched against it today', 'repudiate the "culture of death" that nurtures these attacks', 'love human life as God's precious gift', and 'protect and cherish it' (87).
22. See for instance Brody, 'Abortion and the sanctity of human life'.
23. See for instance Anderson, 'Always care, never kill'.
24. For a critical discussion of this kind of argument see Winston, 'The death penalty and the forfeiture thesis'. Winston argues that the belief common among the many Americans supporting the death penalty that those convicted of capital crimes have forfeited their right to life is 'inconsistent with the belief in universal human rights, with the founding principles of their own country, and with basic beliefs they have about other constitutional rights' (370).
25. 'The right to self-defense was not invented by the American founders but has roots that are older than civilization itself. It is inscribed on every human heart. It is a sacred responsibility – a choice that most mainstream Americans understand' (LaPierre, 'Standing guard', 12). For a critical discussion of the way the language of sacredness is appropriated by the American right, see Dawson, 'Shall not be infringed'.
26. Lame Deer and Erdoes, *Lame Deer, Seeker of Visions*, 131. For further reflection on Lakota spirituality and respect for the sacred, with a special focus on Lakota medicine man Frank Fools Crow, see Chastain, 'Becoming a hollow bone'.

27. Traditionally, the Lakota see all things as inhering soul or spirit – other animals, plants and rocks – an awareness captured in the phrase *Mitakuye Oyasin*, or 'all my relatives' (Lame Deer and Erdoes, *Lame Deer, Seeker of Visions*, 268). Of the buffalo in particular Lame Deer says, 'We Sioux have a close relationship to the buffalo. He is our brother' (131).

28. The Western religious appeal to the idea that human life is sacred because we are made in the image of God (*imago Dei*) recently appeared in a number of articles in opposition to torture: Waldron, 'What can Christian teaching add to the debate about torture?', 338; Antepli, 'An interfaith view of torture', 205; Luban, 'Human dignity, humiliation, and torture', 214–16. Merrihew ('Moral horror and the sacred') also attempts to construct a broader theory of our moral horror with acts such as torture and rape based on the idea that these are violations of the image of God within us.

Bibliography

Anderson, Ryan T. 'Always care, never kill: how physician-assisted suicide endangers the weak, corrupts medicine, compromises the family, and violates human dignity and equality', *The Heritage Foundation Backgrounder* 3004 (24 March 2015): 1–22.

Antepli, Abdullah. 'An interfaith view of torture – a Muslim perspective', *The Muslim World* 103 (2013): 204–8.

Austin, J. L. *How to Do Things with Words*. Oxford: Clarendon Press, 1962.

Barsam, Ara Paul. 'Albert Schweitzer, Jainism, and reverence for life'. In *Reverence for Life: The ethics of Albert Schweitzer for the 21st century*, edited by Marvin Meyer and Kurt Bergel, 207–45. Syracuse, NY: Syracuse University Press, 2002.

Benson, Bruce Ellis. 'Is there such a thing as religion? In search of the roots of spirituality', *Open Theology* 6 (2020): 693–5.

Brady, Emily. *The Sublime in Modern Philosophy: Aesthetics, ethics, and nature*. Cambridge: Cambridge University Press, 2013.

Brody, J. A. 'Abortion and the sanctity of human life', *American Philosophical Quarterly* 10/2 (1973): 133–40.

Brown, Cathy. '15 sacred plants from cultures around the world', Matador Network, 28 July 2014. https://matadornetwork.com/bnt/15-sacred-plants-around-world/ (accessed 1 December 2021).

Burke, Edmund. *A Philosophical Inquiry into the Origin of Our Ideas of the Sublime and the Beautiful*. Oxford: Oxford University Press, 1998.

Chastain, Drew. 'Gifts without givers: secular spirituality and metaphorical cognition', *Sophia* 56 (2017): 631–47.

Chastain, Drew. 'Becoming a hollow bone: Lakota respect for the sacred'. In *The Philosophy of Spirituality: Analytic, continental, and multicultural approaches to a new field of philosophy*, edited by Heather Salazar and Roderick Nicholls, 164–88. Leiden: Brill Rodopi, 2018.

Chastain, Drew. 'Faith, meaning and spirituality without religion'. In *Mind Over Matter*, edited by Roderick Nicholls and Heather Salazar (forthcoming).

Dawson, Jessica. 'Shall not be infringed: how the NRA used religious language to transform the meaning of the Second Amendment', *Palgrave Communications* 5/58 (2019). https://www.nature.com/articles/s41599-019-0276-z.pdf (accessed 1 December 2021).

Durkheim, Emile. *The Elementary Forms of Religious Life*, translated by Karen E. Fields. New York: The Free Press, 1995.

Dworkin, Richard. *Life's Dominion: An argument about abortion, euthanasia, and individual freedom*. New York: Vintage Books, 1993.

Huntington, Ronald M. 'Jainism and ethics'. In *Reverence for Life: The ethics of Albert Schweitzer for the 21st century*, edited by Marvin Meyer and Kurt Bergel, 184–206. Syracuse, NY: Syracuse University Press (2002).

Illich, Ivan. *H₂O and the Waters of Forgetfulness*. London/New York: Marion Boyars, 1985.

James, William. *The Varieties of Religious Experience*. New York: Barnes & Noble Classics, 2004.

Kant, Immanuel. *Critique of Judgment*. New York: Hafner, 1951.

Kant, Immanuel. *Groundwork of the Metaphysics of Morals*, translated and edited by Mary Gregor. Cambridge: Cambridge University Press, 1997.

Lacewing, Michael. 'Can non-theists appropriately feel existential gratitude?', *Religious Studies* 52 (2016): 145–65.

Lame Deer and Richard Erdoes. *Lame Deer, Seeker of Visions*. New York: Pocket Books, 1994.

LaPierre, W. 'Standing guard: Barack Obama's slippery oratory', *American Rifle Magazine* 146/10 (2008): 12.

Lee, Lois. *Recognizing the Non-Religious: Reimagining the secular*. Oxford: Oxford University Press, 2017.

Liptak, Adam. 'In narrow decision, Supreme Court sides with baker who turned away gay couple', *The New York Times*, 4 June 2018. https://www.nytimes.com/2018/06/04/us/politics/supreme-court-sides-with-baker-who-turned-away-gay-couple.html (accessed 1 December 2021).

Luban, David. 'Human dignity, humiliation, and torture', *Kennedy Institute of Ethics Journal* 19/3 (2013): 211–30.

May, William A. 'The sacredness of life: an overview of the beginning', *The Linacre Quarterly* 63/1 (1996): 87–96.

Merrihew, Robert Adams. 'Moral horror and the sacred', *Journal of Religious Ethics* 23/2 (1995): 201–24.

Otto, Rudolf. *The Idea of the Holy*, translated by John W. Harvey. Oxford: Oxford University Press, 1923.

Rilke, Rainer Maria. *Duineser Elegien*. Leipzig: Insel-Verlag, 1923.

Rogers, Ben (ed). *Is Nothing Sacred?* London: Routledge, 2004.

Solomon, Robert. *Spirituality for the Skeptic: The thoughtful love of life*. Oxford: Oxford University Press, 2002.

Taylor, Charles. *A Secular Age*. Cambridge, MA: Belknap Press, 2007.

Waldron, Jeremy. 'What can Christian teaching add to the debate about torture?', *Theology Today* 63 (2006): 330–43.

Watts, Jonathan. 'Oil and gas firms "have had far worse climate impact than thought"', *The Guardian*, 19 February 2020. https://www.theguardian.com/environment/2020/feb/19/oil-gas-industry-far-worse-climate-impact-than-thought-fossil-fuels-methane (accessed 1 December 2021).

Winston, Morton E. 'The death penalty and the forfeiture thesis', *Journal of Human Rights* 1/3 (2002): 357–72.

Index

and brain 55
Descartes on 48, 52–3
distancing from 50–1
dualism 52–6
and emotions 47–8
feeling pain 47, 52
and gender 56, 65–6, 68, 70
losing and replacing parts 47, 55, 60
as a thinking thing 59–62
as a tool 47
as a vessel 46, 49
The Body in Pain (Scarry) 263
The Book of the City of Ladies (Pizan) 72
Bostrom, Nick 247, 249–50, 256
Bradbury, Ray 97–8
Brady, Ian 143
brain 55, 57
Brecht, Bertolt 167
Buddhism 14, 269
buffaloes, as sacred 281–5
Bundy, Ted 143–4

Camus, Albert 17, 21
Capitol Building 270
cats 122–4
causation 11–13, 33–8
Cavarero, Adriana 197n, 198n
Cézanne, Paul 213–14
Chesterton, G. K. 238
childhood 89, 90
    dependency on care-givers 181, 183, 187–8
    invention of 85, 87
Chimakonam, Jonathan 4
Christianity 53, 145, 160, 163, 269
Chu, Andrea Long 68, 71
climate change 14–15, 147, 158n, 245n, 250
Cocking, Dean 222n
Cohen, Leonard 136
colonialism 149
colours 254
concentration camps 147, 149
A Conception of Evil (Formosa) 157n
Confessions (Augustine) 145
connection 17–20
consciousness 105–6, 108; *see also*
    self-consciousness
conversationalism 4
Copernicus, Nicolaus 236
coronavirus pandemic 188
critical judgement 233–4
Cruz, Eduardo R. 198n

Dakota Access Pipeline (DAPL) 270, 272–3, 276
Darwin, Charles 9–10, 49, 53
Dastur, François 197n
death 111, 113–15, 117, 127, 160–79, 186–7
    analagous to separation 164–5, 167
    awareness of own 54, 88
    Epicurus on 163–6
    fear of 160–1, 165, 171, 176n
    and grief 162, 164
    and human extinction 198n
    and illness 196, 198n
    of non-human animals 54, 182, 197n
    penalty 281, 287n
    as a process 187

and suffering 161–2
    transcending 51, 97–9, 173, 191–4, 198n
Death and the Afterlife (Scheffler) 198n
decision-making 37–8
Delaney, Neil 222–3n
dependency
    as adults 188–9
    as babies and children 181, 183, 187–8
Descartes, René 48, 52, 56, 59
Deshaye, Joel 137n
de Sousa, Ronald 221–2n
determinism 15, 27
    and agency 28, 30–3, 37–42
Dewey, John 253
Diamond, Cora 158n
Dick, Philip K. 184–5
digital existence 46
divorce 241
dogs 120–4, 128
    capacity for evil 151–3
    Romanian culls 136n
Doss, Desmond 121–2
dragonflies 137n
    and goodness 130, 133–4
drugs 274
dualism 63n
Dunsworth, Holly M. 197n
Durkheim, Emile 287n
duties 134
Dworkin, Ronald 279

eating disorders 76
Eichmann, Adolf 149, 156n
Ekman, Kasja 79
elections, USA 2020 239
Eliot, T. S. 171–2, 174
Embirikos, Andreas 175
emotions 47–8
The Emperor's New Clothes (Andersen) 267n
endowment thesis 23n
Epicurus 163–6, 169
ethical naturalism 138n
evil 140–59, 252
    as an absence 143–4
    capacity for 132
    distinct from bad or wrong 140–2
    as mental illness 157n
    in non-human animals 148, 150–3
    problem of 140, 142–5
    secondary or structural 149, 151, 155
    seen in eyes/face 143–4, 146–7
    without God 140, 142
evolution 9–11, 49, 56, 60
existence 103, 106, 111

fairness 250
faith 227–46
    as a choice 229–30
    conversion to 237
    definition of 227–9
    doubt and crises of 231–5, 237
    having 'faith in' 239–42
    leap of 228, 231, 238, 244–5n
    and reason 234, 238, 244n
    and religion 227, 235–6;
        fundamentalist 234–5

and shared history 206–7
and shared values 211
for things 201, 213–14, 217–18, 220n
unrequited 215, 220n
'The love song of J. Alfred Prufrock'
(Eliot) 171–2
Lucretius 177n
Luther, Martin 43

MacKinnon, Catharine 72
Marcel, Gabriel 240
Marinetti, Filippo 257–8, 261–3
marriage 218, 223n, 230, 241
arranged 204, 208, 221n
gay 270, 285n
see also love
Martin, Mike 157n
Matador Network 286n
meaning 7–26
and agreement 13–14
and connection 14, 17–21
and making a difference 16–19
linguistic 8–9
memory 106
men, objectified 74
Men Trapped in Men's Bodies (Lawrence) 68
Merton, Thomas 237
Midgley, Mary 1, 3, 4, 43n, 137n
A Midsummer Night's Dream
(Shakespeare) 204
mind(s) 34, 46
and body 52–3
Modern Family 66–7
Monso, Susana 197n
Montaigne, Michel de 94, 94–5, 222n
Monty Python 239, 241
moral entropy 128–9
moral luck 137n
mortality *see* death
Mozart, Wolfgang Amadeus 247, 249, 250
Muhammad 269
murder 141, 143, 148
Murdoch, Iris 137–8n, 222–3n, 261
music 9, 12–13, 17, 23n, 247, 250
Musil, Robert 50
The Myth of Evil (Cole) 157n

Nagel, Thomas 21, 23n, 137n
Nagy, Greg 259
Nazism 149
Nietzsche, Friedrich 17, 158n, 244n
nihilism 22
nonbinary 68, 77–8, 79–80
Nozick, Robert 223n
Nussbaum, Martha 136n, 223n

old age 84–6, 89, 94–7
Otto, Rudolf 234, 286n

pain 47, 52, 192–3, 263
panpsychism 118n
pansacramentalism 277–8
Parens, Erik 4
Pascal, Blaise 229
Peirce, Charles Sanders 228, 244n
Pelosi, Nancy 270

Perez, Caroline Criado 76
pessimism 15, 19, 21–3
Phaedo (Plato) 163, 166
Phaedrus (Plato) 258
phenomenology 63n
Philaster (Beaumont and Fletcher) 167
physicalism 15
pineal gland 53
Pizan, Christine de 72
plants 59, 107, 116, 121, 265
sacred 286n
Plato 46, 136n, 138n, 263, 172, 209, 256,
258, 260
Plessner, Helmuth 63n
Plotinus 253, 260, 267n
poetry 13, 251
Poincaré, Henri 233
population growth 15
pornography 71–2, 76
Portmann, Adolf 197n
pragmatism 245n
Prescott, Paul 156n
Pride and Prejudice (Austen) 224n
prisons, and access to nature 258
Prometheus Bound (Aeschylus) 166–8
pronouns 78, 81, 102–3
prostitution 72, 79
Protagoras (Plato) 136n
Protasi, Sara 220–1n, 223n
Putnam, Hilary 24n
Pythagoreans 46, 253

race, self-identification 75, 77, 99n
racism 155
Raymond, Janice 68
Recognizing the Non-Religious (Lee) 286n
Ricoeur, Paul 232
Rilke, Rainer Maria 276
Rorty, Richard 222n
Rowling, J. K. 82n
Russell, Bertrand 250
Ryan, Sharon 138n

sacredness 269–89
and awe 276, 278
and inviolability 279–80, 282
of life 280–3
of non-human animals 281–5, 288n
of objects and locations 269–70
pansacramentalism 277–8
of plants 286n
as a religious concept 269
as a secular concept 270–4
and spiritual experience 274–5
stronger and weaker uses of the word 273–4
of water 270, 272–3, 276–7, 279
sacrifice 284
Saint-Exupéry, Antoine de 236
Sappho 251
Sartre, Jean-Paul 197n
Scheffler, Samuel 198n
Schopenhauer, Arthur 14, 111, 169–70,
172, 174–5
Schweitzer, Albert 287n
Scruton, Roger 223n
Seacole, Mary 121–2

CPSIA information can be obtained
at www.ICGtesting.com
Printed in the USA
JSHW051920130223
37490JS00015B/29